CW01642701

Cinematic Modernism and Contemporary Film

Aesthetics and Narrative in the International Art Film

Howard Finn

BLOOMSBURY ACADEMIC
LONDON • NEW YORK • OXFORD • NEW DELHI • SYDNEY

BLOOMSBURY ACADEMIC
Bloomsbury Publishing Plc
50 Bedford Square, London, WC1B 3DP, UK
1385 Broadway, New York, NY 10018, USA
29 Earlsfort Terrace, Dublin 2, Ireland

BLOOMSBURY, BLOOMSBURY ACADEMIC and the Diana logo are trademarks of Bloomsbury Publishing Plc

First published in Great Britain 2023
This paperback edition published 2024

Copyright © Howard Finn, 2023

Howard Finn has asserted his right under the Copyright, Designs and Patents Act, 1988, to be identified as Author of this work.

For legal purposes the Acknowledgements on p. ix constitute an extension of this copyright page.

Cover design: Ben Anslow
Cover image: *Burning* (2018), directed by Lee Chang-dong. Shown from left: Yoo Ah-in, Jeon Jong-seo, Steven Yeun (© CGV Arthouse/Photofest)

All rights reserved. No part of this publication may be reproduced or transmitted in any form or by any means, electronic or mechanical, including photocopying, recording, or any information storage or retrieval system, without prior permission in writing from the publishers.

Bloomsbury Publishing Plc does not have any control over, or responsibility for, any third-party websites referred to or in this book. All internet addresses given in this book were correct at the time of going to press. The author and publisher regret any inconvenience caused if addresses have changed or sites have ceased to exist, but can accept no responsibility for any such changes.

A catalogue record for this book is available from the British Library.

Library of Congress Cataloging-in-Publication Data

ISBN: HB: 978-1-7883-1273-8
PB: 978-1-3503-4958-2
ePDF: 978-1-3502-4258-6
eBook: 978-1-3502-4257-9

Typeset by Deanta Global Publishing Services, Chennai, India

To find out more about our authors and books visit www.bloomsbury.com and sign up for our newsletters.

Cinematic Modernism and Contemporary Film

Contents

List of figures vi
Acknowledgements ix

Introduction 1

1 What is modernism? What is cinema? 6
2 Cinema and the modernist arts: The cult of the image 45
3 Cinematic modernism in the silent film era 68
4 Postwar cinematic modernism: From neorealism to the new wave 90
5 Postwar cinematic modernism: Critical perspectives 119
6 The return of cinematic modernism 146
7 Contemporary cinematic modernism: Currents and controversies 168
8 Contemporary cinematic modernism: An international style – commentaries on ten contemporary films 213

Appendix 269
Selected filmography 272
Notes 282
Bibliography 313
Index 321

Figures

1 An everyday moment of intimate realism. *Man with a Movie Camera* (1928), Dziga Vertov © VUFKU (Eureka Masters of Cinema Blu-ray 2017/Lobster Films restoration 2015) 21

2 Documentary realism and formalist abstraction. *Stromboli: Land of God* (1950), Roberto Rossellini © Berit Film, RKO Radio Pictures (*The Rossellini and Bergman Collection*, BFI Blu-ray 2015) 28

3 Jeanne Moreau caught between the vertical and horizontal abstractions of the modern city. *La Notte* (1961), Michelangelo Antonioni © Nepi Film, Sofitedip (Paris), Silver Films (Paris) (Eureka Masters of Cinema Blu-ray 2013) 38

4 Objectifying subjective alienation. *Red Desert* (1964), Michelangelo Antonioni © Film Duemila, Francoriz (BFI Blu-ray 2011) 64

5 The 'objective' kino-eye observes an everyday city street scene. *Man with a Movie Camera* (1928), Dziga Vertov © VUFKU (Eureka Masters of Cinema Blu-ray 2017/Lobster Films restoration 2015) 78

6 Montage not only between frames but within frames. *Man with a Movie Camera* (1928), Dziga Vertov © VUFKU (Eureka Masters of Cinema Blu-ray 2017/Lobster Films restoration 2015) 78

7 'Unmotivated camera mischief'. *Man with a Movie Camera* (1928), Dziga Vertov © VUFKU (Eureka Masters of Cinema Blu-ray 2017/Lobster Films restoration 2015) 79

8 Cameraman and camera as master of reality? *Man with a Movie Camera* (1928), Dziga Vertov © VUFKU (Eureka Masters of Cinema Blu-ray 2017/Lobster Films restoration 2015) 79

9 Maria the maid performing her kitchen chores in real-time durations. *Umberto D* (1952) Vittorio De Sica © Rizzoli Film, Produzione Films Vittorio De Sica, Produzione Film Giuseppe Amato (Cult Films Blu-ray 2017) 96

10 A statue reaches out to Ingrid Bergman. *Journey to Italy*, Roberto Rossellini 1954 © Sveva Film, Junior Film, Italia Produzione Film, Société Générale de Cinématographie, Les Films Ariane, Francinex (*The Rossellini and Bergman Collection*, BFI Blu-ray 2015) 99

11 Political modernism : Brecht, Lenin, Rimbaud. *Le Gai savoir* (1969), Jean-Luc Godard © Anouchka Films, Bavaria Atelier GmbH (*Jean Luc-Godard Politique* Gaumont DVD 2012) 109
12 Staging the encounter between cinema and theatre. *Out 1* (1971), Jacques Rivette © Sunshine, Sunchild Productions, Les Films du Losange (Paris) (*Jacques Rivette Collection* Arrow Academy Blu-ray 2016) 113
13 Gazing into the landscape as a mirror of place and time. *Mirror* (1975), Andrei Tarkovsky © Mosfilm (Criterion UK Blu-ray 2021) 138
14 Minimalist hyper-realism as suspenseful repression. *Jeanne Dielman, 23, quai du Commerce, 1080 Bruxelles* (1975), Chantal Akerman © Paradise Films, Unité 3, Ministère de la Culture Française du Belgique (The Criterion Collection, Blu-ray 2017) 151
15 The female gaze as object of the male gaze of cinema. *Under the Skin* (2014), Jonathan Glazer © Nick Wechsler, JW Films / Sigma Films, Seventh Kingdom Productions Limited, Channel Four Television Corporation, The British Film Institute (StudioCanal Blu-ray 2014) 186
16 Minimalism and expressionism. *Colossal Youth* (2006), Pedro Costa © RTP – Radio Televisão Portugal, RTSI, Arte France Cinéma (Eureka Masters of Cinema DVD 2011) 206
17 Walking the line between sacred and profane. *Birdsong* (2008), Albert Serra © Andergraun Films, Eddie Saeta S.A. (Capricci DVD 2011) 209
18 Frontal Steadicam 'walking shot'. *Sátántangó* (1994), Béla Tarr © MIT, Von Vietinghoff Filmproduktion, Vega Film, Magyar Televízió, Télévision Suisse Romande (Curzon Artificial Eye Blu-ray 2020) 219
19 Steadicam 'walking shot' from behind. *Sátántangó* (1994), Béla Tarr © MIT, Von Vietinghoff Filmproduktion, Vega Film, Magyar Televízió, Télévision Suisse Romande (Curzon Artificial Eye Blu-ray 2020) 220
20 The inexorable zoom. *Sátántangó* (1994), Béla Tarr © MIT, Von Vietinghoff Filmproduktion, Vega Film, Magyar Televízió, Télévision Suisse Romande (Curzon Artificial Eye Blu-ray 2020) 221
21 The driver as figure of alienation. *Taste of Cherry* (1997), Abbas Kiarostami © Abbas Kiarostami Productions (Criterion UK Blu-ray, 2020) 223

22 A static long shot from behind. *Taste of Cherry* (1997), Abbas Kiarostami © Abbas Kiarostami Productions (Criterion UK Blu-ray, 2020) 226

23 A static frontal close-up. *Taste of Cherry* (1997), Abbas Kiarostami © Abbas Kiarostami Productions (Criterion UK Blu-ray, 2020) 226

24 Sublimating slapstick and camp: 'queer deadpan'. *Goodbye, Dragon Inn* (2003), Tsai Ming-Liang Homegreen Films © (Second Run Blu-ray 2020) 234

25 Photographer in focus, background blurred. *Marseille* (2004), Angela Schanelec © Schramm-Film Koerner & Weber (Filmgalerie DVD 2005) 239

26 At the margins of privatized public space. *Marseille* (2004), Angela Schanelec © Schramm-Film Koerner & Weber (Filmgalerie DVD 2005) 239

27 A still life composition. *Still Life* (2006), Jia Zhangke © Xstream Pictures Limited, Hong Kong / Beijing (BFI DVD 2008) 247

28 The protagonist vanishes. *Liverpool* (2008), Lisandro Alonso © 4L, Fortuna Films, Slot Machine, Eddie Saeta S.A., Black Forest Films (Second Run DVD 2012) 258

29 The planimetric image reconfigured. *Burning* (2018), Lee Chang-dong © Pinehouse Film, Nowfilm / NHK (Thunderbird Blu-ray 2019) 261

30 Estrangement: foreground seated figure in focus, background standing figure out of focus. *An Elephant Sitting Still* (2018), Hu Bo © Ltd Beijing Dongchun Films Co. (New Wave Films Blu-ray 2019) 266

Note: images are taken from screenshots by the author from the Blu-ray editions referenced.

Acknowledgements

I would like to thank Morag Shiach and everyone in the School of English and Drama at Queen Mary College, University of London. I also wish to thank Scott McCracken, Laura Marcus, Adam Guy and everyone at the Dorothy Richardson Society. Thank you to Shohini Chaudhuri and the Centre for Film and Screen Media at the University of Essex. Some ideas in this book originated a rather long time ago in discussion with Shohini when we were seeing Iranian films in the 1990s. I would like to thank my editors, Rebecca Barden and Veidehi Hans, at Bloomsbury and the commissioning editor of this book, Madeleine Hamey-Thomas. Thank you to Jules Deering at Queen Mary for technical help with the images in this book. I am grateful to Peter Latham for his thoughts on film and literature over many years and to Andrew Rouse with whom I saw the wind in the trees in Tarkovsky's *Mirror* when we were teenagers. Thank you to Hiromi Horosawa and Monica Kolesnik. Thank you to Alex Davey for her postcards and to Len Massey for his phone calls during the Covid-19 lockdown year in which this book was being written-up.

Introduction

The wind in the trees and the sky in a puddle

In *Theory of Film* Siegfried Kracauer recounts the well-known story of how D. W. Griffith on his deathbed renounced Hollywood and expressed his allegiance to the natural authentic beauty of cinematic realism. Kracauer sees this as evidence for the realist aesthetic which *Theory of Film* espouses:

> I have stressed that films conform to the cinematic approach only if they acknowledge the realistic tendency by concentrating on actual physical existence – 'the beauty of moving wind in the trees', as D.W. Griffith expressed it in a 1947 interview in which he voiced his bitterness at contemporary Hollywood and its unawareness of that beauty.[1]

There is an obvious irony in the story given that Griffith is known as the man who established the conventions of editing, shot composition and techniques like the close-up: the grammar of film, the foundation or building blocks for what became known as the 'classical' Hollywood narrative film, which came to dominate cinema around the world and is still dominant today in the twenty-first century. Griffith's comment has been quoted, paraphrased and translated back and forth between a number of languages and has assumed numerous variations: 'the wind in the trees', 'the wind moving through the trees', 'the breeze rustling the leaves' and so on. The original comment was taken down by a reporter interviewing Griffith for a newspaper in 1948, and according to Griffith's biographer, the original quote, which may or may not have been wholly reliable, was:

> The beauty of the moving wind in the trees, the little movement in a beautiful blowing on the blossoms in the trees. [. . .] We have lost beauty.[2]

Kracauer refers to the 'wind in the trees' and the 'rustling of leaves' throughout *Theory of Film* and declares that cinema 'fulfils itself in rendering the "ripple of the leaves."'[3] Such motifs correspond to his idea of what film should be as a modern art: an encounter between narrative – what he calls the 'light narrative' of the episodic 'found story' – and documentary realism, the aim being to juxtapose human consciousness with the impersonal, fleeting, contingency of reality:

> [Films] open up a dimension much wider than that of the plots which they sustain. This dimension extends, so to speak, beneath the superstructure of specific story contents; it is made up of moments within everybody's reach, moments as common as birth and death, or a smile, or 'the ripple of the leaves stirred by the wind'.[4]

Kracauer notes that right from the beginning of cinema, the realist tendency represented by Lumière's *actualités* was praised by more modernist-minded critics for the rustling leaves as much as for the arriving train:

> Significantly, the contemporaries of Lumière praised his films – the first ever to be made – for showing 'the ripple of the leaves stirred by the wind'. [. . .] It was inevitable that, in the comments on Lumière, 'the ripple of leaves stirred by the wind' should be referred to enthusiastically. The Paris journalist Henri de Parville, who used the image of the trembling leaves, also identified Lumière's over-all theme as 'nature caught in the act'.[5]

Kracauer traces the motif back further still to the emergence of photography:

> About 1860, Cook and Bonnelli, who had developed a device called a photobioscope, predicted a 'complete revolution of photographic art. . . . We will see . . . landscapes', they announced, 'in which the trees bow to the whims of the wind, the leaves ripple and glitter in the rays of the sun'.[6]

Kracauer recounts how the motif is then picked up by realist novelists who, in part as a response to this new invention, the camera, elaborated their new aesthetic of literary realism as a means of capturing that 'something', that essence, which lay in the complex surface of the world and its fleeting infinite detail:

> Nineteenth-century writers called this something nature, or life; and they were convinced that photography would have to impress upon us its infinity. Leaves, which they counted among the favorite motifs of the camera, cannot be 'staged' but occur in endless quantities. In this respect, there is an analogy between the photographic approach and scientific investigation: both probe into an inexhaustible universe whose entirety forever eludes them.[7]

If the realist novel adapted itself to photography, then photography adapted to its precursors in painting and the tradition of the still life. But life isn't still.

A photograph is always static, by contrast film moves and captures movement, and it *can* capture the wind in the trees and the rustling of the leaves.

It is evident from Kracauer's account that the motif of 'the wind in the trees' is situated within a critical discourse on cinema and its relationship to other arts and to the world. The motif suggests that cinema can capture the reality of the world (like a photograph) but capture that reality of the world in movement and in time, in duration. The motif is aligned with modernism in its focus on the transience of the epiphanic moment as the wind passes through the trees, its focus on the 'infinity' of the rippling leaves, and on the uncanniness of reality in its appearance, because the wind cannot actually be filmed: the wind or the breeze is an invisible object only captured by implication through its effect on other objects – it is as if we are watching this invisible life force itself, even though we are merely watching the effect of the wind upon the leaves.

This book has two primary aims. The first is to clarify the relationship between cinema and modernism. Cinema was the most important new artistic medium of the twentieth century and modernism was the most important new aesthetic movement across the arts in the twentieth century. But what exactly is the relationship between cinema and modernism? The second aim of this book is to consider the ways in which cinematic modernism might still inform a prominent strand within contemporary film. Many labels have been applied to this type of film: cinema of stasis, slow cinema, contemplative or reflective cinema, minimalist, sparse and neo-neo realist cinema. These labels have not only their uses but also their limits and can be misleading. Not all films in this trend are 'slow' and slow in what way and to whom? Not all art films are slow, not all are minimalist and not all art films belong to the trend in contemporary cinema with which this book is concerned. The films in this prominent trend are also difficult to categorize within 'alternative' terms like 'indie', 'cult' or 'counter-cinema'.

The argument of this book is that a prominent type of contemporary art film can best be explained, understood and appreciated as an 'international style' (a term *not* synonymous with the broad marketing category of 'world cinema') and that this 'international style' is derived from and explicitly influenced by the cinematic modernism of the mid-twentieth century. There were many different types of postwar cinematic modernism, a diversity which became especially marked in the various new waves of the 1960s, but one trend of postwar cinematic modernism has a particular relevance to contemporary film. This one specific strand emerged out of neorealism and was first identified with Rossellini's trilogy of films starring Ingrid Bergman – *Stromboli*, *Europa 51* and

Journey to Italy – before going on to evolve into an aesthetic corresponding to an 'existentialist' sensibility, beginning in the 1950s with two main variants exemplified by Antonioni and Bresson, and drawing to a close in the 1970s with two equally contrasting variants exemplified by Tarkovsky and Fassbinder. The origins of this strand of postwar film were theorized, at the time its emergence (in the 1940s and 1950s) by André Bazin and Siegfried Kracauer in terms of a *new* self-consciously *modern* cinema and as a combining of genre-based fictional narrative with documentary realism. This same strand of postwar film was later theorized by Gilles Deleuze (in the 1980s) in terms of modern film as the cinema of the 'time image'.

This book aims to show how certain contemporary films are informed by the aesthetics of cinematic modernism and its engagement with the problematics of realism and formalism. The argument will not be that a given film is modernist or an example of pure modernism, but that particular contemporary films utilize and draw selectively on techniques and sensibilities associated with cinematic modernism in an updated form and do so alongside techniques and sensibilities drawn from classical and genre cinema. The point of this book therefore is to tell the story of the relationship between cinema and modernism as a means to contextualize some of the more interesting films of recent years.[8]

The first chapter of the book will provide an overview of the relationship between cinema and modernism as a relationship between shifting critical discourses. Chapter 2 will look at the influence on cinema of early-twentieth-century modernism across the arts, particularly modernism's privileging of the image. Chapter 3 discusses how cinematic modernism developed in the era of silent film and in response to the consolidation of 'classical' Hollywood film. Chapter 4 looks at the postwar new waves and how cinema arrived at its own mature cinematic modernism. Chapter 5 discusses some of the major critical perspectives on cinematic modernism. Chapter 6 looks at the re-emergence of films informed by cinematic modernism in Taiwan, Iran and elsewhere in the 1990s. Chapter 7 discusses various currents, debates and controversies relating to contemporary cinematic modernism. Chapter 8 argues that contemporary cinematic modernism constitutes an 'international style'. This final chapter consists of short readings of ten key contemporary films informed by cinematic modernism.

To the question 'in what ways does cinematic modernism inform contemporary film?' it would be tempting to answer simply that you know you are watching a film informed by cinematic modernism when you see an image of the wind in the trees rustling the leaves, probably filmed by a fixed camera in a long take.

Siegfried Kracauer ends his preface to *Theory of Film* with the following story about the first time he went to the cinema and a particular image in the film he saw:

> Let me conclude with a personal reminiscence. I was still a young boy when I saw my first film. [. . .] And I remember, as if it were today, the marvels themselves. What thrilled me so deeply was an ordinary suburban street, filled with lights and shadows which transfigured it. Several trees stood about, and there was in the foreground a puddle reflecting invisible house facades and a piece of the sky. Then a breeze moved the shadows, and the facades with the sky below began to waver. The trembling upper world in the dirty puddle – this image has never left me.[9]

The image Kracauer remembers from the first film he ever saw is not an image of wind in the trees or of the beautiful sky, but an image of sky and trees reflected in a dirty puddle in an ordinary suburban street, an image which 'wavers' when a breeze ripples the water in the puddle. As this book will explain, Kracauer and Bazin conceive of cinema in terms of its power to 'redeem' reality, but it is a complicated kind of reality. Reality in cinema is always a wavering reflection of reality modified by time and memory and by contingency and indeterminacy. And for contemporary cinematic modernism a redemptive sublime is invariably accessed through an aestheticized reflection of a mundane reality: the image of beauty reflected in a dirty puddle.

1

What is modernism? What is cinema?

A central chapter in Mark Cousins's *The Story of Film* (2004) is entitled 'The Exploded Story (1959-1969): The Breakdown of Romantic Cinema and the Coming of Modernism'. Cousins associates cinematic modernism with the 'exploded story', a radical change in narrative form and he associates this with a decade, the 1960s. The title of Cousins's preceding chapter, an account of 1950s cinema, refers to 'new early-modernist directors' and the succeeding chapter, on film in the 1970s, contains a section headed 'Beyond the New Waves: Political Modernism'. In Cousins's account, therefore, modernist cinema runs across three decades: the 1950s, 1960s and 1970s, decades corresponding to early modernist, modernist and political modernist, respectively.[1]

The Story of Film gives prominence to cinematic modernism, with an emphasis on postwar international 'art' cinema as 'modernist'. In this period the distinctive aesthetic of cinematic modernism serves to represent an existentialist anxiety about the modern world and serves to generate a critique of modern society and, in the parlance of the time, its dominant bourgeois values. The aesthetic of cinematic modernism is primarily a response to a 'crisis of representation' and an attempt to find new modes of realism, the old cinematic realisms – particularly those of 'classical' Hollywood film – considered passé and no longer credible as a means of representing modern life. This aesthetic of postwar cinematic modernism is most evident in its approach to narrative: ellipses, fragmented structure, temporal dislocations, downgrading of plot, unresolved endings, de-dramatization, unreliable storytelling and multiple narrative perspectives – all of which contribute to a general tendency towards narratives marked by uncertainty and ambiguity and all of which correspond to innovations in narrative form associated with the modernist novel from the earlier twentieth century. If in literature the 'exploded story' occurred in the novels of Joyce, Proust, Woolf, Musil and Faulkner in the 1920s, then in cinema the 'exploded story' occurred in the films of Antonioni, Fellini, Bergman and Godard in the 1960s.

The chronology of *The Story of Film* reflects a consensus in film studies that modernist cinema can be aligned with the postwar period, from the early 1950s to the mid-1970s. This consensus is broadly upheld in three contrasting but indicative books. András Bálint Kovács in *Screening Modernism* (2007) insists that cinematic modernism belongs to the postwar 'existentialist' period which, with admirable precision, he dates as beginning with Rossellini's *Journey to Italy* (1954) and ending with Tarkovsky's *Mirror* (1975). Sam Rohdie's *Film Modernism* (2015) is focused almost entirely on canonical postwar European modernists from Rossellini, Bresson and Bergman to Antonioni, Pasolini and Godard (plus a few Hollywood auteurs canonized by *Cahiers du cinéma*: Welles, Hitchcock, Ford, Hawks, Ray). D. N. Rodowick in *The Crisis of Political Modernism* (1994) also dates cinematic modernism to the postwar period but focuses on 'political modernism' as a consequence of the shift from existentialism to Marxism in the immediate aftermath of May 1968. This is the moment of political radicalism, the self-reflexive 'Brechtian turn' undertaken by Godard, Fassbinder and Straub-Huillet and promoted by *Cahiers du cinéma* in its 'Maoist' phase and '*Screen* Theory' associated with the British film journal *Screen*. Beginning in 1968 the period of 'political modernism' lasted barely a decade, being all but exhausted by the late 1970s.[2]

Notwithstanding their different emphases, taken together the accounts of Kovács, Rohdie and Rodowick are representative of how in film studies modernism is identified with international postwar art cinema and the accounts are compatible with the description of the development of cinematic modernism across the 1950s, 1960s and 1970s outlined by Mark Cousins in *The Story of Film*.[3]

However, this periodization of modernist film makes cinema something of an anomaly in the arts. In painting modernism is usually dated from Picasso's *Les Demoiselles d'Avignon* and the beginning of cubism circa 1907. In music modernism is commonly dated from the scandal surrounding the Paris premiere of Stravinsky's *Rite of Spring* in 1913. In literature modernism is usually dated to the period of the First World War through to the peak of 1922, the year of *Ulysses*, *Jacob's Room* and *The Waste Land*. Whereas film studies generally dates cinematic modernism to the postwar period, in art and literary studies attention has been directed towards the early twentieth century and the interaction between modernist painters and novelists and the new medium of film. From this perspective cinematic modernism is silent film: Eisenstein, Vertov, Murnau; Soviet montage, German expressionism and the 'art' films endorsed by modernist-affiliated film journals of the 1920s such as *Close Up*.

Laura Marcus has given a comprehensive account of the relationship between modernist literature and cinema in the silent film era in *The Tenth Muse: Writing about Cinema in the Modernist Period* (2007).[4] In *Cinema and Modernism* (2011) David Trotter qualifies this approach, arguing that the new medium of film reflected modernity primarily through Griffith, Chaplin and Keaton: it was popular (Hollywood) film, along with the inherent properties of the medium of film (the mechanical recording of reality), that in the silent era corresponded to the concerns of modernism across the arts, rather than the art or avant-garde film.[5]

This chapter will ask 'what is modernism?' with reference to the early modernist theories of Roger Fry and the postwar promotion of modernism as an aesthetic by Clement Greenberg. The chapter will then ask 'what is cinema?' with reference to the postwar theories of film offered by André Bazin and Siegfried Kracauer. The chapter includes a short commentary on Stanley Cavell's *The World Viewed*, a book which remains, alongside Deleuze's two *Cinema* books, the best-known attempt by a philosopher to ask 'what is cinema?'; less well remembered perhaps is that Cavell attempts to answer this question, in part, by way of modernism and its aesthetics. The chapter closes by looking at Miriam Bratu Hansen's study of Kracauer, Benjamin and Adorno's writings on cinema, modernity and modernism, *Cinema and Experience* (2012), and offering some comments on Hansen's essay, 'The Mass Production of the Senses: Classical Cinema as Vernacular Modernism' (1999), her influential critique of cinematic modernism as a critical discourse.

Part I: What is modernism?

A basic premise of this book is that 'modernism' is a 'critical discourse', meaning a set of developing critical ideas, and that modernism constitutes an 'aesthetics', meaning a set of ideas about artistic representation and form. There are dozens of major 'general' theories of the modern, modernity and modernism. Four of the best-known theorists – Marshall Berman, T. J. Clark, Fredric Jameson and Raymond Williams – each see modernity as a concept closely linked to the development of capitalism, democracy and socialism and see the fortunes of modernism as tracking the fortunes of Marxism, regardless of the politics of a given modernist artist or writer.[6] This book assumes the background provided by these major theories but focuses on modernism as a critical discourse about aesthetics and in terms of how cinematic modernism might relate to other modernist arts including painting, poetry, drama and, especially, the modernist novel.

A critical discourse is an ongoing discussion, conversation or argument about a thing or object. 'Modernism' is not an inherent or essential property of a particular object, be it a Joyce novel, a Picasso painting, a Le Corbusier building, an item of Bauhaus furniture or an Antonioni film. Modernism is a critical discourse which seeks to describe and understand art objects primarily within the cultural context of modernity. A critical discourse is a set of ideas *about* its object, a set of ideas incorporating conflicting viewpoints, but within agreed parameters which ensure a basic coherence to the discussion. If the viewpoints within a discourse become too heterogeneous and conflicted, the discourse collapses or is superseded by another. A critical discourse such as 'modernism' shifts and evolves over time and sometimes changes abruptly in response to new theoretical paradigms or simply in response to changing intellectual fashions, but equally this type of critical discourse is often determined by institutional factors to do with the requirements of universities, academic journals and publishers.[7] It is important to emphasize that 'modernism' is a critical discourse because it differs from labels associated with modernism such as cubism, Dada, futurism, vorticism, imagism and surrealism. These movements were declared by artists themselves at the time the artists were consciously producing cultural work aligned with these labels. Manifestos were issued. Programmes announced. Polemics undertaken. To put it in contemporary terminology, artists 'self-identified' (with greater or lesser degrees of comfort) with these labels. By contrast, painters, novelists, poets, dramatists or filmmakers in the first half of the twentieth century only very occasionally described themselves as 'modernist'.

Modernism is a critical discourse I: 1910

The predominantly Anglo-American critical discourse of modernism has its source in 'post-impressionism', a term used by Roger Fry for the 1910 London exhibition *Manet and the Post-Impressionists* which he curated. This was the exhibition reputed to have outraged critical and public opinion but which introduced to England the paintings of Cézanne, Van Gogh, Gauguin and Seurat. The 1910 exhibition and its 1912 and 1913 successors would also introduce the more current and radical art of Picasso and Matisse under the post-impressionist label. 'On or about December 1910', wrote Virginia Woolf, 'human character changed.'[8] This laconic remark is commonly understood to assert that with the 1910 Post-Impressionist exhibition the twentieth century had arrived and the nineteenth century had been banished. Modern art and therefore modern culture had finally arrived in London, albeit a decade or so after Paris – the actual polemical point of Woolf's essay being that it was time for the novel to leave behind the outmoded 'realism' of Arnold Bennett, H. G. Wells and John Galsworthy and catch up with painting by developing a new realism, a literary equivalent of Cézanne; it was time for the novel to become modern. Woolf's Bloomsbury friends Roger Fry and Clive Bell explained the aesthetic, informing the paintings in the 1910 Post-Impressionist exhibition, especially the paintings of Cézanne, to an initially perplexed public and in doing so mapped out the basic ideas which would provide a starting point for the critical discourse of modernism. Clive Bell writes:

> There must be some one quality without which a work of art cannot exist; possessing which, in the least degree, no work is altogether worthless. What is this quality? What quality is shared by all objects that provoke our aesthetic emotions? What quality is common to Sta. Sophia and the windows at Chartres, Mexican sculpture, a Persian bowl, Chinese carpets, Giotto's frescoes at Padua, and the masterpieces of Poussin, Piero della Francesca and Cézanne? Only one answer seems possible – significant form. In each, lines and colours combined in a particular way, certain forms and relations of forms, stir our aesthetic emotions. These relations and combinations of lines and colours, these aesthetically moving forms, I call 'Significant Form'; and 'Significant Form' is the one quality common to all works of visual art.[9]

Bell stresses that he is not arguing for totally abstract art.[10] Painting is likely to continue to be representational and should be grounded in reality, but it is the application of 'significant form' to the rendering of the object in a painting that objectifies and universalizes the emotion generated by the artwork. Roger Fry argues that there is 'actual life' and 'imaginative life'. Realist artists go too far in trying to record and represent actual life, while the impressionists go too far in trying to record and represent the imaginative life of subjective consciousness and perception. The modern artist, beginning with Manet and exemplified by Cézanne, reconciles these tendencies by accessing and representing reality through a significant form. Form objectifies both the physical object and the subjective consciousness and perception of the object and in doing so sublimates 'actual life' into the 'imaginative life' that is the primary realm of art.

In a 1909 essay, Fry links his theory of modern art to the new medium of cinema. He notes that the cinematograph presents 'actual life', for example a street scene, in all its concrete reality, yet we the viewers do not see it as we might in reality. Because the scene is shot from a particular angle and *framed*, it provides a selective view of the scene, one which activates our powers of observation and imagination.

> The result is that in the first place we see the event much more clearly; see a number of quite interesting but irrelevant things, which in real life could not struggle into our consciousness.[11]

'Irrelevant' here is not a derogatory term, Fry is approving of cinema's ability to mechanically record and capture reality in all its contingent detail in a scene, to capture details unnecessary to the main event in Lumière-style *actualités* or 'irrelevant' to the story in a drama film. Fry goes on to suggest that the cinematographic image acts like a mirror, and when we watch a street scene in a film it is as if we are looking at the street scene in a mirror, rather than looking at the actual scene in real life:

> The frame of the mirror, then, does to some extent turn the reflected scene from one that belongs to our actual life into one that belongs rather to our imaginative life. The frame of the mirror makes its surface into a very rudimentary work of art, since it helps us to attain the artistic vision. For that is what, as you will have already guessed, I have been coming to all this time, namely that the work of art is intimately connected with the secondary imaginative life, which all men live to a greater or lesser extent.[12]

The primacy given here to the frame and flat surface will become crucial to how Clement Greenberg will conceive modernist aesthetics in relation to painting and will also have an importance in later film theory. For Roger Fry the frame separates art from life *even in cinema, where it is 'reality itself' in all its quotidian detail that has been recorded and presented.* Art is 'the expression of the imaginative life rather than a copy of actual life' and the difference resides in form.[13] Artists may deploy forms derived from or related to the forms of nature, but the kind of 'significant form' found in Cézanne and endorsed by Fry and Bell manifests the consciousness and emotions of the artist (something not found in nature) and is more likely to generate 'that intense disinterested contemplation that belongs to the imaginative life'.[14]

The modernist concept of form initially appears to be something material and concerned with refining the presentation of reality. But there is a tension in Fry and Bell's theory of modern art, which will also be evident in later modernist aesthetics, between form as something which frames and abstracts from reality and form as something which leaves reality behind and provides access to an ideal or transcendental realm. The Kantian idea of form as an object of detached contemplation can lead to the idea that form might provide access to some kind of 'essence' within or beyond reality; the Kantian thing-in-itself here conflated with the Kantian sublime behind which, for Fry, Bell and the modernists, lie the Platonic ideal forms, the problem being not artistic representation as such but that *reality itself* is a secondary representation of the ideal forms. Fry, Bell and Woolf along with most of the early abstract painters like Kandinsky and many of the later American Abstract expressionist painters share this tendency: they are less interested in form-for-form's-sake than in form as a means of accessing a transcendental or existential essence, a sublime (or its opposite, an abyssal abject). In early modernist critical discourse, 'reality' comes to be figured not so much as the material world of physical objects but as Platonic Ideal, Hegelian Spirit or Schopenhauerian/Nietzschean Will. If music is a direct manifestation of Spirit/Will rather than mere representation, might abstract painting, pure form, aspire to the condition of music and have a similarly direct relationship with Spirit? For Roger Fry and Clive Bell 'significant form' ultimately seems to lead less to Kantian disinterested contemplation than to a Dionysian oneness with the unrepressed. As Bell puts it in relation to Cézanne:

> Everything can be seen as pure form, and behind pure form lurks the mysterious significance that thrills to ecstasy. The rest of Cézanne's life is a continuous effort to capture and express the significance of form.[15]

In taking up modernism as a critical discourse in the 1940s, Clement Greenberg's task was to rescue the materialist idea of 'significant form' from the mystical baggage attached to it by Fry and Bell, by early modernist abstract painters and by most of the postwar American Abstract expressionist painters Greenberg was busy promoting.[16]

Modernism is a critical discourse II: 1945

In the postwar period Clement Greenberg popularized the word 'modernism' (usually with a capital *M*) as a term denoting a critical discourse about twentieth-century modern art. Greenberg's theories gained ground in New York just as Abstract expressionism was being promoted as the most advanced art in the world, signalling New York taking over from Paris as the centre of modern art and culture. Acknowledging the influence of Fry and Bell from the early twentieth century, Greenberg's ideas related to painting but found a resonance across the arts, even in literature where the American school of New Criticism focused on 'immanent' interpretation of the 'autonomous' poem and its form. Confusingly, in cinema, his ideas have been more directly influential on 'avant-garde' and 'experimental' film than on what this book is defining as 'cinematic modernism', and it is necessary to briefly outline Greenberg's ideas in order to understand how modernism was initially consolidated as a critical discourse in the postwar period. Greenberg declares:

> Modernism includes more than just art and literature. By now it includes almost the whole of what is truly alive in our culture. It happens, also, to be very much of a historical novelty. Western civilization is not the first to turn around and question its own foundations, but it is the civilization that has gone furthest in doing so. I identify Modernism with that intensification, almost the exacerbation, of this self-critical tendency that began with the philosopher Kant. Because he was the first to criticize the means itself of criticism, I conceive of Kant as the first real Modernist.[17]

Greenberg saw modernism as synonymous with a stage of Western civilization in which everything, including the very foundations of that civilization, is open to question, to critique. Modernism is the modern tendency towards ongoing self-critique.[18] Greenberg's fundamental idea is that modern philosophy since Kant has developed via immanent critique, logic is used to critique logic, reason is used to critique reason. As far as art is concerned therefore, each modern art should follow modern philosophy in developing via self-criticism, via a dynamic internal to the aesthetic 'logic' of a given stage in the development of an art form – and it is the *form* rather than representational content through which this aesthetic logic unfolds. The parameters of form are in turn determined by medium specificity, which in the case of painting is materiality of paint and canvas, the frame (usually rectangular) and two-dimensionality, flatness. Greenberg is not against representation per se but he believes that in painting the representational involves illusions of space, depth and volume and such illusions, having been subjected to immanent critique since cubism, are no longer credible; modern painting as a self-reflexive art must acknowledge frame, flatness and surface, these are the determining conditions of painting as a medium-specific art.

A number of objections could be raised against Greenberg's basic premise. Art is not (yet) philosophy. Perhaps one day all arts will arrive at the purely conceptual, which according to Hegel would mark the end of art and its incorporation into philosophy. A conceptual turn did of course occur in painting and sculpture in the 1960s, but more generally the different arts continue to perform many different functions – representing reality, accessing the transcendental, generating aesthetic ecstasy, providing emotional consolation, expressing a political or ideological position, decorative pleasure and so forth. Why should such functions be determined by a grand narrative of unfolding self-critique? And anyway the conceptual in art is 'in the final analysis' itself representational (representing a concept) and therefore at odds with the Greenbergian stress on medium materiality. Although Kant in the *Critique of Judgement* applies rational critique to the concept of the aesthetic, Kant's assumption is that the aesthetic itself is a realm distinct from and outside the realm of critical reason – that is the whole point: the aesthetic is the 'free play of the faculties', the 'purposeless' play of the imagination. It should also be noted that abstract art in most cultures is not anti-representational, the abstract when not decorative represents the unrepresentable – God, the absolute, the beyond, the sublime – and, *contra* Greenberg, most modernist abstract painters, from Kandinsky and Malevich to Rothko and Barnett Newman, have explained their work in similar terms, the painting as gateway to the ineffable beyond.

Nevertheless, despite such objections, Greenberg's ideas remain, like Bell and Fry's, a useful marker of how modernism became constituted as a critical discourse and helps to explain why the best modern art often occurs as part of a wave which is founded upon a critique of a preceding set of artistic conventions, as driven by a Greenbergian logic of self-reflexive critique. This can be seen in cinematic modernism. For example, the various postwar new waves generally defined themselves by a withering critique of preceding cinematic aesthetics, and auteurs like Bergman, Antonioni, Pasolini and especially Godard are associated with an extended series of films in which each film develops out of, yet critiques, the form of the preceding film.

It is also possible to reconcile Greenberg's modernism with Bazin and Kracauer's theories of cinema. Bazin and Kracauer would argue that the essence of cinema resides in the 'ontology of the photographic image' – the complex relationship between film and reality and the complex relationship between the recording of reality and the reconstitution of that reality via montage. If so, then modernism in film would be primarily concerned with how a 'reality' immanent to cinema unfolds by way of a critical development of cinematic form within realist modes, rather than by way of the materiality of the cinematic apparatus itself (the medium-specific 'essence' which has been the concern of avant-garde and experimental film).

In proposing that the 'autonomy' of the modernist artwork resists assimilation to mass culture (and therefore capitalist commodification), the politics of

Greenberg's modernist aesthetic resembles that of Adorno in certain respects. For Greenberg, writing in the mid-twentieth century, American mass culture is commodified 'kitsch' (his term), a kind of opium of the people replacing religion as a means by which the elites control the masses – Hollywood film for both Greenberg and Adorno being an example of an instrument through which a kitsch culture, as a vehicle for reactionary ideas, is disseminated throughout American (and global) culture. Greenberg contended that modernist art opposes kitsch (a binary which postmodernism would reverse or dismantle). Modernist art must resist passive consumption and encourage critical conceptualization and interpretation on the part of the viewer. In Paris, in this same postwar period, similar ideas were being propagated by Roland Barthes in relation to literature. Barthes argued that a distinction should be made between 'readerly texts' passively consumed by the reader and 'writerly texts' with which the reader must critically and creatively engage.[19] From Joyce's *Ulysses* to Beckett's *Trilogy* and the *nouveau roman*, the modernist novel resists easy interpretation and passive consumption and is supposed to encourage an active critical participation by the reader in the act of generating meaning.

In the postwar period modernist art becomes identified with art that reflects critically on itself and which to some degree challenges and resists mass 'commodity' culture and mass public taste. Rather than offering accessible representations of reality, modernist art creates aesthetic forms which obstruct accessibility and resist assimilation into mass culture.[20] If an argument along these lines is accepted then a number of questions arise. Does 'realism' as a representational mode across the arts naturalize, normalize and consolidate existing constructions of 'reality', that is, the reality of capitalism and the assumptions and prejudices of bourgeois ideology? If so, should all modernist art reject 'naturalistic' realism? Should cinema, if it wants to be considered a modernist art, embrace formalism in order to create a critical distance between its modes of representation and what passes for 'realism'? Should cinema embrace modernist aesthetics as a means of resisting assimilation into the 'opium' of mass culture, of which Hollywood is the prime example? Should cinematic modernism set out to challenge its viewers and resist providing the easy pleasures of classical Hollywood film?

By the mid-1960s the predominantly Anglo-American critical discourse of modernism was becoming ubiquitous across diverse areas of art and culture. In doing so, the relatively coherent principles of Clement Greenberg concerning immanent critique, medium specificity, abstraction, form and autonomy had given way to a wide range of arguments about how modernism might be understood in relation to various mediums and artworks, in relation to popular culture and in relation to politics. It is at this point that Frank Kermode (best known as a literary critic) attempts what was almost certainly the first account of modernism *as a critical discourse*.

The emergence of modernism as a critical discourse

In his 1966 essay 'Modernisms' Frank Kermode noted the increasing prevalence of the terms 'modernism' and 'avant-garde' across the arts along with a new(ish) term 'postmodernism'. Much of the essay consists of Kermode casting a sceptical eye over various accounts of these terms.[21] He finds there to be general agreement that 'the modern' designates an historicization of the present, a self-consciousness about the idea that the present is somehow radically new and different from the past and that tomorrow will be different again from today, these differences manifesting themselves in art and culture as well as in science, technology, economy, politics, philosophy, morality and sensibility, or in a combination of some or all such fields. Although a corresponding term can be found in antiquity, there seems to be general agreement that 'the modern', as we might understand it, first becomes evident in the sixteenth and seventeenth centuries and has something to do with the Renaissance, the Enlightenment and the emergence of capitalism, that is to say has something to do with a long transition from the static and cyclical certainties of religion and feudalism to ideas of development, progress and evolution, driven primarily by technological and economic factors. Beyond those basics Kermode finds little consensus. Figures nominated as signifying the birth of 'the modern' range from Descartes, Rousseau, Kant, Hegel, Marx and Nietzsche to Shakespeare, Goethe, Byron, Wagner and Baudelaire. Events asserted as crucial to the birth of 'the modern' range from the Reformation and the English Civil War to the French and Russian Revolutions.

If 'the modern' remains a contested concept, then Kermode finds agreement that the word 'modernism' is essentially retrospective, emerging in the postwar period as a way of talking about modern art and culture from the early twentieth century. The word 'modernism' itself was not used very much in the 1920s and when it was it had specific contexts and connotations somewhat different from its postwar usage.[22] The term 'avant-garde' had been in currency since the aesthetes and Symbolists of the *fin de siècle* and while ostensibly designating art which was ahead of its time – ahead of and marking a break with the nineteenth century and signalling the arrival of the twentieth century, the future – in practice 'avant-garde' had long been synonymous with modern art which intentionally sets out to destabilize the art world and its values, shock the public and scandalize conservative bourgeois taste.

Kermode considers the argument that the postwar consolidation of modernism as a 'disciplinary field' was linked to its institutionalization within American universities and cultural life and that this was in turn bound up with the postwar promotion of modern art as an initiative of American cultural imperialism, sponsored by security agencies within the context of the Cold War as part of the battle to spread 'American' values of freedom and progress against communist totalitarian art and culture. This aspect of the promotion of modernism was a particularly painful point for Kermode who, when writing his essay on modernism in 1966, was about to resign as editor of the cultural and political magazine *Encounter* after it emerged that it had received funds from a front for the CIA.[23]

Kermode proceeds to offer his own perspective on modernism and, admitting that he is 'more in favour of continuities than of schisms', his account downplays the manifestos and polemics of futurists, Dada and the like and instead stresses continuities between modernism and the modern art movements of the second half of the nineteenth century: impressionism and post-impressionism, Manet and Cézanne, the Symbolist poets from Baudelaire and Rimbaud to Yeats, the (social) realist theatre of Ibsen and the realist formalism of novelists like Flaubert – the key characteristic of modernism, Kermode suggests, is 'its Flaubertian alliance of formal experiment and realism', a characteristic more important than shock, protest and 'making it new'.[24] Yet Kermode acknowledges that several radical turns if not 'schisms' do occur as conventionally marked by *Les Demoiselles d'Avignon* (1907), *The Rite of Spring* (1913) and *Ulysses* (1922). And a comparable radical turn occurs after 1945 with Abstract expressionism, *Waiting for Godot*, the *nouveau roman*, Stockhausen and Boulez. To which list might be added Rossellini, Antonioni, Fellini and Godard.

Kermode's conclusions can be summarized as follows: modernism has its roots in the late nineteenth century, in the new intensified engagement with issues of realism and the turn to formalism as a means to radicalize realist modes of representation. There is also a continuity between modernism and late-nineteenth-century aesthetics in the *privileging of the image*, whether as the primary unit of the new negotiation with reality and search for new realist modes or as a transcendental, almost alchemical portal through which the truth and the universal can be accessed.

Acknowledging that 'modernism' is a shifting and unstable critical discourse, the following definition might be offered as a counter to any narrow emphasis on modernism as anti-representational and anti-realist. Such a 'corrective' definition may be useful when considering cinema as a modernist art, given the central idea proposed by both Bazin and Kracauer that the 'essence' of cinema resides in its intrinsic relationship with concrete reality: *Modernism is essentially 'realist' – a critical engagement with objective reality and subjective consciousness of that reality – but, through its tendency towards abstraction of form, modernism maintains a critical distance from reality (ontological and social), manifesting an 'alienation' from reality – an estranged consciousness – while sustaining the redemptive utopian impulse of the formalist aesthetic 'sublime'.*

Part II: What is cinema?

> *The Cahiers axiom is this: that the cinema has a fundamental rapport with reality and that the real is not what is represented – and that's final.*
>
> – Serge Daney[25]

Cinema, like modernism, is a critical discourse. When in 1958 André Bazin asked the question 'what is cinema?' (his choice of title for projected volumes of his selected writings) he was not referring to films in general or theatres and studios, he was referring to an ongoing critical conversation about film with participants ranging from the early days of cinema to Bazin's contemporaries, participants including Béla Balázs, Rudolf Arnheim, Sergei Eisenstein, Vsevolod Pudovkin, Dziga Vertov, Siegfried Kracauer, Jean Epstein, Germaine Dulac, Jean Mitry, Lotte Eisner, Louis Delluc, Alexandré Astruc, Roger Leenhardt and Cesare Zavattini. Bazin didn't address all of these figures directly, but in his writings he is in dialogue with this broader critical discourse.

From the key thinkers in the critical discourse on cinema Siegfried Kracauer has been placed alongside Bazin for the purposes of this book, for the obvious reason that they are both known for having grappled with the problematic relationship between film and reality and also because they tentatively proposed a similar aesthetic derived from Italian neorealism, from *Paisà*, *Umberto D* and *Journey to Italy*, an aesthetic which constituted the initial basis for 'modern film' – and they did so *before* the arrival of the ground-breaking films of Fellini, Antonioni, Bergman and the *nouvelle vague*, that eclectic range of films commonly identified as achieved examples of cinematic modernism. In addition, the aesthetic proposed by Bazin and Kracauer – basically an encounter of documentary realist modes with modernist formalism, producing an 'informal formalism' – is a source of the dominant aesthetic in recent art film.

André Bazin

He [Bazin] had a curious way of taking off from the false to arrive at the true.
– Robert Bresson[26]

André Bazin (1918–58) wrote thousands of film reviews and essays for various journals and newspapers in the 1930s and 1940s, notably the liberal Catholic journal *L'Esprit*, Sartre's *Les Temps modernes* and a daily newspaper *Le Parisien libéré*. He also organized *ciné clubs* and networks. Through his writing and active promotion of film, Bazin came into contact with many of the important figures of his day including Sartre and Malraux. In 1951 he founded a new film journal *Les Cahiers du cinéma* with Jacques Doniol-Valcroze and recruited as writers for *Cahiers* young cinephile regulars at Henri Langlois's Cinémathèque Française, including Truffaut, Godard, Rivette, Rohmer and Chabrol. Although never producing a theoretical book as such, shortly before his premature death Bazin compiled a selection of his articles and essays as a thematically organized four-volume series entitled *Qu'est-ce que le cinéma?* (1958–62), which appeared in English as *What Is Cinema?* in two volumes (1967–71) translated by Hugh Gray with prefaces by Renoir and Truffaut.[27]

Bazin chose to open the first volume of *What Is Cinema?* with 'The Ontology of the Photographic Image', an essay which according to Dudley Andrew went through numerous drafts, gradually being refined down to its dense final version in 1945.[28] Like Benjamin's similarly endlessly interpreted essay 'The Work of Art in the Age of Mechanical Reproduction', the essay 'Ontology' is full of stimulating insights and speculations which are partly an effect of the essay's inscrutability as a whole, an inscrutability which has only increased with the countless layers of critical exegesis accrued over the decades. Bazin is often characterized as having been anti-montage, but the essay 'Ontology' reads like a would-be montage of different fragments from different, probably incompatible, discourses: Catholicism of various hues, Sartrean existentialism, Marxism, anthropology, Egyptology. The clash of abrupt juxtapositions is worthy of Eisenstein but closer to Bazin's own aesthetic in generating indeterminate effects, ending with a lone stray laconic sentence: 'On the other hand, of course, cinema is also a language' – a sentence which doesn't seem to relate to anything in the preceding essay and might even contradict the main argument, but like the freeze frame at the end of *400 Blows* forever places an ambiguity, an openness to interpretation, over the text. Bazin's other writings are generally approachable and, in his prescient endorsement of Rossellini and Bresson, it is relatively easy to reconstruct Bazin's aesthetic at the time of his death, at the moment cinema was on the cusp of cinematic modernism.

Film is a medium which mechanically and objectivity records reality unfolding in time, in duration. Yet film is an artificial reconstruction of reality whether through Soviet montage or Hollywood continuity editing. In addition, film is a mass-cultural medium, a popular entertainment driven by narrative and genre requirements. Film becomes 'cinema', becomes a modern art, when it develops realist modes of representation which incorporate and balance the recording of reality in duration, the formal interest of montage and the narrative and genre requirements. If the main characteristic of modernism since Cézanne is the application of 'significant form' to reality in order to abstract or reveal the 'essence' of reality, rather than the shift to pure formalism (including pure abstraction) characteristic of the avant-garde, then modern film can develop its own cinematic modernism, with a unique interest or tension, namely that any formalism must negotiate the particularly intense relationship film as a medium has with reality, with what Bazin conceives as 'the ontology of the photographic image'. What this means in terms of Bazin's aesthetic of modern film is a preference for a formalism, like Roger Fry's 'cinematographic frame', which subtly *reveals reality* (and therefore an 'essence', however defined, immanent to that reality) rather than a formalism which imposes itself upon reality (Figure 1).

Siegfried Kracauer

> *It has become necessary to point out that genuine realism consists in the interpretation of the raw material of experience by means of significant form and that therefore a concern with unshaped matter is a melancholy surrender rather than a recovery of man's grip on reality.*
>
> – Rudolph Arnheim, 'Melancholy Unshaped' (review of Kracauer's *Theory of Film* 1963)[29]

The association of Siegfried Kracauer (1889–1966) with the Frankfurt School went back a long way: he was tutor to the young Adorno, guiding his pupil through the rigours of Kant's *Critique of Pure Reason*. Kracauer himself seems to have kicked away the ladder of philosophy in the early 1920s, turning to

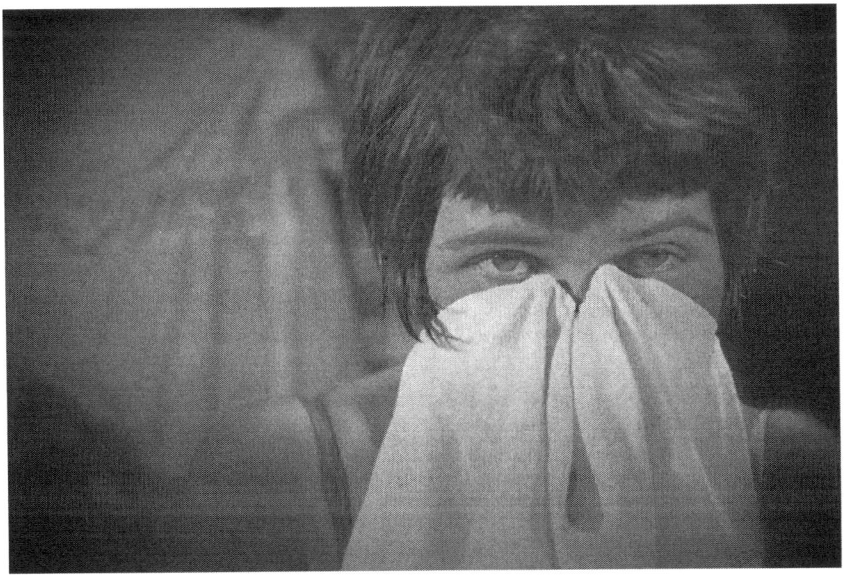

Figure 1 *Man with a Movie Camera* (1928), Dziga Vertov.
Morning in the modern city of the young Soviet Union and a woman washes her face. A casual everyday moment of intimate realism and eyes which look back at the camera/viewer. Reality as self-reflexive *before* Vertov's montage imposes itself upon that pro-filmic reality.

sociology and to writing influential essays on modern mass culture – many written in dialogue with Adorno and Benjamin – while working as a journalist on the *Frankfurter Zeitung*, including several hundred film reviews, not quite as many as Bazin's estimated three thousand reviews, but more than enough evidence of an intensive cinephile engagement with film in the 1920s.

When Hitler came to power Kracauer migrated to Paris and, like several other Frankfurt School associates, went to Marseille during the war, awaiting a passage to New York. As a refugee in limbo in Marseille he began planning his book *Theory of Film*. Miriam Bratu Hansen recounts a darkly humorous exchange about whether the refugee Jewish intellectuals would end up having to kill themselves to avoid a worse fate at Hitler's hands, to which Walter Benjamin responded:

> What will happen to us cannot be easily predicted. But of one thing I'm sure: if anyone will *not* kill himself, it's our friend Kracauer. After all, he has to finish writing his encyclopedia of film. And for that you need a long life.[30]

Unlike Benjamin, Kracauer did escape Europe, making the voyage to New York, where he established his reputation with *From Caligari to Hitler: A Psychological*

History of the German Film (1947), a book that reads German expressionist and Weimar-era films as revealing a political unconscious in which the national anxieties, fears and delusions that would give rise to Nazism in the 1930s were already prefigured. In 1948 Kracauer resumed work on *Theory of Film* and, in her introduction to the current edition, Hansen traces the development of the project through various notebooks and drafts along with summaries and proposals for publishers. Suffice to say the book had a long gestation between Marseille 1941 and its eventual publication as *Theory of Film: The Redemption of Physical Reality* in 1960. Having researched the drafts, Hansen suggests that a subtext of the book – redeeming the reality of the Holocaust – is gradually and almost entirely erased, the final book containing just one enigmatic reference towards its close:

> [In] the litter of tortured human bodies in the films made of Nazi concentration camps, we redeem horror from its invisibility behind the veils of panic and imagination. And this experience is liberating in as much as it removes a most powerful taboo. Perhaps Perseus' greatest achievement was not to cut off Medusa's head but to overcome his fears and look at its reflection in the shield. And was it not precisely this feat which permitted him to behead the monster?[31]

This difficult comment might be glossed as follows: cinema has the capacity to create an impersonal mechanical objective record of the reality of the concentration camps, such a recording of reality would not succumb to the tasteless and mystifying effects of other kinds of artistic representation but provide clarity as to the nature of the horror and would have the potential to 'redeem' the otherwise lost or invisible reality of the camps and incorporating the redemptive power to fight back and destroy the monster (Fascism).

Both Bazin and Kracauer foreground the idea that cinema, because of its unique relationship to reality and time, can somehow redeem reality. Their respective theories of modern film are theories of redemption. In Bazin's case, the theological baggage is evident and for both Bazin and Kracuer there is a traumatic historical consciousness attached to the idea of reality and its redemption, but in Kracauer's *Theory of Film* redemption is rendered into secular 'materialist' terms. For Kracauer reality is physical reality, however, this 'vulgar' materialism barely conceals the underlying extension of reality to include existential reality, our relationship to the 'flow of life' – one of Kracauer's favourite phrases. By the end of *Theory of Film* it is evident that what is important about cinema is not its capacity to record physical reality per se, but its capacity via its peculiar temporal dimensions, including duration, to represent quotidian reality as an integral element of this 'flow of life', a flow which only the moving image, film not the photograph, can record. Kracauer sees the uniqueness of cinema not only as located in its capacity to record the everyday, the typical and the contingent 'in themselves' but also as part of a flow both temporal and existential, and to present fragments of reality within the flow of life in a way which may indicate metonymically matters of greater significance, whether psychological, historical, political, philosophical or of a cosmic order. Redemption of reality lies in the way cinema can transmit everyday reality and the moment, in the immediacy of its presentness, into this realm of greater existential significance.

Theory of Film wears its philosophical background lightly, neither is it particularly sociological, only occasionally referring to audiences and matters of reception. Benjamin had it right when he referred to Kracauer's 'encyclopedia' of film – the book is essentially a classification and typology of different aspects of film: types of narrative, types of genre, types of actor and acting, different uses of music and sound, and so on. The book begins by laying out the classic binary: '*the realistic tendency*' represented by Lumière and '*the formative tendency*' represented by Méliès; the documentary tendency towards recording reality and the opposing tendency towards creating stylized representations of reality or the fantastic and all points between. The subsequent history of film will be a history of how these two tendencies, the realistic and the formative, relate and interact. Most of *Theory of Film* consists of charting this relationship, Kracauer arguing that film must never lose its primary reference to reality but that certain types of narrative, story and even plot, are necessary to elicit this reality. Kracauer's own eclectic taste in films doesn't always conform to his strictures on the right balance between the realistic and the formative (requiring numerous qualifications to his typology) but that balance is finally achieved with neorealism and *Umberto D*, De Sica's film being a constant reference point throughout *Theory of Film*.

Bazin and Kracauer

> *Cinephilia questioned the categories of artistic modernism not by deriding high art but by restoring a closer and less obvious linkage between the types of art, the emotions of the narrative, and by discovering the splendour that the most commonplace objects could acquire on a lighted screen in a dark auditorium: a hand lifting a curtain or fumbling with a door handle, a head leaning out of a window, a fire or car headlights in the night, drinking glasses glittering on a bar . . . it introduced us to a positive understanding, in no way ironic or disillusioned, of the impurity of art.*
>
> – Jacques Rancière[32]

Bazin and Kracauer were both cinephiles. They resented the low cultural status accorded to cinema and worked to secure its position as a modern art form and as a subject worthy of serious study and deserving of institutional support from the academy and state. At the same time, however, they appreciated the fact that cinema was a living mass-cultural form and not a rarefied art reduced to a sterile afterlife in the university, museum or gallery. They saw and reviewed films mostly for a popular newspaper readership. They were interested in all films, whatever the nationality, whatever the period, whatever the genre. A bad film might be worth watching because it contains one scene of interest. For the true believer all films, even the most debased, have a right to exist in the church of cinema. Paradoxically, but not unusually, this extreme liberalism in practice was accompanied by a sometimes doctrinaire theory as to what constitutes 'true' cinema and what 'true' cinema should become, after the war, as it begins to correspond to a modernist art.

Bazin and Kracauer converge in their basic liking for Hollywood and various types of mainstream genre cinema (the Western, film noir) and in their misgivings about so-called 'quality' and 'artistic' film of the theatrical and literary adaptation type. Both revere D. W. Griffith and Chaplin. Both have a vexed relationship with Hitchcock. Bazin has criticisms of Soviet (montage) film and German expressionist film. Kracauer is critical of Eisenstein, though less so than Bazin. Perhaps because he had been a German film critic in the Weimar, Kracauer is far more sympathetic than Bazin to expressionism and German silent film in general. Bazin and Kracauer share a degree of scepticism towards the avant-garde film. They, especially Kracauer, find certain individual avant-garde films interesting, but both see avant-garde film as overly influenced by trends in modern art (painting) and as estranged from cinema in its rejection of narrative and realism. They both reject formalist excess; form in cinema should facilitate the unfolding of reality not its disavowal. They both reject any notion of 'pure cinema', the aesthetic they endorse is always going to be a hybrid of genre-based narrative modes and realist documentary modes.

Bazin and Kracauer do not ignore the technical, commercial or historical contexts which determine filmmaking, nevertheless in their more theoretically inclined writing their prime concern is to try and identify a particular cinematic aesthetic which is grounded in the ontological (Bazin) or material (Kracauer) status of reality itself. This is not the medium-specific materiality of the cinematic apparatus and modification of the celluloid film stock characteristic of avant-garde or experimental filmmakers, but the 'pro-filmic' material reality of what the film medium records, the reality of its content (a train arriving at a station, the look on a face, the wind in the trees, the play of reflections in a puddle in the street) and the temporal duration of that content, that event. Yet both Bazin and Kracauer recognize that there is a complicated passage from the recording of reality on film to the cinematic representation of reality. Their respective theories of film are an extended grappling with what the relationship between 'pro-filmic' reality and cinematic representational reality might be. They see film as a modern art emerging in the encounter of 'classical' Hollywood modes with documentary modes and modernist formalism.

Light narrative

The 'staged' encounter of 'classical' narrative modes with documentary 'realist' modes is prefigured in any number of films from cinema's early years and from the documentary movements of the 1920s and 1930s. Bazin and Kracauer emphasize the importance of *Nanook of the North* (1922) and Flaherty's subsequent films as early indicators of the kind of aesthetic they are searching for: an encounter between reality itself and the discreet staging of that reality structured by a minimal 'light narrative' to use Kracauer's term. And what are the characteristics of this new aesthetic emerging from the encounter of narrative and documentary modes? Bazin and Kracauer converge most of all in their enthusiastic engagement with Italian neorealism, seeing the key characteristics of neorealism as being light narrative, loose plotting and elliptical episodic narrative structure, along with casual or informal intrusions of 'reality' and contingency. These will be the foundational elements of their preferred aesthetic of modern cinema.

Bazin's well-known writings mostly date from the mid-1940s to the mid-1950s. Although Kracauer published *Theory of Film* in 1960, two years after Bazin's death, there is a sense that he was less up to date than Bazin, a sense that the regular cinema-going of his Weimar days was long gone and that by the 1950s he was only seeing a relatively small number of films; many of the most interesting films of the 1950s go unmentioned in *Theory of Film*. Bazin understands that neorealism marks a break and a shift in the history of cinema, as creating the conditions for a new kind of modern cinema which has come into being specifically with Rossellini and Bresson. Kracauer sees neorealism as exemplifying his preferred aesthetic largely on the basis of *Umberto D* and certain episodes in *Paisà*, but seems unsure about its broader significance and, some discussion of Fellini and Bresson aside, unsure about where cinema is heading. Towards the end of *Theory of Film* there are a few brief tantalizing references to *Seventh Seal* and *Wild Strawberries*, presumably late additions to the text. However, perhaps because he was based in America, Kracauer seems better informed than Bazin about the American experimental film scene, giving qualified praise to Maya Deren (*Meshes of the Afternoon* 1943) and Stan Brakhage (*Loving* 1957).

Together *What Is Cinema?* and *Theory of Film* share a similar small canon of films. *Rashomon* seems to be the only Japanese film Kracauer has seen, and Japanese films don't appear in the two English volumes of *What Is Cinema?* (although they do in Bazin's annual *Cahiers* lists). Satyajit Ray's *Pather Panchali* (1955) and *Aparijito* (1957) are the only major Indian films discussed. Leaving Hollywood, including Welles and Hitchcock, to one side, the following list (almost identical to *What Is Cinema?* and *Theory of Film*) suggests the mostly European reference points for the common aesthetic Bazin and Kracauer are developing independently of one another and includes the key postwar films Bazin and Kracauer are writing about:

Partie de campagne (Renoir 1936, released 1946)
La Règle du jeu (Renoir 1939, rereleased 1956)
Ossessione (Visconti 1943)
Paisà (Rossellini 1946)
Bicycle Thieves (De Sica 1948)
La terra trema (Visconti 1948)
The Third Man (Reed 1949)
Stromboli (Rossellini 1950)
Story of a Love Affair (Antonioni 1950)
Los Olvidados (Bunuel 1950)
Diary of a Country Priest (Bresson 1951)
Umberto D. (De Sica 1952)
Europa '51 (Rossellini 1952)
I vitelloni (Fellini 1953)
Viaggio in Italia (Rossellini 1954)
La strada (Fellini 1954)
Ordet (Dreyer 1955)
Pather Panchali (Satyajit Ray 1955)
A Man Escaped (Bresson 1956)
Aparijito (Satyajit Ray 1957)
Nights of Cabiria (Fellini 1957)
Wild Strawberries (Bergman 1957)

This list confirms the centrality of Italian neorealism but shows that Bazin and Kracauer, despite their theoretical adherence to 'reality' and their continued loyalty to Flaherty, recognized that documentary realism was in itself unsatisfactory. Genre-based narrative modes derived from Hollywood needed to be introduced into documentary realism in order to elicit 'reality' and create 'true' formative and imaginative cinema. This was the case with what is usually credited as the first neorealist film, Visconti's *Obsession* – gritty social realism with plenty of what Kracauer would call 'physical reality' but also a noir thriller, a story of erotic passion and murder, an early adaptation of James M. Cain's *The Postman Always Rings Twice.*

Stromboli *(1950)*

The defining encounter of Hollywood and Italian neorealist 'reality' is staged when Rossellini introduces Ingrid Bergman, at the time Hollywood's biggest and most glamorous star, into the shot-on-location reality of the small volcanic island of Stromboli (near Sicily) and its cast of non-professional actor inhabitants. Ingrid Bergman plays a refugee character Karin, displaced by the war, who finds herself in an allied internment camp but gains release by marrying an Italian prisoner of war and agreeing to go with him to Stromboli. Life on the rocky island is harsh and the inhabitants hostile to this foreign stranger and her modern ways. She plans an escape from the island but then experiences a redemptive epiphany – existentialist and religious – while climbing the side of a volcano, clambering amid the volcanic ash. Filmed on location there are several 'documentary' sequences about working lives on the island, including an extended fishing scene in which Karin participates. *Stromboli* was a flop on release, a 1950 review in *Variety* being typical:

> Given elementary-school dialog to recite and impossible scenes to act, Ingrid Bergman's never able to make the lines real nor the emotion sufficiently motivated to seem more than an exercise. [. . .] The only visible touch of the famed Italian director is in the hard photography, which adds to the realistic, documentary effect of life on the rocky, lava-blanketed island. Rossellini's penchant for realism, however, does not extend to Bergman. She's always fresh, clean and well-groomed.[33]

The critical reputation of the film was rescued by Bazin and positive notices in *Cahiers*, but the *Variety* review inadvertently captures what is interesting about the film. It is not so much in the encounter of the character Karin with the island and its inhabitants within the narrative that 'reality' lies. It is in the 'staged' encounter of Ingrid Bergman the actress with her surroundings that a defamiliarized reality emerges: Ingrid Bergman in this completely, to her, alien rocky physical reality of the island and the otherness of its inhabitants – a Hollywood star struggling with a non-Hollywood location, script and acting style, with none of the support she was used to having when shooting in a Hollywood studio and little support from her own new husband, the director. By all accounts Ingrid Bergman found the filming of *Stromboli* and her time on the island a deeply unsettling and uncomfortable ordeal. As the *Variety* review puts it: 'Rossellini's penchant for realism, however, does not extend to Bergman. She's always fresh, clean and well-groomed.' But it is in this encounter between a well-groomed Bergman, the Hollywood star, and the neorealist mode, along with a rough-hewn formalist abstraction in the image composition, that a complex reflexive reality is generated (Figure 2).

Bazin himself did not often use the term 'modernist' for several reasons. He associated 'modernism' with developments in painting which favoured

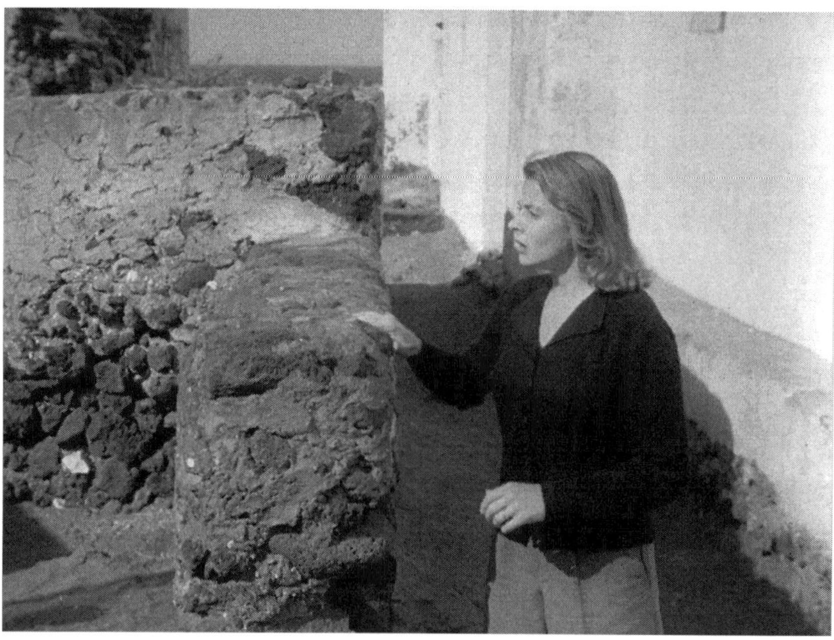

Figure 2 *Stromboli: Land of God* (1950), Roberto Rossellini.
Beyond neorealism: not only in staging an encounter between Hollywood icon Ingrid Bergman and a location setting with non-professional cast in an island community but in the encounter between documentary realism and a rough-hewn formalism often tending towards abstraction – in this case a composition featuring Bergman within vertical and horizontal lines, rectangular blocks and a play of white, black and shades of grey.

ideas of medium-specific purity and total abstraction with which he was not in sympathy or felt to be unsuited to cinema. He had reservations about modernist film – German expressionism and Soviet montage – from the silent era and a degree of antipathy towards the avant-garde or experimental art film. In the immediate postwar period he was involved in heated polemics with the proto-Situationist *Lettrists*, who upheld the perennial Dadaesque provocative strategies of the avant-garde. More generally, in French art criticism the terms 'modern' and 'modernity' tended to cover what is in Anglo-American criticism called 'modernism'. However, terminological confusions aside, it is evident that Bazin was rather more aware than Kracauer that postwar developments in film, especially what was emerging out of neorealism, marked a threshold on the other side of which lay a cinematic aesthetic corresponding to developments in modern art, in particular the modernist novel of the 1920s: Joyce, Faulkner, Hemingway. According to Bazin 'the modern film' dates from Italian neorealism and the transition from *Paisà* and *Umberto D* to *Stromboli* and *Journey to Italy*. This transition is identified by a self-reflexivity inherent in juxtaposing a documentary reality (real locations, non-professional actors, long takes) with 'light' fictional narrative form (episodic, loosely plotted) in recognizable cinematic genres (thriller, melodrama, romance, quest), combining non-actors with star actors, and deploying a formalism including montage (cuts, ellipses) that structures and reconfigures narrative time without undermining the integrity of real-time duration. These characteristics become the key features of cinematic modernism.

Stanley Cavell: A world screened

Stanley Cavell's *The World Viewed* (1971) is informed philosophically by Heidegger (and existentialism), its approach to modernism is informed by Clement Greenberg (and Michael Fried) and its approach to cinema is informed by André Bazin. Cavell's first love was the classical Hollywood film he grew up with, but the main reference points in the book are modernists: Vigo, Renoir, Dreyer, Bresson, Bergman, Antonioni, Truffaut and Godard. Cavell also discusses what he calls 'neo-Hollywood': *Bonnie and Clyde*, *The Graduate*, *Petulia*, *Point Blank* and *Rosemary's Baby* (films from 1967–9; Cavell was writing before the 'New Hollywood' of Altman, Coppola, Scorsese, Malick et al. had broken through).[34]

The basic argument proposed in *The World Viewed*, which Cavell acknowledges is derived from Bazin, can be summarized as follows: the purpose of art is to reveal the world in its being, presence and immediacy of 'presentness'.

On the one hand, photography marked an absolute break in the history of art because it records mechanically without human intervention the world itself. But the photographic still is torn out of time and consequently, for better or worse, seems artificial, theatrical or an imitation of painting. Cinema, on the other hand, not only has the 'ontological' virtues of photography (the automatic mechanical recording of the world itself, presentation rather than representation) but also records duration; it reveals the world in its temporal and ontological 'presentness' as continuity (Cavell agrees with Bazin that montage as a formalist device should be used sparingly).

Film records the world mechanically without human intervention and film is watched by viewers who are invisible to it, watching a screening of the world into which they cannot intervene. The viewer passively watches the world unfold on the screen, but this means that the viewer is an outsider who views the world in its 'thereness'. This opens up a fundamental 'alienation' (the first of many) because although cinema presents the world 'as it is' the viewer is separate from that world, essentially a voyeur. The revealing of the 'thereness' of the world may not be a bad thing but it is not 'hereness' and certainly not 'oneness'. Similarly the 'presentness' of cinema is a peculiar thing because screening is in the present but the world being screened is in the past: the viewer watches a present in its pastness or the past in its presentness. Either way, it is evident that cinema reveals not 'presentness' or 'being in time' but a series of temporal dislocations within a virtual present of screening/viewing, or as Bazin and Deleuze might say, a film is mummified in (multiple) sheets of presentness and sheets of pastness.

Cavell engages with the obvious objections that arise to the basic Bazinian argument of *The World Viewed*.[35] However, what is of particular interest is Cavell's schema (writing in 1971) of early cinema, classical Hollywood cinema and modernist cinema. Cavell begins conventionally enough by aligning modernity with modernist aesthetics by way of Baudelaire:

> Baudelaire called for a realization of the other half of art whose first half is 'the eternal and unchangeable'. The half he wanted he named 'modernity', that which is 'ephemeral, fugitive, contingent upon occasion', the 'description of contemporary life', and in particular the 'nature of beauty in the present time'. And he says: 'The pleasure we derive from the depiction of the present arises not only from the beauty in which it can be attired, but also from its essential quality of being the present.'[36]

An art in its early stage, argues Cavell, involves a playing with the novelties of a new medium, while an art in its classical stage has refined its means of processing a given medium and is satisfied by its representation of the world. An art enters its modernist stage when it is no longer satisfied by its modes of representation and turns back to an interrogation of its medium, which usually means questioning processes and stripping away all that is extraneous or not specific to a given medium.

> For what has made the movie a candidate for art is its natural relation to its traditions of automatism. The lapse of conviction in its traditional uses of its automatism forces it into modernism; its potentiality for acknowledging that lapse in ways that will redeem its power makes modernism an option for it.[37]

Cavell takes his definition of modernism from Greenberg's analysis of modernist painting; however, neither Clement Greenberg nor Michael Fried had much to say about cinema, they considered its populism, mix of high and low registers and technologically over-determined development antithetical to modernism. By contrast Cavell sees cinema as obeying the laws of artistic development laid down by Greenberg, but extends the idea of medium specificity (automatism) beyond the material medium and apparatus to include aesthetic forms; through innovation of form the new modernist cinema of Antonioni and Godard is 'interrogating' the conditions of possibility of film as an art and as a medium. In other words, technical innovations in film can generate new aesthetic forms. Unlike painting, where technical innovations involving the very materiality of painting as a medium are comparatively rare, in cinema technical innovations are frequent and impossible to separate from the new aesthetic forms to which they give rise.

Cavell discusses at some length examples of such innovations which are both technical/medium specific and formalist: use of slow motion, the freeze frame (especially for a film's closing image), flash insets (flash edits of the Resnais type), split-screen, use of documentary or newsreel inserts, experimentation with camera position/perspective, use of silence and overlapping dialogue. Cavell notes that these devices have already become the clichés of modernist film and have fed into mainstream film and television drama, but defends them as the necessary means by which cinema becomes a modernist art by questioning its own conventions and traditions and its own basis as a medium:

> Our sudden storms of flash insets and freeze frames and slow-motions and telescopic-lens shots and fast cuts and negative printing and blurred focusings – unlike the use of such experiments in the early period of film – are responses to an altered sense of film, a sense that film has brought itself into question and must be questioned and openly confessed.[38]

Cavell defends these technical/formal devices as 'modernist' not just when such devices are 'forms' integrated into the narrative 'content' of a given film but when used by a film which has an overall 'integrity' – in which case the devices function as a self-reflexive critique or interrogation of film form. He gives the example of Truffaut's *Jules et Jim* (1962) in which 'modernist devices' are used in an unexpected way not in keeping with a period drama, but for that precise reason mark a modernist interrogation of the conventions of romantic period drama, of genre, of 'classical' cinematic representation. By this point Cavell has taken an awkward Heideggerian turn in his response to problems with his basic Bazinian argument and is now evaluating films on the basis of their integrity and refusal of bad faith. The modernist interrogation of classical cinema strips away the falseness and the extraneous forms of a now passé classicism and brings film back to its essence, which is its capacity to record and then 'exhibit' (screen) reality – the world – in all its detail:

> To satisfy the wish for the world's exhibition we must be willing to let the world as such appear. According to Heidegger this means that we must be willing for anxiety, to which alone the world as world, into which we are thrown, can manifest itself; and it is through that willingness that the possibility of one's own existence begins or ends.[39]

This seems unduly programmatic. In practice Cavell appreciates cinema for the same reason as Bazin, Kracauer and most of the other critics and theorists in this book: what modernist cinema since neorealism has retained from the founding cinematic myth of the automatic recording of unfolding reality in duration is the emergence of a particularity of detail within quotidian existence – and the epiphanic potential of such details within a narrative:

> Early in its history the cinema discovered the possibility of *calling* attention to persons and parts of persons and objects; but it is equally a possibility of the medium not to call attention to them but, rather, to let the world happen, to let its parts draw attention to themselves according to their natural weight. This possibility is less explored than its opposite. Dreyer, Flaherty, Vigo, Renoir, and Antonioni are masters of it.[40]

Classical Hollywood cinema calls attention to a detail of its 'reality effect' to a precise degree required by dramatic/narrative ends – story, plot, characterization – while cinematic modernism and its precursors allow reality in its detail a relative autonomy from narrative requirements. In cinematic modernism a given object may have no overt significance, but in eliciting a response from a viewer it may take on a significance for that viewer:

> [Sparing] our attention wholly for *that* thing *now*, in the frame of nature, the world moving in the branch.[41]

Cavell doesn't quite refer to Griffith's 'wind in the leaves' but in seeing 'the world moving in the branch' perhaps goes further. The quotidian detail or object, whether in its thingness or in its uncanny ineffability, may take on significance for the viewer but this should remain beyond verbal communication, beyond the sayable. The cinematic image aspires to the condition of poetry but resists pre-determined symbolism. Moreover, the detail or object in the cinematic image is in movement and this seems to lead away from a symbolic function and towards the evocation of fleeting mood and memory:

> I have rather in mind the pulsing air of incommunicability which may nudge the edge of any experience and placement: the curve of fingers that day, a mouth, the sudden rise of the body's frame as it is caught by the color and scent of flowers, laughing all afternoon mostly about nothing, the friend gone but somewhere now which starts from here – spools of history that have unwound only to me now, occasions which will not reach words for me now, and if not now, never.[42]

This sounds less like the automatic recording and screening of a world into which I am thrown and more like the romantic epiphanies of a certain type of postwar cinematic modernism: to be precise, a quintessential 1960s *nouvelle vague* movie.

Miriam Bratu Hansen: Cinema, modernity and modernism

> *Cinema, like no other medium, can register material phenomena in their otherness, their opaque singularity.*
>
> – Miriam Bratu Hansen[43]

In addition to her role in explicating Kracauer's work and rehabilitating it from relative critical neglect, Miriam Bratu Hansen is significant to this book in that she was a contemporary critic who always asserted the importance of modernity and modernism, even when these terms have been unfashionable in academia, and always asserted the centrality of cinema to any discussion of modernity and modernism. Hansen's 2012 book *Cinema and Experience* attempts to undercut the familiarity of the respective positions concerning modernity, modernism and cinema commonly assigned to Siegfried Kracauer, Walter Benjamin and Theodor Adorno, and instead show how their positions interact, shift and develop. Earlier, in the 1999 essay 'The Mass Production of the Senses: Classical Cinema as Vernacular Modernism', the question of how cinema might fit into the relationship between modernity and modernism led Hansen to elaborate the idea of 'vernacular modernism'. Of the many revisions of modernism as a critical discourse which have emerged in the last twenty years or so, vernacular modernism is perhaps the most influential. The following remarks indicate some key points in Hansen's account of cinema, modernity and modernism in *Cinema and Experience* before suggesting why the idea of vernacular modernism presents a challenge to the aesthetic of contemporary cinematic modernism.

Kracauer, Benjamin and Adorno start out sharing the widely held premise of the period after the First World War that modernity marked the decline of Western civilization. Hansen writes:

> Kracauer's writings prior to the mid-1920s by and large participate in the period's pessimistic, lapsarian discourse on modernity. Within a predominantly philosophical and theological framework, modernity appears as the endpoint of a historical process of disintegration, spiritual loss, and withdrawal of meaning from life, a dissociation of truth and existence. Expelled from a traditional order of life and a corresponding religious sphere, the individual is 'thrown into the cold infinity of empty space and empty time', a state summed up in Georg Lukács's phrase 'transcendental homelessness'.[44]

Although Kracauer identified positive aspects to the new mass culture, Hansen begins *Cinema and Experience* by charting how his writing on film in the 1920s comes to reflect increasingly pessimistic sociological and ideological considerations:

> Kracauer's early film reviews are actually cinema reviews, in the sense that they include remarks on theater design, performance practices, musical accompaniment, and audience response. From 1925 on he began to reflect on the cinema more generally as a catalyst of a new kind of public, symptomatic of the culture of leisure and consumption that he saw emerge in Germany with the introduction of principles of mass production and the concurrent mushrooming of the class of white-collar workers or employees. When, toward the end of the decade, his writings on film and cinema increasingly shifted from a materialist physiognomy of modernity to a critique of ideology – prefiguring the approach of *From Caligari to Hitler* (1947) – it was because, in the face of the mounting political crisis, contemporary cinema was failing on two counts: it neither advanced the negativity of the historical process, or 'self-sublation' of modernity, nor lived up to the liberating, egalitarian impulses in which Kracauer had discerned the contours of a democratic mass public.[45]

While Kracauer becomes disillusioned about the progressive potential of film in the late 1920s, Hansen sees Benjamin as becoming more interested in cinema as a mass-cultural form – culminating in various versions of the essay 'Work of Art in the Age of Mechanical Reproduction' – because he thought that film might have a positive cultural role in two ways.[46] First, by being therapeutic, by allowing audiences – the masses – to find a cathartic outlet for their grievances and frustrations in cinematic fantasies that might otherwise take on more dangerous fascistic forms in the real world. Second, by allowing audiences to become conscious of the everyday conditions of their estrangement, particularly as regard to work and technology. The first argument is informed by psychoanalysis and Benjamin's penchant for surrealist aesthetics, the second argument is informed by Marxism and Brecht. Brechtian aesthetics, with their extradiegetic disruptions and estrangement effects, not only corresponded to Benjamin's reading of Soviet cinema as a cinema of defamiliarization but also led to a reconsideration of Hollywood slapstick and its disruptions of plot, its parodic subversions of the 'experience' of modernity. Animation took kinetic physical comedy to a new extreme. In the first Mickey Mouse film *Steamboat Willie* (1928) everything is in motion; the human, animal and everyday objects are constantly morphing into each other; bodies extending, contracting and fragmenting. Liberated from the technical restrictions of live action and sound coordination, the early Disney films combine the shapeshifting anti-naturalism of animation with sound to create what Benjamin proposes is an aesthetic primarily of rhythm, parodying the delirious rhythms of modern life and technology. The idea that (early) Mickey Mouse might be subversive was not unusual – Eisenstein was a fan – but Hansen argues that Benjamin goes much further, seeing Mickey Mouse, like Chaplin and Keaton, as an 'allegorical' figure with which audiences identify and through which audiences resist – through laughter – their fear of modernity and its technology and do so as a 'compact mass' in a cinema. This positive collective experience, along with the humour and absurdism of slapstick, is not only subversive in relation to capitalist rationalism but is diametrically opposed to the pomposity of fascism and its construction of a disempowered dehumanized mass.

The attribution of significant cultural value to popular Hollywood cinema in relation to modernity complicates the distinction between high and low culture. According to Benjamin, modernist 'high' art alienates a mass audience, while supposedly 'low' culture, such as a Hollywood film, can deliver a progressive engagement with modernity which is accessible to a mass audience through a new mode of reception:

> The reactionary attitude toward a Picasso painting changes into the progressive reaction toward a Chaplin film. This progressive reaction is characterized by the direct, intimate fusion of visual and emotional enjoyment with the orientation of the expert.[47]

Adorno found Benjamin's speculations on the progressive character of humour in Chaplin and Disney unconvincing, as Hansen explains:

> Adorno cautions Benjamin emphatically against romanticizing the barbarism manifested in mass-cultural reception: 'The laughter of a cinema audience . . . is anything but salutary and revolutionary; it is full of the worst bourgeois sadism instead'. He extends this verdict even to Chaplin, who had been a political good object, after all, not just for Kracauer but generally in leftist-intellectual and avant-garde circles of the time.[48]

The following statement, quoted by Hansen from Adorno's controversial letter to Benjamin (18 March 1936) criticizing the 'artwork' essay, is often taken as summing up his view of the debasement of both high and low culture under conditions of capitalist modernity:

> Both [the highest and the lowest] bear the stigmata of capitalism, both contain elements of change (but never, of course, the middle-term between Schönberg and the American film); both are the torn halves of an integral freedom, to which however they do not add up.[49]

What tends to go unremarked about this statement is that 'American film' stands for the lowest kind of mass culture. Although Adorno is in fact suggesting that high and low culture have validity, in that they bear the 'stigmata' of capitalism in a way middle-brow bourgeois culture doesn't, he insists that projecting high modern culture – modernism – onto low mass culture (as, one might say, a 'vernacular modernism'), in this case onto Hollywood film, even Chaplin, is misguided romanticism:

> The idea that the reactionary is turned into a member of the avant-garde by expert knowledge of Chaplin's films strikes me as out-and-out romanticization. For I cannot count Kracauer's favourite director, even after *Modern Times*, as an avant-garde artist (the reason will be perfectly clear from my article on jazz), nor do I believe that any of the decent elements in this work will attract attention. One need only have heard the laughter of the audience at the film to know what is actually happening.[50]

Hansen begins her main discussion of Adorno by summarizing the basic analysis of Adorno and Horkheimer's *Dialectic of Enlightenment* (1947):

> There, to recall, the authors excoriated the culture industry as a system of secondary exploitation, domination, and integration by which advanced capitalism subordinates any cultural practice, low or high, to a single purpose: to reproduce the spectator/listener as consumer. If the culture industry voraciously commodified human experience and reduced all art to advertisement, any attempt to make a difference was doomed to be assimilated and to validate the system as a whole; no alternative practice of film (or any other technologically based mass medium) seemed conceivable.[51]

This damning appraisal of the culture industry informs Adorno's negative view of cinema. Turning to Adorno's scattered writings specifically on cinema, Hansen focuses on the essay 'Transparencies on Film' (1966).[52] According to Hansen the essay was written 'in solidarity' with the Young German Cinema declared by the 1962 Oberhausen manifesto (this group of young filmmakers were aligned with other international new waves and evolved into the New German Cinema of Kluge, Schlöndorff, Fassbinder, Herzog, Wenders and von Trotta). If so, then the essay is a very Adorno-like act of solidarity. He sympathizes with the Oberhausen group's disgust at established German cinema but is caustic about the Oedipal rhetoric of young new waves rebelling against 'Daddy's Cinema'. He appears ambivalent about the new permissiveness associated with films 'peddling Parisian libertinage' (the *nouvelle vague*?) and criticizes Schlöndorff's 1966 film adaptation of Musil's *Young Törless*, arguing that modernist literary texts are incompatible with film, particularly film dialogue. Adorno makes a passing complaint about Kracauer's *Theory of Film* for practising 'sociological abstention' and criticizes both Kracauer and Benjamin for fetishizing cinema 'as the discoverer of the beauties of daily life'.[53] Although Hansen sees Adorno as interested in the international new waves, he condemns neorealism for its belief in the immediacy of film's rendering of reality (a criticism also aimed at Kracauer and Benjamin) because reality and nature are themselves now – in modernity – lost to experience, are themselves commodified ideologically mediated constructs. At the same time, he condemns the anti-realist techniques associated with art cinema, such as soft focus, superimpositions, flashbacks, abstraction and radical montage. He sees these techniques as crude would-be analogues for formalist techniques in other modernist arts, cinema invariably reducing such techniques to mannerism.

Nevertheless, Adorno accepts that for better or for worse cinema is a crucial medium to modernity and believes that cinema, to become a modernist art, would have to negate or self-reflexively critique its basic nature as a medium, in the way other postwar modernist arts, such as Beckett in theatre or Boulez

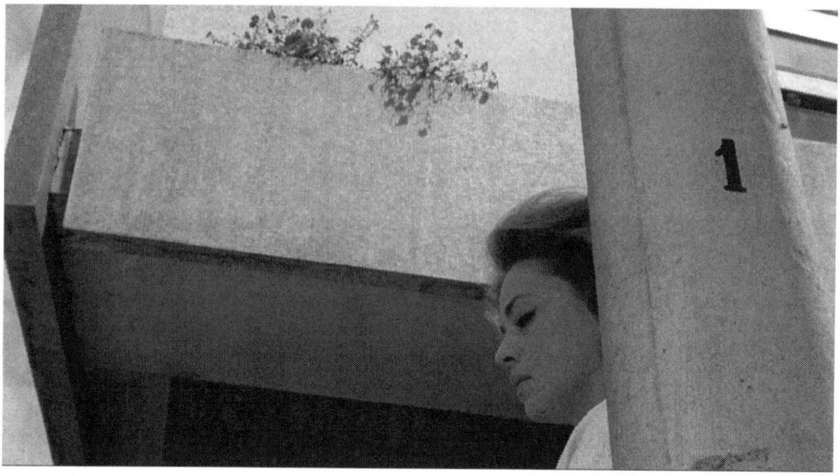

Figure 3 *La Notte* (1961), Michelangelo Antonioni.
Jeanne Moreau caught from below at a tentative angle overwhelmed by the verticals and horizontals – and concrete blocks – of the modern city. But what impressed Barthes, Cavell, and even Adorno was the way Antonioni's formalism somehow objectified subjectivity and threw into relief the ambivalent *presence* of 'being' in modernity, the 'little histories' or epiphanies of the individual marked not only by alienation but by fleeting moments of spontaneous pleasure, curiosity, melancholy and ambivalence.

and Stockhausen in post-serial music, had done. From this perspective Adorno does, in the 1960s, seem to believe – tentatively – that cinema could become a modernist art. For example, he is impressed by Antonioni's *La Notte* (1961) not just because it portrays the supposed alienation of modern life, but because it allows stasis and emptiness within the image to negate the movement/immediacy inherent in the medium, a negation which emerges as something immanent to Antonioni's genre-based (romantic melodrama) cinematic realism (Figure 3). Similarly, Antonioni's films are plot-driven yet tend to negate their own narrative drive – the plots slowly unravel and remain unresolved. More generally, in 'Transparencies on Film' Adorno seems to envisage loosely structured, episodic narrative films containing moments which circulate gently defamiliarized images rendering the immediacy of the everyday world as it appears to an interior subjective consciousness – an aesthetic which might recall the 1920s modernist stream-of-consciousness novel and might also resemble the cinematic aesthetic endorsed in the 1950s by Kracauer and Bazin:

> The aesthetics of film will do better to resort to a subjective mode of experience that film, indifferent toward its technological origin, resembles and that constitutes its artistic character. For instance, a person who, after a year in the city, spends a few weeks in the mountains abstaining from all work may

> unexpectedly experience colorful images of landscape consolingly coming over or moving through him or her in dreams or daydreams. . . . . Such movement of [interior] images may be to film what the visible world is to painting or the acoustic world to music. Film could be art as the objectivating re-creation of this mode of experience.[54]

Despite his theoretical misgivings, the idea of film subjectifying the objective (and vice versa) and the fleetingly epiphanic stylistics of the image described by Adorno in the above passage are not so dissimilar to the standard romantic stylistics of postwar cinematic modernism.

Cinema and Experience concludes with a reading of Kracauer's *Theory of Film*, in which Hansen sees Kracauer, having overcome the ideologically grounded pessimism of his prewar writing on film, as gradually eliminating the socio-historical framework from the text in favour of what purports to be a theory of cinema as a medium of immediate reality, but is in practice a recognizably modernist aesthetic:

> Kracauer's book is usually discussed in the context of postwar theories of cinematic realism, notably the work of Bazin and writings surrounding Italian neo-realism. Yet, unlike nineteenth-century concepts of realism centering on referential verisimilitude and formal closure that were invoked (more wrongly than rightly) by semiotic critiques of realist film theory, Kracauer's realism has a distinctly modernist inflection, emphasizing film's truck with contingency, indeterminacy, and endlessness, with the fortuitous, fragmentary, ephemeral, and ordinary.[55]

Hansen suggests a set of reference points for contextualizing *Theory of Film*, which range from existentialism, Bazin, neorealism and the new waves to Susan Sontag's 'Against Interpretation'. Put simply, *Theory of Film* reflects a *postwar* version of cinematic modernism:

> Kracauer's book, like Bazin's writings, has to be considered as part of an international cineaste culture that inspired and supported new wave movements in France, Germany, Italy, Eastern Europe, Japan, India, and other parts of the world.[56]

One aspect of Kracauer's alignment with postwar cinematic modernism and increasing distance from the avant-garde is his assertion of the importance of narrative in *Theory of Film*, albeit a very particular type of 'loose' narrative structure, described by Hansen as follows:

> Kracauer extols loosely composed, 'porous', 'permeable', open-ended forms such as the episode film and the found story, types of narrative that leave 'gaps into

> which environmental life may stream'; and he gives qualified approval to the convention of 'happy' or, more precisely, 'nontragic', 'provisional' endings.[57]

The structure of *Cinema and Experience*, with sections on Kracauer framing sections on Benjamin and Adorno, adds to the sense that Hansen is reading Benjamin and Adorno *through* Kracauer, through the problematics of realism and postwar international art cinema. From this perspective it is possible to see Benjamin as having prefigured Kracauer's idea that cinema 'redeems' the everyday reality of modernity – the banality of modern life as lived in nondescript urban spaces – as something meaningful:

> We may truly say that with film a new realm of consciousness comes into being. To put it in a nutshell, film is the only prism in which the immediate environment – the spaces in which people live, pursue their avocations, and enjoy their leisure – are laid open before their eyes in a comprehensible, meaningful, and passionate way. In themselves these offices, furnished rooms, bars, big-city streets, stations, and factories are ugly, incomprehensible, and hopelessly sad. Or rather, they were and seemed to be, until the advent of film. The cinema then exploded this prison-world with the dynamite of its fractions of a second, so that now we can set off calmly on journeys of adventure among its scattered ruins.[58]

Benjamin wrote this in 1927, inspired no doubt by the defamiliarization of everyday modern life through the explosive shock of radical montage in Eisenstein and Vertov, yet the broader aesthetic envisaged here is a 'calm journey of adventure' among the 'offices, furnished rooms, bars, big-cities, stations, and factories' of the modern city and finding beauty and strangeness – and passion – amid the sadness, alienation and ennui. All of which sounds closer to Antonioni than Eisenstein.

In reading Benjamin and Adorno through Kracauer's *Theory of Film* Hansen downplays their tendency towards reading images as allegorical or as signs of over-determined ideological meaning and she instead draws out from their writings those aspects more amenable to ambiguity and the 'opaque singularity' – the otherness – of reality. Kracauer is in dialogue with Proust throughout *Theory of Film* but, finally, Hansen sees the difference between Kracauer and Proust as key:

> Kracauer repeatedly invokes Proust's image of the 'ghostly trees that seem to impart a message to him', an image he adduces to distinguish the 'material continuum' of life that film is able to convey from the mental and language-bound continuum of the novel: '[Proust's] affinity for the cinema makes him sensitive to transient impressions, such as the trees which look familiar to him; but when

> he identifies the trees as yet undeciphered phantoms of the past "appealing to me to take them with me, to bring them back to life[,]" he exchanges the world of cinema for dimensions alien to it'. Kracauer wants those trees to remain trees, rather than 'rebuses' or decipherable messages. Cinema, like no other medium, can register material phenomena in their otherness, their opaque singularity. 'Snatched from transient life, [these ideograms] not only challenge the spectator to penetrate their secret but, perhaps even more insistently, request him to preserve them as the irreplaceable images they are'. Preserving such images for memory comes closest to what I take Kracauer to mean by *redemption*.[59]

Cinema and Experience reads Kracauer – and to an extent Benjamin and Adorno – retrospectively in terms of a standard narrative of cinematic modernism, from Soviet film of the 1920s and Brechtian defamiliarization to the postwar new waves emerging out of neorealism. By contrast Hansen's 1999 essay 'The Mass Production of the Senses: Classical Cinema as Vernacular Modernism' is a polemical expression of her dissatisfaction with the standard narrative of modernism across the arts, calling for this narrative to be opened up, expanded and diversified. The essay reflects the period of postmodernism in which modernism had been characterized as narrow and elitist, a critique initiated by debates in architecture, a field in which a particularly dogmatic and purist version of modernism had been dominant since Le Corbusier, and the idea of a 'vernacular' style of architecture and design had developed as part of the postmodernist reaction against modernism. Hansen borrows this idea of 'vernacular' but uses it to reconfigure modernism rather than identifying it with postmodernism. In the essay she defines 'vernacular' as follows:

> I take the study of modernist aesthetics to encompass cultural practices that both articulated and mediated the experience of modernity, such as the mass-produced and mass-consumed phenomena of fashion, design, advertising, architecture and urban environment, of photography, radio, and cinema. I am referring to this kind of modernism as 'vernacular' (and avoiding the ideologically overdetermined term 'popular') because the term vernacular combines the dimension of the quotidian, of everyday usage, with connotations of discourse, idiom, and dialect, with circulation, promiscuity, and translatability.[60]

In film studies the idea of a 'vernacular modernism' is complicated by the term 'classical' having been applied to Hollywood film in a way which has little to with Enlightenment formulations of classical aesthetics. Instead, the term essentially denotes the fact that Hollywood foundational techniques or 'codes' governing the shooting and editing of narrative film, as elaborated after 1908 by D. W. Griffith, became dominant across almost all genres of filmmaking and almost every national cinema by the late 1920s, even before the arrival of the sound film, and have remained dominant ever since. In 1970s film studies 'political modernism' and *Screen* theory situated classical Hollywood film as analogous to nineteenth-century bourgeois realism in the novel (as critiqued by Roland Barthes) and promoted an oppositional Brechtian cinematic modernism – Vertov, Godard, Straub-Huillet – and positioned certain traditions, such as pre-1908 early cinema ('the cinema of attractions') and 1930s Japanese cinema under fascism, as 'other' to classical Hollywood.[61] Hansen writes:

> In cinema studies, the juncture of the classical and the modern has, for the most part, been written as a bifurcated history. The critique of classical cinema in 1970s film theory took over a structuralist legacy of binarisms, such as Barthes's opposition between the 'readerly' and 'writerly', which translated into the binary conception of film practice as either 'classical-idealist', that is, ideological, or 'modernist-materialist', that is, self-reflexive and progressive. This is particularly the case for the theory and practice of 'counter cinema' that David Rodowick has dubbed 'political modernism' – from Jean-Luc Godard and Peter Gidal through Noël Burch, Peter Wollen, Stephen Heath, Laura Mulvey and others – that owes much to the revival or belated reception of the 1920s and 1930s leftist avant-garde, notably Bertolt Brecht.[62]

Although herself strongly invested in political modernism and the early cinema movement, Hansen argues that film studies has set up misleading terms and a series of false oppositions, against which she insists that 'classical' Hollywood cinema was a development out of early cinema not its opposite or its betrayal, neither was the sound film a betrayal of silent film – dramatic discontinuities in the story of film occur against a backdrop of underlying continuity – and at its best classical Hollywood film was engaged with modernity as it was experienced by the masses and was capable of generating modernist aesthetic strategies – *Citizen Kane* being an obvious example. Early film might be an example of 'vernacular' cultural production, but Hollywood film itself is 'vernacular' rather than 'classical' in its aesthetic and mode of mass reception.

Rather than reducing modernism to a set of formalist aesthetics, Hansen advocates opening up the category of modernism to all cultural production which engages with modernity. For Hansen this would facilitate the beneficial destabilizing of the orthodox canon of modernism, with its exclusions of class, race, gender and geography, and would destabilize the distinction between 'high' and 'low' culture:

> Modernism encompasses a whole range of cultural and artistic practices that register, respond to, and reflect upon processes of modernization and the experience of modernity, including a paradigmatic transformation of the conditions under which art is produced, transmitted, and consumed. In other words, just as modernist aesthetics are not reducible to the category of style, they tend to blur the boundaries of the institution of art in its traditional, eighteenth- and nineteenth-century incarnation that turns on the ideal of aesthetic autonomy and the distinction of 'high' vs. 'low', of autonomous art vs. popular and mass culture.[63]

The claim that American 'classical' cinema, in the international reach of its engagement with modernity, was the 'first global vernacular' may be uncontroversial, but does Hansen's thesis work for *modernism*?[64] Does the logic of the thesis mean that all modern culture is potentially a vernacular modernism? And therefore the critical and institutional field of modernist studies can now expand and subsume any modern cultural production it wishes?

In fact, the previous quoted passage from 'Mass Production of the Senses' retains an important distinction between vernacular modernism and modern cultural artefacts in general, namely that vernacular modernism is modernist because it refers to 'cultural and artistic practices that register, respond to, and reflect upon processes of modernization and the experience of modernity'. Hansen wishes to privilege an inclusive 'reflexivity', defined as 'respond to', yet her definition of 'reflect upon' as a 'paradigmatic transformation of the conditions under which art is produced, transmitted, and consumed' suggests a residual 'self-reflexivity' with its Brechtian and Godardian political modernist overtones. While Chaplin's *Modern Times* explicitly 'responds to' modernity, most Hollywood films might merely 'register' various aspects of modern life. But even *Modern Times* is not 'self-reflexive' about its own form the way *Citizen Kane* is – which is why modernism might not be a helpful category through which to read Chaplin but might be appropriate to Welles, in which case the problem might not be the obvious one that vernacular modernism is too broad and inclusive to be a sustainable category, but rather that it simply recapitulates the standard parameters of cinematic modernism.[65]

The 'Mass Production of the Senses' essay also raises a question pertinent to the discussion of *contemporary* cinematic modernism. Twenty-first-century cinema has been increasingly dominated by a CGI-driven 'cinema of sensation', such as the various superhero film franchises with their ultra-rationalized modes of monopoly production and distribution. These films are denigrated by many cineastes as the lowest kind of film and recently Martin Scorsese and Francis Ford Coppola have questioned whether such films even deserve to be called 'cinema', arguing that they represent an aesthetic experience more akin to a Disneyland theme park – a perspective from which the twenty-first-century 'cinema of sensation' may bear a resemblance to the pre-1908 'cinema of attractions'.[66] In such a context, the 'international style' of contemporary cinematic modernism represents an attempt to create a distinctive *art* cinema, dependent on film festival patronage not mass audiences, and embracing a 'slow' aesthetic which is the antithesis of commercial 'fast' film. It could be argued that the dominant long-take aesthetic of contemporary cinematic modernism, largely derived from either Antonioni or Tarkovsky, with its emphasis on the contemplative, resists the aesthetics of the vernacular and has instead taken on the character of a cult or sacred object accompanied by a ritualistic mode of reception. What has been derived from Tarkovsky in particular is a stylistic repertoire intended to generate not the 'opaque singularity' and 'otherness' (Hansen's terms) of reality in its everyday and material forms as described by Kracauer, but the auratic effects of the rarefied art object as described by Benjamin – but which, according to Benjamin, can of course only ever be ersatz auratic effects in the age of mechanical reproduction.[67]

2

Cinema and the modernist arts

The cult of the image

If cinema was a new art for the twentieth century, was it distinct from the other arts or was it closely related to modernist developments in the other arts? This chapter will look at how early cinema interacted with the other modernist arts.

Architecture and design were overt in their embrace of the twentieth century as an era requiring a modernist aesthetic of clean, minimalist, geometric design fulfilling a utilitarian purpose and in their corresponding rejection of excessive ornamentation and clutter, things associated with the dark and dingy nineteenth century. These aesthetic values would go on to inform a particularly dogmatic modernist 'international style' in architecture lasting well into the second half of the twentieth century, before the advent of a postmodernism equally dogmatic in its negation of modernist aesthetics. While the other arts shared many of the aesthetic preferences of modernist architecture, a greater eclecticism and tension between conflicting tendencies is evident. In the paintings of Cézanne and post-impressionism 'significant form', tending towards abstraction as a means to represent reality in terms of geometric space and volume, is combined with an aesthetic which is not uncluttered or minimalist but colourful and rough-hewn. Notwithstanding the crucial importance of the 'pure' formalist moment of analytical cubism, the combination of rigour and rough looseness of form identifiable in Cézanne, Picasso and Matisse is indicative of new realist modes marked by an 'informal formalism' as important to the development of modernism as the intermittent moments of attempted 'pure form' or 'total abstraction' which sometimes dominate discussions of modernism. In both its early twentieth century and its postwar periods, modernist painting will be a site of tensions between pure subjective expression and pure objective form, between realism, formalism and an expressionism often incorporating folk, 'primitivist' and non-Western references, a tension which is usually sublimated via a stylistics of abstraction into a supposed 'significant form'. The very label

'Abstract expressionism' voices the tension. While the genealogy of Jackson Pollock's *Number 1A* (1948) is readily explicable in the context of modern art history, the vulgar question remains: Is *Number 1A* an extreme subjectivist and individualistic outpouring of the self, the ego, the unconscious, or is it a purely objective painting, incorporating contingency, a flat surface covered in markings which signify nothing beyond the fury of this display of their materiality?

Similar tensions are evident in music. Modernism was identified with early Stravinsky (*The Firebird* 1910, *Petrushka* 1911, *Rite of Spring* 1913) in which modern urban rhythm and dissonance is juxtaposed with folk themes, the Dionysian primitivist and the archaic. Both Picasso and Stravinsky embrace the juxtaposition of fragments, an aesthetic of montage (Picasso literally so in his turn to collage). This expressionist aesthetic of dynamic montage – the juxtaposition of clashing materials, objective and subjective, modern and archaic – when taken to an extreme intermittently gives way to its opposite, sublimation into synthetic form: analytical cubism and abstraction in painting or Schoenberg, the Second Viennese School and twelve-tone serialism in music. As with painting, this modernist trajectory towards abstract formalism in music continues and in some ways culminates in the postwar avant-garde, in Boulez and Stockhausen and the Darmstadt School, where the romantic and archaic elements and the tendency towards an aesthetic of collage are still discernible within the formalist post-serialism of works like Stockhausen's *Gruppen* (1957) or Boulez's *Le Marteau sans maître* (1955), a formalism which in the 1960s will frequently cross over to its apparent opposite in the improvisational and Dadaesque leanings of the Cage/Fluxus tendency.

Modernism in painting, sculpture and music has had an important influence on avant-garde or experimental film, less so on what this book is presenting as cinematic modernism, a modernism which never disavows its links to naturalism and realism. The modernist arts to which cinematic modernism has a close relationship would be theatre, poetry and the novel and it is to these relationships that this chapter will now turn.

Modernism and theatre

> *Late-nineteenth-century Naturalism, in practice, was the first phase of Modernist theatre [. . .] What is most clear in modernist Naturalism – from Ibsen through early Strindberg to Chekhov – is its challenging selection of the*

> *crises, the contradictions, the unexplored dark areas of the bourgeois human order of its time.*
>
> – Raymond Williams[1]

In *The Politics of Modernism* Raymond Williams argues that for Ibsen, Strindberg and Chekhov, naturalism and realism provided the aesthetic means to address modern social, political and psychological issues through a new emphasis on the following: the contemporary, an everyday setting (a room), everyday speech forms and the 'everyday' itself (the metonymic 'slice of life' standing in for a whole way of life), along with characters representing a broad range of social classes. Williams notes that this naturalism will become the basis for cinema, to which such naturalistic modes are better suited than to theatre; however, he also notes that this naturalism in the theatre quickly developed into a recognizable modernism – *there is a continuity between naturalism and modernism rather than an opposition.* The limitations of naturalism gave rise to dramatic forms, often anti-naturalistic, that are associated with what Williams refers to as avant-garde drama, but without dispensing with realist representational modes and their grounding in social and psychological reality:

> Social and economic crises in the wider society had their effects back in the living room, but dramatically only as reports from elsewhere, off-stage, or at best as things seen from a window or as shouts from the street. Similarly, crises of subjectivity – the privacies of sexuality, the uncertainties and disturbances of fantasies and dreams – could not be fully articulated within the norms of language and behaviour which, for its central purposes, the form had selected.
>
> This was an ironic result in a form which had gained its main energies from its selection and exposure of deep crises and hitherto dark areas. And in fact each of the three major Naturalist dramatists moved to continuing experiment to overcome these limitations. Ibsen and Chekhov used visual images beyond the room to suggest or define larger forces (*The Wild Duck*, *The Cherry Orchard*). Ibsen, in his last plays and especially in *When We Dead Awaken*, and Strindberg, from *The Road to Damascus* through *Dreamplay* to *Ghost Sonata*, actually inaugurated the methods, later known as Expressionism, which were to be the main elements of the drama and theatre of the avant-garde. Here again, and centrally, the essential continuity between the thrust of modernist Naturalism and the campaigns of the avant-garde is historically evident.[2]

If by 'avant-garde' Williams is referring primarily to expressionism then the influence of this continuity is also felt in silent cinema, but perhaps the more important parallel is with postwar cinema and the centrality of naturalistic neorealism as the origin of what would develop into the cinematic modernism of Rossellini, Fellini, Antonioni and Pasolini.

Williams suggests that the centrality of naturalism to modernism was lost because the politicized (Marxist) critical discourse on modernism in the theatre, particularly after 1968, favoured the overtly self-reflexive anti-naturalism of Brecht (and to an extent Beckett) and a diametric opposition between realism and modernism. The critical discourse rejected naturalism as a bourgeois 'reality effect' and therefore marginalized realist modes, a rejection which was repeated with similar dogmatism for cinema in *Screen* and *Cahiers du Cinéma* in their respective Brechtian and Maoist phases.

Theatre and early cinema

Theatre provided an initial model and resource for cinema – 'filmed theatre' or 'filmed vaudeville' – and early film often referred to existing dramatic works, transferring plays from the theatrical stage to the film studio and the camera. However, once cinema had established its basic modes of staging, filming and editing, it became obvious that cinema was a radically different medium to theatre and required not only a different type of 'non-theatrical' acting but also a radically different aesthetic. This was true for early Hollywood, including the most popular films such as the comedies of Chaplin and Keaton, which were derived from the practices of music hall and vaudeville but adapted to meet the technical and stylistic demands of the new medium of film.

The difference between theatre and cinema was a particular issue for modernism, less because of a principle about medium specificity, but rather because early cinema, being silent, really did have to develop a different aesthetic to dialogue-based theatre. This requirement to develop an aesthetic in some ways in opposition to theatre excited modernists in that it offered the possibility of a dramatic form of the image not overly determined by speech or a given language. Could an art cinema be like the globally popular films of Chaplin and create images that transcended language barriers? This reliance on the purely visual image made cinema different to language-based theatre and different also to the novel and poetry. Silent cinema created the possibility of a non-linguistic art with mass popular appeal which could be internationalist, universal.

Expressionist theatre is usually dated from 1910 (Oscar Kokoschka, *Murder Hope of Women*, 1909) to the mid-1920s and centred in Germany (although enjoying an intermittent vogue elsewhere, including the United States).

Expressionist drama was characterized by plots, dialogue, staging, sets and acting styles which are anti-naturalistic, simplified yet accentuated or heightened in order to represent an extreme psychological state. Aside from the dramatically artificial sets which suited primitive studio production, expressionist drama, with its privileging of physical gesture and facial expression over speech, was eminently suited to the close-ups of the face and figure that were such a startling new feature of cinema. The general influence of expressionism can be discerned in much silent cinema, including Soviet film, and of course expressionist drama in Germany is almost unique in being a form of theatre which translated directly and successfully into film in the form of German expressionist cinema and its modernist classics such as Robert Weine's *The Cabinet of Dr. Caligari* (1919) and Murnau's *Nosferatu* (1922).

Impressionism is not a label that has been widely applied to drama. However, it is possible to detect something analogous to impressionism in modernist drama which sets out to suggest a mood or ambience and to portray psychological states in a rather more introspective way than expressionism. Chekhov's narratives (in both his short stories and his plays) are realist slices of life but decontextualized, with no beginning and, crucially, no closure, tending instead towards open endings. Chekhov's plays *The Seagull* (1896), *Uncle Vanya* (1898), *Three Sisters* (1901) and *The Cherry Orchard* (1904) have an elliptical episodic form which tends towards a 'static drama' aesthetic, not exactly de-dramatization but a kind of sublimation of the 'dramatic' into a loose organic form, the purpose of which is to strip back the causality of plot and instead foreground undercurrents of mood reflecting the consciousness (desires and delusions) of the characters.[3] Chekhov's drama also displays the tendency of naturalism to generate its apparent opposite, the Symbolist. It is as if naturalism invariably points beyond itself, as if what it represses returns via the realm of the allegorical. In the case of Chekhov, the allegorical alludes to universal existential issues but with specific historical, social (class/gender) and political resonances. By contrast in Symbolist drama such resonances are all but lost in an 'autonomy' of form which negates reality and attempts to access the ineffable. The idea of a Symbolist drama as a stylized playing out of an impressionistic mood, an unconscious or a higher 'reality', is epitomized by the *fin de siècle* popularity of Maeterlinck and his 'static drama' (initially a marionette theatre) in plays such as *Pelléas and Mélisande* (1893) and *Interior* (1895) through to *The Bluebird* (1908): elliptical episodes, dislocations of time and place and faux-historical settings, and a de-dramatization of plot, action and dialogue in favour of mood and impression. Maeterlinck's drama had some influence on early conceptions of silent cinema as an art cinema creating the ambience of an uncanny dream state on the screen and in the mind of viewers in the darkened auditorium (although the silent film adaptations of Maeterlinck tend to be disappointingly sentimental and melodramatic if endearingly strange).

The plays of W. B. Yeats in his period of closest alignment with Ezra Pound and modernism such as *At the Hawk's Well* (1916) are altogether more ascetic than Maeterlinck, acted upon minimalist sets in impromptu spaces but, like the Symbolist drama, Yeats's plays are constructed around the formalized static staging of two or three archetypal figures (rather than realist characters) performing gestural movements rather than realistic actions, in elliptical tableaux-like scenes. Like so much modernism, Yeats's plays are both modern, influenced by the imagist aesthetics of the period, and yet archaic, drawing on Irish folk tales and Celtic mythology. Moreover, the whole conception of *At the Hawk's Well* is influenced by the Japanese classical Noh theatre, a theatre of ritualized slowness and stasis, including non-naturalistic declaimed speech and elements of dance. As with Maeterlinck, Yeats's theatre is usually described as Symbolist, but in its emphasis on representing ambiguous epiphanic moments through static images and the dream-like juxtaposition of tableaux-like scenes, this drama could be construed as belonging to a kind of impressionism.

A cinema of poetry I: Imagism

An 'Image' is that which presents an intellectual and emotional complex in an instant of time.

– Ezra Pound (1915)[4]

The most influential modernist movement in poetry of the First World War period was imagism. The various imagist manifestos by Ezra Pound and F. S. Flint outline a characteristic set of modernist rules: 'To present an image (hence the name: "Imagist")'; 'To produce poetry that is hard and clear'; 'Direct treatment of the "thing," whether subjective or objective'; 'Use no superfluous word, no adjective, which does not reveal something'; 'Go in fear of abstractions'; 'Use either no ornament or good ornament'; 'To use the language of common speech, but to employ always the exact word, not the nearly-exact nor the merely decorative word'; 'language is made out of concrete things. General expressions in non-concrete terms are a laziness'.[5]

Imagist aesthetics privilege the autonomy of the image, an image marked by clarity and stasis which is then brought into dynamic and elliptical juxtaposition with other such images. The haiku-like combination of images renders an impression, a mood. According to Ezra Pound, the image oscillates between an objective rendering of reality and a subjective rendering of the perceiving consciousness. Notwithstanding Pound's rhetoric of mean and lean clarity, the overall effect of a poem lies less in the cumulative effect of 'realist' images than in the ambiguity generated by the juxtaposition of images. The poetry resides neither in the image nor in the order of images (as in continuity editing in film) but in the ellipsis itself.

The network of personal connections and influences linking the beginning of an Anglo-American critical discourse on cinema with imagism is epitomized by the figure of poet Vachel Lindsay who, while aligned with imagism, wrote what is considered to be the first book on the aesthetics of cinema, *The Art of the Moving Image* (1915).[6] In *The Tenth Muse: Writing about Cinema in the Modernist Period* Laura Marcus gives the following account of Lindsay:

> His writing had been taken up by Harriet Munroe and published in *Poetry* magazine in 1913; aligned, for a period, with the Imagists, Lindsay would propose an 'Imagist photoplay' in *The Art of the Moving Picture*, which would, in his words, bring 'Doric restraint' (a term that echoes throughout H.D.'s film articles for *Close Up*) into the 'overstrained' and 'overloaded' world of even the finest photoplays. Calling attention to the significance of the Imagists – Lindsay named Ezra Pound, Richard Aldington, John Gould Fletcher, Amy Lowell, F.S. Flint and D.H. Lawrence – Lindsay writes that:
>
>> The imagist impulse need not be confined to verse. . . . There is a clear parallelism between their point of view in verse and the intimate-and-friendly photoplay. [. . .] Read some of the poems of the people listed above, then imagine the same moods in the films. Imagist photoplays would be Japanese prints taking on life, animated Japanese paintings, Pompeian mosaics in kaleidoscopic but logical succession, Beardsley drawings made into actors and scenery, Greek vase-paintings in motion. . . . Scarcely a photoplay but hints at the Imagists in one scene.
>
> 'The Imagists are colorists', Lindsay added, suggesting that the use of varying shades of 'photographic black, white and gray' might be aspects of Imagist film-making, though 'to use these colors with definite steps from one to the other does not militate against an artistic mystery of edge and softness in the flow of line'. In literary terms, the qualifying phrase might suggest the desire for more fluid versions of the chiselled images of imagism (at work in H.D.'s poetic revisions of

> Imagist tenets). It also suggests an Impressionistic aesthetic ('an artistic mystery of edge and softness in the flow line') running parallel to the pictorial poetics and intense visualisations of Imagist aesthetics, in art, literature, and the discourses of the cinema.[7]

The Art of the Moving Image reflects the period of aesthete taste for exoticized classicism and contains a prescient if crude discussion of how cinematic images can be seen as structured like (Egyptian) hieroglyphics, a cross between picture and sign, and therefore have the potential to become a universal Esperanto.[8] The book also stresses the crucial quality of movement and how all cinematic images contain a dynamic of movement, speed and stasis. Lindsay's overall message is that, in 1915, films are becoming too grandiose or too overloaded with action and plot, too melodramatic and mannered, too cluttered; instead he prefers the simplicity of early Griffith and promotes a kind of minimalistic aesthetic, derived from poetic imagism, of restraint and intimacy, combining a naturalistic precision of image with an impressionistic mood of ambiguity or mystery.

The most obvious connection between modernist poetry and modernist film is, first, the primacy of the image as an autonomous unit and, second, the juxtaposition of images, that is to say, montage. The connection is explicit in Pound and Eisenstein's recourse to then current theories about Chinese and Japanese theatre and poetry and, via Fenollosa, theories about the Chinese written script centring on the basic units of that script, the hieroglyph and the ideogram. The ideogram or 'character' functions less like a letter in an alphabet, a signifier in a closed chain of twenty-six signifiers, and more like a sign in a cumulative 'open' system of characters, without limit; in the classical Chinese script there are thousands of characters, of which a great many have to be learnt to be at all conversant in the script. China and Japan use the same script, including the same set of ideograms or characters, as a 'classical' written script, alongside regional, vernacular and 'Westernized' scripts. This classical script (hanzi) originated in China and transferred to Japan (kanji), although over the centuries the ideograms in Japan, although still much the same as the Chinese, have taken on different meanings – something which should immediately alert us to the fact that, contrary to what Pound and Eisenstein wanted to believe, we are probably not dealing with signs derived from the literally 'pictorial', but 'arbitrary' signifiers of a type we find in the written scripts of most languages. What interests both Pound and Eisenstein, however, is the idea that each character or sign represents an *image*, or for Pound a sequence of images in a poem and for Eisenstein shots within a montage sequence. Eisenstein gives the following simple example. In Chinese script when the character for 'eye' is placed next to the character for 'water' it creates a concept: 'weeping'. Sometimes this concept or third meaning will be a 'synthesis' of the two initial character-images combined or superimposed, and sometimes the third meaning will be entirely different, something produced by a conflictual dynamic between the two images. In relation to imagist poetry Pound calls this dynamic a 'vortex'. Meaning is created by juxtaposition as combination, superimposition or *in the cut*: the very cut between the two characters or images creates an ellipsis from which the third ideogram, image, meaning or concept emerges.

Imagism and montage

Even more exciting for Pound and Eisenstein was their belief that the primacy of imagistic montage inherent in the Chinese system of writing and thinking influenced the forms taken by Chinese and Japanese arts, most obviously in the haiku, which obeyed a rigorous form (including syllable stress) attractive to modernists and their cult of significant form, but did so with an equally attractive concentration, brevity and modern-seeming laconic tone. Pound and Eisenstein, perhaps not fully grasping the heavily intertextual allusive nature of Chinese and Japanese classicism, saw the haiku as two or three images juxtaposed, the 'meaning' of the juxtaposition determined retrospectively by the combination of all three lines (including the title), as in Pound's own famous 1913 poem:

> 'In a Station of the Metro'
>
> The apparition of these faces in the crowd;
> Petals on a wet, black bough.[9]

In keeping with the post-1910 modernist distancing of itself from *fin de siècle* Symbolist, aesthete, Romantic and impressionist forbearers, Ezra Pound's various imagist manifestos promote imagism as an aesthetic of directness, of objectivity, opposed to the blurry aesthetic of impressionism, which is one reason why in London after 1910 what is today called modernism was known as post-impressionism. Modernism was essentially defined by its position as superseding impressionism. Yet imagism in practice is surely an impressionistic poetry. Pound's imagist poem and *faux* haiku 'In a station of the Metro' presents us with three lines, the poem's setting stated plainly in the title, followed by two disparate images, cut by a semi-colon. It is the semi-colon, the cut, that creates the abruptness of the juxtaposition, in which the third line becomes an unexpected defamiliarizing image retrospectively superimposed upon the title and second line and determining the impression generated by the poem as a whole. It is in the dynamic created by the three lines, effectively three images, which not only modify each other but feed back into each other to create a vortex (to use Pound's 'Vorticist' terminology): a circuit of impressions of being in a crowded metro station in Paris one day in 1913. But only the first line, the title, is straightforwardly realist. The faces in the crowd are an 'apparition' and the petals on the wet black bough do not belong in a modern Parisian metro station and neither does the line belong in this poem, it belongs to a different (*Japonisme*) poetic register, although it is this last line which, in unexpected juxtaposition with the first two lines, generates the defamiliarized evocation of the metro station. This impression relies on the instability introduced by the cut, the juxtaposition, in which each line is left to oscillate against the other two lines, never to be resolved. The superimposition is not a synthesis and despite its apparent static sharpness and 'frozen moment' quality, the poem remains an 'apparition', an unsettled fleeting impression, a sequence of images irreducible to over-determined meaning and closure.

Eisenstein's interest in Chinese and Japanese hieroglyphs, characters and ideograms and the haiku was similar to that of Ezra Pound. In the haiku three 'objective' images (shots) when combined in a sequence (montage) produce a psychological or emotional 'subjective' impression in the reader. This is continuity editing as elaborated by Kuleshov, Pudovkin, Griffith and Eisenstein himself but, in his 1920s polemics with Kuleshov and Pudovkin, Eisenstein argues that continuity editing is not merely a brick-by-brick 'building block' technique for representing a sequence of causally linked dramatic actions, but a technique for producing complex psychological effects in the viewer. Eisenstein writes:

> The *haiku* is a concentrated impressionist sketch:
>
> A lonely crow
> On leafless bough,
> One autumn eve.
>
> – Bashō
>
> What a resplendent moon!
> It casts the shadow of pine boughs
> Upon the mats.
>
> – Kikaku
>
> An evening breeze blows.
> The water ripples
> Against the blue heron's legs.
>
> – Buson

It is early dawn.
The castle is surrounded
By the cries of wild ducks

– Kyoroku

From our point of view, these are montage phrases. Shot lists. The simple combination of two or three details of a material kind yields a perfectly finished representation of another kind – psychological.

And if the finely ground edges of the intellectually defined concepts formed by the combined ideograms are blurred in these poems, yet, in *emotional quality*, the concepts have blossomed forth immeasurably. We should observe that the emotion is directed towards the reader, for, as Yone Noguchi has said, 'it is the readers who make the *haiku's* imperfection a perfection of art.'[10]

In a manner almost identical to Pound's 1913 imagist manifesto, Eisenstein stresses that what he calls 'laconic' images (lean, concrete, quotidian) are 'perfect' in themselves but in sequence contain a blur or imperfection, *the openness of ellipsis*. It is the ellipsis that creates a space for the active participation of the viewer whose subjectivity interacts not just with the images but also with the cut or blur of their juxtaposition and it is this that generates an impression or emotion.[11] For Eisenstein the cut as violence, fragmentation rather than continuity, and juxtaposition as conflict or collision, leads in practice to an expressionistic rather than impressionistic or imagistic aesthetic and ultimately leads to an interest in a deterministic montage of conflicting images from which, via materialist dialectics, would be produced crystal-clear messages to his audience: the clash of images generating strictly determined political meaning *or concepts*. The potential to juxtapose images within montage to obtain a strictly determined *abstract* concept was precisely the thing that Pound wished to avoid. If Eisenstein had ever filmed Pound's 'In a Station of the Metro', the concept derived from the juxtaposed images of station, faces and petals might have been something like 'this is the alienation of the individual in the anonymous modern crowd in the cities of capitalism'.[12] At different points in his thinking, Eisenstein seems torn between montage as a means of creating impressionistic emotional and psychological effects and montage as an expressionistic means of achieving (political) conceptual clarity.

Modernist poetry quickly moves on from the evocation of imagistic moments set in a quasi-classical Greek backdrop (the Hellenic cliffs, rocks and whirlpools of imagism) and by the end of the First World War modernist poetry arrives at the rendering of the modern city dweller and his or her estranged consciousness.

The proto-existentialist sensibility of modernity (glimpsed obliquely in Pound's 'In a Station of the Metro') emerges in T. S. Eliot's 'The Love Song of J. Alfred Prufrock' (first published in 1915) and 'The Waste Land' (1922). And in modernist cinema the emergence of German expressionism corresponds to this shift towards the alienated and estranged consciousness of modernity as the focalizing consciousness; the elliptical images now broken into fragments in a jagged urban backdrop, the images no longer make sense, or rather make too much sense: the logic of madness as the only sane response to an insane world – the cell of the lunatic asylum in *The Cabinet of Dr Caligari* as the appropriate site for representing the breakdown of the estranged consciousness of modernity.

Neurosis, alienation and madness were not the kind of 'concepts' of modernity that Eisenstein had wished his montage to produce, although such effects might be appropriate to a montage characterizing the breakdown of a Kerensky or the representatives of a decaying aristocratic or bourgeois class. If Soviet montage cinema can be identified as a current of expressionism, it is an expressionism that deals with the consciousness of social and class types, caricatures, and for all the complexity of their montage Eisenstein's 1920s films have little psychological depth. This is not a criticism – dealing in types and caricatures may have been politically necessary and conducive to the Brechtian turn in Eisenstein's thinking, inspired by his experience of seeing Chinese opera and Japanese Kabuki and which would, later, have some bearing on the highly stylized theatricality of *Ivan the Terrible* (1944).

Nevertheless, the question arises: Do Eisenstein's films – and Soviet montage film – qualify as fully achieved cinematic modernism? Bazin thought not. Or at least he considered Soviet montage cinema a fascinating and necessary phase in the infancy of cinema, in which the novelty of new techniques, new effects – new toys – run riot, after which the toys must be returned to the box and only brought out later, by the grown-ups, when sound, the long take and depth of field will allow montage to be 'sublimated' within a mature modern cinematic form. In modern cinema *editing* will be in the classical Hollywood manner, transparent, not drawing attention to itself, functional in the service of narrative; in the modern art-film *montage* (the aestheticization of editing) will largely occur either *within* the image, for example within the long-take sequence shot, maintaining the ostensible integrity of temporal duration, or *between* episodes, the 'between' strongly marked by ellipsis. For Bazin, Soviet montage cinema imposed montage as an aesthetic form upon the representation of 'reality', upon narrative, whereas montage in the postwar modernist film serves narrative requirements within a realist mode and has the appearance of something immanent to and emerging from the unfolding image in time.

From the point of view of an attempt to distinguish a central identifiable genealogy of cinematic modernism, it might be proposed (at the risk of sounding like Zhdanov) that Eisenstein, Vertov and the Soviet montage cinema made great films but with a few exceptions – certain films by Pudovkin and Dovzhenko – represent a 'formalist' side-track, subsequently marginalized by cinematic modernism's interest in representing the immediacy of reality, time (duration), consciousness, alienation and sexuality; a set of interests which required one step back to impressionism and two steps forward: first, towards a new kind of elliptical narrative corresponding to that of the modernist novel (Joyce, Woolf, Proust, Faulkner), towards narrative ambiguity and psychological depth, and second, forward to neorealism and the postwar modernism of Rossellini as elucidated by the Bazinian aesthetic. Where Soviet film does retain its importance to the general development of cinematic modernism in its attention to everyday reality – modes of realism – and to its investigation of the image and the relationship between images; in its privileging of the image itself Soviet cinema is clearly aligned with the broader privileging of the image in modernist aesthetics across the arts.

Early modernist aesthetics in the form of imagism, primarily imagist poetry, sparked an interest in Chinese and Japanese classical aesthetics, including the elliptically structured image-sequences of the haiku and the de-dramatized, ascetic, slow, elliptically structured extended scenes of the Noh drama (which would influence a rarefied strand of modernist theatre from Yeats through to Beckett). This imagist tendency in modernism also informed the modernist interest in cinema, for example the modernist film journal *Close Up* in the 1920s was largely written by ex-imagist poets and novelists. To sum up: the imagist strand within early modernism provides a context for the almost mystical or transcendental status attributed to both the image itself and to the juxtaposition of images, not merely the sequence or order of images within an accepted convention of continuity editing but the status of the cut or ellipsis. This investment in the image, the ambiguous juxtaposition of images and the elliptical cut is carried over from imagism to cinematic modernism.

Cinema and narrative

Given the anxieties surrounding 'filmed theatre' in early cinema, the critical consensus is that as film began to codify the means (such as continuity editing) to create narrative, film began to turn away from theatre and towards the novel. The popular silent cinema prioritizes action – slapstick, the chase, the gun fight, the kiss – and by 1906 or thereabouts cinema was quickly developing techniques that provide *continuity* of actions from shot to shot and this facilitated the development of narratives in which to place the actions. By the end of the First World War, with Griffith, more complex narrative structural conventions have been established for filmmakers and have become legible to audiences. Even before the arrival of the sound film in the late 1920s, popular 'classical' Hollywood cinema was formulated as heightened moments of action (spectacle) against the backdrop of narrative (story, plot). The narratives are adapted from various sources, including the popular fiction and plays of the day, but it is possible to generalize and say that the narratives of the 'classical' Hollywood era correspond to the narrative conventions (storylines, plots, characterizations) of the nineteenth-century novel, while the art film, especially postwar and contemporary cinematic modernism, corresponds to the early-twentieth-century modernist novel.

The modernist novel

Writing concerned with the modification of vocabulary, the disruption of syntax and subversions of typographic layout belonged to the avant-garde wing of modernism, only coming into contact with the main current of the modernist novel in parts of *Ulysses*, all of *Finnegans Wake* and a handful of novels such as Gertrude Stein's *Three Lives*.[13] The 'revolution of the word' had some alignment with experimental film, but the main current of innovation in the modernist novel takes place not at the level of the word, syntax or typography but at the level of *narrative*: narrative structure and narrative perspective, ellipsis, the episodic, fragmentation, temporal dislocations, unstable characterization, focalizing consciousness, multiple narrative perspectives and so on. It is this central current of modernist fiction that has had a long-standing influence on cinematic modernism.

The lineage of the modern novel is usually traced back to Flaubert (*Madame Bovary* 1856) and the stripping away of stylistic excess and intrusive narrative commentary. Ostensibly an acutely focused realism, this neutral objective anti-style was paradoxically the height of stylistic sophistication. Rather more overtly stylized, key immediate precursors to literary modernism are Henry James (*The Ambassadors* 1903) and Joseph Conrad (*Heart of Darkness* 1899), novelists who experiment with (unreliable) narrative perspective, ambiguity, representations of consciousness and display a self-reflexivity with regard to the act of narrating itself. These archetypal modernist concerns become defining features of the modernist fiction which emerged, in Europe, just before the First World War, continuing through to the 1920s, with 1922 – the year of James Joyce's *Ulysses* – commonly cited as modernism's peak year. This period would include the early fiction of Joyce (*Dubliners* 1914 and *A Portrait of the Artist as a Young Man* 1915), Dorothy Richardson (*The Tunnel* 1919), Ford Madox Ford (*The Good Soldier* 1915), Wyndham Lewis (*Tarr* 1918), Virginia Woolf (*Jacob's Room* 1922) and the short fictions of Katherine Mansfield (*Bliss and Other Stories* 1920). Outside of the London epicentre of literary modernism, a list of European and American writers producing fiction commonly categorized as modernist would include Proust, Gide, Musil, Thomas Mann, Kafka, Stein, Faulkner, Fitzgerald, Dos Passos, Djuna Barnes and, in his early writings, Hemingway.

The connections between early cinema and the novel are well documented. Maxim Gorky's newspaper review, often considered to be the first piece of serious film criticism, written after seeing a presentation of Lumière films in 1896 and in which Gorky initially finds the cinema, its images drained of colour and sound, to be a monotonous grey 'kingdom of the shadows' redolent of an afterlife inhabited by ghosts who must repeat exactly the same actions and gestures into eternity. H. G. Wells's entanglement in the development of the early cinematic apparatus, his numerous commentary pieces on film and the many fictions, from *The Time Machine* (1895) on, which are considered as 'prophesying' or responding to aspects of cinema. Eisenstein's discussion of how cinematic techniques such as parallel editing or cross-cutting first occurred in the novels of Flaubert and Dickens – and Eisenstein's discussion of *Ulysses* and the stream-of-consciousness technique and his meeting with Joyce. Joyce opening Ireland's first cinema, the Volta Electric Theatre in Dublin in 1909. Virginia Woolf's 1926 essay 'The Cinema', which expresses her excitement at how film can capture 'reality' and the details of the everyday as fleeting and contingent – a feather blown by the wind, the play of light and colour, the chaos of the street – or perhaps cinema can present the world of dreams and the unconscious? The films for which Woolf expresses an antipathy are those based on heavy-handed literary and theatrical adaptations.

An authoritative and comprehensive account of the critical discourse on the relationship between the modern novel and early cinema is given by Laura Marcus in *The Tenth Muse*, and Marcus recounts how much of the discussion has followed the example of Eisenstein by looking at how new cinematic techniques such as the close-up, zoom, parallel editing or cross-cutting, the tracking shot and point-of-view shot were prefigured by 'equivalent' techniques in literature, in the novels of Balzac, Dickens and Flaubert, or alternatively how such equivalent literary techniques were a response by the modernist novel of Joyce, Woolf and Stein to the challenge and example of early film.[14]

The following remarks on the modernist novel relate more to postwar and contemporary cinematic modernism than to early cinema and address a more general yet fundamental question: How do issues concerned with narrative structure and perspective in the modernist novel inform cinematic modernism?

Narrative structure

With regard to narrative structure, the influence of the modernist novel on cinematic modernism is straightforward. The modernist novel tends to be episodic, each episode dominated by a few, often just one, extended Chekhovian scene – usually a social gathering like a dinner, a party, a meeting or salon, involving interaction and dialogue between characters – and this scene is rendered in a way that simulates or evokes real-time duration. Although the scene may lack dramatic action or plot twists ('nothing happens') and instead be filled with 'everyday' social interactions, a subtext will develop culminating in a revelation or acknowledgement that something of narrative significance *has* occurred, and so the scene is transformed into a crucial narrative event.

These episodes and extended scenes are rarely linked to a preceding or subsequent episode or scene through direct causal links or transitional narrative passages. Instead, the episodes are juxtaposed with each other via a radical ellipsis, although in modernist novels and the main current of cinematic modernism this radical ellipsis is not actually presented as sharp, violent or expressionistic, but instead as something apparently naturalistic.[15] The modernist novel therefore resembles cinematic modernism in that both favour an episodic montage structure, in which each episode centres on an extended scene evoking real-time duration, and through which episodes are juxtaposed via an ellipsis, introducing temporal, spatial and narrative ambiguity and discontinuity.

Virginia Woolf: Time passes

Virginia Woolf's *To the Lighthouse* (1927) consists of three narrative blocks. The first, 'The Window', is set in the early years of the century and takes place at the Ramsay family holiday home, where a guest, the artist Lily Briscoe, begins a painting of Mrs Ramsay. A large part of this first narrative block is taken up with an extended dinner scene at which all the characters – the family and guests – are present and are presided over by Mrs Ramsay. From the apparently trivial conversation various significant things about each person at the dining table become evident, including truths about the power dynamics in the marriage of Mr and Mrs Ramsay, which at the end of the scene take on the aspect of what might be described as 'existential' truths about life and mortality (in fact these truths will later be revealed as misguided and illusory). There is then an abrupt 'cut' to the second narrative block, titled 'Time Passes' and which takes place during the First World War at the holiday home but with all the family members and guests absent. This 'recording' of the summerhouse with nobody there (except the housekeeper and some occasional cleaners, a social class nuance on Woolf's part) is often read as influenced by the uncanny dialectic of presence and absence attributed to cinema. It also suggests the idea of the automatic camera-eye recording the 'time image' of the house in the absence of human presence.[16] 'Time Passes' is thought to be influenced by cinema in another way, because what in a traditional novel would be major events, such as the death of Mrs Ramsay, are given as short parenthetical statements resembling an intertitle in a silent film. At the end of 'Time Passes' there is another cut to the third block of narrative 'The Lighthouse', which takes place at the holiday home after the war and sees the surviving characters reunite. Much of this episode is taken up with an extended scene of the characters interacting in the garden of the house as Lily Briscoe resumes and completes her painting of the now absent – long deceased – Mrs Ramsay.

Woolf initially sketched the structure for *To the Lighthouse* as two large vertical blocks bridged by a narrow horizontal block (the 'Time Passes' section), the novel presenting its episodic blocks, extended 'real-time' scenes, ellipses and drastic temporal cuts in a particularly explicit way. Most modernist novels after *Ulysses*, *Pilgrimage* and *À la recherche du temps perdu* use a similar narrative structure, if in less programmatic ways, and episodic juxtaposition, elliptical cutting and the privileging of extended duration scenes later becomes the default structure of cinematic modernism from Rossellini, Antonioni and Fellini through to contemporary filmmakers like Abbas Kiarostami, Hou Hsiao-hsein, Bela Tarr and Nuri Bilge Ceylan.

Nothing happens: Dorothy Richardson's hyperrealist everyday

Dorothy Richardson's *Pilgrimage*, the first part of which was published in 1915, is generally considered to be one of the first modernist novels. May Sinclair's seminal 1918 essay 'The Novels of Dorothy Richardson', published in both the London *Egoist* and the New York *Little Review*, introduced the term 'stream of consciousness' to literary criticism and sums up Richardson's radical new type of novel:

> In this series there is no drama, no situation, no set scene. Nothing happens. It is just life going on and on. It is Miriam Henderson's stream of consciousness going on and on. And in neither is there any grossly discernible beginning, middle or end. In identifying herself with this life, which is Miriam's stream of consciousness, Miss Richardson produces her effect of being the first, of getting closer to reality than any of our novelists who are trying so desperately to get close.[17]

Sinclair argues that the modernist novel rejects the omniscient narrator and intrusive narrative commentary, all but dispenses with beginnings, middles and ends and the need to set up situations and resolve story lines, and indeed assigns a drastically reduced status to story, plot, drama and action. In terms of structure *Pilgrimage* consists of lengthy scenes evoking the continuous present, something akin to real-time duration. However, *Pilgrimage* is also episodic – blocks of narrative both long and short are juxtaposed by abrupt cuts – radical ellipsis emerging as the key structuring device in *Pilgrimage* as a whole. So while it might seem that 'nothing happens' in *Pilgrimage* and that it is formless, just 'life going on and on', this formlessness is actually a new kind of form in which a great deal happens, albeit often at a sub-textual level, numerous major and minor narrative events occurring in the lengthy scenes and also in the ellipses through which the scenes – and episodes – are juxtaposed.

The idea that 'nothing happens' in *Pilgrimage*, meant by Sinclair as a compliment, became something of a clichéd comment on modernist novels, usually meant pejoratively, and has similarly become a cliché about cinematic modernism since the riotous response to Antonioni's *L'avventura* at the 1960 Cannes Film Festival, Antonioni's film upsetting viewers of the time by apparently setting up a thriller romance only to frustrate any such expectations of plot and story. At Cannes in 1975 a hostile response met Chantal Akerman's *Jeanne Dielman* for much the same reasons, a notoriety attached to the film acknowledged by the title of Ivone Margulies's critical monograph *Nothing Happens: Chantal Akerman's Hyperrealist Everyday*.[18] The idea that 'nothing happens' has become particularly attached to contemporary cinematic modernism, especially in its 'slow cinema' variant. Of course, *Pilgrimage*, *Portrait of the Artist*, *To the Lighthouse*, *L'avventura* and *Jeanne Dielman* are all carefully structured and a great deal happens; it is just a different type of narrative structure, a different type of event and rendered in a different way to conventional plot-driven narratives in novel and film. In her essay May Sinclair says that Richardson must render reality directly without the distractions of imposed plot, contrived storylines or an intrusive narrator:

> Obviously, she [Richardson] must not interfere; she must not analyse or comment or explain. Rather less obviously she must not tell a story or handle a situation or set a scene; she must avoid drama as she must avoid narration. And there are some things she must not be. She must not be the wise, all-knowing author.[19]

By eliminating the contrivances of plot and drama Richardson, like other modernists, literary and cinematic, allows the representation of reality itself to unfold, in extended durations but marked by intermittent epiphanic 'moments of being' (to use Woolf's term).[20]

Narrative perspective

Literary historians tell us that the 'classical' nineteenth-century novel, regardless of genre, conformed to a 'realism' whose narrative conventions upheld a consistency of diegetic time and place and the validity of causal links between events, as well as a reliability of characterization. The stability of the relationships between narrative elements was embodied in an omniscient narrator or reliable first-person narrator – even if a first-person narrator has a mistaken perspective on an aspect of the story, the reader can rely on that mistake being genuine to the character and that the mistake will be corrected in the resolution to the story. By the early twentieth century the internal diegetic consistency of the novel had begun to break down, reflecting a loss of certainty in narrative perspective. In the fiction of Joseph Conrad and Henry James, the omniscient narrator had all but disappeared as had the reliable first-person narrator, replaced by multiple narrative frames (with different narrators), non-intrusive third-person narrators (who never comment on or explain what they are narrating), observer/witness narrators who may comment a great deal on their narration but have a partial and imperfect perspective on the story they are narrating, or variations on free indirect narration, either aligning a narrative with the perspective of a character, who James called a 'centre of consciousness' or 'focalising consciousness', or opening up a gap between the narrative and the unreliability of a character's subjective and partial perspective. Modernist novels tend to utilize a combination of some or all of these techniques; however, free indirect discourse/narration is commonly cited as the key distinctive innovation of the modernist novel.

To put this in cinematic terms, in classical cinema the camera occupies a position and perspective analogous to that of an omniscient narrator with absolute control over the whole narrative and *incorporating* the perspectives and point-of-view shots of various characters. Usually the camera will be seamlessly aligned with the perspective of a central character (a Jamesian focalizing consciousness) facilitating the viewer's identification with the perspective of this central character. In cinematic modernism, as in the modernist novel, the 'transparent' direct or free indirect alignment between the camera and central character starts to fissure, a tension or gap is introduced as the viewer becomes aware that the camera has a perspective distinct from any character perspective or any omniscient narrator function. In many postwar modernist films – Antonioni from *L'avventura* on – the camera seems to share the perspective and sensibility of a character but starts to split away and gain an autonomy, including 'point-of-view' shots not that of a character or omniscient narrator but that of the camera-eye itself, a surveillance camera with no one – a void – behind it, for example the archetypal modernist shots held for several seconds before or after characters have entered or exited the frame. This gaze without a consciousness behind it became the gate through which the director returned as auteur, the camera-eye becoming the parametric sign of the auteur's vision, a stylistics

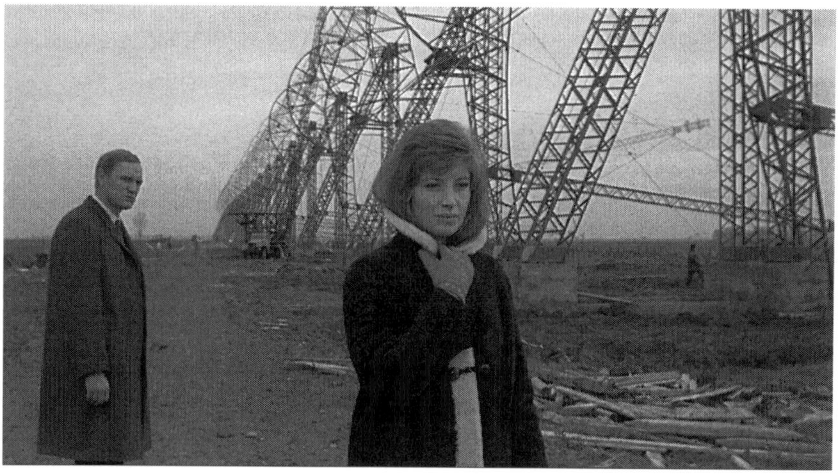

Figure 4 *Red Desert* (1964), Michelangelo Antonioni.
According to Pasolini, *Red Desert* takes the subjective mental sickness of Giuliana (Monica Vitti) and then objectifies it by making the landscape and the industrial constructions correspond to Giuliana's distorted view. In doing so, Antonioni and the auteurs of cinematic modernism attempt to objectify their own bourgeois alienation through a 'delirious aestheticism'.

determined by reference to the auteur's other films, to his or her oeuvre. Free indirect narration becomes not only a formalist mode but also a vehicle for the consciousness of the auteur (Figure 4).

The cinema of poetry II: Pasolini and free indirect discourse

The exasperated tracking-shots [. . .] the shots that remain interminably on the same image.

– Pasolini (1965)

In 'The Cinema of Poetry' (1965) Pier Paolo Pasolini argues along the lines of Bazin and Kracauer that cinema unlike other arts uses reality itself to represent reality. Film is grounded in the reality of physical objects, people and landscapes. Prefiguring Deleuze, Pasolini also argues that images are grounded in reality, images even when representational are themselves real, images are a part of reality and in our ordinary lives we are surrounded by images, we learn how to read them or respond to them, and a film consists of a world of images to a large extent recognizable as the world of images we live in. Pasolini adds that memories and dreams also have their repertoire of images which cinema can access.

Film is not therefore a language, images are not a set of fixed units or signifiers which take on meanings in relation to an overall sign-system; film draws on an open-ended accumulation of images, each with a referent in the real and yet each as image with a degree of autonomy. However, the ways in which images are selected and arranged within films adheres to conventions not dissimilar to a syntax which, in film, Pasolini sees as essentially stylistic rather than as bound by 'grammatical' rules. The use of images in stylistically unconventional, unrealistic, surreal or abstract arrangements aspires to be a poetic cinema but Pasolini, again like Bazin and Kracauer, sees this kind of avant-garde or experimental film as a side-track. True cinematic poetry emerges instead, paradoxically, out of a cinema of prose grounded in realism and narrative conventions like those of the novel:

> Classic cinema was and is narrative, its language is that of prose. Its poetry is an inner poetry, as, for example, in the narratives of Chekhov or Melville.[21]

In the mainstream classical Hollywood-type film a deadening cinema of prose without 'inner poetry' has come to dominate; in the modernist cinema of prose, however, a greater degree of inventive freedom in the image repertoire and image 'syntax', along with an ambiguity and multiplicity of perspective, creates a space for poetry to emerge. By modernist cinema Pasolini means films since neorealism, beginning with Rossellini and leading on to Antonioni and Fellini and then on to the new waves of the 1960s. So, Pasolini's initial points are that, in cinema, modernism and realism are or should be reconciled and that he sees a 'cinema of poetry' emerging out of a 'cinema of prose', out of the post-Rossellini modernist art film, not out of the experimental avant-garde.[22] Pasolini then makes a further point: that the cinema of poetry is linked to the emergence of a stylistics of what he calls 'free indirect discourse' in film corresponding to that of the modernist novel. Without straying too far into the complexities of narratology or addressing all the contentious details of Pasolini's presentation, his basic argument is as follows. The modernist film is marked by formalist devices which draw attention to the camera and its perspective:

> The primordial characteristic of these indications of a tradition of the cinema of poetry consists in a phenomenon which technicians define normally and tritely as 'making the camera felt'. In sum, the maxim of wise filmmakers in force up till the '60s 'Never let the camera's presence be felt' has been replaced by its opposite. [. . .] Thus one feels the camera, and for good reasons. The alternation of different lenses, a 25 or a 300 on the same face, the abuse of the zoom with its long focuses which stick to things and dilate them like quick-rising loaves, the continual counterpoints fallaciously left to chance, the kicks in the lens, the tremblings of the hand-held camera, the exasperated tracking-shots, the breaking of continuity for expressive reasons, the irritating linkages, the shots that remain interminably on the same image, this whole technical code was born almost of an intolerance of the rules, of the need of unusual and provocative liberty, a diversely authentic and pleasant taste for anarchy, but it immediately became law, a prosodic and linguistic heritage which concerns all the cinemas in the world at the same time.[23]

Cinematic modernism – a cinema of poetry emerging within or out of a cinema of prose – had, by 1965, become an international style, with the potential to consolidate, for better or for worse, in a new law, a new code or set of self-reflexive stylistic conventions.[24] In Antonioni's *Red Desert* (1964) every element of the film adheres to the overall design, even real trees and real grass were painted different shades of green to fit in with the colour scheme of the film. Pasolini emphasizes the tendency in the modernist art film to have one central 'focalising consciousness' with which the perspective of the whole film is aligned through a mode of narration analogous to the most common mode of free indirect narration in the modernist novel, what Pasolini terms 'free indirect subjective narration'. In Antonioni's *Red Desert* the central character Giuliana (played by Monica Vitta) is a neurotic experiencing a breakdown and so, according to Pasolini, the whole film is aligned with and filtered through the distorted perception of this estranged *subjective* consciousness. Pasolini sees this as a successful film because instead of imposing an objective autonomous formalist aesthetic upon the film, in *Red Desert* alienation is immanent to the focalizing consciousness of the central character and the aesthetic formalism is therefore a free indirect subjective narration aligned with this neurotic alienated consciousness. Such an alignment invariably leads to auteur theory because the alignments of perspective can be traced back to the camera-eye, behind which is either a void, a Deleuzian 'camera consciousness', or the director. Pasolini favours the latter option: the formalism of *Red Desert* expresses and 'objectifies' the subjective neurotic alienation of not just its central character but of Antonioni the auteur.[25] However, Pasolini is unsure whether, in Lukácsian terms, Antonioni's cinematic modernism with its combination of naturalism and formalism provides a 'realist' portrait of a decaying neurotic bourgeois class within an implied totality of class relations in Italy's postwar 'economic miracle' or whether such cinematic modernism, and its alignment of objective formalism with an estranged subjective focalizing consciousness, represents a 'recuperation' of modernist aesthetics by a late-capitalist aesthete bourgeois culture.[26]

The debate opened up by Pasolini in 1965 is particularly relevant to contemporary cinematic modernism, which is so often criticized as merely a now overly codified retro international style or aestheticism. Does a film like Kiarostami's *Taste of Cherry* (1997) with its combination of naturalism and formalism, its free indirect subjective narrative mode, its narrative ambiguity, its portrait of the existentialist angst of the individual, provide, via its aesthetic, access to the broader and inner realities of contemporary Iranian society? Or is the film a refusal to address the realities of Iran and globalization, a retreat into a contemplative, aesthete, formalist international style divorced from the particulars of social life? Or is such a modernist aesthetic 'refusal' itself, as Adorno and Greenberg would argue, a radical act, currently the only possible radical aesthetic act?[27]

3

Cinematic modernism in the silent film era

The previous chapter looked at how cinema emerged at the same time as modernism and the various ways in which aesthetic innovations associated with modernism across the arts, particularly in theatre, poetry and the novel, related to the development of film. The influence of modernism encouraged the idea that film might come to constitute not only a mass entertainment medium reflecting modernity but also a modernist art. This chapter gives a concise historical account of how the relationship between cinema and modernism led to the first period of cinematic modernism after the First World War, customarily associated with movements such as German expressionist cinema, French Impressionist Cinema and Soviet Cinema, and films like *The Cabinet of Dr. Caligari*, *Battleship Potemkin*, *The Passion of Joan of Arc* and *Man with a Movie Camera*. To what degree was the cinematic modernism of the 1920s influenced by the main currents of modern art, such as expressionism and impressionism? To what degree was cinematic modernism influenced by trends associated with the avant-garde, such as abstract art, Dada and surrealism? To what degree was early cinematic modernism, as the sound film approached, influenced by the increasingly dominant 'classical' Hollywood cinema?

The birth of cinema

In *The Story of Film* Mark Cousins refers to a 'shambolic race' to develop the cameras, projecting machinery and film stock to make still photographic images move: a race involving many inventors across many nations and concluding on 28 December 1895, in Paris, when the Lumière brothers screened *L'Arrivée d'un train en gare de la Ciotat/The Arrival of a Train at La Ciotat Station*, following which they dispatched their representatives, equipment and films around the world to over fifty counties, including Russia, India, Argentina, Mexico,

Japan, Thailand, the Philippines, Iran and Senegal.[1] By 1900 film was a global phenomenon. The documentary one reel/one shot *actualités* of a real event like a train arriving at a station were followed by the development of slapstick 'one gag' scripted scenarios and then the emergence of the fiction or narrative film deploying staging, in-camera effects and editing tricks, epitomized by Méliès and films like *Le Voyage dans la Lune/A Trip to the Moon* (1902).

Between 1895 and 1908 the basic grammar of film developed – film shots, edit/cuts, close-ups and camera angles and movements – alongside rapidly evolving ideas about how to stage figures, objects and background sets within the filmic frame. It is generally agreed by early film scholars that film quickly came to be seen as a low-brow popular entertainment offering 'attractions' – unusual, exotic, bawdy or risqué images – competing with the offerings of the amusement arcade, fairground or circus. Early film scholars also agree that almost all the basic camera shots and basic editing techniques that would, when fully achieved, provide the 'language' for 'classical' Hollywood film were already in place in early film. This 'grammar' needed a commonly comprehensible 'syntax', a consolidated relationship of continuity between images, that is to say an established practice of sequencing images through editing, a refined practice of montage. The moment at which editing starts to become consolidated is usually dated to 1903 and the complicated editing history of Edwin Porter's *The Great Train Robbery* (USA 1903) and *The Life of an American Fireman* (USA 1903). As Cousins puts it in *The Story of Film*, 'filmmakers learnt to say "Once upon a time . . .", and "Then this happened . . ." or "Meanwhile".'[2] The building blocks of classical cinema were developed in early film by a process of trial and error, largely determined by technological factors, but driven from 1903 onwards by a commercially motivated desire to go beyond the gag or individual scene towards something resembling an equivalent to theatre, that is to say a sequence of scenes and dramatic events with a story and plot, with narrative.

The birth of the art film

Mark Cousins sees 1908 as a watershed year in the development of a consciously 'art' cinema, with the success of the French *Film d'Art* company being part of a wider movement in Europe to establish a cinema based on literary narrative rather than isolated thrills and sensations:

> Andre Calmettes and Charles le Bargy directed *L'Assassinat du duc de Guise* for the French company, *Film d'Art*. Although not the first film company to look

> to adapt novels and plays for the screen, its self-consciously highbrow cinema, aimed at theatre-going audiences, was better marketed and more successful than most. The so-called heritage films made by Merchant-Ivory in Britain in the 1980s and 1990s are the progeny of *The Assassination of the Duc de Guise*, often deriving from literature and emphasizing diction, set design and verbal nuance.[3]

Cousins remarks that variations on the 'Art Film' movement became established across Europe, especially in France, Germany and Scandinavia. In 1919, the one-hour film *Les Amours* (Henri Desfontaines and Louis Mercanton), starring icon of the theatre Sarah Bernhardt, was exported from France to America:

> Cinema had opened its doors to new, wealthier audiences, who would demand more comfortable and stylish cinemas than the nickelodeons, shop-front outfits and music hall auditoria which had hitherto been the sites for cinema. They wanted weightier subjects too, and the film world would accede to this. Within a generation, movie palaces or atmospherics would be built; places where ordinary people could feel like royalty for a night and where film became a medium of contemplation as well as sensation.[4]

In Cousins's account, the art film and film adaptations of novels and plays represented social and cultural respectability for cinema, a medium which, after the initial widespread interest in the Lumière films in the 1890s, had almost immediately fallen to the status of low novelty. If the art film played an important role in elevating and broadening the appeal of cinema, it did so alongside the rapid development of various genres, especially the epic, initially Italian (*Cabiria* 1913) but quickly mastered by Hollywood in the films of D. W. Griffith and Cecil B. DeMille. In addition, slapstick comedy, a mainstay of early cinema, also developed in sophistication as Chaplin and Keaton took leave of Mack Sennett and Keystone to direct their own films in which the comedic gags were integrated into narratives full of sharp social observation, as well as a sometimes almost Dickensian humanist poignancy and pathos. The broad mass (and global) appeal of cinema following the First World War enabled the development of the technical apparatus for making and screening films alongside the consolidation of the conventions or codes of narrative form, leading in turn to the consolidation of the so-called 'classical' or 'romantic realist' aesthetic, all of which would soon ensure the dominance of Hollywood with its industrial studio system, its star system, its talent pool and its worldwide distribution.

While the art film may have helped to consolidate 'classical' Hollywood in the silent era as a respectable mass entertainment medium, the art films in themselves were not so successful in establishing cinema as a viable modern art form. The theatrical or literary film gave its narrative forms to the mainstream Hollywood romantic, action and comedic drama film, but the theatrical *Film d'Art* remained problematic: too static, too stodgy, *too nineteenth century*. It may have been art film but it was the wrong type of art. Modernist writers and artists generally preferred Chaplin and Keaton to *Film d'Art*: the mainstream popular Hollywood film was more authentically *modern* than the filmed-theatre art film – a preference that would go on to be asserted repeatedly within the critical discourse of cinematic modernism.

Despite the preferences and prejudices of modernists and cineastes, the literary adaptation has remained a popular mainstay of 'art' cinema. For British cinema (and television) 'quality' literary adaptation and costume drama are still ubiquitous today and still provide a reliable and crucial financial support for the film industry. Cousins's account in *The Story of Film* registers a disapproving cineaste attitude towards this type of mainstream art film – a lineage he traces from *The Assassination of the Duc de Guise* in 1908 through to the internationally popular Merchant-Ivory films of the 1980s and 1990s. When Truffaut and his fellow *Cahiers* critics lambasted the cinema against which they wished to rebel in the mid-1950s, they did not have in mind Hollywood films, on the contrary they located genuine 'art' and authentic cinematic modernism in Hollywood studio B-movie thrillers, including the cheap and trashy; instead they singled out the French postwar 'cinema of quality' for their vitriol.[5] This recurring pattern of an artistic avant-garde disapproving of relatively mainstream and conventional middle-brow art films of the 'quality' literary type goes back to the 1920s. The modernists were looking for art and cinematic modernism but didn't find it in the *Film d'Art*.

Cousins's commentary also evinces a preference for films that facilitate and elicit 'contemplation as well as sensation'.[6] Although modernists are often portrayed as anti-mass culture (which they often were) they were equally likely to profess a love for the vulgar, sensation and cheap thrills (the music hall, fairground, the circus) and endorse 'sensation', especially as a means of shocking the bourgeoisie and provoking a scandal. However, it has been more common for cinematic modernism to adopt, as Cousins suggests, an aesthetic of contemplation, a preference for films constituted by the primary unit of *the image* to be scanned, read and interpreted by the viewer, contemplated in its otherness like a modernist painting. This contemplative aesthetic was prevalent in the modernist cinema of the silent era, also in the postwar art-house era, and has been particularly dominant in twenty-first-century cinematic modernism.

'Filmed theatre' with its ensemble casts has usually meant tableaux in which the actors frontally face the camera: static actors, static camera and a flat mise-en-scène. In other words, the art film in the form of 'filmed theatre' gave rise to a rather stodgy uncinematic cinema. And the very fact that plays are essentially verbal created an obvious problem for silent film. The slapstick film consisting of visual gags barely needed intertitles, but an adaptation of a play would seem to require actors mouthing at the camera for inordinate lengths of time punctuated by even longer intertitles, transcriptions of the playscript. But it was these very demands made by the 'art film' that necessitated not just technical advances (Cousins gives the example of reverse angle shooting) but aesthetic solutions: a move towards a stylization of the image and a stylization of figurative or facial expression that could, as it were, 'stand in' for a thousand words. Similarly, as editing developed, the 'cut' could stand in for a transition or passage of time that might in a novel take a page and a half to describe. The consolidation of film grammar and syntax occurred between 1909 and 1912 over the course of the dozens of short films D. W. Griffith made for Biograph in which he developed innovations like the close-up, long-shot, cross-cutting and the flashback. When, in 1935, the well-known modernist and film critic Iris Barry became the first curator of the film department of the Museum of Modern Art in New York, she began collecting and restoring films from the silent era, most of which had long since ceased to have any appeal to audiences even before the coming of the sound film, and she established a canon of American cinema with Griffith firmly at its centre as the director who transformed cinema into a popular *art* form. As she writes in her 1940 Griffith monograph for MOMA:

> In 1912 Griffith was ready to progress further. He found himself with plenty to say and a new ease in saying it. Social problems had not ceased to interest him and, late this year, he made one of his finest short pictures, the *Musketeers of Pig Alley*. Whether as a study in realism, as an ancestor of the gangster films of later decades, or as an exercise in motion-picture composition this is a remarkable piece. The photography is extraordinary and the whole film predicts what was to come in the modern section of *Intolerance*. Another noteworthy picture of that year was *The New York Hat*, with Lionel Barrymore as Mary Pickford's champion. This film uses cut-backs, close shots and sharply edited scenes with ease and mastery: close-ups made acting a matter of expression and minute gesture instead of the stereotyped gestures of the popular theatre. The plot for this charming little picture had been submitted by Anita Loos, a sixteen-year-old stage actress in San Diego. At this period, ideas for films were commonly

> bought from outsiders and members of the company alike. Mary Pickford, Mack Sennett and others contributed many of the plots Griffith used.[7]

The fact that Iris Barry was curating this collection of Griffith for the Museum of Modern Art confirms that the popular mass entertainment medium of silent film was by the 1930s, retrospectively, attaining the institutionally endorsed status of a modern art:

> [T]he men who make films today know who it was that taught them the basis of their craft. The American public, which for forty-five years has so keenly enjoyed and supported the motion picture, has been somewhat reluctant to allow it the status of an art. Now, gradually, they too are recognizing that in Griffith they have one of the greatest and most original artists of our time.[8]

But was Iris Barry correct in equating Griffith with other modernist artists in the MOMA collection like Cézanne, Picasso and Matisse?

The first era of cinematic modernism

The ghosts of cinematic modernism exist in silent film and they can still charm, but do they strike us as modern in the sense that Picasso and Braque's cubist paintings, Joyce's *Ulysses* or T. S. Eliot's 'The Waste Land' retain their modern sensibility even in the twenty-first century? The argument of Bazin, Deleuze, Pasolini and many others is that a fully achieved cinematic modernism began after the Second World War with Rossellini and Welles. If this argument is accepted, then what can be recuperated from the first era of cinematic modernism in the silent film era?

Hollywood

D. W. Griffith may have remarked on his deathbed in 1944 that Hollywood talkies had lost the true art of cinema: to capture the wind in the trees, but today it is difficult to see the wind in the trees in Griffith films, because the films are so weighed down with old-fashioned moralism, melodrama and sentimentality, as well as what might charitably be called ideological currents of their time – endearingly so perhaps in the case of socialistic films like *A Corner in Wheat* (1909) but less so in the now more than ever unpalatable *The Birth of a Nation* (1915). The early art cinema epic – even *Intolerance* (1916) despite its many virtues – often seems clunky with its undigested theatrical and historical baggage. Late Hollywood classics of the silent era like Von Stroheim's *Greed* (1924), King Vidor's *The Crowd* (1928) and perennial critical favourite Murnau's *Sunrise* (1927) may still be loved by cineastes, may still be great cinema, but more generally the 'pre-classical' Hollywood art film has not fared well as modern art; their *modernism* is of a rather crude kind when compared to the modernist painting, novel, poetry and drama of the time. More in keeping with modernist taste are the residual traces of the *actualitiés*, traces of reality and contingency still to be found in early cinema prior to the consolidation of classical Hollywood and the sound film. Iris Barry notes that in 1940, when she was writing, Griffith's historical films appear unconvincing and dated while the contemporary films have moments which prefigure an authentically modern realism:

> It is remarkable to what an extent Griffith's films of contemporary life appear, in retrospect, to excel his period or costume pieces. This is chiefly due to the unconvincingness of the coiffures, costumes, gait, gesture and general air of the actors in period films, whereas the contemporary material has, by now, the un-mistakable veracity of photography by an Atget or a Brady.[9]

From this point of view, it is the elements of informal realism in Griffith's early Biograph shorts, including the use of locations and backgrounds set among real working lives, that point towards cinematic modernism rather than the achievement of radically structured epic narrative in film. According to Kracauer, the only 'modernity' that remained for Eisenstein in his recollections of Griffith was in these moments of passing reality:

> Yet if the street episodes of the 'modern story' [of *Intolerance*] involve the depiction of mass violence, they do by no means exhaust themselves in it. Eisenstein praises them for something less glaring – the way in which they impress upon the spectator the fortuitous appearances and occurrences inseparable from the street as such. In 1944, all that he remembered of these episodes was an ephemeral passer-by. After having described him, Eisenstein continues: 'As he passes he interrupts the most pathetic moment in the conversation of the suffering boy and girl. I can remember next to nothing of the couple, but this passer-by who is visible in the shot only for a flashing glimpse stands alive before me now – and I haven't seen the film for twenty years! Occasionally', he adds, 'these unforgettable figures actually walked into Griffith's films almost directly from the street: a bit-player developed in Griffith's hands to stardom; the passer-by who may never again have been filmed'.[10]

The Hollywood films amenable to modernism lay not so much in the would-be art film as in the popular film. Like the rest of the world, (most) modernists loved Chaplin and Keaton. This was not just an affectation of populist taste. In the first two decades of the twentieth century, modernists genuinely felt that Chaplin and Keaton were subversive artists, challenging and satirizing the staid conventions of bourgeois life and morality, and its class hypocrisies – attacking modernism's arch enemy: the nineteenth century. Chaplin and Keaton engaged with modernity, as both its celebrants and its victims. They represented the poor against the rich and their mode of attack, balletic slapstick, could be construed as absurdist, Dadaesque and surreal. In terms of cinematic form, Chaplin and Keaton were felt to embody the movement and mobility which was specific to film as a medium, yet in their acting and demeanour they represented a very modern and non-theatrical intimacy and informality.

In films ranging from *Shoulder Pads* (1918) to *Modern Times* (1936), Chaplin's engagement with the modern and the sensibility of modernity is ironically detached from the trauma of modernity the films represent (trench warfare in the First World War and Fordist industrialization respectively).[11] Even when caught up in an event like waking up in a flooded trench or working on a factory conveyor belt, Charlie is always outside looking on at the absurdity and it is with this comedic critical detachment that the viewer identifies, not the suffering. When Chaplin tries to foreground Charlie's suffering, the point of identification for the viewer becomes sentimentalized, something audiences came to resist and this quickly dated Chaplin's later films. It is in the little casual moments, a seemingly improvised half-gag or gesture or expression, that reality, life and the quotidian break through and which prefigure neorealism and the Bazinian aesthetic, and many such moments can be found in the best of the Essanay and Mutual shorts from 1915 to 1918, like the truly anarchic *Work* (1915) as well as in the more highly developed narrative films like *Easy Street* and *The Immigrant* from 1917. Similarly in the best of Buster Keaton's short films, *One Week* (1920) immediately springs to mind, the kinetic event – the gag – is highly formalized yet rendered casual within the seeming looseness of the beautifully unaffected narrative of a young newly-wed couple and their attempt to assemble a build-it-yourself house. The real present-time dimension of the gags is combined with the fresh novelty of cinematic technique, including self-reflexive cinematic jokes, such as the bath scene in which Seely (Buster's young wife) has to retrieve the soap from outside the bath and the cameraman covers the lens to protect her modesty. The modernity of *One Week* lies not only in its representation of modern life with its technologies (gadgets), its new social (and sexual) living arrangements and its (self-reflexive) cinematic techniques but in its focus on real-time moments within a loose narrative of contingent events and in the spontaneity and informality of its de-dramatized acting style.

The silent avant-garde

If literary and theatrical adaptation proved problematic for the early art film, a more cohesive association developed between painting and the avant-garde cinema, indeed avant-garde films were usually made by painters and tended to be short non-narrative films concerned with the materiality of the medium: the mechanics of the camera and projection as well as the properties of film stock. The avant-garde films of the silent era also tend towards a 'pure' formalism, such as images of semi or complete abstraction.[12]

Debates over the relative merits of silent versus sound film and the relative merits of avant-garde versus modernism mark recurring schisms in the critical discourse on cinematic modernism. Peter Wollen's influential 1975 essay 'The Two Avant-Gardes' attempted to clarify both schisms:

> Painting, I think it can be argued, played the leading role in the development of modernism in the other arts. The break, the *coupure* – to use the Althusserian terminology – the shift of terrain that marked the substitution of one paradigm or problematic for another, the beginning of modernism, the work of the historic avant-garde, was a break that took place in painting pre-eminently, with the discoveries of Cubism. It is not hard to show how painting affected the other arts, how early Cubism had a decisive impact on Gertrude Stein and Ezra Pound, for example, in literature, and later on William Carlos Williams, Apollinaire, Marinetti, Mayakovsky, Khlebnikov – all were influenced at a crucial point by their encounter with Cubism. The innovations of Picasso, and Braque, were seen as having an implication beyond the history of painting itself.[13]

Wollen argues, in the post-structuralist mode of the time, that in painting there was a 'break' – cubism – in which the relationship between signifier and signified was comprehensively destabilized while in the literary arts this destabilization remained intermittent, the signified remained dominant; basically this means that painting no longer referred beyond itself to a referent in the real or in the transcendental, while literature remained grounded in realist narrative. Wollen admits that things were not quite so clear cut, given that abstract painters tend to refer to the ultimate signified in the form of a transcendental absolute or sublime. Nevertheless, his argument is that early attempts to create an art out of the new medium of film split between an avant-garde following painting into a rejection of representation, narrative and realism, and another avant-garde following the novel into new kinds of realist narrative. The first cinematic avant-garde flourished during the silent era:

> One powerful influence has come from painting, bringing with it a tendency to abstraction – pure light or colour; and non-figurative design – or deformation of conventional photographic imagery, involving prismatic fragmentation and splintering, the use of filters or stippled glass, mirror-shots, extreme and microscopic close-ups, bizarre angles, negative images, all of which are to be found in twenties films.[14]

The key filmmakers of the 1920s avant-garde are listed by Wollen as Léger-Murphy, Picabia, Clair, Eggeling, Richter, Man Ray and Moholy-Nagy.[15] The second avant-garde, although often using radical editing techniques or special effects, remained firmly grounded in the literary, in narrative and in realism, and this list would include German expressionists like Murnau, French impressionists like Jean Epstein and Soviet directors like Eisenstein and Pudovkin, but with the significant exception of Vertov (Figures 5–8):

> The Soviet directors of the twenties, though they saw themselves in some sense as avant-garde, were also preoccupied with the problem of realism. For the most part they remained within the bounds of narrative cinema. The most clearly avant-garde passages and episodes in Eisenstein's films (experiments in intellectual montage) remain passages and episodes, which appear as interpolations within an otherwise homogeneous and classical narrative. There is no doubt that the dramaturgy is modernist rather than traditional – the crowd as hero, typage, *guignol* – but these are not features that can be attributed to a break with rather than a renovation of classical theatre. They are modes of achieving a heightened emotional effect or presenting an idea with unexpected vividness or force. In Eisenstein's work the signified – content in the conventional sense – is always dominant and, of course, he went so far as to dismiss Vertov's *Man with the Movie Camera* as 'formalist jackstraws and unmotivated camera mischief', contrasting its use of slow motion with Epstein's *La Chute de la Maison Usher*, in which, according to Eisenstein, it is used to heighten emotional pressure, to achieve an effect in terms of a desired content or goal. Vertov's film was, of course, a milestone for the avant-garde and it is a sign of its richness that it can be seen as a precursor both of *cinema-verité* and of structural film, though also, evidently, a sign of its ambiguity, of its uncertainty caught between an ideology of photographic realism and one of formal innovation and experiment.[16]

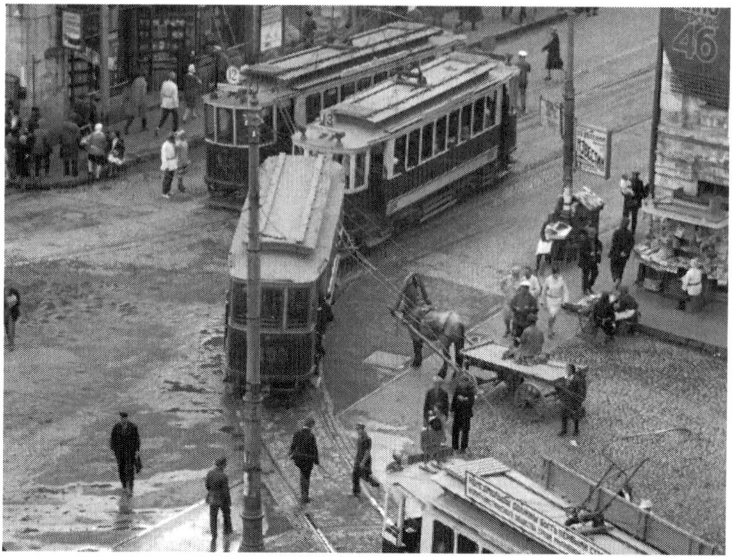

Figure 5 *Man with a Movie Camera* (1928), Dziga Vertov.
Documentary realism. The 'objective' kino-eye observes (from above) an everyday city street scene and the modern trams sharing space with bustling pedestrians and a horse and cart.

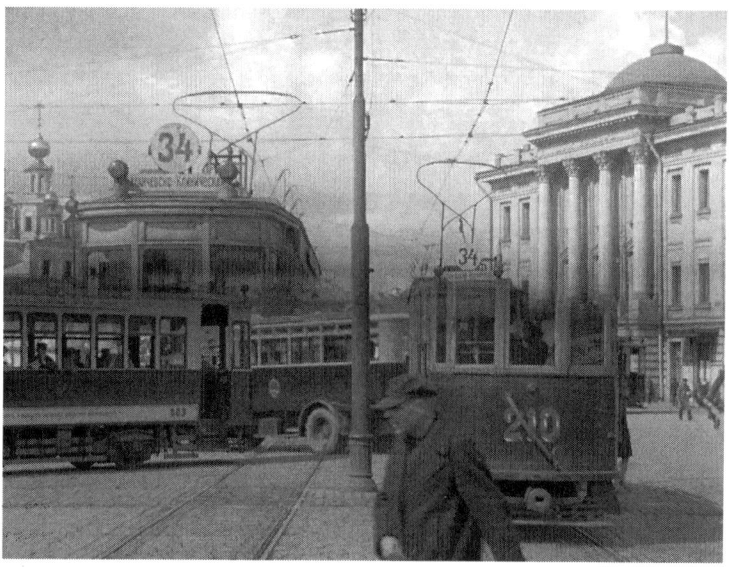

Figure 6 *Man with a Movie Camera* (1928), Dziga Vertov.
Documentary realism has now given way to a futurist and expressionist aesthetic: montage not only between frames but within frames, the trams and streets now divided and superimposed to denote the chaos of time, space and movement, the delirious mechanistic rhythms of modernity.

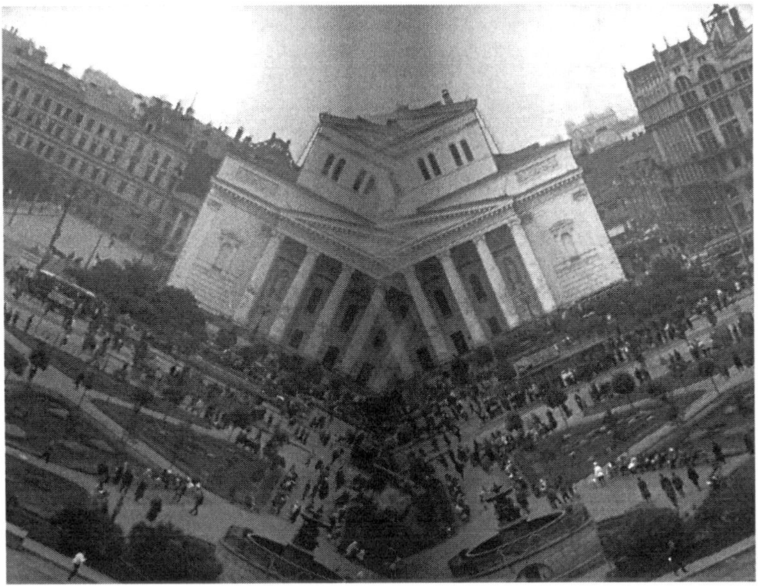

Figure 7 *Man with a Movie Camera* (1928), Dziga Vertov.
The image is now violently distorted to evoke a hallucinatory defamiliarization of reality – Eisenstein called this 'formalist jack-straws and unmotivated camera mischief'.

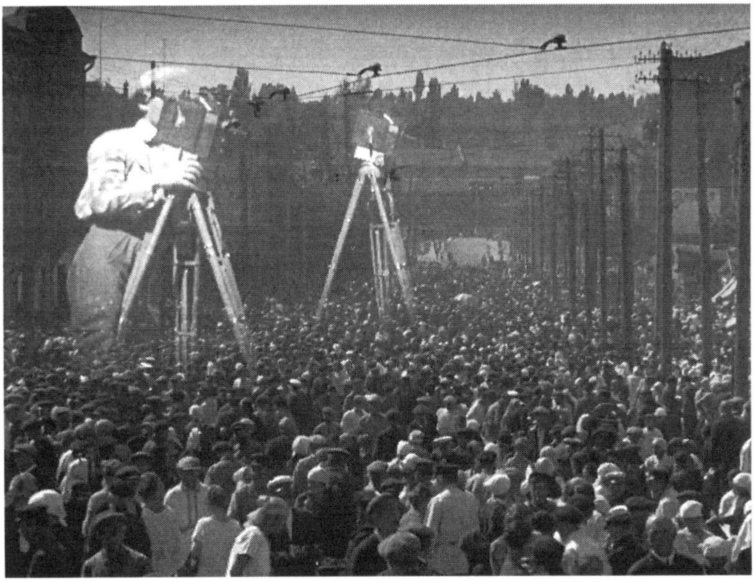

Figure 8 *Man with a Movie Camera* (1928), Dziga Vertov.
Montage and its formalism having been imposed upon reality, the auteur/director, cameraman (and editor) and his machine – the camera – emerge as master of reality: transcendent and all-seeing above the masses.

The first avant-garde flourished in the silent era precisely because it privileged the visual image over verbal language, and this anti-verbal, anti-narrative 'silent' legacy continued into the postwar (New York and London) experimental film:

> Primarily of course verbal language was missing and also narrative. During the silent period, the absence of language was not foregrounded; it seemed a natural quality of film, but in retrospect its significance can be seen. Language is still excluded from an enormous number of avant-garde films, which are shown either silent or with electronic or other musical tracks. Again, there are real technical and financial reasons for this, but these practical disincentives coincide with an aesthetic itself founded on concepts of visual form and visual problems that exclude verbal language from their field, and may be actively hostile to it.[17]

It is not surprising that once sound arrived, the second avant-garde (for which narrative and dialogue were an integral part of the aesthetic) became predominant and it is this avant-garde that feeds into the postwar cinematic modernism of Rossellini, Antonioni and the new waves of the 1960s. The premise of this book is that the two avant-gardes do still exist and within the critical discourse are commonly distinguished as experimental film and cinematic modernism. Peter Wollen's argument is that a radical reconciliation between the two avant-gardes would be desirable and was almost achieved by Vertov in the 1920s and Godard in the 1960s, particularly in the post-1968 films, in the period of what is now called 'political modernism'. Wollen writes:

> In a sense, Godard's work goes back to the original breaking-point at which the modern avant-garde began – neither realist or expressionist, on the one hand, nor abstractionist, on the other. In the same way, the *Demoiselles d'Avignon* is neither realist, expressionist, or abstractionist.[18]

This is less of a reconciliation than a return to the moment before the 'break' and is perhaps better described as an overlap between different tendencies. There is clearly also an overlap between the avant-garde film and Dada and an overlap between Dada and surrealist film. The overlap is evident in the introduction of objects and figures in place of pure abstract shapes, and the introduction of narrative, however absurdist. As such, surrealist film may constitute a transitional space between the avant-garde and cinematic modernism. Or to put it another way, Dada and surrealist film lead away from the avant-garde and move towards cinematic modernism – but without necessarily arriving there.

In a summary of the 1920s avant-garde, Murray Smith discusses Clair's *Entr'acte* and notes the overlap between the artistic movements, between painters, musicians and filmmakers, and he also notes that aesthetically the 'site' of the overlap was the question of narrative:

> The most accomplished Dada film – completed some time after the movement had disintegrated – was Rene Clair's *Entr'acte* (France, 1924). Two aspects of the film stand out. First, while the outlines of a narrative can be found – involving the shooting of a man and his subsequent funeral – the energies of the film are invested in a variety of non-narrative strategies which cut across and often completely submerge its progress. Since narrative is a form of rationality – we explain ourselves through stories revealing our reasons for doing things – it becomes an object of attack, along with standards of propriety (scattered across the film are 'crotch-shots' of a ballerina, ultimately revealed to be a bearded man in drag). Narrative logic is replaced by an unpredictable mix of associative and abstract links. Second, the film was originally conceived and projected as part of a larger performance: the film acted as an intermission (the literal meaning of 'entr-acte') within the Dada ballet *Relâche* ('Cancelled'). The scenario for the film was the creation of the painter Francis Picabia, who wrote the ballet with the composer Erik Satie (the two of them also 'star' in the film). Thus, although the film was directed by a figure who was to sustain his career as a film director, it emerged very much out of collaboration with artists working in the plastic and musical arts. This was typical of the avant-garde film production in the 1920s, and to a lesser degree continued to be so throughout its history.[19]

There are several ambiguities here. Is narrative being deployed in order to be subverted and attacked? Or is the attempt to subvert and repress narrative actually the back-door through which narrative returns and through which the avant-garde and Dada transitions to surrealism and from there to narrative-based cinematic modernism or, in Rene Clair's case, mainstream popular cinema? In *Un Chien Andalou* (1929) we don't have abstraction and non-narrative; Bunuel and Dali give us a full-blown anti-narrative. But, structured by negation, anti-narrative is a form of narrative and moreover one that is easy to recuperate along traditional lines as dream logic, the (ir)rationality of the unconscious, parody of old-fashioned narrative tropes or as satire of bourgeois culture. The long career of Jean Cocteau culminating in *Orphée* (1950) is perhaps the best example of a surrealist fellow-traveller who creates a body of work which in its investment in conventional realist narrative, albeit stylized to render the desires, fantasies and fears of dream, finally belongs to cinematic modernism more than it belongs to the tradition of avant-garde film.

For the purposes of clarification, the following admittedly crude distinction might be offered:

- *Avant-garde film* is non-narrative, is related to developments in painting rather than literature, is shown in exhibition spaces not cinemas and is associated with a lineage of auteurs from Richter and Man Ray to Brakhage and Mekas.
- *Modernist film* is narrative (even when subverting, obstructing or deconstructing narrative), is related to developments in literature rather than painting, is shown primarily in cinemas, deploys a cinematic aesthetic (mise-en-scène) and is associated with the lineage of film auteurs from Dreyer, Renoir and Vigo to Rossellini, Welles and Tarkovsky.

If the avant-garde film has a problematic relationship with cinematic modernism, perhaps, as already noted in the previous chapter, a more sympathetic relationship can be discerned in the influence of expressionism and impressionism on cinematic modernism?[20]

Expressionism and impressionism

In *Screening Modernism* András Bálint Kovács argues for the importance of expressionism as the first real attempt to create a cinema corresponding to then-contemporary developments in the art world, as the inaugural attempt at creating a cinematic modernism:

> Early modern filmmakers critiqued not so much popular narrative cinema as the artistic utilization of cinema, which they themselves were busy modernizing. Because cinema did not have an artistic tradition proper to its medium to modernize, there were different ways to achieve this goal. One way to bring out the artistic potential of cinema was to create cinematic versions of modernist movements in the fine arts, theater, and literature, or simply fit cinema in with narrative and visual forms of the national cultural heritage. In this sense, early modernism was cinema's reflection on artistic and cultural traditions outside of the cinema. German expressionism was the first appearance of that kind of modernism in the cinema.[21]

While specialists in German film continue to argue about which films from the 1920s were actually expressionist, cineastes continue to be quietly confident that they know expressionism when they see it and happily apply the term to all kinds of films, including those of Welles, Bergman and many others. Nevertheless, regarding German expressionism of the 1920s, Georges Sadoul remarked on a distinction in German film commentary from the period between the movement proper with a capital 'E' and the ongoing dispersal and modification of stylistic traits spelt with a small 'e'. Thus 'expressionism' dates from 1919 to 1927, beginning with *The Cabinet of Dr Caligari* (Wiene 1920) and *Nosferatu* (Murnau 1922) and ending with *Faust* (Murnau 1926) and *Metropolis* (Fritz Lang 1927), while 'expressionism' continues into Lang's *M* (1930) and *Testament of Dr Mabuse* (1932) and from there on to being an important stylistic component in Hitchcock, Hollywood horror and film noir.[22]

Derived primarily from both expressionist painting (Beckmann, Kokoschka, Nolde, Schiele) and expressionist theatre (Oskar Kokoschka, *Murderer, Hope of Women* 1908), cinematic expressionism is an aesthetic of chiaroscuro lighting, disorientating camera angles and strange stage sets marked by sharp vertical lines, diagonals and off-kilter horizontals. The overall effect is that of distorted vision reflecting a disordered psyche (and society).

Hitchcock was heavily influenced by his time at UFA and there is an evident expressionist influence on *The Lodger* (UK 1926) and, as with Lang, expressionist elements reappear across Hitchcock's career through to *Psycho*. Much of Eisenstein and the Soviet montage films deploy a kind of expressionist aesthetic in the melodramatic staging and acting and also in the dynamic distortions and fragmentation of reality inherent in the 'montage of attractions'. The influence of expressionism from the silent era in Germany is then carried over the Atlantic to Hollywood to become a staple trait of horror and then film noir, not only the chiaroscuro lighting but also a more general influence on the mise-en-scène and the idea of the individual falling into paranoid delusions when faced by the conspiratorial madness of the modern world. Kovács points out that the influence of expressionism on Hollywood after the coming of the sound film was in many ways a continuation of expressionistic styles that had existed in Hollywood in the silent era since Griffith:

> [T]he modernity of expressionism is not to be found in how it differs from the canonized norms of narrative cinema. In fact, as far as narrative is concerned, German expressionist films were not at all subversive, and they respected most classical rules. The extremely unrealistic character of some of their narratives was probably unusual in Hollywood terms, but they were not at all anti-Hollywood in their principles. Expressionist films were in fact the first models of some of the most popular Hollywood genres, such as vampire and monster movies and psycho-thrillers. Even their unusual and extravagant visual devices turned out to be familiar to the Hollywood visual universe. On the one hand, the success of German filmmakers who emigrated to Hollywood in the 1930s shows that their cinematic culture in fact harmonized well with the Hollywood way of thinking. On the other hand, the stylistic renewal of the American cinema by Orson

> Welles and film noir in the 1940s had its foundation precisely in expressionist cinematography. Later on, the formal principles of other modernist and avant-garde movements appear in the cinema as well, such as surrealism (Fernand Léger, Luis Buñuel, Salvador Dali, Man Ray, and Germain Dulac), futurism (Vertov), Dadaism (Clair, Francis Picabia, Hans Richter) and cubism (Marcel L'Herbier). However, only expressionism and surrealism had a lasting impact on the development of cinema.[23]

Early cinema borrowed and reacted to all the surrounding art movements which would now be categorized as modernist, but the avant-garde (anti-narrative) influence remained limited to avant-garde film, often made by avant-garde artists who had made their reputations first and foremost as painters prior to turning to filmmaking. By contrast, expressionism and surrealism would go on to influence popular and mainstream film, including Hollywood, from Hitchcock to Lynch. However, Kovács then goes on to argue that, while expressionism and surrealism fed into mainstream film, a third modernist aesthetic – impressionism – has had the most abiding influence on cinematic modernism:

> There is yet a third way in which modernism informed the cinema of the 1920s. This trend was the least spectacular, but its impact was the most important for the future development of cinematic modernism. This is the movement that Henri Langlois named 'French impressionism'. Auteurs like Germaine Dulac, Louis Delluc, Jean Epstein, Abel Gance, and Marcel L'Herbier are counted among its representatives. The idea of proving that cinema is a modern art form in its own right is the driving force of this movement, but like German expressionists, French impressionists did not deny the narrative nature of cinema and did not look for cinema's 'essence' in abstract visuals and sequential principles.[24]

As David Bordwell notes, impressionist film seems close to the modernist novel in its focus on consciousness, memory and time:

> To a degree unprecedented in international filmmaking, Impressionist films manipulate plot time and subjectivity. To depict memories, flashbacks are common; sometimes the bulk of a film will be one flashback or a series of them. Even more striking is the films' insistence on registering characters' dreams, fantasies, and mental states. Dulac's *La souriante Madame Beudet* (1923) consists almost entirely of the main character's fantasy life, her imaginary escape from a dull marriage. Despite its epic length (over five hours), Gance's *La roue* (1923) rests essentially on the erotic relations among only four people, and the director seeks to trace the development of each character's feelings in great

> detail. Impressionism's emphasis on personal emotion gives the films' narratives an intensely psychological focus.[25]

It is from the overlap between impressionism and the other counter-cinemas of the silent era, such as surrealism and the documentary, an overlap exemplified by the films of Jean Epstein, that impressionism generated a French 'poetic realism' which would provide a basis for cinematic modernism in the sound era in the films of Vigo: *Zéro de conduit/Zero for Conduct* (1933), *l'Atalante* (1934) and Renoir: *Une Partie de campagne/A Day in the Country* (1936) *Le Règle du jeu/The Rules of the Game* (1939).[26] In their poetic realism, their formal awareness and informality of tone, these films point towards the Bazinian aesthetics of postwar cinematic modernism, something acknowledged when Renoir dedicated the acclaimed 1959 restoration of *Le Règle du jeu* to the memory of the recently deceased Bazin.[27]

The emerging critical discourse on cinema as an art

According to David Bordwell the critical discourse of film history from the 1920s down to the present has been dominated by what he calls the 'The Basic Story':

> The Basic Story tells us that cinematic style developed by abandoning the capacity of the motion picture camera to record an event. According to the Story, in the course of the 1910s and 1920s particular film techniques were elaborated that made cinema less a pure recording medium than a distinct means of artistic expression.[28]

The novelty of recording 'reality' – trains arriving at stations, workers leaving factories – wore off, the Lumière *actualités* gave way to the trick photography, staging and special effects of Méliès in the service of narrative as something imaginary and unreal. Edwin S. Porter and then D. W. Griffith establish the basic rules for combining separate pieces of film or shots in sequences representing continuity in time and space and representing causality between events as a means of creating narrative. Hollywood, with Chaplin and Keaton at the forefront, becomes the dominant world cinema alongside a succession of national cinema movements which, led by key auteurs, proceed to suggest the aesthetic possibilities inherent in and specific to cinema: Scandinavian cinema with its use of landscape and light; French impressionism with its use of stylized camera work to suggest the moods and vicissitudes of subjectivity; the French avant-garde with its experiments in abstraction and rhythm; German expressionism with its extreme anti-naturalism in order to present disordered and distorted 'alienated' psychological states; Soviet montage cinema with its use of elaborate dynamic rhythmic editing techniques to deliver political messages about class conflict.

In the 1920s and 1930s film clubs and film journals around the world, especially in Paris, London, Berlin and New York, consolidate and disseminate this 'Basic Story' of how cinema became a narrative form and then a 'poetic' means of aesthetic expression, a modern art, which can be understood in terms of the development of the other arts in the age of modernism. Bordwell sees Paul Rotha's seminal account as epitomizing the story of how cinema went from being a derided vaudevillian sideshow to a modernist art:

> All these tendencies find compact expression in Paul Rotha's 1930 *The Film Til Now*, the most ambitious and influential English-language film history of the era. A short chapter surveying the development of film as a means of artistic expression points to several milestones: *The Great Train Robbery* as launching the story-based film; the Film d'Art; the work of Griffith; *The Cabinet of Dr. Caligari* as the decisive break with realism; *The Last Laugh*, which 'definitely established the film as an independent medium of expression'; and the Soviet masterworks. In the remainder of the book Rotha devotes a chapter to each significant film-producing nation, organizing his account according to the oeuvres of major directors.
>
> From nation to creator to individual work: by the end of the silent era, this basic art-historical breakdown had become commonplace in synoptic film histories. More surprisingly, in certain respects the development of this mass-market entertainment seemed to parallel the history of modernism in other arts. Like contemporary art historians who glanced from country to country in search of the latest break with tradition, champions of the new medium presumed that the Basic Story would exhibit those leaps from 'vanguard to vanguard' that pushed an art forward. In the 1920s, the ball of cinematic progress seemed obviously to pass from America to Germany to France to the USSR. Ever since the Basic Story was articulated, each research program has had to reconstruct the idea of aesthetic modernism in a fresh way.[29]

Rotha's book confirmed how, among the international cineaste community in the 1920s, a critical discourse on film as an art developed, which defined film as an art in relation to the other arts with reference to then current modernist aesthetics. In other words, the attempt to reinterpret this 'mass-market entertainment' of cinema as an art was bound up with film's relationship to modernism. Cinema, conceived as a modernist aesthetic, progressed on multiple fronts and interacted with a full range of other modernist arts but – and this is perhaps the most important point – cinema was a modernist art that remained bound up with 'mass-market entertainment' to a far greater degree than any other art. And, while this has often been a source of embarrassment and exasperation, it is this relationship to a popular mass entertainment medium that has given cinematic modernism an inclusivity and impurity that modernism in the other arts struggled to retain when not working to actively exclude. Cinema was also unique among the arts in being able to represent modernity with the latest technology of modernity, indeed cinema was itself one of the key features of modernity to which modernism was responding. The closeness of cinema to modernism in the other arts is explicit in the names of the various film movements, almost all of which correspond to modernist movements in the arts: impressionism, expressionism, Dada and surrealism. Within the critical discourse of film as an art there was also an emerging consensus that the conception of cinema as an art was based on two awkwardly related fundamental ideas:

- Film, more than any other art, not only represents but records and presents reality, has a direct relation to ontological reality.
- Film, more than any other art, can modify and distort reality through staging, trick photography and special effects. Through editing – montage – film can deconstruct and reconstruct reality.

If the apogee of film as a (supposedly) direct recording of reality would be the documentary movement (Flaherty, *Nanook of the North* 1922), then the apogee of film as 'reality reassembled' was Soviet montage (Vertov, *Man with a Movie Camera* 1929). It is probably true to say that during the later silent film era the art film leaned towards the stylization and reassembling of reality rather than documentary realism, in part because by its very nature silent film was non-naturalistic – it lacked sound – it therefore tended towards the elaboration of the purely visual image and the arrangement of visual images to compensate for the lack of sound and speech and the marginalization of text, and this emphasis on the image as something non-verbal and universal – not bound by national languages but internationalist – was part of the utopian appeal of silent cinema for modernists. Towards the close of the 1920s there was reasonable confidence that cinema had proved itself to be an art, albeit only in a small minority of films – an up to the minute, global and in many ways inclusive modernist art.

But then everything changed. By 1928 the 'talking pictures' had arrived, and the silent film era was over.

Bazin and the sound film

For many modernist artists and writers involved with cinema, the sound film signalled the end of cinema as an art. According to Rudolf Arnheim in *Film as Art* (1933) language and speech distracted from, undermined and directly contradicted the aesthetics of the silent cinematic image.[30] The poetry of the cinematic image was over. In the silent era cinema had established itself as an art by shaking off the baggage of 'filmed theatre', now it would become 'filmed theatre' at a much more literal level, or worse still 'filmed novel', dominated by dialogue, storylines and characterizations borrowed from and imitative of the (non-modernist) novel. The internationalist Esperanto of the image would be replaced by a dependency upon the verbal and with that would come the global dominance of the English language and the American film – Hollywood. And, in a way, the advocates of silent film were right: after straightening out the initial technological problems, Hollywood 'talkies' did foreground dialogue, story/plot and characterizations, largely derived from the novel (whether high-brow, middle-brow or low-brow). Acting styles would now become more 'naturalistic' in a way that retrospectively made the acting styles of the silent film seem a parodic exaggeration of the overwrought gestural stylistics of stage melodrama. The 'talkies' established a set of conventions which rendered editing and stylization 'invisible' to an audience that soon took these conventions for granted. According to Rudolf Arnheim and the unrepentant partisans of the silent art film, the Hollywood film of the 1930s was designed to create a window, a transparency through which an audience could directly access a story, a plot, and so escape into the immersive 'world' of that story and the aura of its stars. The mass entertainment medium became exclusively that, a popular entertainment medium; it had lost its art, its aesthetic specificity and its modernism.

Rejecting the idea that the shift from silent film to sound film marked a fundamental break, André Bazin argues instead that the silent era was a kind of accelerated working-through of all the visual possibilities of the new medium, along with influences derived from older arts. By the late 1920s the formalism represented by German expressionism and Soviet montage was already – during the silent era – exhausted, reduced to mannerism and passé technical trickery. At the same time, the refinement of cinematic codes of narrative-based realism – incorporating stylistic elements when required from expressionism – was already being consolidated in Hollywood before the talkies arrived. With provocative bravado, Bazin declares:

> [T]he invention of the sound track is just a fortuitous scientific phenomenon and not the aesthetic revolution people always say it is [. . .] the history of cinema

> before and after 1928 is an unbroken continuity. It is the story of the relations between expressionism and realism.[31]

In other words, the addition of sound merely completed the process by which 'classical' Hollywood romantic realism with its expressionist thriller elements became dominant. 'Classical' cinema is synonymous with the 'golden age' of Hollywood, the 1930s and 1940s, but when, immediately after the war, Bazin and his colleagues in Paris were able to catch up with the latest fare from Hollywood – Welles, Wyler and Hitchcock, especially *Citizen Kane*, *The Little Foxes* and a little later *Rope* – it seemed evident that 'classical' film was being superseded by a new more troubling and sophisticated phase. Behind the technophile fetishization of depth of field and the long take lies something more significant: a new psychology, a modern (postwar) sensibility and a (re)turn to modernist formalism in the service of rendering that new sensibility. What these films signified was a shift to a new psychological sensibility, one reflective of the war and its aftermath – in the parlance of the time, an existentialist sensibility of estrangement and uncertainty. Or to put in another way, if classical Hollywood film resembled the nineteenth-century novel, cinematic modernism had, belatedly, caught up with the twentieth-century modernist novel.

In an extreme-seeming juxtaposition, alongside the slick sophisticated new fare from Hollywood and while grappling with *Citizen Kane*, Bazin was also able to see the early wave of neorealist films from Italy: Visconti, De Sica and Rossellini – *La Terra Terma*, *Bicycle Thieves* and especially *Paisa* and *Umberto D*. It is a tribute to Bazin's perspicacity that instead of seeing Welles and Rossellini as diametrically opposed, he saw them as complementary, as both marking a transition for cinema, as moving beyond the now 'classical' Hollywood film and, albeit from opposite ends of the spectrum, *as moving towards cinematic modernism.*

4

Postwar cinematic modernism

From neorealism to the new wave

Across three chapters in *The Story of Film* Mark Cousins distinguishes three different phases of postwar cinematic modernism:

- a 'new early modernism' (example: Rossellini) emerging out of neorealism and marked by the attempt to cast off a redundant realist mode, such as 'classical' Hollywood realism, in order to develop a more authentic realism that is both objective and subjective
- 'modernism' (example: Antonioni) in which the representation of consciousness, existence and time leads to a tension between realist and anti-realist modes and the undermining of 'reality' itself, undercut by the 'estranged' subjective vision and sensibility of the auteur as manifested in formalist stylistics
- 'political modernism' (example: Godard), a post-1968 self-reflexive critical cinema, deploying Brechtian strategies and influenced by Soviet montage cinema of the 1920s (Vertov)[1]

This chapter looks at what is generally agreed to have been the heyday of cinematic modernism during the postwar period and tracks the emergence and development of cinematic modernism across the three phases outlined by Cousins in terms of neorealism, the new wave and political modernism.

Part I: From neorealism to cinematic modernism

Rossellini and Welles

When Roberto Rossellini and his young assistant Federico Fellini ventured out into the rubble of Rome to film *Rome, Open City/Roma città aperta* in 1945, it is doubtful if they were thinking about how their film might be situated in the history of modern art or modernism. Orson Welles was a performer and director of everything from Shakespeare to H. G. Wells in practically every medium. Welles therefore had an acute self-consciousness about art and modernity, but chose cinema precisely because he thought it was the key mass medium for culture in the twentieth century, superseding the theatrical stage and the novel, a living popular cultural form not a rarefied academic realm of modern art. As he made *Citizen Kane* Welles may have thought he was bringing a modern artist's sensibility to the mainstream cinema of Hollywood, but he was probably not thinking of *Citizen Kane* as itself an artefact of high modernism.

The idea that Rossellini and Welles represent the new beginning of cinematic modernism was not initially apparent to the directors themselves or inherent in their films, but is rather an idea generated by a particular critical discourse on modern cinema in a particular place, Paris, at a particular time – the immediate aftermath of the Second World War.

Postwar Paris: The critical context

A critical discourse on modern aesthetics and cinema already existed in Paris, conducted by André Malraux and Roger Leenhardt under the influence of Sartre's existentialist investment in authentic lived reality and Merleau Ponty's phenomenological investment in the primacy of perception and bodily sensory-motor functions. This philosophical background helped privilege cinema as providing a direct access to the real, to lived existence as it is experienced and perceived – seen (and heard) by the spectator – and possibly access to reality in itself as recorded by the machine (camera). Malraux wrote 'Sketch for a Psychology of Film' in 1940 and Leenhardt had written 'Little School of the Spectator' in 1936. Together these articles assumed an evolutionary view of the arts, arguing that film was leaving behind its infancy and moving towards a more mature stage which involved discarding the old avant-garde idea that the unique quality of cinema was to reconstruct reality (as manifested in Soviet montage and German expressionist staging and special effects). Instead the unique quality of cinema is to record and directly represent reality. Montage should serve continuity (via '*decoupage*') rather than disrupting it. Expressionism should serve a realist mise-en-scène rather than being imposed upon it as stylistic excess. 'Classical' Hollywood had long assimilated montage and cinematic special effects into a 'realist' aesthetic governing editing, shot composition and mise-en-scène, arriving at a cinematic realism which had triumphed all over the world – which is why Hollywood film was, for most French critics in the 1940s, more advanced than the 'art film'. But mainstream Hollywood films lacked psychological and aesthetic sophistication; the advanced stylistic techniques were prone to serve vulgar action, sensation or melodrama. 1930s French cinema, Renoir and Vigo, had shown the way forward and now, together, Italian neorealism and the new Hollywood film of Welles, Wyler and Hitchcock were pointing cinema towards its maturity.

Malraux, among his many accomplishments, was a novelist and his demand for cinema to capture the reality of the everyday was based both on the example of the modern novel and on the unique quality of the cinematographic image, a demand which would be answered by neorealism and which was summarized by Leenhardt as early as 1936:

> Malraux defined a new literary aesthetic which would rely on ellipsis in opposition to the ancient art of metaphor. This aesthetic is the aesthetic of cinema. It corresponds to the stage of precision which human information has achieved – photography is only one of its forms – and to a taste for the matter-of-fact, the document, which characterise modern times. . . . Ultimately, it reveals a new method in the interpretation and the expression of the world. . . . Not the studied search for a 'meaning' through acting or décor but a simple work of 'rendering.' Not an artistic exercise in expression but a technical effort of description.[2]

This then was the critical discourse that had begun to emerge in the 1930s: accepting the sound film, accepting Hollywood, accepting the correspondence of modern cinema to the modern novel, distancing modern cinema from the plastic-arts influenced avant-garde of the silent film era. Above all, the aesthetic of cinema in its modern stage will be realist, open, elliptical; a *rendering* of matter-of-fact reality in all its ambiguity rather than the imposition of 'studied' closed totalities of meaning.

In terms of an aesthetic of cinematic modernism, the direction of travel set by Malraux and Leenhardt is clear and will arrive at its destination in the late 1940s in the pages of *Esprit*, *Les Temps Modernes* and film journals like *Le Revue du Cinema* and *Les Amis du Cinema* and cine-clubs ranging from Objectif 49 and Ciné-Club du Quartier Latin to Henri Langlois's Cinémathèque Française. It was from this vibrant Parisian film scene that André Bazin and Alexandre Astruc would emerge as the instigators of a critical discourse on modern cinema which, requiring an outlet and forum, would soon lead to the founding of rival film journals *Cahiers du cinéma* in 1951 and *Positif* in 1952.

Following the liberation of France, a flood of films and novels that had been banned by the Nazis suddenly arrived in Paris, stimulating the culture-starved intelligentsia. The importance of the American novel at this specific postwar moment means that 'modernism' as a literary reference point in France is not so much Joyce or Woolf but Hemingway, Fitzgerald and especially Faulkner. There was also a vogue for the American hard-boiled fiction of Dashiell Hammett, Raymond Chandler, James Cain and their many imitators, books popular not just with the French literati but with the younger Parisian cineastes who would come under Bazin's influence, write for *Cahiers du cinéma*, promote film noir and Hitchcock and go on to create the French New Wave. The tastes of Parisian cineastes after 1945 were transformed by the impact of exposure to a backlog of recent Hollywood films, as described by Mark Cousins in *The Story of Film*:

> After four years with no releases from Hollywood, Parisian audiences gorged on an influx of American movies. After *Gone with the Wind* (USA, 1939) there came, in July 1946 alone, Orson Welles' *Citizen Kane* (USA, 1941), John Huston's *The Maltese Falcon* (USA, 1941), Billy Wilder's *Double Indemnity* (USA, 1944) William Wyler's *The Little Foxes* (USA, 1941) and *The Best Years of our Lives* (USA, 1946). This feast of deep-staged films was a revelation, even in the homeland of Jean Renoir. The critic André Bazin argued that deep staging in such films enabled them to express the real world's complex realities. He detested what he perceived as naively stylized films such as *The Cabinet of Dr. Caligari* (Germany 1919) and as a Christian and a profoundly moral critic, he likened deep space almost to an act of worship or a genuflection before a transcendentally designed universe. It seemed that Hollywood cinema had begun to gain credibility in Europe and certain French filmmakers soon used deep staging themselves.[3]

Cousins goes on to argue that deep staging, facilitated by the technical advances (primarily in camera lenses) that made depth of field and deep focus possible, led directly to the long-take sequence shot cinema of Hitchcock in the late 1940s (most obviously *Rope* 1948), although the flowing long-take sequence shot had precursors such as Mizoguchi (who was about to become an important reference point to French critics in the 1950s). Cousins also notes an irony in Bazin welcoming the new Hollywood film noir, pulp thrillers and B-movies, influenced directly or indirectly by expressionism, Bazin having previously rejected the overtly modernist cinema of 1920s German expressionism.

In addition, Parisian cineastes after the war had access to the new films from Italy, the neorealist films produced in even more traumatic postwar circumstances – defeat, devastation and ruin – than those faced in Paris. There had been close connections between the Italian and French film industries before the war, including associations between Italian and French directors and critics, and after the war the Italian critics and theorists like Zavattini and Aristarco had already theorized neorealism as a (Marxist) counter-cinema rendering the banal realities of everyday life, marginalizing the artificial contrivances of story and ideally eliminating plot entirely.

Italian neorealism

Italian theorists like Zavattini tended to view reality and reality staged and filmed as more or less the same thing, this was because in practice 'reality' was a political and moral construct – reality only became reality if it was filmed from the correct political and moral point of view. Bazin is broadly in sympathy with the stylistics of neorealism promoted by Zavattini and thought that neorealism showed the possibility of a kind of modern cinema that could show everyday life unfolding in duration, could reveal the reality of ordinary life, that reality that Hollywood and mainstream film represses and disavows. As Cousins explains:

> This is the sea-change that neorealism brought about, and it is not always understood. Conventional film historians argue that the films of De Sica, Visconti and Rossellini (who all started their careers in the Fascist era) used natural lighting extensively and were visually gritty, but *Shoeshine*, and neorealism's great precursor, *Ossessione/Obsession* (Visconti, Italy, 1943), are full of stylised lighting. In addition, these films were not always shot on real streets or with non-professional actors as is sometimes claimed. However, the attitude at this moment in cinema was new. Zavattini said 'when we have thought out a scene, we feel we need to remain in it, because . . . it can contain so many echoes and reverberations'. In a well-known sequence in *Umberto D* a young housemaid (Maria Pia Casilio) lights a fire in the kitchen, sweeps the floor, relights the fire, looks outside, sprays some ants and starts to make coffee, all in silence. We watch her ordinary chores, of no consequence to the story, while she is alone with her thoughts and routines. The camera remains in the scene. In mainstream Hollywood cinema, such extraneous details would have been rigorously removed, creating 'life with the dull bits cut out', as Hitchcock reputedly said. In many of these Italian films, the apparently dull bits remain and consequently, time is expanded in them.[4]

Neorealist films should be structured by unfolding scenes and loosely and elliptically arranged events, rather than events reduced to dramatic action and linked by the contrived causality of plot. The idea of 'remaining' in the scene to document the unfolding of time (duration), to document the quotidian and to catch the contingent will become an abiding principle of the neo-Bazinian aesthetic that can be tracked through so much modernist cinema of the 1960s and 1970s, and so many films in the dominant strand of cinematic modernism today. For Deleuze, remaining in the unfolding scene necessitates real-time duration and provides the impetus for the modernist cinema of the 'time image' distinct from the plot and action-driven 'classical' film of the 'movement image'.

For all the novelty of its location shooting, rough mise-en-scène and deployment of non-professional actors, *Rome, Open City* had key scenes filmed in the studio, had a cast headed by star actors and was in many respects a mainstream melodrama – and was a commercial hit movie. It later became known that stylistically the film's unusual features were to an extent a result of circumstances (lack of money, lack of film stock, lack of basic film production facilities) and that the film had important continuities with Rossellini's previous films made as fascist propaganda during the war, almost all the leading figures of postwar Italian film – Rossellini, Fellini, Antonioni – having had their start under the beady eye of film fan and dictator's son Vittorio Mussolini. It could also be argued that much postwar Italian neorealist film and subsequently neorealist film from all over the world, often remains at the level of either sentimental melodrama, crude political or social allegory, or the equivalent of naturalism in the nineteenth-century novel.

Paisà (1946) rather than *Rome, Open City* is a genuinely radical film in its loose episodic structure, its rough mise-en-scène, juxtaposition of discontinuous scenes and its resistance to overly determined ideological judgement or *meaning*, it being left to the viewer to interpret the relationship between the episodes. For Bazin *Umberto D* (1952) is the key neorealist film because it represents a pinnacle of the cinema inaugurated by *Rome, Open City* and *Paisà*, and he was probably the first of the many commentators to have analysed the scene with Maria the maid doing her chores – a modest scene as Cousin's account suggests, but a scene with enormous implications in terms of attention to the quotidian, to de-dramatization and to the side-lining of story and plot – and in terms of the scene consisting of a maid, a woman, doing household chores, distantly prefiguring Chantal Akerman's *Jeanne Dielman* (1975), Marguerite Duras's *Nathalie Granger* (1972) and a whole strand of feminist filmmaking (Figure 9).

Neorealism and the Bazinian aesthetic

To understand Bazin's take on neorealism it is necessary to recap two fundamental ideas of cinema as an art in the silent film era. Bazin agrees with the ideas but radically re-evaluates them:

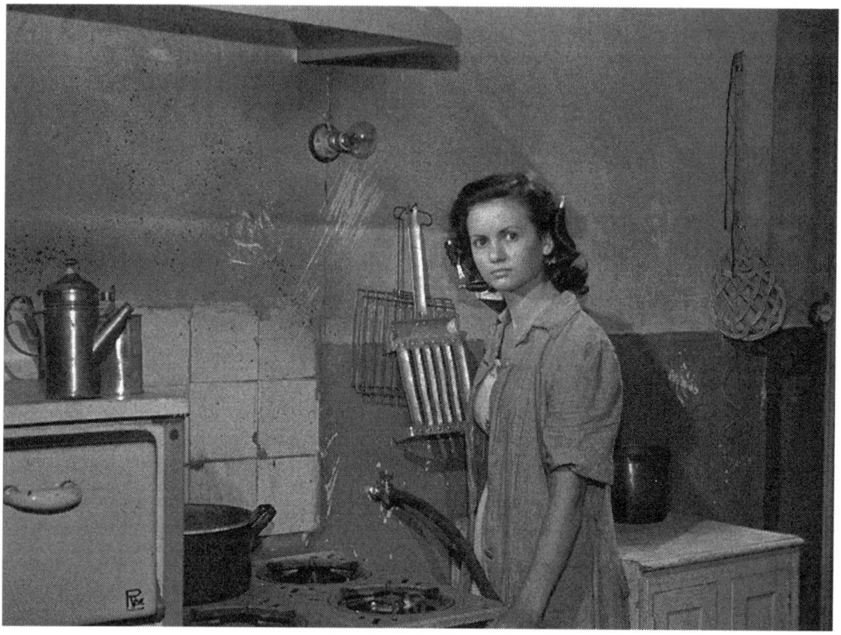

Figure 9 *Umberto D* (1952), Vittorio De Sica.
Maria the maid in the kitchen performing her daily chores in real-time durations. Yet this apparent 'dead time' in which 'nothing happens' acts as a repressed correlative for dramatic undercurrents – including her revelation to Umberto, in this scene, that she is pregnant.

- First, film more than any other art not only represents but records and presents reality and has a direct relation to ontological reality.
- Second, film more than any other art can modify and distort reality through stylized cinematography, staging, 'trick' photography and special effects. Through editing – montage – film can deconstruct and reconstitute reality.

It may well be that Bazin felt that the second fundamental – montage – had become intrusive and excessive in avant-garde and Soviet film of the 1920s, but he recognizes that montage is an essential aspect of cinema. Similarly, although positing the idea that cinematic reality is reality 'mummified' – not a symbolic representation of the body but the body itself, frozen in time – Bazin recognizes that what we see on the screen is not simply 'reality', but reality mediated by the technology and aesthetics of cinema, is in fact an *aesthetic representation*, albeit one that uses *reality itself* as a prop. This uncanny doubling of reality with the representation of reality – including the doubling of time, of temporal duration – in the cinematic image can never be entirely disavowed in the experience of watching a film. The Soviet montage film wished to analyse, deconstruct and then reconstruct reality in the service of an imposed ideological reality. Bazin is less bothered about the rights and wrongs of propaganda than about the attempt to take control of the cinematic image in order to banish its otherness. The Bazinian aesthetic endorses instead the movement away from the imposed montage of the explicit cut towards a montage of continuity *within* the long-take sequence shot, this allows reality and its otherness to unfold, to be revealed, and not subjected to overt intrusive control. What Bazin is looking for is a narrative-based aesthetic that compliments the uncanny relationship of film with ontological reality. This means an aesthetic which acknowledges reality as 'being', as 'existence' and which acknowledges time.

What connects sophisticated technically advanced Hollywood films like *Citizen Kane* and *Rope* with loose, rough Italian neorealist films like *Paisà* and *Umberto D* is the shift towards an aesthetic that foregrounds being (existence of people and objects), space (the spatial forms of a landscape, city or a room), time and duration, including more or less arbitrary everyday real-time duration activities with a degree of autonomy from plot, such as the scene of Maria the maid working in the kitchen from *Umberto D*. However, Hitchcock's elevation of everyday activities with *seeming* autonomy from the plot is peculiar because even the 'reality effects' – the marginal activities and details of his scenes – tend to contain sub-plots of their own, ultimately serving the requirements of suspense. The more irrelevant and innocent the detail, the more likely it turns out to be the vital clue to the entire underlying conspiracy structuring the film. This is presumably one of the reasons why Bazin had reservations about Hitchcock and the enthusiasm of the *Cahiers* Hitchco-Hawksians. If, after the silent film era, Hitchcock is modernist, then it is a modernism within and at the service of mainstream 'classical' Hollywood modes. The only consistently viable space for modernism in Hollywood was film noir, the genre that incorporated an encounter between European expressionism and the hard-boiled American detective tradition.[5] Welles was able to occupy this space with *Lady from Shanghai* and *Touch of Evil* but was otherwise obliged to stage the encounter not in Hollywood but in Europe with *Mr Arkardin* and *The Trial* – the latter film being one of the more self-conscious attempts at an explicitly modernist cinema.

An encounter between Hollywood and neorealism did take place, but in Italy not Hollywood: in Rossellini's films featuring Bergman. In a well-known story Ingrid Bergman, then Hollywood's biggest, most glamorous star, saw a screening of *Rome, Open City* and experienced an epiphany, deciding that instead of Hollywood confections she wanted to make real films about real people in real places. She fell in love with neorealist films and then fell in love with Rossellini.

Amid scandal, she left Hollywood and her marriage and came to Italy to make films with Rossellini.

In the Bazinian aesthetic it is through the juxtaposition or encounter of fiction with documentary modes that reality might be revealed. And this is one reason why Bazin, almost alone of the critics of his time, enthused about Rossellini's films with Ingrid Bergman. Embodying the sophisticated aura not just of Hollywood stardom but of the classical Hollywood narrative melodrama, Ingrid Bergman encounters the harsh lives of an Italian island fishing community in *Stromboli*, encounters various strata of the Italian urban working class in *Europa '51*, and the otherness of Italy archaic and modern in *Journey to Italy*, the latter film being the first full-fledged example of postwar cinematic modernism, something which Rossellini may have been conscious of given the film's various references to James Joyce: the bickering Bergman-Sanders couple being 'the Joyces' and aspects of the storyline being borrowed from Joyce's *Dubliners* novella *The Dead*, there are even some slightly clumsy attempts at stream-of-consciousness/interior monologue in scenes where Bergman is driving her car and her scattered thoughts are rendered via her voiceover. Prefiguring *Hiroshima mon amour* by several years, *Journey to Italy* stages an encounter between a modern couple with their romantic difficulties and a documentary reality, in this case the documentary filming of, and commentary on, the archaeological site at Pompei. This sets up a key moment in the film: the petrified skeletal figures of the ancient couple, frozen in flame the moment the Pompei eruption reached them, their bodies mummified, preserved down the ages by volcanic ash. Katherine (Bergman) realizes that she and Alex (Sanders) resemble that couple – petrified, frozen, dead – they need to release themselves emotionally and find each other and their love in order to live again.

For Bazin there is an additional frisson to the story of the couple frozen by heat in an embrace in Pompei thousands of years ago, a couple preserved in the most intimate moment of the everyday by layers of volcanic ash. Is this not what film can do? Preserve and mummify the dead and time so that they live again in their presence and present-ness every time the film is shown. Ingrid Bergman's encounter with the remains of the ancient lovers in Pompei is a very modernist and very Joycean story and also displays a typical postwar existentialist sensibility: you are thrown into this world, you are estranged from your environment, you must acknowledge this and take responsibility for your actions in order to truly exist, to be authentically alive (Figure 10). But is that still possible? What if the miracle that resolves a situation is false? What if an epiphany is merely fleeting? The miracles at the end of Rossellini's Bergman films are as moving as those in Dreyer's films but more fragile and ambiguous, closer to the 'negative' epiphanies with which

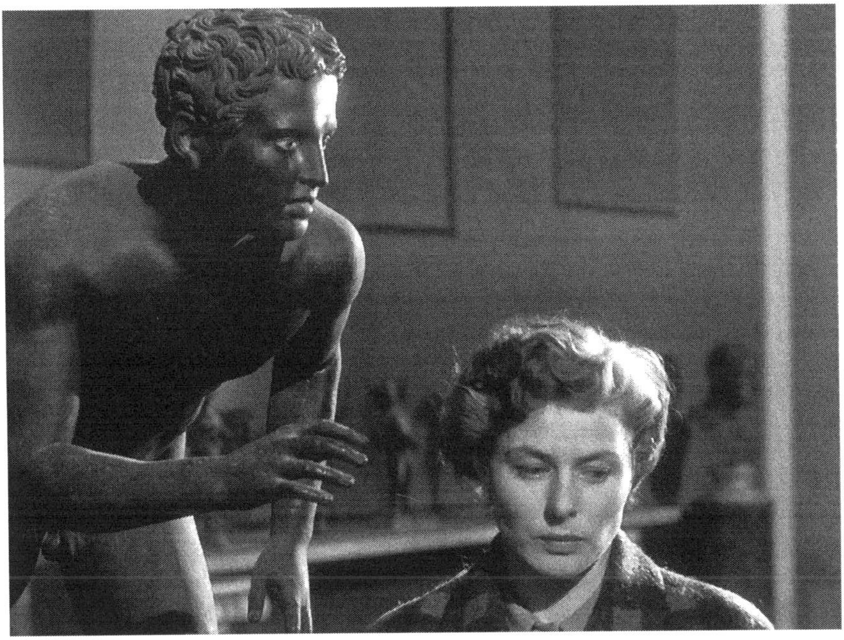

Figure 10 *Journey to Italy* (1954), Roberto Rossellini.
A wry image of a statue reaching out to Ingrid Bergman. Visiting the ruins and museums of Italy, Katherine Joyce (Ingrid Bergman) comes to see a resemblance between the frozen statues caught forever in the moment and the living death of her marriage, of her own sense of self being frozen and in need of a miraculous act of redemption in order to live again.

Antonioni will end his films. It is a short step from Ingrid Bergman's three films with Rossellini to the cinema of Antonioni and the popular existentialism of the period: psychology and consciousness as marked by an alienation caused by not only social reality (class struggle) and trauma (the war) but also the contingency of existence. Not the certainty of reality but its contingency and its ambiguity: its alien and alienating aspect.

Stromboli, *Europa '51* and *Journey to Italy* represent an encounter between Hollywood romantic classicism and neorealism, an encounter which produces the next stage beyond both classicism and neorealism, what this book is calling a 'neo-Bazinian aesthetic' and in doing so produces a template for cinematic modernism.

Part II: Postwar cinematic modernism

Bazin and Deleuze posit a 'break' in film history circa 1945 represented by the new films of Welles, Wyler and Hitchcock in Hollywood and by Italian neorealism and the films of Rossellini and De Sica. These two very different cinemas, Hollywood and Italian neorealist, provide the parameters for a new kind of 'world' cinema informed by the primacy of the 'time image' and the loosening of causal links between images and within a de-dramatized elliptical narrative structure, an aesthetic corresponding to that of modernism in other arts, especially the modernist novel. Kracauer in *Theory of Film* doesn't propose such a break, but he does clearly endorse a similar emerging aesthetic to Bazin: a realist aesthetic which leans towards the combining of unstaged and staged elements, non-professional actors with stars, juxtaposing documentary realism with episodic 'light narrative' and so on. The new modern cinematic aesthetic is discussed by Kracauer in terms of Italian neorealism, its precursors in France (Vigo, Renoir) and related developments elsewhere (Bresson, Dreyer, Satyajit Ray, Kurosawa). From Bazin and Kracauer's discussion of postwar film in *What Is Cinema?* and *Theory of Film* a limited set of key films emerges common to both texts, corresponding to what Mark Cousins calls the 'new early modernist directors' and the first phase of cinematic modernism:

Citizen Kane (Welles 1941), *Magnificent Ambersons* (Welles 1942), *The Little Foxes* (Wyler 1941), *Notorious* (Hitchcock 1946), *The Lady from Shanghai* (Welles 1947)

Stromboli (Rossellini 1950), *Story of a Love Affair* (Antonioni 1950), *Umberto D* (De Sica 1954), *Journey to Italy* (Rossellini 1954), *La Strada* (Fellini 1954)

Los Olvidados (Bunuel 1950), *Diary of a Country Priest* (Bresson 1951), *Ordet* (Dreyer 1955), *Rashomon* (Kurosawa 1950)

Bazin and Kracauer were able to offer preliminary responses to Ingmar Bergman and to the first vogue for Japanese film – Kurosawa, Mizoguchi – and to align these directors with the new cinema, but both Bazin and Kracauer have a frame of reference which draws to a close in the mid-1950s. Bazin died on the same day that Truffaut began shooting *The 400 Blows/Les Quatre Cents Coups* (1959), the film which is generally seen as inaugurating the *nouvelle vague*, a new cinema which would come to exemplify cinematic modernism. Truffaut dedicated *The 400 Blows* to Bazin, and we can assume Bazin would have approved of Truffaut's film on the basis of his enthusiastic review of Agnès Varda's 1954 debut *La Pointe Courte*, which he called 'miraculous' and praised in ways which prefigure the appeal of the new wave:

> There is a total freedom to the style, which produces the impression, so rare in the cinema, that we are in the presence of a work that obeys only the dreams and

> desires of its auteur with no other external obligations. If *La Pointe Courte* is an avant-garde film, it is not in the real sense of the word, which is always confused with the followers of surrealism, or to say the least, with the decomposition of anecdotes or storytelling. Agnès Varda's story is the most simple in the world, and it is a love story. [. . .] It naturally brings to mind Rossellini's *Journey to Italy* (which obviously could not have influenced Agnès Varda for chronological reasons), where there is a similar counterpoint between the heroes' feelings and the human and geographical environment. This affinity honours both films. However, Agnès Varda's film is quite different in terms of tone and technique. First and foremost it is a film by a woman, in the same way you recognize a book is written by a woman, and this creates something rather unique in film.[6]

Note how Bazin praises Varda and *La Pointe Courte* by aligning her with Rossellini and *Journey to Italy* while deprecating the avant-garde, surrealism and the 'decomposition of anecdotes or storytelling'. It can only be speculated how Bazin would have responded to the films which arrived in the year after his death: *Hiroshima mon amour*, *L'avventura*, *La Dolce Vita*, *Breathless*. Godard's early films are closely engaged with the Bazinian aesthetic but in an Oedipal fashion, ultimately reacting against Bazin, reasserting not only the centrality of montage but 'dialectical' montage as a means of 'deconstructing' realist modes (including the decomposition of storytelling) along Brechtian lines.[7] Similarly, although Bazin had endorsed Resnais's early short films, it is difficult to know what he would have thought of the extreme formalist stylization of *Last Year at Marienbad* and *Muriel*, the latter a film which filters realism through formalist 'serial' or 'mosaic' montage.

The development beyond neorealism and beyond the Bazinian aesthetic occurred in Italian cinema during the 1950s, arriving at an overt self-conscious cinematic modernism with Antonioni's *L'avventura* (1960) and Fellini's *8½* (1963). This development took place within a commercial film industry aimed at a mainstream audience. When such films met with a negative response from audiences and critics, it was the critical discourse initiated by Bazin at *Cahiers du cinéma* which came to the support of these films and their directors and helped to generate an international audience for this type of cinema. *Cahiers du cinéma* and its rival *Positif* were also directly involved in the creation of the *nouvelle vague* (itself split into two wings aligned with each journal). A number of countries were developing an 'art' cinema along the lines of the *nouvelle vague* and, following the French example, countries began to market their art films in terms of national cinema 'waves' and 'auteurs'. This new art cinema which exploded around the world in the 1960s initially took three basic forms: variations on neorealism, 'youth' pastiche films of an early *nouvelle vague* type and existentialist modernist films of a Bergman/Fellini/Antonioni type. The new wave cinemas of France, Italy, Poland, Czechoslovakia, Hungary, Yugoslavia and Germany and the auteurs of postwar 'world cinema' are familiar enough not to require any introduction here.[8] The following brief comments refer to three somewhat anomalous 'new waves': Japan, the United Kingdom and the United States.

Japan

Japanese cinema had always been aware of trends in American, European and Russian films and in the silent and early sound film eras had its own expressionist, impressionist and proletarian social realist tendencies, all of which displayed a confident assimilation of the most advanced 'Western' film and, like its Western counterparts, often reflected a modernist aesthetic. A well-known example is Kinugasa's *A Page of Madness* (1926) set in an asylum and largely visualized from the perspective of mad inmates, an extreme exercise in expressionist montage and camerawork. Mizoguchi and Ozu both worked their way through the popular genres and through these 'advanced' styles, moving away from expressionism to a more naturalistic impressionism that has some resemblance not only to 1930s European films (Vigo, Renoir) but also to postwar neorealism, Sadao Yamanaka's *Humanity and Paper Balloons* (1937) being a 'modernistic' film of this type. If Japanese film culture was knowledgeable about world cinema, Western film culture seems to have been largely ignorant about Japanese film, not excepting Eisenstein.[9] The eventual international success of Japanese film in the 1950s was partly due to the appeal of a *japonisme* that was exotic and 'other', yet cinematically not 'primitive' but corresponding to modernist aesthetics (Western film culture repeating the paradoxes of the reception of *japonisme* in the impressionist arts of the 1870s). Following the success of *Rashomon*, with its multiple narrative perspectives on the same uncertain event, at the Venice Film Festival 1951 and at the Academy Awards 1952, a canon of Japanese film quickly developed leading to the polemical battle between adherents of Kurosawa and adherents of Mizoguchi among the *Cahiers* cineastes, Bazin brokering a compromise by arguing in a letter to Truffaut that appreciation of Mizoguchi's long take and tracking shot aesthetic did not require rejecting Kurosawa's Hollywood-style montage and action aesthetic:

> I'm sorry I couldn't see Mizoguchi's films again with you at the Cinematheque. I rate him as highly as you people do and I claim to love him the more because I love Kurosawa too, who is the other side of the coin: would we know the day any

> better if there were no night? To dislike Kurosawa because one loves Mizoguchi is only the first step toward understanding. Unquestionably anyone who prefers Kurosawa must be incurably blind but anyone who loves only Mizoguchi is one-eyed. Throughout the arts there runs a vein of the contemplative and mystical as well as an Expressionist vein.[10]

The Japanese New Wave, which arrived circa 1959, was quite diverse, ranging from violent 'youth' films and 'exploitation' films to complex Brechtian deconstructions of the Japanese political situation in relation to the legacy of the war and vis-à-vis the continuing dominance of American interests, military and otherwise, long after formal occupation had ended. As in Europe, the Japanese New Wave films became more radical in the late 1960s, particularly after many of the best-known directors, including Oshima, Imamura, Yoshida, Shinoda and Matsumoto, left the established studio system and went independent by forming the Art Theatre Guild in 1967. Even more than in Europe, the new wave films tended to reflect and find their audience amid the radicalized student demographic.

The reception of Japanese film within the international postwar critical discourse of cinematic modernism was complicated by two factors. First, the Japanese New Wave rejected as old fashioned and reactionary the very directors – Kurosawa, Mizoguchi and Ozu – who were acclaimed internationally as radically modern.[11] Second, in the post-1968 'political modernism' period when radicals endorsed culture perceived as somehow outside 'Western' (imperialist) bourgeois ideology, film theorists like Noël Burch began their search for films which did not conform to the classical Hollywood 'codes' of editing, shooting, mise-en-scène and narrative. Burch acknowledged the militant intentions of the Japanese New Wave but preferred Japanese film from the late 1930s and the war period during which Japan actively resisted Western culture. Although the reasons for this resistance were bound up with the ideology of a reactionary nationalist military regime, Burch argued that advanced film directors of the time, thoroughly conversant with modern cinema, suddenly had to find a new cinematic formalism which rejected Hollywood modes and, in certain respects, drew on traditional pre-capitalist Japanese and Chinese aesthetics. Burch therefore argued, controversially, that the best films by Mizoguchi, Kurosawa and Ozu were those made in the 1930s – Mizoguchi's *The Story of the Last Chrysanthemums* (1939) with its fluid long-take sequence shots being his prime example. The internationally famous postwar films like Kurosawa's *The Seven Samurai* (1954) by contrast reflected the American Occupation and its re-imposition of Hollywood action film modes and bourgeois liberal humanism. Although mistaken and perverse in its generalizations – struggling to account for postwar films as formally radical as Mizoguchi's *Life of Oharu* (1952) and the entirety of Ozu's oeuvre – Burch's theory did help to add prewar Japanese cinema to the acknowledged influences on international cinematic modernism. Nevertheless, the Japanese films which had and continue to have the greatest influence on cinematic modernism internationally are the 'classical' postwar films, rather than prewar or new wave, Ozu having emerged as one of the most important reference points for contemporary cinematic modernism.

The United Kingdom

Bazin and Kracauer had a regard for British film which was decidedly not shared by the *Cahiers* 'Young Turks'. In fact Bazin and Kracauer see David Lean's *Brief Encounter* (1945) and Carol Reed's *The Third Man* (1949) as part of the new neorealist-inspired European cinema. Kracauer pays attention to the fantastical cinema of Powell and Pressburger – *Black Narcissus* (1947) and *The Red Shoes* (1948) – and both Bazin and Kracauer endorse Olivier's Shakespeare adaptations, especially *Hamlet* (1948), but modern British film quickly became synonymous with social realism. Lindsay Anderson formed the Free Cinema movement in 1956, directly influenced by Italian neorealism and the new Polish films. Free Cinema crossed over into the wave of 'kitchen sink' realist films associated with Woodfall productions which, in turn, crossed over into what is now retrospectively called the 'British New Wave' of the 1960s, Ken Loach being the most accomplished and challenging director to emerge from the social realist side of this 'new wave'. British film struggled to achieve international critical acceptance as a modernist cinema (and even in 2007 Kovács in *Screening Modernism* can only bring himself to include eleven British films in his corpus of 240 European modernist films). This may be partly because British cinema has been a genre-based national cinema – horror, science fiction, historical and costume drama, literary adaptation and romantic comedy – rather than, with a few exceptions, auteur-based.

There were, however, directors, either British or working within the British film industry, making films informed by cinematic modernism. Joseph Losey (American but working in Britain) is particularly regarded for his collaborations with Harold Pinter and Dirk Bogarde, and *Accident* (1967) is influenced by the 'serial' or 'mosaic' montage of Resnais and Robbe-Grillet, complete with flash edits and ellipses large and small that rendered the main storyline ambiguous and impossible to resolve. Nic Roeg almost warrants a co-director credit on Richard Lester's foray into Hollywood *Petulia*, set in San Francisco in 1967 and also deploying serial montage derived from Resnais, which Roeg himself called 'psychic montage', meaning that the editing evokes a kaleidoscopic associative stream of consciousness, including fragments of fantasy and memory, an experiment in montage taken even further in the radical in every way *Performance* (Roeg and Cammell 1968/1970). *Walkabout* (1971) is perhaps Roeg's most successful film as regards integrating 'psychic montage' into a storyline, a set of thematic concerns and, not least, a representation of the Australian landscape. Roeg continued into the 1980s with his singular aesthetic of 'psychic' cinematic modernism and his experiments with new forms of elliptical montage in a run of classic films: *Don't Look Now* (1973), *The Man Who Fell to Earth* (1975) and *Bad Timing* (1980). John Boorman's most successful film in terms of cinematic modernism was achieved not in England but in Hollywood with *Point Blank* (1967), like Roeg's *Performance*, a modernist take on the noir gangster thriller deploying a fractured time-line, destabilized point-of-view shots, ellipses and geometric framing.

The United States

The critical discourse of cinematic modernism has its grand narrative, and a crucial episode in that narrative is Orson Welles having *The Magnificent Ambersons* taken out of his control by studio henchmen and re-edited, 'mutilated', so as to be more conventional in the context of classical Hollywood and more accessible to mainstream audiences. Welles was banished from Hollywood and sent into, not the wilderness exactly, but Europe and an itinerant exile. Bazin had lauded Welles, Wyler and, with reservations, Hitchcock as being as important to the birth of a new cinema as Rossellini, De Sica and the Italian neorealists but, with the apparent closing down of the new cinema in Hollywood, by the mid-1950s the centre of gravity for cinematic modernism had shifted decisively to Europe. There are obvious qualifications to be made of this narrative: Welles continued to work in Hollywood in various capacities and as a director made some of his best films there (*Lady from Shanghai* and *Touch of Evil*), Hitchcock enjoyed his 'golden period' (*Notorious* to *The Birds*) and there were many worthy genre films – film noir, westerns, melodramas – produced by Hollywood. Bazin recognized this and the 'Hitchco-Hawksians' at *Cahiers* found much of their inspiration for a modern cinema in auteurs working within the Hollywood studio system.

Although increasingly out of touch with contemporary cinema by the mid-1950s, Kracauer in *Theory of Film* acknowledges the American experimental film scene, including Stan Brakhage, Maya Deren and Kenneth Anger, and gives a tentative endorsement of Brakhage's *Loving* and Deren's *Meshes of the Afternoon*.[12] Bazin and *Cahiers* do not appear to have been interested in the American experimental filmmakers, presumably seeing them as a throwback to the avant-garde of the silent era or analogous to the Lettrist and Situationist avant-garde in France with whom Bazin had a largely hostile relationship. A dialogue of sorts between American experimental/'underground' cinema and Bazinian realism did, however, occur in the field of documentary film, with the overlap between the 'direct cinema' movement, privileging objective fly-on-the-wall style documentary, and the more interventionist *cinéma vérité* movement.

In the early 1960s the success of Bergman, Fellini and the French New Wave created a vogue for the intellectual and often risqué international art film in America and art-house cinemas popped up in most major US cities and college towns, creating an audience for a range of films derived from the canon drawn up by Bazin and *Cahiers* a decade earlier in Paris. From the perspective of *Cahiers* and Europe the only true pioneer of modernist filmmaking in the United States (and who would also turn out to be the father of American indie film) was John Cassavetes (*Faces* 1968). By the late 1960s the influence of the European art film was beginning to be discerned in mainstream American filmmaking, in films such as *Bonnie and Clyde* (Arthur Penn 1967) and *The Graduate* (Mike Nichols 1967). After a commercial breakthrough with films aimed at the late 1960s counter-culture like *Easy Rider* (Hopper 1969), a belatedly arrived American cinematic modernism appeared to be on the verge of taking over Hollywood itself in the mid-1970s: *Badlands* (Malick 1973), *The Conversation* (Coppola 1974), *Nashville* (Altman 1975) and *Taxi Driver* (Scorsese 1976). Unfortunately Martin Scorsese, Francis Ford Coppola and the others were stopped in their tracks by the global success of their former film school cohorts: Spielberg's *Jaws* and Lucas's *Star Wars*.[13] The popular blockbuster, the contemporary 'cinema of sensations', has been seen as a revival of the family action movie of classical Hollywood or, in Deleuzian terms, a regression to the cinema of the 'movement image' as opposed to the 'time image'. It could even be seen as a return to the 'cinema of attractions' from the pre-narrative early silent film era. Scorsese and Coppola now consider the contemporary blockbuster fantasy action film to not be *cinema* at all.[14] The blockbuster action film of the 1970s and 1980s, whether American, European or Asian, did not in fact mark the end of the art film per se (Scorsese, Coppola, Altman and Malick all survived to enjoy long careers in

Hollywood) but it did seem to represent the eclipsing of the aesthetic associated with postwar cinematic modernism.

World Cinema and Third Cinema

The postwar period was the heyday of 'world cinema' as an aesthetic and marketing category overlapping with 'art-house film'. The cinema of many regions of the world gained a degree of recognition in the fertile film culture of the 1960s: Africa (especially Senegal and Mali), the Middle East, India, East Asia and South and Latin America. Many of the films from 'developing countries' had a relationship of influence and interaction with neorealism and the *nouvelle vague*. Today 'world cinema' remains associated with art film and cinematic modernism within cineaste and film festival culture, but elsewhere it has taken on a much broader set of associations and functions as an important if amorphous marketing category; 'world cinema' today might include mainstream popular film, genre film, horror, erotica, trash and cult film.

During the period of the postwar art film, the relationship of directors and films from 'developing nations' to European-centred cinematic modernism was inevitably filtered through varying perspectives on colonialism and cultural imperialism. Labels like 'world cinema' and 'art film' are obviously problematic in this context. Each national film culture in the developing world had its own diverse trends and tendencies in the postwar period, however one generalization that can be made from a 'world cinema' perspective is that each film culture seemed to experience a split in its art film between neorealism and modernism; in each film culture there was a fraught debate over which type of cinema was 'authentic' (as opposed to alien import or symptom of cultural imperialism) and which was the best vehicle for propagating 'progressive' ideological values (whether nationalist, humanist or Marxist). With a few exceptions like King Hu's martial arts movies (*Touch of Zen* 1970), popular mainstream film from developing nations was, for the international art-film audience, of little or no interest, while directors in developing nations who attempted to make overtly modernist films, such as *Memories of Underdevelopment* (Tomás Gutiérrez Alea, Cuba 1968) – films with a challenging Antonioni-style aesthetic and portraying the existential crises of intellectuals or urban alienation – were often seen as inauthentic, as mimicking films from Paris and Rome. It is possible to argue, therefore, that from the 1950s through to the 1970s, both Hollywood and European modernism were viewed as ideologically suspect, and so neorealism remained the default template for alternative cinema in most developing countries, a neorealism that rejects the transition to modernism as elitist, alien and alienating. *Rome, Open City*, *Bicycle Thieves* and *Bitter Rice* remain viable options, while *Journey to Italy*, *L'avventura* and *La Dolce Vita* are either rejected or merely occasional models for contrived imitation.

Filmmakers in developing nations aligned with the anti-colonial and anti-imperialist movements of the 1960s, such as directors associated with Brazil's *Cinema Novo* wave, issued various manifestos calling for a radicalization not only of film aesthetics but in the way films are made, distributed and shown. *Towards a Third Cinema* (1969), by the Argentinian directors Fernando Solanas and Octavio Getino, unsurprisingly rejected Hollywood film, declaring it 'First Cinema' and denouncing it as a means of exporting American imperialism and inculcating American imperialist ideology in the consciousness of its victims, the populations of the third world.[15] Solana and Getino also denounced the modernist cinema of the European new waves as the 'Second Cinema', a bourgeois cinema in its rarefied formalist aesthetics, its cult of the individual genius auteur, and its primary concern with the existential angst of the bourgeois individual. As its title suggests, *Towards a Third Cinema* argues for a 'Third Cinema' (of the 'Third World') broadly following the example of Italian neorealism as regards cinematic style but tapping into a specific given local culture, deploying mythical and folkloric elements and also seeking to collectivize and democratize the filmmaking process outside of the commercial film industry. The best-known films of the Third Cinema movement include Glauber Rocha's *Antonio das Mortes* (Brazil 1969), Jorge Sanjines's *Blood of the Condor* (Bolivia 1969) and Fernando Solanas and Octavio Getina's *Hour of the Furnaces* (Argentina 1968).[16]

The idea of a Third Cinema had an influence on some national cinemas in Africa, the Middle East and Asia, and there has been a long-running debate about which films and filmmakers belong to the movement. For example, is Gillo Pontecorvo's *The Battle of Algiers* (1966) Third Cinema when its production and reception was that of a radical Italian art-house film about Algeria rather than being itself a radical Algerian film?

Towards a Third Cinema remains relevant to twenty-first-century filmmaking in the 'cultural decolonization' era because contemporary cinematic modernism is often criticized in ways which echo the critique of Second Cinema in the 1960s: criticized as being politically opaque and made in an international modernist style for an elite international audience, rather than being made in an accessible indigenous style for a local or mass audience.

In retrospect 'Third Cinema' films from the 1960s and 1970s tend towards variations on a neorealist template while those consciously following a militant

Towards a Third Cinema agenda tend to be in complicated dialogue with folkloric 'magical realism' or new wave cinematic modernism of the Godardian (Brechtian) type.

1968: Political modernism

A political radicalization of filmmakers similar to that articulated by *Towards a Third Cinema* occurred in Europe, the United States and Japan. In Paris (then, arguably, the centre of 'world' film culture), a major break occurred in the critical discourse about modern cinema, and this gave rise to what is known as 'political modernism' (Figure 11). Equivalents to this radicalization of artistic content, form and practice occurred across the arts, particularly in drama, performance art and music, but only in film did the label 'political modernism' emerge denoting the period of radicalization from 1968 to the mid-1970s and only in film has this label retained its meaning and historical reference into the twenty-first century.

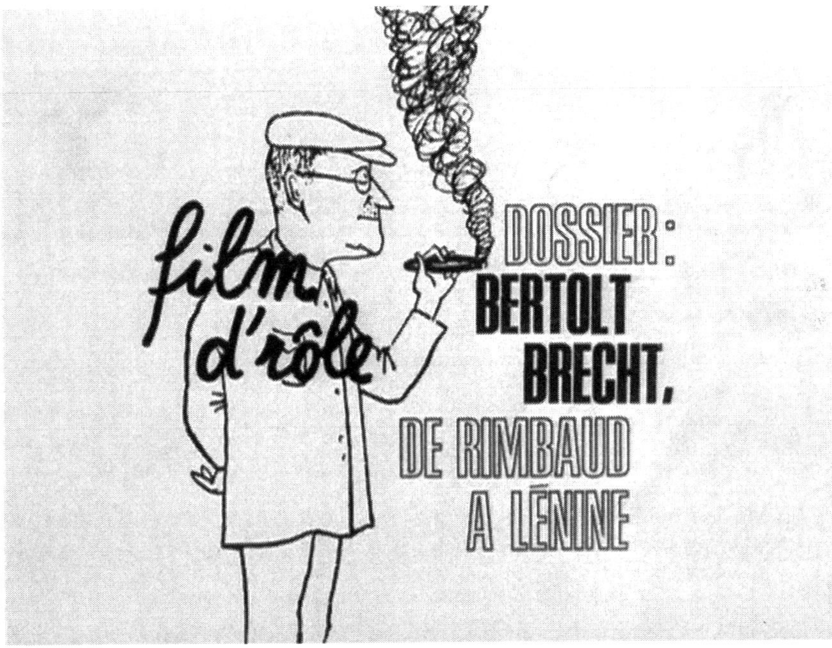

Figure 11 *Le Gai savoir* (1969), Jean-Luc Godard.
One of the final images from *Le Gai savoir* declares the manifesto of 1968 and 'political modernism': to combine the artistic practice of Brecht with the political rigour of Lenin and the subversive, anarchic spirit of Rimbaud. But in subsequent films associated with political modernism, Brecht dominated, Lenin gave way to Parisian cultural Maoism and Rimbaud's visionary poetics would be marginalized.

The close link between the *événements* of 1968 in Paris and the radical shift in film culture was manifested in a number of incidents which have entered into film-lore, such as the furore over the attempted sacking by the French government, by André Malraux, of Henri Langlois at the Cinémathèque Française and the attempted closing down by radicals of the Cannes Festival in 1968. The militant break was announced explicitly in the films of Jean-Luc Godard, whose trajectory in this period began with him satirizing young middle-class Parisian Maoist sects in *La Chinoise* (1967) and ended with him embracing an idiosyncratic French Maoism of the post-structuralist variety with *Wind from the East* in 1969. The closing credits of *Weekend* (1967) followed 'End of Story' (*fin de conte*) with 'End of Cinema' (*fin de cinéma*), implying the end not just of this film but of this type of cinema, that is to say all bourgeois cinema (including the *nouvelle vague*), while *La Gai Savoir* (1968) featured Jean-Pierre Léaud and Juliette Berto sitting in a studio 'deconstructing' the conventional deployment of image and sound in cinema and discussing how to put image and sound back together in a revolutionary way. For Godard this meant embracing self-reflexive Brechtian strategies and the formalism of structuralist film while rejecting or superseding Bazinian neorealism, parodied by two infamous scenes in *Weekend*: the reputedly 'longest tracking shot in film history' of a traffic jam (long in terms of not only time – eight minutes – but also the length of tracks that had to be laid down for the camera). However, the Bazinian 'ontological integrity' of this long take is sabotaged by being interrupted by intertitles at regular intervals. The other scene features *nouvelle vague* provocateur Paul Gégauff playing, haltingly, while delivering a rant about the failure of avant-garde music, Mozart's KV 506 piano sonata on a grand piano in the middle of a farmyard surrounded by bored rustics. The scene is shot in structuralist film style in slowly circling 360-degree movements in alternate directions.[17]

Post-1968 radical film was characterized by a number of strategies, but whereas Godard tended to deploy all the strategies in satiric juxtaposition in a single film, most filmmakers followed one or two particular strategies: 'dialectical' montage (on the Soviet montage model), extreme long takes, non-synchronous sound and visual image, breaking the fourth wall (addressing the camera), undermining diegetic reality (the world within a given film), interrupting the narrative and 'action image' with intertitles or commentary on how the narrative is functioning, flouting the basic codes of Hollywood realism (shot/reverse shot, matching eye-line) and flouting continuity editing between images. Many of these strategies have a tendency to reverse 'dialectically' into each other, for example the realist long take if carried to an extreme, such as the traffic jam or farmyard Mozart recital scenes in *Weekend*, and almost every Godard film contains at least one such scene, reverses into structuralist formalism of the Michael Snow type (*Wavelength* 1967; *Back and Forth* 1969). Although the strategies were many, the post-68 cinema of political modernism can be summarized as following four basic tendencies:

- Dialectical montage (derived from either Eisenstein or Vertov)
- Brechtian strategies of self-reflexivity, distancing, estrangement, obstructing viewer identifications and frustrating the pleasure principle
- The encounter of cinema with theatre – improvisation-based – influenced by both Brecht and Living Theatre-type real-time event or happening
- Extreme neorealist or *cinéma vérité* documentary modes (often embedded within a particular community or subculture)

The diminishing returns of the first two tendencies partly explains the exhaustion of political modernism by the mid-1970s. Radical montage, whether dialectical, rhythmic, associational, serial or mosaic, became something of a period mannerism, along with subliminal edits and jump cutting, and was not developed successfully by many directors other than Godard himself. Similarly Brechtian strategies, which work so well on stage addressing a present audience, tended to become a stilted period mannerism in cinema (e.g. in the films of Lindsay Anderson). The refusal of viewer pleasure (voyeuristic or otherwise) or entertainment was a feature of 'political modernism' into the 1970s, notably in the New German Cinema, but ran into the predictable problem of alienating, boring and therefore losing the audience and so, rather than obstructing viewer identification, radical filmmaking has tended to opt for modifying, subverting or transferring identification along gender or ethnic lines, challenging the 'male gaze' and so forth. However a combination of the third and fourth tendencies in the foregoing list did become predominant after 1968: the idea of 'realism' being produced or revealed in the encounter between documentary and fictional narrative is, in post-68 radical cinematic modernism, replayed as 'realism' being produced by an encounter between the theatrical and the cinematic or, to use Kracauer's terms, 'staged' and 'unstaged'. What connects the post-68 cinema of Rivette at one extreme and Herzog at the other extreme is the idea that *the making of a film is in itself a theatrical or 'staged' event* from which improvised, unexpected, contingent, 'unstaged' reality emerges, a reality which is then revealed in the editing process and rendered 'cinematic' rather than 'theatrical'. Unstaged reality emerges from the staged event. If cinematic modernism is primarily influenced by the modernist novel (elliptical representations of consciousness and time), 'political modernism' in the cinema was closely linked to developments in theatre and was in some ways a belated response to developments in drama since Brecht.

Postwar drama: Staging reality

By 1968 theatre across Europe and America was galvanized by an avant-garde revolt which, like its anti-institutional equivalents in film, the novel and music tended to be referred to as 'experimental'. The experimental theatre ranged from the wildly surreal to stringently Brechtian agit-prop but, even in its quasi-institutional guises under directors like Peter Brook, tended towards variations on the example of Artaud's 'theatre of cruelty'. This type of theatre of cruelty (or ecstasy) might also be considered hyperrealist in that it was constituted by the 'real' enactments of role-playing and ritual on stage in real-time duration, often involving or demanding the active participation of the audience (in effect, a blurring of the lines between actor/'role' and actor/audience); theatrical representational drama is replaced by the psychodrama of the encounter group session.

Fassbinder's post-1968 troupe in Munich called itself an 'anti-theatre', in which an ironic parodic distancing towards theatrical artifice undermines the illusory 'reality' of the stage, the suspension of disbelief, but (*contra*-Brecht) provides for an audience not so much a critical objectivity but rather a raw access to the 'reality' of the performers in the act of playing their roles. Fassbinder would later carry the aesthetic and ethos of the anti-theatre as 'real' role-play over to his early films, in which the performance is itself the event whose documentation becomes the basis for the eventual film. A similar collision of cinematic and theatrical signs had been deployed by Jacques Rivette ever since his debut film *Paris Belongs to Us* (1961) but became more extreme with *L'amour fou* (1969). Dispensing with scripts and screenplays, Rivette cast members of the Marc'O experimental theatre group rehearsing Racine's *Andromaque*, while being filmed for a television documentary – Rivette filming both the theatre group and the television crew. Various improvised scenes, characters, relationships and events emerged, most of which blur the line between acting, role-play and real life or at least blur the lines between different diegetic levels within the narrative. The final film, *L'amour fou*, is Rivette's edit, producing a 'realism' incorporating the different fictional, theatrical and documentary elements.

One of the quintessential products of the post-1968 period, the twelve-hour *Out 1* (1970) takes Rivette's method further, an improvised film featuring two experimental theatre groups 'staging' exercises and rehearsals, mostly filmed in

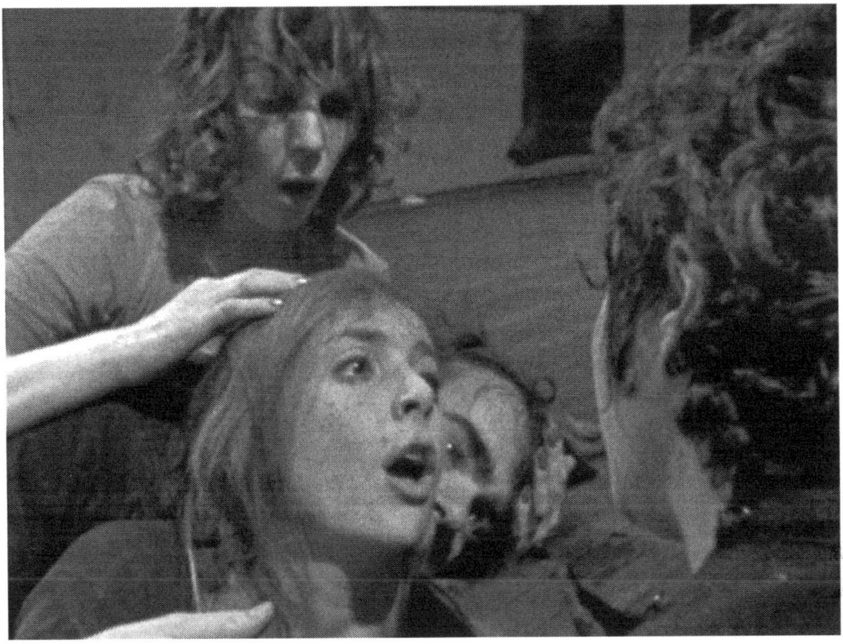

Figure 12 *Out 1* (1971), Jacques Rivette.
The camera records in long takes – and often in close-up – a 'primal' improvisational theatrical event. Cinema and theatre have long been uneasy bedfellows, enemies even. After 1968 an encounter between the cinema and theatre (often of the Living Theatre/performance 'happening' type) was staged by a number of directors, including Pasolini, Fassbinder and Angelopoulos. Jacques Rivette had long been interested in deriving cinema from the 'pro-filmic' performances and rehearsals of theatre groups, something taken to an extreme in *Out 1* in which the lines between theatrical performance and the diegetic world of the film blur and then break down almost entirely. All life becomes a role-play.

very long takes, juxtaposed with a fictional story loosely derived from Balzac about a shadowy revolutionary vanguard organization. The various elements in the film gradually encounter each other, generating sub-plots, but few of the actors had any idea about how the stories fitted together until they saw the final film, the stories only really emerging in the editing process. The blurring of the line between acting, role-play, reality and the narrative constructed in the editing process, by montage, create a strange mise-en-abyme layering effect for the viewer, in which what is theatrical becomes real and what is real becomes theatrical, *but the merging of real, theatrical and fictive is a cinematic affect* (Figure 12).

The New German Cinema (Herzog, Fassbinder, early Wenders) developed variations on this idea that the process of making the film becomes the event that generates material for the eventual film and its reality, its truth. For Herzog, the final film is not a *cinéma vérité* documentation of the making of the film, but the making of a film becomes the 'real' event – for example, taking a boat, actors, film crew and local inhabitants down Amazon tributaries in the Peruvian rainforest in *Aguirre, the Wrath of God* (1972), or hauling a boat over a mountain in *Fitzcarraldo* (1982). It is this real event which throws into relief, as it were, the 'theatrical' acting out of a story and plot and it is out of the encounter between the 'theatrical' event and the 'real' event of making the film that the final film – a cinematic event – is generated via the editing process.

This sense that the 'authenticity' of a film is derived from the experience (the ordeal, even) of the 'event' of making the film becomes an important feature of contemporary cinematic modernism, from Béla Tarr to Lisandro Alonso and Lav Diaz.

Political modernism: Theory

The label 'political modernism' applies less to the relatively small and unsuccessful number of films associated with the revolutionary aspirations of 1968 than to film theory and the critical discourse on modernism, a phase in this discourse which has been extensively discussed in the writings of D. N. Rodowick.[18]

A lineage of film theory had existed since the early days of cinema – from Balázs and Arnheim to Kracauer and Bazin – but 'Film Theory' as a major theoretical and academic discourse is bound up with 1968 in the sense that the new film theory – particularly that of Christian Metz – resulted from interaction with the other theories emerging in Paris in the 1960s and which are generally grouped under the heading of 'post-structuralism' – Althussarian Marxism, Lacanian psychoanalysis, Barthes's new literary criticism, Foucault's new histories, Deleuze's new philosophy, Derrida's deconstruction and so on. *Cahiers du cinéma* embraced some, in fact most, of these theories at one point or another and in the immediate aftermath of 1968 adopted a militant Maoist-structuralist line.

In Britain and the United States such theories were shunned by academia, including respectable long-established humanities departments. By a largely accidental combination of factors the new and not yet well-established discipline of film studies became the gateway for these latest theories from Paris to be imported and to then gradually enter into Anglo-American academia. Barthes, Lacan, Derrida, Kristeva and the rest were first assimilated and popularized by film theory and the critical discourse which became known as 'political modernism', after which these thinkers and their 'isms' went on to have a huge and ongoing influence on Anglo-American academia across the disciplines.

The revival of interest in the Frankfurt School and its debates over the relationship between aesthetics and politics – Adorno, Benjamin, Brecht, Lukacs – also occurred within film theory of the 1970s. As a result, in Anglo-American academia, film theory became a filter for many radical theorists and thinkers of the time, especially in relation to feminism and questions of sexuality and gender. The British film journal *Screen* remains the best-known site for the theoretical debates of the period, '*Screen* theory' being all but synonymous with 'political modernism'. The conceptual edifice of *Screen* theory is elaborate but, as is often the case, the edifice is founded upon a fairly rudimentary premise which we can sum up as follows:

- Capitalism maintains its power by normalizing and naturalizing its social relations (including relations of class, gender and race) through bourgeois ideology, in which citizens or subjects are embedded and with which they identify – the ideology 'interpellating' or appearing to address its subjects as individuals, consolidating the processes by which subjects internalize the dominant ideology. Subjects are not merely dominated forcibly by capitalist social relations but internalize and identify with the dominant bourgeois ideology.
- Cinema lulls its viewers into a passive dream-like state through which they become immersed in the reality – however fantastical – of the film. Unconsciously viewers identify with the perspective of certain characters and align their own perspective with that of the camera, with that of the dominant 'gaze'. Cinema therefore becomes a good metaphor for how subjects internalize the dominant perspective (i.e. dominant ideology). Moreover, film became the great mass-cultural medium of the twentieth century and it was no coincidence that the new dominant world superpower, the United States, developed the dominant cinema, Hollywood, which not only proceeded to act as an opium of the people in Marx's sense but also provided a means of imparting capitalist values to the world and acting as a vehicle for disseminating American culture in support of American imperialism, especially during the Cold War period.
- To contest Hollywood cinematic 'codes' and the dominant ideology, and in order to make visible or block the 'normalizing' processes of viewer identification, films informed by *Screen* theory adopted the range of Brechtian and formalist strategies discussed earlier in relation to post-68 cinema and Third Cinema. A well-known British example, directly involved with *Screen*, is *Riddles of the Sphinx* (Laura Mulvey and Peter Wollen 1975),

> a feminist film juxtaposing gritty realist and agit-prop content with the formalist strategies of structuralist film. Although such Brechtian or Godardian strategies fed into some of the alternative film of the 1970s, in practice most politically radicalized filmmakers in Britain, often working collectively in co-ops or workshops, tended to leave aesthetic formalism to the 'experimental' filmmakers and instead returned to the models of neorealism and *cinéma vérité* documentary modes – Ken Loach epitomizing the rejection of Godard in favour of the consolidation of a social realist aesthetic and normalizing humanist modes of audience identification as a means of contesting bourgeois ideology in a way accessible to a mainstream or working class audience.

From the point of view of contemporary cinematic modernism, the legacy of political modernism is not Brechtian strategies or Godardian montage, but rather the combination of de-dramatization, long-take minimalism and (structuralist film) formalism, a combination associated with, for example, Chantal Akerman. This combination which seemed so forbidding and alienating in the 1970s has over time become more accessible to a broader audience, become more comprehensible, perhaps because of its influence on popular directors like Jim Jarmusch. 'Minimalist formalism' can be discerned not only in much contemporary cinematic modernism but in millennial indie and cult movies, often as a stylistic vehicle for deadpan irony.[19]

Postwar cinematic modernism and today

A precursor of and influence on today's cinematic modernism is a small group of French films from the 1970s and 1980s which are now seen, retrospectively, as part of a renewal of the realist tradition in French cinema, a return to the neo-Bazinian aesthetic after the wilder formalism and stylistics of the *nouvelle vague* and post-68 political modernism. Agnès Varda's *Vagabond* (1985), the films of Jean Eustache, such as *La Maman et la putain* (1973) and *Mes petites amoureuses* (1974), and Maurice Pialat, especially *À nos amours* (*To Our Loves* 1983), carry the spirit of Bresson but without Bresson's rigorous formalism, aspiring instead to a rough, naturalistic, improvised ambience: long takes and elliptical narratives loosely structuring the rendering of characters and dramatic events. This is an aesthetic close to that prized in Rossellini by Bazin and the *Cahiers* critics back in the early postwar era. Pialat's films are not documentary realism but a staged realism, in which the intensified dynamics of the cast and the provocations of the director are designed to trigger and generate unexpected events – usually conflict, sometimes tenderness – beyond the letter of the script and pushing actors out of their comfort zone. As Noël Herpe wrote in a 2003 tribute in *Positif* upon Pialat's passing, Pialat's aesthetic is a 'naturalism that was born of formalism' but which then complicates this naturalism by a formalist turn in the *process* by which the films are made.[20] Pialat is often compared with Cassavetes because of their shared focus on the intricate dynamics of sex, power and recognition within a small social milieu and because of the methodology of setting up the shooting of a film as the 'situation', as the quasi-improvisational 'reality' from which a 'truth' will emerge – variations on this methodology or process are common to many of the directors of contemporary cinematic modernism.

Looking at films informed by cinematic modernism from the 1990s through to the second decade of the twenty-first century today and comparing them with the postwar 'golden age' of the modernist film one main observation can be made. Postwar modernist film began with developments out of neorealism, with Rossellini and Bresson, which quickly evolved into the existentialist 'formalist' film of Antonioni and the 'ornamental' surreal existentialism of Fellini. After the French New Wave, the art film in the 1960s diversified into multiple stylistic strands. Although neorealism, the French New Wave and the existentialist modernism of Antonioni and Fellini remained primary influences, each national film culture developed its own version of cinematic modernism. After 1968, the already eclectic stylistics of cinematic modernism are subject to a further set of radical (Brechtian) developments. Simplifying the classifications of postwar art film offered by Kovács in *Screening Modernism*, we can propose four broad categories of cinematic modernism: naturalist (Rossellini), minimalist (Bresson), theatrical (Rivette) and ornamental (Fellini); and two basic archetypes of form: continuous (Antonioni) and discontinuous/fragmented (Godard).[21]

By contrast, contemporary cinematic modernism of the period 1990–2020 has belonged to *one* primary aesthetic strand, what can be called the 'neo-Bazinian aesthetic'. This aesthetic maintains its roots in neorealism, the naturalism of Rossellini and the encounter of the documentary with fictive narrative, the interaction of staged and unstaged. This aesthetic today also exhibits the influence of Bresson and Ozu in the rigorous 'minimalist' formalism of the image and de-dramatized (non-expressive) acting style, along with the influence of Antonioni and Tarkovsky in the elliptical episodic structures and continuous durations of the long-take sequence shot aestheticization of the Deleuzian 'time image'.

Hou Hsiao-hsien, Abbas Kiarostami, Bela Tarr, Pedro Costa, Tsai Ming-Liang, Jia Zhangke and almost all the directors we might identify as working in a mode of cinematic modernism today can be located within an overlap of three categories: naturalist, minimalist and continuous. Rossellini, Bresson, Ozu, Antonioni, Fassbinder, Akerman and Tarkovsky: these are the key postwar reference points for contemporary cinematic modernism.

5

Postwar cinematic modernism

Critical perspectives

'Modernism' in this sense is not a period or phase of art history, but rather a mode of experience: how we experience or inhabit duration as the passing of present time. In this respect, modernism in art characterizes a style of questioning that, rather than seeking essences, stable forms, or identities, expresses the constant doubt that we don't know what art is, and so the artist must continually recreate new conditions of existence for it. And if film is the most modern of arts, this is because it presents to us, or perhaps sustains us temporally in, just this mode of epistemological questioning and self-(re)evaluation.

– D. N. Rodowick (2007)[1]

This chapter looks at critical perspectives on cinematic modernism with reference to the film theory which has flourished alongside it. The chapter begins with Bazin and Deleuze and then, after a brief clarification of the relationship between cinematic modernism and avant-garde or experimental film, outlines the perspectives of Fredric Jameson and David Bordwell, concluding with András Bálint Kovács's recent consolidation of the concept and category of (postwar) modernist film and Jacques Rancière's rather more sceptical view of the validity of the now orthodox story of a Bazinian/Deleuzian cinematic modernism.

Bazin and modern cinema

In *What Is Cinema?*, especially in the pieces on Rossellini and Bresson, André Bazin is developing an idea of a new genuinely modern cinema, but a terminological confusion arises because Bazin wasn't keen on terms like 'modernism' and 'avant-garde' mainly for reasons connected to the usage and connotations of these labels in the French critical context. Bazin would certainly have rejected Greenberg's idea of modernism as a focus on medium specificity, the autonomy of the artwork, the move towards total abstraction and pure form. Bazin explicitly rejected any idea of 'pure' film and any idea of the totality or autonomy of a film as an individual artwork. Moreover, Bazin was engaged in sometimes fraught polemics in which he rejected the avant-garde art film (including the French 'Cinéma pur' movement and the proto-Situationist 'Lettrist' film) and instead endorsed mainstream cinema – the authentically 'modern' was more likely to be found in a film noir B-movie than in an abstract or surrealist art film. This was not an unusual view among film theorists, Kracauer shares the taste for genre film and argues that moments of 'art' can be found in otherwise bad or trashy films. And the preference for mainstream Hollywood or films from the wrong side of the tracks over 'quality' and 'art' film became a defining characteristic of the younger *Cahiers du cinéma* critics who would go on to become the *nouvelle vague* and the instigators of auteur theory, the initial point of which was to highlight the work of maverick directors within and on the margins of the Hollywood studio system rather than art-film or avant-garde directors.

As discussed in the previous chapter, the important break in film history, between 'classical' and 'modern', occurs for Bazin not in the 1920s with the end of silent cinema and the arrival of the sound film but in the 1940s when a new kind of cinematic realism emerged, taking divergent forms: Welles, Wyler and Hitchcock in Hollywood and Rossellini, Bresson and neorealism in Europe. Bazin was especially receptive to Rossellini's films with Ingrid Bergman, partly because these films staged an encounter between Italian neorealism and Hollywood and partly because these films, particularly *Journey to Italy*, represent the shift from neorealism to something akin to (literary) modernism: the explicit assertion of reality as a site of contemplation and decipherment for an estranged consciousness, the destabilizing of the relationship between real and fictive, the breakdown of narrative causality – all of which are experienced in *Journey to Italy* by Ingrid Bergman's character, who exhibits this estranged consciousness attempting to decipher and, as Kracauer might put it, 'redeem' reality – not only physical and material but also psychological and spiritual reality. From *Journey to Italy* it is a short step to Bresson on one side and Antonioni on the other side, and if neorealism was the crucial break in cinema history then Bazin sees in Rossellini's *Journey to Italy* the emergence of modern cinema or, as Jacques Rivette proclaims in his 1955 'Letter on Rossellini' in *Cahiers du cinéma*, 'If there is a modern cinema, this is it.'[2]

Deleuze and modernism

In the two *Cinema* books Gilles Deleuze takes up the Bazinian premise of a 'break' in the history of cinema circa 1945, out of which modern cinema emerged, but he reconceptualizes this 'break' (marked primarily by Italian neorealism) as the beginning of a shift from the 'movement image' of classical Hollywood film to the 'time-image' of the predominantly European modernist art-house film.[3]

Deleuze follows conventional film history in seeing early cinema as influenced by vaudevillian traditions and theatre, narrative cinema becoming established a little later with D. W. Griffith. With the coming of the sound film, Hollywood consolidates the narrative film around a set of conventions or 'codes' governing the representation of plot-based narrative realism. Each image is linked in a chain of causal relationships, which, codified by a set of technical, formal and narrative conventions, constitute a dramatic narrative, derived less from theatre than from nineteenth-century novelistic modes. In addition to plot and character, the novel provided a template for exciting scenes of action and movement which film could adapt and reproduce on screen, whereas theatre tended to be bound by the restraints of the stage, tended to be 'stilted', based around static actors talking or performing stylized actions that did not transfer well to the screen. Deleuze sees the mass popularity of cinema in the 'golden age' of Hollywood as based on this capacity of film to foreground spectacular action and he also sees 'classical' cinema as inherently kinetic in its ability to translate plots and characterization into action and movement on screen – montage being a means, specific to film and unavailable to theatre, to break down movements into units and then reconstitute them to represent a dynamic action or action sequence, the 'action' being purely an effect of editing. Designating classical Hollywood film 'cinema of the movement-image' Deleuze recasts the Bazinian break in film history, manifested in 1945 by neorealism, as a shift from the 'movement-image' to the 'time-image', the latter term denoting not only the foregrounding of duration but the fragmentation of space, the weakening of causal relationships between images and a loss of narrative coherence. Whereas Bazin stresses the importance of the Liberation of Italy (and Europe) as a positive context for the neorealist cinematic break with classical Hollywood film, Deleuze stresses the traumatic aspect of Italy's experience of fascism, occupation, collaboration and wholesale destruction in the war, a trauma generating a collapse of ideological coherence, a sense of all-pervasive loss, fragmentation and estrangement.[4]

Deleuze sees Italian neorealist films as displaying a new set of narrative conventions in which there is a blurring of the line between what is documentary and what is fictive, and this can enable quotidian reality to break through the fictional narrative framework, for example in the scene of Maria the maid in her kitchen in *Umberto D*, ostensibly a non-professional actor performing real everyday actions in a real location in real time, a scene that is a template for what will become the cinema of the 'time image', a defining feature of cinematic modernism. Deleuze agrees with Pasolini that another feature of modernist cinema is that the viewer's perspective will be filtered through the confused and alienated consciousness of a central protagonist (similar to that at the centre of many modernist novels) and which exists in alignment with the assumed omniscient perspective of the camera-eye and *auteur*. More generally, cinema of the time image is not reducible to the real-time long take, instead it opens out to the reconfiguring of time, often as a reflection of the stream of consciousness or the fragmentation of memory and free association – a common characteristic of postwar cinematic modernism in films such as Alain Resnais's *Last Year at Marienbad* and *Muriel* or Nic Roeg's *Walkabout* and *Bad Timing*. The time image therefore is not only about how particular films represent temporal duration or this or that moment of time but about how time starts to saturate the cinematic image. If the classical Hollywood film or 'movement image' film uses a kinetic image to disavow the passing of time – an exciting film is one in which the viewer completely forgets about time – then the modernist film of the time image tends to make the viewer aware of film as uniquely representing the passing of time not just as duration or in the *frisson* or pathos of the ephemeral and fleeting, but as an uncanny experience bound up with memory and death.

This theory of the shift from movement-image to time-image is analogous to the idea, popularized by Roland Barthes, that the nineteenth-century novel was founded upon a set of narrative conventions denoting realism, with stable characterization, causal links – plot – and strictly determined reader identification, all guaranteed by the authority of an omniscient narrator.[5] The novel form is itself supposedly a product of the emergence of capitalism and this version of reality rendered by the nineteenth-century novel reflected the rise of the bourgeoisie and its national, colonial and patriarchal confidence. Once the social and economic fabric began to unravel and ideological coherence was lost, so the conventions of nineteenth-century realism began to lose authority and it was against the discredited realism of the nineteenth-century novel that the new realisms of the modernist novel were a response and a reaction. Deleuze transposes this chronology of an ideologically and historically determined break in realist representation from the novel to cinema, with classical Hollywood film reflecting American political hegemony and ideological confidence while postwar cinematic modernism manifests a challenge to that confidence and its 'realism'. Cinematic modernism after the Second World War fulfils a role similar to that played by literary modernism after the First World War and, as with the Barthesian 'writerly text', it is the elliptical openness and ambiguity of cinematic modernism that, so the argument goes, problematizes realism, blocks passive consumption and enables the active conscious and critical participation of the viewer in the interpretation and production of meaning.

Although the category of the time image lends itself to a Bazinian aesthetic of minimalism, stasis and long-take evocations of duration, it can also incorporate a stylistic diversity ranging from existentialist noir to Godardian montage – in other words, the time image is primarily a conceptual category referring to the interrogation of temporal and spatial representation, not an exclusive set of particular stylistic devices. Nevertheless, for Deleuze, an aesthetic and historical correspondence between the time image and a cinematic modernism informed by Bazinian aesthetics can be taken as a basic assumption. Deleuze barely acknowledges the avant-garde or experimental film in the *Cinema* books, his canon of directors and films is very selective and almost wholly aligned with that of *Cahiers*: Hollywood silent film and Soviet film; classical Hollywood; Welles and Hitchcock; Ozu, Mizoguchi and Japan; and then cinematic modernism and the time image – Rossellini, Bresson, Antonioni, Resnais, Rivette, Godard and Tarkovsky.[6]

Avant-garde, experimental and modernism: Poggioli, Bürger and Wollen

The label 'avant-garde' is said to have emerged out of French military and political terminology denoting a vanguard military unit or operation, becoming by the early twentieth century the favoured term for describing art which is 'ahead of its time', an artwork in the progressive vanguard, that is to say modern. Avant-garde also often has connotations of a self-conscious attempt to shock, outrage and disturb mainstream cultural norms and tastes. There have been three well-known theoretical attempts to define 'avant-garde': Poggioli, Bürger and Wollen – the latter's concept of 'avant-garde' was discussed in Chapter 3 regarding the relationship between film and the other modern arts in the silent film era and is discussed again here, this time in relation to postwar art cinema and 'political modernism'.

Two or three avant-gardes

In *Theory of the Avant-Garde* (originally published in Italian in 1962 and in English in 1968) Renato Poggioli relates 'avant-garde' to a decadent bohemian social formation which came to prominence with Rimbaud, Verlaine and the French symbolists and the wilder currents of the *fin de siècle* across Europe and America. Poggioli argues that from the time around the First World War the avant-garde becomes responsible for almost all the most *original* and *modern* art, and therefore the concept of the avant-garde needs to be broadened to encompass all the essential modern art of the twentieth century from Picasso, Stravinsky, T. S. Eliot and Joyce to Pasternak, Beckett and the *nouveau roman*. Many of the names on Poggioli's various lists of avant-garde artists will strike the twenty-first-century reader as decidedly non-avant-garde, tamely conservative even.[7] For Poggioli 'modernism' refers to a minor tendency within the avant-garde, exemplified by Italian futurism, which abandons the critical stance and instead fetishizes modernity. This romantic idealization of modernity which Poggioli calls 'modernism' can also be found outside the avant-garde in mass culture (e.g. in Hollywood science fiction films) and indeed he sees this shallow 'modernism' as ultimately incompatible with the serious 'avant-garde'.

Poggioli's definitions are almost the exact opposite of those of Greenberg and Adorno, for whom it was the avant-garde that was associated with futurism, Dada-esque radical novelty and shock provocations. And in the twenty-first century the understanding of these two terms is almost exactly the reverse of Poggioli's. Today, in most academic fields, 'modernism' has come to stand for the broad range of modern art, while 'avant-garde' tends to be seen as an extreme tendency, whether formalist, romantic or nihilistic, of modernism.

Peter Bürger's *Theory of the Avant-Garde* (1974) is very much a product of the post-1968 moment within a German context and the tangled legacy of the Frankfurt School.[8] The basic argument is that 'avant-garde' refers to a particular phase within the history of modernism, after the First World War, the period of Dada then surrealism. This was the period when 'avant-garde' became aligned with revolutionary aspirations. Avant-garde art is therefore primarily modern or modernist art which is politicized. The crucial feature of the avant-garde is its attempt to think through politically and radically not just the artwork itself (its form) but its production, distribution, modes of reception and its wider social and political function. For Bürger the early-twentieth-century avant-garde failed precisely because as art it was so successful, the artworks quickly became institutionalized within art markets and systems of patronage and through gallery and museum networks. The avant-garde then became assimilated into and institutionalized by the critical discourses of academia. Bürger goes on to argue that the postwar 'neo-avant-garde' (his term) fetishized Greenbergian aesthetic autonomy, and that Abstract Expressionists and their successors such as Jasper Johns and Robert Rauschenberg were always depoliticized, always already institutionalized. The neo-avant-garde of the 1950s paves the way for pop art and then postmodernism, in which political radicalism itself is reduced to a commodified pastiche style or gesture.

Notwithstanding Greenberg's promotion of the term 'modernism', from the early 1950s to the late 1960s 'avant-garde' was revived as the popular default term for modern art or for the more extreme end of modern art. To take the example of music, *Deutsche Grammophon* had a famous label called *Deutsche Grammophon Avant-Garde* which issued records by Stockhausen, Boulez and the post-serial composers. Some of this music was indirectly political but almost all of it adhered to abstraction and an 'autonomy of form' aesthetic and it was institutionalized through government funding and patronage via higher education, public radio broadcasting, concert halls and record companies. The rival avant-garde music (anti-serial) of John Cage and Fluxus was equally institutional, usually transmitted via galleries and the art world, and adhered even more strongly to the ideal of autonomous form and an aesthetic of indeterminacy and was *less* political. The most extreme music of the 1960s, for example the downtown New York minimalists or the predominantly European free improvisation movement called themselves 'experimental' or 'underground' (with close links to the 'experimental film' scene), distinguishing themselves from the 'avant-garde' and 'modernism', both of which they denounced as too tied to art institutions or, in the parlance of the time, as 'straight'.[9] Similar accounts could be given of postwar modern art movements in painting, dance, theatre, literature and film. In which case is Godard, before or after 1968, a 'classical' modernist or a genuine revival of the (politicized) avant-garde – or just another voguish product of Bürger's pop art 'neo-avant-garde'?

An attempt to answer that very question is the starting point for a third attempt to define 'avant-garde', that of Peter Wollen. As discussed in relation to silent cinema in Chapter 3, Wollen's 1975 essay 'The Two Avant-Gardes' argues that modernism begins in the first decade of the twentieth century, primarily in painting, with cubism marking a break with mimesis and realist modes of representation and marking the shift towards art that reflects on its own materiality, its own process of creation and its modes of representation.[10] Wollen explains this shift as a destabilizing of the signified and referent, and a freeing of the play of the signifier, resulting in the undermining of conventional codes of realist representation.[11] Painting and the associated arts followed a path towards the free play of the signifier, which in practice usually meant abstraction or the conceptual, but literature, or at least the novel, 'fell back', as Wollen puts it, into conventional realist modes, novelistic narrative being unable to do without the realist referent and experimental techniques such as 'stream of consciousness' serving to enhance rather than undercut representational realism.

When modernism emerged across the arts, Wollen writes, cinema 'was still in its infancy, scarcely out of the fairground and the nickelodeon, certainly not yet the Seventh Art'.[12] When it tried to establish itself as a modernist art in the 1920s, the attempt split cinematic modernism into two avant-garde tendencies. The first followed pictorial modernism into abstraction, Dada and surrealism, indeed most of these filmmakers were painters or photographers. The second avant-garde, as represented by Eisenstein and the Soviet directors, also used formalist techniques derived from futurism, cubism and constructivism but only as a means of defamiliarization within essentially realist narrative modes derived from the classical Hollywood 'codes'. The integration of formalist devices within realist narrative was also a consequence of the necessity to engage with a mass audience, largely illiterate, in order to inculcate the political ideology of the new communist state. Eisenstein denounced *Man with the Movie Camera* as 'formalist jack-straws and unmotivated camera mischief' because he perceived Dziga Vertov as having abandoned the realist narrative and the masses and gone over to the side of self-reflexive formalism and the bourgeois art elite.[13] Peter Wollen, however, sees Vertov as representing a utopian possibility: *the convergence of the two avant-gardes in an art that is revolutionary in both form and content.*

It is not until 1968 that cinema makes another attempt to catch up with what Picasso and Braque had achieved in painting back at the start of the century and what Vertov achieved in film in the 1920s. Once again, according to Wollen, cinema had split into these two avant-gardes, the first epitomized by Stan Brakhage and the underground 'Co-op' or 'loft' filmmakers who followed the free play of the signifier into abstraction in line with the Greenbergian conceptual and 'materialist' turn in modernist painting. The other avant-garde is epitomized by Godard and Straub-Huillet and in which classical realist narrative modes are not only retained but also radically defamiliarized via formalist devices, with Godard emerging as the equivalent to Vertov in the extremism with which he engages with classical cinema while simultaneously trying to subvert it in the name of a revolutionary Marxist project. From Wollen's point of view, it is entirely appropriate therefore that Godard should in 1968 abandon commercial filmmaking and work within a co-op under the collective name of the 'Dziga Vertov Group' (pro-Vertov, anti-Eisenstein). Bazinian and mainstream postwar cinematic modernism – Wollen names Bergman, Antonioni and Bunuel – are all but dismissed.[14]

However, Wollen's conclusion is that once again the utopian moment passes and 1968 actually represents a consolidation of the split between the two avant-gardes: the first reverting back into formalist sterility and largely apolitical 'experimental' film (which would eventually find a home in the gallery) while the second, rejecting the 'deconstructive' example of Godard and Straub-Huillet, reverts back into narrative realism and an aesthete cinematic modernism (Antonioni).

Fredric Jameson and the chronologies of cinematic modernism

Bazin and Deleuze both posit a broad chronology of film history divided by a break which occurs after the war at a particular time, 1945, and in a particular place, Italy. In his major essay on film history 'The Existence of Italy', Fredric Jameson writes that 'Film history can be clarified, or at least usefully estranged, by period theory'.[15] He goes on to propose that the periods in question can be identified as realism, modernism and postmodernism, aligned with stages in the other arts in accordance with formal and stylistic criteria. These stages are, in turn, governed by 'the historic logic of the three fundamental stages in secular bourgeois or capitalist culture as a whole', that is to say, cultural stages underpinned by a periodization of economic, social and political developments within capitalism.[16] Thus realism corresponds to the national/local era of capitalism, modernism to the monopoly/imperialist stage and postmodernism to the multinational era of globalization. To conceive of periods in art and culture without reference to the economic would be 'yet another form of idealist history', but Jameson accepts that tracing the mediations between formal or aesthetic categories and historical periods is fraught with difficulties.[17]

These difficulties are immediately apparent when it comes to film history. It is relatively straightforward to relate film aesthetics to technological changes within the cinematic process itself, such as the transition of silent to sound film, black and white to colour, and changes in cameras, lenses, film stock, as well as changes in production, projection and distribution, or wider contexts of communications such as the rise of television, the digital, the internet and so forth. But it is much harder to relate film aesthetics to the broad periodization of capitalism. The most obvious sign of this difficulty, Jameson notes, is that the chronology of film history being 'virtually coterminous with the twentieth century [. . .] signally fails to coincide with any of the rhythms or coordinates of development in the other arts or media' or with a broad periodization of capitalism dating back to the nineteenth and eighteenth centuries and beyond.[18] If it is true, he argues, that nineteenth-century realism in literature corresponds to national capitalism or that Baudelaire and *fin de siècle* modernity are a response to the stage of imperialism, then these stages, these correspondences, all but predate cinema. So how can film history possibly be synchronized with the history of other arts or with any broad periodization of capitalism?

The answer, according to Jameson, is that film history is 'semi-autonomous', a 'microchronology' which 'recapitulates something like a realism/modernism/postmodernism trajectory at a more compressed tempo'.[19] What Jameson is proffering is the idea that 'realism' is a foundational category for culture within capitalism; later developments in capitalist culture in the twentieth century will be construed as 'social moments' in which the aesthetics of realism are replayed, reworked or reacted against, in forms corresponding to realism, modernism and postmodernism – each of which is now conceived as a primarily aesthetic category rather than as strictly chronological stages. 'The formal self-consciousness of the modern', Jameson writes, 'draws its abstractions from the content of an older realism' while the postmodern 'ransacks all the preceding cultural moments for its new forms of "cultural credit"'.[20] In this view, modernism and postmodernism in film do not necessarily 'reflect' or 'correspond to' broad social and economic determinants, not because they have achieved a classical autonomy but rather because they are mediated by the 'accumulated cultural capital' of realism. It is the primacy of realism that facilitates the ostensible 'semi-autonomy' of modernism and postmodernism. And, perhaps more than with any other art, film history is therefore to be seen as a 'recapitulation' of the realist, modernist, postmodernist periodization in the form of non-synchronous microchronologies or moments, scrambled, as it were, by immediate aesthetic, social, technological and commercial factors. Or to put it another way, film history is primarily a 'semi-autonomous' history of stylistic responses to realism. To complicate matters further, Jameson acknowledges that it might be necessary to posit two separate histories, one for silent film and another for the sound film, each with its own playing out of the realism/modernism/postmodernism trajectory. Jameson even muses that the postwar experimental film (Stan Brakhage, Maya Deren) might represent the postmodern phase of silent film rather than being subsumed into the modernist stage of the sound film.[21]

If film history is a compressed recapitulation, it is unsurprising that it lends itself to continuous reconfiguration. Each definition of a term like 'realism', 'classical' or 'modernism' is likely to be determined by a particular passing critical context, as well as by their unstable, constantly changing relationship to each other. Which is why Bazin and Deleuze could recognize the birth of cinematic modernism in the problematic of realism inaugurated by 1940s Italian neorealism (rather than in the self-professed modernism of the 1920s avant-garde) and why Jameson argues that, as the *Cahiers* critics struggled towards their own modernist filmmaking practice in the 1950s, they could reconfigure 'classical' Hollywood as a modernist precursor to the French New Wave.[22] More generally, from Jameson's analysis, the following points emerge:

- Film history, being 'virtually coterminous with the twentieth century', does not correspond to the broader 'three-stage' development of capitalism rooted in the nineteenth century and is chronologically not synchronized with the development of other, older, arts.
- Cinema 'recapitulates' the stages of realism, modernism and postmodernism from the other arts as semi-autonomous categories of form and style and reworks them in reconfigured relationships determined by aesthetic, technological or commercial factors. Broader historical determinants, as envisaged by the 'three-stage' theory of capitalism, are largely mediated by 'social moments' relating to local, immediate factors.
- Realism as the foundational category of capitalist aesthetics quickly became the dominant mode of 'classical' cinema (Hollywood) regardless of what was happening in other arts and despite initial efforts to import (avant-garde) modernist ideas into silent cinema in the 1920s. Only when realism on the Hollywood model had become dominant could modernism develop as a response and a reaction in the form of Italian neorealism.

If the history of cinema often resembles a series of condensed and scrambled microchronologies in the way Jameson suggests, it helps to explain why contemporary cinematic modernism could return with Abbas Kiarostami, Hou Hsiao-hsien, Bela Tarr and Alexander Sokurov in the 1990s *after* postmodernism. That is to say, cinematic modernism returns as yet another interrogation and problematization of realism (with its continued 'cultural capital') and modernist formalism, both supposedly having been rendered obsolete by postmodernism, and as a further 'recapitulation' of the stages of realism, modernism and postmodernism. Cinematic modernism returns as a response to a new crisis of capitalism (globalization, collapse of the 'new world order', the failings of neoliberalism, the 2008 financial crash) and as a semi-autonomous category of form and style (reacting against the stylistic eclecticism of the postmodernist art film and the hyper-kinetic blockbuster aesthetic).

David Bordwell and the trouble with modernism

In their various set-books for film studies David Bordwell and Kristin Thompson have offered several approaches to the question of an art cinema distinct from both classical Hollywood cinema and avant-garde/experimental film. Bordwell has also addressed the issue in a number of articles, beginning with his influential 1979 essay 'The Art Film as a Mode of Film Practice'.[23] In this piece Bordwell suggests that while there had been attention to art cinema as an institutional mode in terms of production, distribution, marketing and exhibition, art cinema also constitutes a distinct aesthetic or style.

> *La Strada* (1954), *8½* (1963), *Wild Strawberries* (1957), *The Seventh Seal* (1957), *Persona* (1966), *Ashes and Diamonds* (1958), *Jules et Jim* (1962), *Knife in the Water* (1962), *Vivre sa vie* (1962), *Muriel* (1963): Whatever else one can say about these films, cultural fiat gives them a role altogether different from *Rio Bravo* (1959) on the one hand and *Mothlight* (1963) on the other. They are 'art films', and, ignoring the tang of snobbishness about the phrase, we can say that these and many other films constitute a distinct branch of the cinematic institution. [. . .] In the long run, the art cinema descends from the early *film d'art* and such silent national cinema schools as German Expressionism and Neue Sachlichkeit and French Impressionism. (A thorough account of its sources would have to include literary modernism, from Proust and James to Faulkner and Camus.) More specifically, the art cinema as a distinct mode appears after World War II when the dominance of the Hollywood cinema was beginning to wane.[24]

Bordwell then catalogues the primary features of the art-film style: an uneasy combination of realism and expressionism – realist in objective situation and subjective psychology, but the latter brings to the fore expressionist tendencies in the rendering of existentialist alienation and estrangement, while cause-effect linkage of events becomes loose and tenuous.[25] The distinctive characteristic of art-film style can be summarized as elliptical narrative in the service of narrative ambiguity and the open-ended play of thematic interpretation. This narrative ambiguity in turn serves as a vehicle for the 'estranged' vision or perspective of the auteur.

Bordwell's analysis of the art film and his catalogue of stylistic and thematic features is familiar, and this book follows Bordwell's analysis in many respects. However, Bordwell prefers to stick with the label 'art film' and distrusts labels like 'modernism', 'postmodernism' or 'avant-garde'. It might be argued that 'art film' only makes sense in terms of the aforementioned 'institutional mode' regarding production, distribution and above all marketing and exhibition. In other words, the idea of the art film became synonymous with the idea of art-house film: the place of exhibition – the independent art-house cinema. However, art-house cinemas have nearly always had an eclectic curating policy. Founded in London in 1925 and curated by Ivor Montagu and Iris Barry, the Film Society in Regent's Street showed German expressionist films, abstract avant-garde films and strongly promoted the new Soviet film, but the Society also showed documentaries along with revivals of Chaplin, Keaton and early Hollywood slapstick. When the Society premiered *Battleship Potemkin* in November 1929, it was supported by a new Mickey Mouse film *The Barn Dance* from Disney (Eisenstein probably approved).[26] In the 1950s the Cinémathèque Française under the curatorship of Henri Langlois and Lottie Eisner showed an even wider range of films and similarly eclectic programming was the norm rather than the exception at art-house cinemas in London, Paris, New York and elsewhere in the 1960s, 1970s and 1980s. Ever since the critically maligned pre–First World War *Film d'Art* movement and through to Truffaut's attack on the 'cinema of quality' in his 1954 'A Certain Tendency in French Cinema' *Cahiers* article, much art cinema has been derided by cineastes as bad cinema and bad art, while mainstream, commercial and Hollywood films, from Chaplin to Ford, Hawks and Hitchcock, have been critically revered as attaining the status of art and have taken their place in art-house programming. Bordwell's attempt to establish a stylistics of the art film is therefore problematic because labels like art film, art-house film, world cinema and cult film are categories based on institutional, exhibition and marketing factors rather than common stylistic features. The culminating stylistic feature towards which Bordwell's analysis develops – elliptical narrative in the service of narrative ambiguity – is not common to all, or even most, films marketed as art films or films shown in art-house cinemas; it *is*, however, a key characteristic of modernism, especially (as Bordwell notes) literary modernism, and it is a common feature of the main strands of cinematic modernism. As the essay draws to a close Bordwell acknowledges this issue by arguing the reverse:

> We cannot construct the art cinema in isolation from other cinematic practices. The art cinema has neighbors on each side, adjacent modes which define it. One such mode is the classical narrative cinema (historically, the dominant mode). There also exists a modernist cinema – that set of formal properties and viewing protocols that presents, above all, the radical split of narrative structure from cinematic style, so that the film constantly strains between the coherence of the fiction and the perceptual disjunctions of cinematic representation. It is worth mentioning that the modernist cinema is not ambiguous in the sense that the art cinema is; perceptual play, not thematic ambivalence, is the chief viewing strategy. The modernist cinema seems to me manifested (under various circumstances) in films like *October* (1928), *La Passion de Jeanne d'Arc* (1928), *Lancelot du Lac* (1974), *Play Time* (1967), and *An Autumn Afternoon* (1963). The art cinema can then be located in relation to such adjacent modes [. . .] the art cinema represents the domestication of modernist filmmaking. The art cinema softened modernism's attack on narrative causality by creating mediating structures – 'reality', character subjectivity, authorial vision – that allowed a fresh coherence of meaning. Works of Rossellini, Eisenstein, Renoir, Dreyer, and Ozu have proven assimilable to art cinema in its turn, an important point of departure.[27]

So, confusingly, cinematic modernism fractures causality and strains coherence but is *not* marked by ambiguity, while art cinema retains the fundamentals of narrative realism and maintains a 'coherence of meaning' yet *is* marked by ambiguity and ambivalence: 'the modernist cinema is not ambiguous in the sense that the art cinema is.' Echoing Peter Wollen's discussion of the two avant-gardes, Bordwell is basically arguing in a post-1968 'political modernism' vein that cinematic modernism undermines representational realism but produces clearly determined political meaning or critique, while art film is a bourgeois aesthete cinema. But how does modernism's political clarity equate with the privileging of 'perceptual play' as an end in itself? If this is recapitulating Eisenstein's debate with Vertov over *Man with a Movie Camera* then Bordwell, like Wollen (and Godard), is siding with Vertov and supportive of 'formalist jack-straws and unmotivated camera mischief' as indicative of the true revolutionary aesthetic and is opposed to Eisenstein's 'revisionist' realism. Wollen's two divided avant-gardes are displaced by Bordwell onto a split between modernism and art film but with a similar resolution: 'historical materialist film' announcing a radical return to modernism as a means of rejecting the bourgeois aesthete art film; perceptual play as opposed to narrative and thematic ambiguity.

'Historical materialism', a term with a complicated genealogy in Marxism, here refers to the post-1968 political/aesthetic paradigm, largely theoretical and involving a rehabilitation of Brechtian strategies, Russian Formalism, Lukács and Frankfurt School theory, alongside various post-structuralist and Situationist currents of the time. In Anglo-American academia the post-1968 paradigm was imported from Paris by way of the new field of film studies, rather than literary, philosophical or political studies, and was developed as 'film theory' via journals such as *Screen* and this paradigm is what is still currently termed, at least in film studies, 'political modernism'. Whether labelled 'historical materialist' (Bordwell) or 'political modernism' (Rodowick) the post-1968 paradigm endorsed cinema which purported to show the material reality of class relations free from the mystifications of bourgeois ideology as perpetuated by Hollywood romantic realism and its passive modes of viewer identification. Today 'historical materialism' and 'political modernism' remain associated with Godardian 'deconstructive' strategies and Brechtian de-dramatized 'distanced' treatments of history in films like *The Taking of Power by Louis XIV* (Rossellini 1966) and *Othon* (Straub-Huillet 1969). Bordwell gives a brief account of how directors in the 1960s, such as Resnais, Straub and Huillet, Oshima, Godard, 'dissolve' causality and 'shatter' character subjectivity in order to critique art cinema ambiguity from the point of view of a return to (political) modernism or historical materialism and a radical 'third cinema' type rejection of reactionary aesthete 'second cinema', the essay ending with a, by 1979 rather late, call-to-arms flourish:

> If, as some claim, a historical-materialist order of cinema is now appearing, the art cinema must be seen as its necessary background, and its adversary.[28]

This book adheres to much of Bordwell's stylistic analysis but reverses, as it were, his terminology and argues that 'art film' (or art-house film) is a very loose category determined not by a particular style but by factors of institution, exhibition and marketing; cinematic modernism is a more specific term which may be applied to films influenced primarily by literary modernism and which are characterized by a configuration of narrative ambiguity, thematic ambivalence *and* perceptual play: elliptical narrative in the service of narrative ambiguity. 'Historical materialist' film (or 'political modernism') from Vertov to Godard is a subset of or localized reaction *within* (even if sometimes a reaction *against*) the aesthetic lineage of cinematic modernism, a reaction governed by immediate ideological demands, particularly in the post-1968 moment, rather than the aesthetic properties of a given film.

For his 1985 book *Narration and the Fiction Film* Bordwell revised and expanded the 1979 art-film essay into three chapters on 'Art-Cinema

Narration', 'Historical Materialist Narration' and 'Parametric Narration', respectively.[29] By revisiting 'historical materialism' in 1985 Bordwell evinces a continuing sympathy for the post-1968 'political modernism' paradigm. 'Parametric narration' means cinematic representation constructed by way of a recognizable style external to the requirements of a given narrative. This usually means the recognizable style of an auteur; a particular type of shot, staging or motif consistent from film to film regardless of the different content of each film; *leitmotifs* by which an auteur's work is recognized in terms of an *oeuvre*. As such, parametric narration is a feature of numerous films – classical, modernist, postmodernist – in many genres and largely synonymous with auteur theory. However, Bordwell's elaboration of a concept of parametric narration (derived from Noël Burch's *Theory of Film Practice* 1973) focuses on films in which a particular motif, object, colour, sound, camera movement or angle, image or type of image, is 'distributed' across a film according to a prior plan conceived in 'serial' terms. The distribution of parametric units governs image and sound 'cells' according to a pattern or formula and this 'generates' the film and its structure. Burch took this idea from modernist serial music, the twelve-tone composition technique of Schoenberg, but of more relevance to postwar film were the works of then-contemporary post-serial composers such as Boulez and Stockhausen in the 1950s, compositions in which timbre, length of note, volume, tempo and other 'parameters' were set in advance to govern the distribution of notes or sounds across a score according to mathematically inflected structures. Although various *nouveau roman* writers adapted this idea of generative cells and the distribution of parametric units to the construction of narrative, only Robbe-Grillet used it in a sustained way, both in novels (*Jealousy* 1957) and films (*Eden and After* 1970), but he did so with the ironic sensibility of a pastiche modernism in the service of erotic fetishism. The idea of the parametric works best with music and abstract art (and perhaps structuralist film) but has limited application to realist and narrative modes, whether literary or cinematic. Nonetheless Bordwell's idea of parametric narration does provide another way of approaching the foregrounding of repetitive structure as style, not just in obvious examples such as Resnais (*Last Year at Marienbad* 1961, *Muriel* 1963) but in Ozu and Bresson, and therefore provides an explanation as to why certain directors from quite different cultural and cinematic contexts, in the case of Ozu the context of mainstream Japanese commercial cinema, have been viewed as having something in common from the perspective of cinematic modernism.

The problem of modernism

The expanded version of the essay 'The Art Film as a Mode of Film Practice' in *Narration and the Fiction Film* concludes with a section entitled 'The Problem of modernism':

> Throughout this book I have refrained from using the term 'modernism'. By spelling out the differences among various modes and norms, we can see that several different sources of narration could qualify as 'modernist'. If we look to the traditions of twentieth-century fiction and drama, running roughly from James, Proust, Joyce, and Kafka through to Faulkner, Camus, and the Theatre of the Absurd to Cortázar and Stoppard, we find that art-cinema narration could be called modernist; for these are among its important sources. If we take modernism to be more closely allied with the experimental work of political artists like Grosz, Lissitsky, Heartfield, Brecht, and Tretyakov, then historical-materialist narration will be a better candidate for the label. And if we consider parametric narration as a distinct mode, its modernist pedigree can be traced back to the work of the Russian Formalists – a movement deeply involved with contemporary avant-garde poetry and fiction – and to the continental serialism and structuralism of the 1950s and 1960s. Thus parametric films might be considered modernist.[30]

From this it seems as if the most important techniques, sources and aesthetic genealogies Bordwell is ascribing to the postwar art film are, in fact, modernist, but Bordwell is reluctant to use the label 'modernist' and instead resorts to the category of 'certain problematic films':

> For reasons that will have to be explained in each particular context, filmmakers in widely differing periods and cultures have utilized parametric principles. Some have done so consistently (Ozu, Bresson), others sporadically (Lang, Dreyer, Fassbinder, Godard). Whether we call this 'modernism' is not as important as recognizing that only after an aesthetic was formulated explicitly was it possible for critics and spectators to construct an extrinsic norm that helps us grasp certain problematic films.[31]

In 1985 Bordwell is writing at a time when postmodernism appeared to have superseded modernism and he was distancing himself from grand post-structuralist theorizing and becoming identified with 'post-theory' empiricism and the study and classification of particular techniques in particular films. Bordwell sees 'modernism' as carrying the baggage of an unverifiable zeitgeist and prefers to elevate a particular technique – parametric narration – as the key 'extrinsic norm' through which we can identify 'certain problematic films', whether we call them modernist film or art film. More recently, in his 2007 collection *Poetics of Cinema*, Bordwell reprinted his original 1979 essay 'The Art Film as a Mode of Film Practice' supplemented by a new Afterword in which he accepts that the 'faith in an emerging 'historical-materialist' cinema' turned out to be ill-founded and that there has instead been a global revival of art film in the 1990s and into the twenty-first century, from Taiwan to Iran and beyond:

> Many of these newer traditions, it seems, replay at an accelerated pace the trajectory of European art cinema. An indigenous realist movement, somewhat comparable to Italian neorealism, becomes more conscious of the conventions involved in realism, and develops more abstract experiments in form. The emergence of Iranian cinema is a remarkable instance. Budgets are bare-bones by Western standards, and by using non-actors and locations, filmmakers have presented post-Shah Iranian culture to a world that knew little of it. The humanistic strain of neorealism finds echoes in films like *The Key* (1987), *The White Balloon* (1995), *The Apple* (1998), *The Child and the Soldier* (2000), and *Blackboards* (2000). At the same time, and often within the same films, we find sophisticated games with cinematic technique. *The Mirror* (1997) starts with a little girl's frustration with trying to cross a busy intersection, then shifts its story action almost wholly to the soundtrack when she barricades herself behind her household gate and refuses to meet the camera. Mohsen Makhmalbaf's *Moment of Innocence* (1996) shows him staging a film based on a crime he committed in his youth, and the result is a dizzying *mise en abyme* reminiscent of *8½*.[32]

This account resembles Jameson's idea that film history recapitulates its developments in accelerated non-synchronous 'microchronologies' and acknowledges the emergence of a contemporary international cinema which combines realism with formalism in a manner 'replaying' developments out of Italian neorealism in the postwar art film. *On the History of Film Style*, a 1998 film studies set-book presenting a history of cinema by way of Bazin and Burch, sees Bordwell frequently applying the term 'modernism' to films, largely as synonymous with 'art film', and analysing predominant features of contemporary cinematic modernism such as the long take (both static fixed-camera and fluid sequence shot) and 'planimetric image' (the flat frontal shot).[33] Despite his understandable reservations over many years, it would seem that Bordwell has come to accept the usage of 'modernism' as a valid term to describe a significant type of contemporary art cinema.[34]

András Bálint Kovács: A taxonomy of cinematic modernism

In his 2007 book *Screening Modernism: European Art Cinema, 1950-1980* András Bálint Kovács upholds the centrality of Bazin and Deleuze's chronology: the break in cinema history represented by Italian neorealism. He also concurs with Bazin's problematization of the real and with Deleuze's orthodox canon of *auteurs*, which begins with Rossellini and evolves via Bresson and Antonioni into a full-fledged cinematic modernism which ends in the mid-1970s with Tarkovsky. However, Kovács is also writing a history which assumes the validity of Jameson's category of the postmodern – Kovács is attempting to clarify what cinematic modernism was, as a historical phase belonging to the past, from the vantage point of what superseded it: postmodernism.

Using Bordwell's stylistic classifications as his starting point, Kovács presents a detailed analysis of postwar art cinema. He addresses the diversity of art cinema by dividing it into four broad categories of style: minimalist, theatrical, ornamental and naturalistic; and two basic archetypes of form: continuous and fragmented.[35] Kovács also outlines three basic categories of content or meaning: disconnection and alienation of the individual, critical redefinition of the concept of reality, disclosure of nothingness behind surface reality.[36] To this existentialist paradigm of the (lack of) meaning he adds the later critical (self)reflexivity and post-1968 Brechtian 'political modernism'.[37] Kovács draws up a 'historical taxonomy' of common features and characteristics – long take, sequence shot, serial montage, fragmented narrative, ellipsis, indeterminate perspective – and then offers a corpus of 240 films to which the taxonomy can be applied. On the basis of this analysis Kovács proposes that the postwar art film was a modernist cinema, closely related to the modernism that had developed in other arts in the early decades of the twentieth century, especially the modernist novel.

According to Kovács, modernist film began with Rossellini, notably *Journey to Italy*, and ended with Tarkovsky's œuvre – to be precise, between *Mirror* and *Stalker*. Tarkovsky's *Mirror* manifests the end of cinematic modernism: a vivid enactment of the shattering and fragmenting of the 'mirror' – the modernist project to reflect reality through the personal vision of an *auteur*, the psychological authenticity of the individual artist and his/her inner life as aligned with a representation of the grand narrative of history – in the case of *Mirror*, the collective history of Soviet Russia and indeed the whole world in mid-century (Figure 13). *Mirror* (1974) is still modernist because it is anchored to the *auteur*'s position within reality and history, whereas *Stalker* (1978) presents a 'parallel universe as an empirical experience inseparable from everyday reality' and so

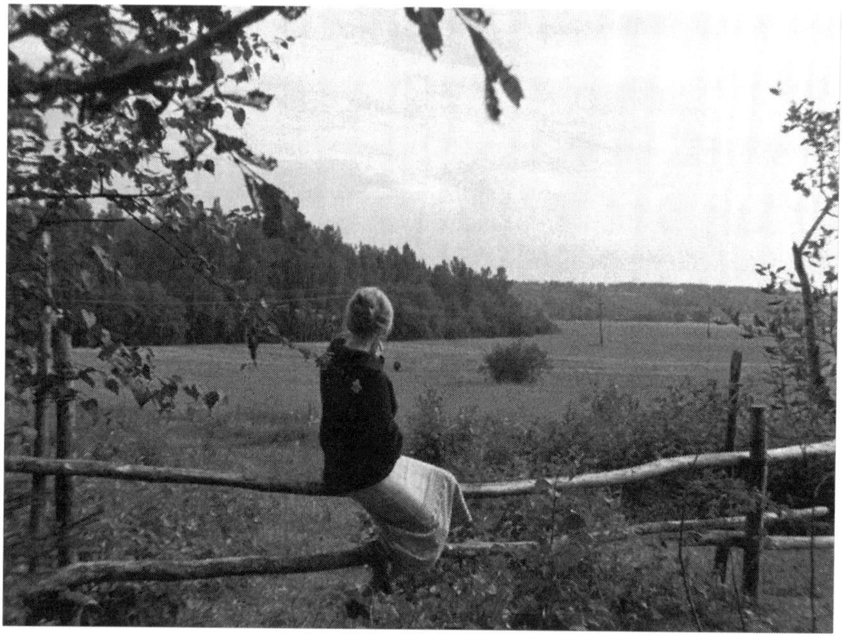

Figure 13 *Mirror* (1975), Andrei Tarkovsky.
Gazing into the landscape as a mirror of place and time(s). Filmed from behind, a woman (daughter, mother, grandmother) sits on a fence, smoking, staring into the fields, bushes and trees, and remembering the wind rippling the leaves. She gazes at a landscape as an uncanny void to be filled variously by nature, by Soviet history, by love, marriage and motherhood, and by the self – the attempt to reconstruct the fragmented reflections of the self into a whole. *Mirror* might be structured by the man's (Tarkovsky's) narcissistic broken mirror, but it is the women across the generations whose reflections cohere.

'that is where Tarkovsky transgressed in his œuvre the thin and almost invisible borderline between modern and postmodern'.[38]

Although his taxonomy provides a comprehensive description of stylistic traits common to art films made in Europe from the mid-1950s to the mid-1970s, Kovács concludes that the defining feature of a specifically modernist cinema is, finally, not to be found in particular formal qualities but in its philosophical subtext. Whether or not a strand of modernist film follows a neo-Bazinian aesthetic, all modernist films are in one way or another a Bazinian meditation on the representation of reality in the cinematic image and, by extension, an investigation of reality itself. This Bazinian problematic of the ontology of the cinematic image finds its correspondence in an existential doubt that characterizes the sensibility – existentialism – which most acutely reflects the social reality of the period. Antonioni is the definitive modernist director because he carried on where Rossellini and Visconti had left off by combining neorealism with film noir and romantic melodrama, leading to the destabilization of these genres (the emptying of plot and characterization into narrative indeterminacy) and sustaining a representation of reality while throwing it into confusion and doubt. The resulting 'uncanniness' of reality is, in Antonioni, linked up to the existentialist sensibility of the period (the uncanniness of being) and a concrete historical context (Italy in transition from postwar trauma to economic miracle). Far from being a superficial and modish supplement, 'existentialist alienation' is essential to Antonioni and modernist film and is glossed by Kovács as follows:

> [T]he common aspect of modernist forms is a sense of empirical reality existing behind the aesthetic form, even if this reality is conceived of as an abstract and conceptual entity. The idea of nothingness became in modernism the only verifiable reality behind the surface of the empirical world.[39]

In other words, while in most modernist directors there is the possibility of truth, meaning and transcendence, whether ideological, political, religious or sexual, their realization is increasingly thrown into doubt as the probability of nothingness increases. In Antonioni nothingness itself becomes the tangible reality that lies behind the empirical surface and it is this recognition of nothingness that becomes the common subtext defining cinematic modernism: nothingness as a critique of social being, nothingness as itself a 'transcendental value', albeit a negative one.[40] What marks postmodernism in opposition to modernism is therefore, in Kovács's striking phrase, 'the disappearance of nothingness' – there is, in postmodernism, no longer a common knowledge of or interest in 'what is missing'.[41]

Rancière: From one image to another

In *Film Fables* Jacques Rancière provides a concise summary of the story of how modern cinema came into being.[42] It is worth quoting here as a recap of the assumptions from which this chapter and indeed this book take their cue.

> Let's assume that there is a cinematographic modernity and that it confronted the classical cinema of the link between images for the purposes of narrative continuity and meaning with an autonomous power of the image whose two defining characteristics are its autonomous temporality and the void that separates it from other images. This break between the two ages of the image has two model witnesses: Roberto Rossellini, the creator of a cinema of the unexpected that confronts classical narrative with the essential discontinuities

> and ambiguities of the real, and Orson Welles, who broke with the tradition of narrative montage through the creation of deep focus. And it is also has two model thinkers: André Bazin, who in the 1950s, a religious agenda firmly in the background, deployed the arsenal of phenomenology to theorize the artistic advent of the essence of cinema, which he identified with cinema's 'realistic' ability to 'reveal the hidden meanings in people and things without disturbing the unity natural to them'; and Gilles Deleuze, who in the 1980s set about articulating a theory of the break between these two ages based on a rigorous ontology of the cinematographic image. The correct intuitions and theoretical approximations of the occasional philosopher Bazin find their solid foundation in Deleuze's theorization of the difference between two types of images, the movement-image and the time-image. The movement-image, the image organized according to the logic of the sensory-motor schema, is conceived of as being but one element in a natural arrangement with other images within a logic of the set [*ensemble*] analogous to that of the finalized coordination of our perceptions and actions. The time-image is characterized by a rupture with this logic, by the appearance – in Rossellini – of pure optical and sound situations that are no longer transformed into incidents.[43]

In classical (Hollywood) cinema temporal and spatial relations are ostensibly stable as are relations of causality between events and these relations are rendered through conventions or 'codes' governing how each shot is set up (e.g. in terms of point of view) and how each shot relates to the next (conventions of continuity editing). These conventions structuring the image and order of images are in accord with the structure of the narrative – its story, plot and internal consistency of time, place and characterization. Rancière's gloss on Deleuze tells us that the 'natural' arrangement of images in film is 'analogous' to the coherence our perceptual apparatus imposes upon the world, including the realm of immediate sensation, and which allows us to make sense of the world. Modern cinema begins when these conventions governing the relationship between images breakdown; temporal, spatial and causal relations are called into question and certain images take on a heightened degree of autonomy from the surrounding images and from the requirements of narrative. This breakdown in the coherence of the arrangement of images in cinema corresponds to an actual dysfunction in the 'sensory-motor schema' through which people – after the trauma associated with the Second World War – interacted with the world. Images become 'pure optical and sound situations' estranged from conventional causal relations, they are 'no longer transformed into incidents', they are no longer events with a causal purpose within a narrative. And so, liberated from classical cinema's conventions of cause and effect and temporalities determined by the requirements of plot, the image in modern cinema achieves a high degree of autonomy from story, plot, events, causal relations and other images; each image becomes a site of autonomous temporality, each image has its own duration:

> The time-image founds modern cinema, in opposition to the movement image that was at the heart of classical cinema. Between the two there is a rupture, a crisis of the action-image or a rupture of the 'sensory-motor link', which Deleuze ties to the historical rupture brought about by the Second World War, a time that generated situations that no longer fit the available responses.[44]

The basic idea is clear: in modern cinema the image (and scene/episode) has a higher degree of autonomy from dramatic narrative than was required by the conventions of classical cinema and this autonomy is felt most keenly through the rendering of time and duration rather than dramatic action.

Rancière's account will be, by now, very familiar, but of course Rancière is only assuming and summarizing this account of Bazin, Deleuze and the birth of modern cinema in order to then offer a critique. The critical discussion takes place in Part III of *Film Fables*, 'If There Is a Cinematographic Modernity' (note the loudly equivocal 'if') and chapter (note the equally sceptical question mark) titled 'From One Image to Another? Deleuze and the Ages of Cinema'. So what are Rancière's main points of criticism? Rancière is sceptical about the idea of a particular 'break' in the organization of the cinematic image occurring in Italy in 1945 and sceptical of such a break being a direct manifestation of a traumatized breakdown in the 'sensory-motor schema' of the Italian psyche. The continuities in the cinematic practice of Rossellini before and after the fall of fascism are well known, and any number of similar objections could be made: Is the birth of modern cinema in Hollywood (Welles) also due to some traumatic event? And how does this story of modern cinema relate to modernism across the arts? Are not the main characteristics of modern cinema – fragmentation, ellipses, destabilizing of identity and narrative – already present in modernist literature decades earlier? Did the First World War produce a similar shock to the 'sensory-motor schema'? If so, why did the revolution in modern painting (Cezanne and post-impressionism to Picasso and cubism) occur *before* the trauma of the First World War? Even if the focus is kept to cinema, it might be argued that lots of nations suffered from the trauma of the Second World War, so why didn't other national film cultures – for example Germany – develop a similar wave of neorealism? It might also be remembered that Bazin and Deleuze actually have almost diametrically opposed explanations for selecting Italy 1945 as the point of the break between classical and modern cinema. For Bazin Italy 1945 was a year zero marking the Liberation, a blank slate of possibility and a utopian dream of creating a new progressive national culture; for Deleuze Italy 1945 is a year zero marked by the trauma of fascism, occupation, bombed-out cities, devastation and defeat.

Nevertheless it is true that neorealism emerged in Italy in the late 1940s and was received around the world as something radically new and it was this Italian cinema that went on to develop into various kinds of cinematic modernism. Clearly there are concrete reasons specific to Italian film culture that facilitated neorealism and subsequent developments out of neorealism. There are also more idiosyncratic explanations such as Godard's stress in *Histoire(s) du cinéma* on the link between the cinematic image in Italy and the painterly culture of Italy, a culture of the image, together with the custom of the Italian film industry to continue with post-synchronized sound long after other national film cultures abandoned it. Godard argues that Italy alone maintained the primacy of the image from the silent film era into the era of the sound film, sound and text remaining strictly secondary to the image.[45] For Rancière such empirical objections may be valid but are in themselves trivial, he has a more fundamental objection, that Deleuze (intentionally) oscillates between conceptualizing the image as a 'virtual' variation on doubling/representation and conceptualizing the materiality of the image:

> What, then, is an image? It is not what we see, nor is it a double of things formed by our minds. Deleuze develops his reflections as a continuation of the philosophical revolution started by Bergson, so what is the principle of that revolution? It is to abolish the opposition between the physical world of movement and the psychological world of the image. Images are not the doubles of things, but the things themselves. [. . .] This 'philosophy of cinema', in other words, takes on a paradoxical turn from the very beginning. Cinema had generally been thought of as an art that invents images and the arrangement between visual images. And along comes this book [Deleuze's *Cinéma*] with its radical thesis. What constitutes the image need not be constituted at all. It exists in itself. It is not a mental representation, but matter-light in movement. Conversely the face looking at the images and the brain conceiving them are dark screens that interrupt the movement in every direction of images. Matter is the eye, the image is light, light is consciousness.[46]

Rancière is sympathetic to this as part of Deleuze's philosophical project, but problems arise when the argument is translated back to actual film history and a familiar debate arises, a familiar Bazinian quandary. If an image as a thing in itself is more important that any representational function, then images themselves are the primary reality, are at one with reality however we might define that given reality (as physical, psychological, social, spiritual, etc.). If so, should cinema be constructing images and reconstructing them through montage, in the manner of Eisenstein, Vertov and Godard, to present a political and ideological critique of a given reality? In other words, should cinema be creating new images and defamiliarizing old images? Or, alternatively, is it cinema's main purpose to reveal the reality that is within images? Whatever the philosophical issues, two options at a stylistic level are evident: the reconstitution of reality through the reconfiguration of images versus finding images and allowing the reality immanent within them to emerge, to be revealed (e.g. through long take, sequence shot and deep focus). Rancière points out that both options assume that the image is fallen, has lost its reality, lost its truth and, whether through montage or the long take, the job of cinema is to restore truth to the image:

> The proposed [Deleuzian] 'classification' of film images is in fact the history of the restitution of world-images to themselves. It is a history of redemption.[47]

Which brings us back to Bazin and Kracauer and the idea that cinema is an essentially redemptive art: redeeming reality, redeeming lost time, redeeming the present, redeeming the past, redeeming history and redeeming the human soul. But from the point of view of this book the most pertinent aspect of Rancière's critique is his discussion of the historical schema, his take on the idea that there are at least two ages of cinema – the classical and the modern – and that there is a break after 1945 – Rossellini and Welles – which marks a transition from one age to the next. Rancière has his own key concepts, namely 'the aesthetic regime' and the 'redistribution of the sensible' which elaborate the idea of a shift from representational art imposing itself on reality to art which through form manifests the contradictions within reality.[48] Unlike the idea of a classical age being superseded by a modern age via a particular break or transitional moment, Rancière's conceptual schema discerns overlapping tendencies and is less determined by historical periodization or linearity. Without going too far into Rancière's conceptual apparatus, the conclusion can be put simply: *basically Rancière is uncomfortable with the idea of the modern and modernism.* He uses the two terms more or less interchangeably in *Film Fables* but seems to see modernism as a recent Anglo-American ideological mystification of the already problematic Franco-German idea of the modern. The issue of the relationship between a break in the character of images in cinema (the time image) and a supposed break or event in actual history (Italy after the Second World War) is symptomatic of how 'modernism' fetishizes discontinuity, breaks, schisms, the shock of the new, as a means of explaining the relationship of supposed 'modern' art to a supposed 'modernity' at an historical level, something, according to Rancière, symptomatic of 'what is fundamentally equivocal in "modernist" thought':

> In its most general garb, this form of thought identifies the modern revolution in the arts with each art's manifestation of its proper essence. The novelty of the 'modern' is that the essence of the art, though it had always been active in the art's previous manifestations, has now gained its autonomy by breaking free of the chains of *mimesis* that had always fettered it. The new, considered in this light, has always already been prefigured in the old, and the 'rupture', in the end, is nothing more than a required episode in the edifying narrative through which each art proves its own artistry by complying with the scenario of a modernist revolution in the arts wherein each art attests to its own perennial essence. For Bazin, Rossellini's and Welles' revolutions do no more than realize cinema's autonomous vocation for realism – which was already manifest in Murnau, Flaherty, or Stroheim – through their opposition to the heteronomous tradition of a cinema of montage illustrated by Griffith's classicism, Eisenstein's dialectic, or the spectacularism of expressionism.[49]

This account of Bazinian cinematic modernism as the redemptive realization of a realism immanent to the cinematic image rehearses a straw-man programmatic Greenbergian version of modernism far removed from the now more common eclectic and inclusive versions. The privileging of purity, autonomy and teleology presents a version of modernism which Bazin, Rivette, Truffaut and most of the *Cahiers du cinéma* critics and new wave *auteurs* rejected as an alien modernism or avant-gardism imported into cinema by artists from the world of painting in the early years of cinema, during the silent era, when film theorists obsessed over Lessing's *Laocoon* (1767) and whether film was a new 'art' and if so what was its relationship to the existing arts. How was film, in Lessing's terms, distinct, specific and autonomous? As discussed at various points in this book, Lessing's criteria for the classification of the arts was revived by Greenberg's 'Towards a Newer Laocoon' (1940) with reference to painting in the postwar period and from there went on to have great influence across the arts. Bazin and *Cahiers* believed that cinema was an art and they also recognized that with Rossellini and Welles a modern cinema had been born, but they rejected what in the French context was regarded as the purist formalist dogmas of the French avant-garde and Anglo-American modernism. Instead, as is well known, Bazin endorsed an 'impure' cinema. Nevertheless Rancière's argument that there is an archetypal modernist tendency at the core of Bazin's thinking helps to explain why in retrospect it seems so obvious that what Bazin is describing in his account of Rossellini (and

Welles and Bresson) is not just modern cinema but what this book is referring to as cinematic modernism. Or as Rancière puts it: 'For Bazin, Rossellini's and Welles' revolutions do no more than realize cinema's autonomous vocation for realism.' From the perspective of Bazin and Kracauer, modernism in cinema does *not* primarily concern the realization of abstract form or the materiality of the cinematic apparatus – conceptualizations of form and materiality imported from other arts and alien to the realist essence of cinema. However, if realism is the problematic essence of cinema, then modernism in cinema is the realization of this essence, is the problematization of realism via modernist form.

Rancière is sceptical about this line of reasoning but it does help to contextualize the perspectives of Bazin, Kracauer and Deleuze. What is clear is that Bazin saw cinema as having a particularly complex relationship with reality (the ontology of the photographic image) and whereas the role of formalism ('significant form') within most other modernist arts tended towards the anti-representational, anti-mimetic and above all anti-realist, the role of formalism within cinematic modernism was to respect this complex ontology and facilitate the revealing of a reality immanent or latent within the image – the Deleuzian time image – rather than to construct, reconstitute or deconstruct reality through, say, expressionistic montage, dialectical or otherwise. Whatever its theoretical validity, a particular aesthetic combining realist and formalist modes flows from this argument and it is this aesthetic that has generated a recognizably neo-Bazinian cinematic modernism today.

6

The return of cinematic modernism

András Bálint Kovács in *Screening Modernism* is unequivocal: cinematic modernism was specific to the post-Second World War period in Europe and centred on the investigation of a traumatized uncertain reality and the existentialist search of the alienated individual for lost meaning.[1] According to the dominant critical discourse of the 1980s and 1990s, postmodernism had superseded modernism and was no longer focused on this search for lost meaning. There is neither transcendental absolute nor void, there is no hidden secret truth or definitive meaning, no Rosebud.

This chapter looks at how ideas of postmodernist film and cinematic modernism can inform rather than negate each other, and argues that a contemporary cinematic modernism, usually taking the form of what this chapter proposes as a 'neo-Bazinian aesthetic', first emerged in Taiwan and Iran and then internationally in the 1990s.

Whatever happened to postmodernism?

Postmodernism is commonly conceived as being a cultural response to the stabilization of capitalism and liberal social-democracy in the 1970s following the end of the Vietnam War, the management of the oil crises, the winding down of the Cold War, the capitalist turn in China and the eventual collapse of communism and the Soviet bloc. The implication of these events was summed up in Francis Fukuyama's 1989 proclamation of the 'end of history' with no alternative, no outside or 'other' – no more history in the Hegelian sense of a major new development leading to a qualitatively different or 'higher' stage, just 'internal' modification, readjustment and reform.[2] The account of postmodernism as a cultural and aesthetic movement 'reflecting' so-called late capitalism enjoyed a wide consensus by the mid-1980s, partly on the basis of Fredric Jameson's theoretical framework.[3] According to Jameson, the aesthetic of postmodernism rejected the signified in favour of the play of the signifier, which in practice meant scepticism towards any 'pure' realism or formalism as representing existential truths and the endorsing instead stylistic eclecticism and the circulation of intertextual tropes as ludic pastiche.

From the point of view of today, however, the historical context of postmodernism seems to have been that period of 'late capitalism' extending from the mid-1970s to the early 2000s, a period now (since the 2008 financial crash) popularly denoted by the labels 'neoliberalism', 'financialization' and 'globalization'. These labels refer to theoretical constructs aiming with varying degrees of accuracy to describe and explicate the ongoing processes through which 'free markets' attempt to reproduce themselves in conjunction with powerful social formations (class elites) and the ceaseless flux of these ongoing processes, as well as particular technological or cultural developments.[4] Today postmodernism is generally seen as the cultural and aesthetic reflection of a phase in these ongoing processes not their end.

The rapid decline of the postmodernism thesis corresponds almost exactly to the rapid decline of the 'end of history' thesis, while the return of modernism corresponds to the perceived return of extreme existential crises generating a sensibility of radicalized existentialist doubt and an acute awareness of the loss of meaning and agency. Kovács argued in *Screening Modernism* that postmodernism manifested the 'disappearance of nothingness', the disappearance of 'what is missing'.[5] If so, then it might be said that 'nothingness' and an awareness of 'what is missing' have reappeared with a vengeance, and at a cultural level this provides a key thematic basis for contemporary cinematic modernism. Instead of superseding modernism, postmodernism is today regarded rather as a passing foil to modernism, the latter now extending into the twenty-first century under a proliferating variety of academic guises: contemporary modernism, meta-modernism, neo-modernism, global modernism, vernacular modernism, late modernism, the new modernism, to name just a few.[6] What these new theoretical versions of modernism have in common is that they reflect not only the anxiety of 'existential' crises but also early-twenty-first-century ideological concerns by making modernism inclusive in terms of gender and sexuality, geography and ethnicity, and inclusive in terms of historical periodization. Whether or not such an all-inclusive version of modernism is conceptually sustainable remains to be seen.

A brief history of postmodernist cinema

The archetypal characteristics of modernist and postmodernist aesthetics were played out in explicit fashion in cinema. By the end of the 1970s the modernist art-house film that had flourished in the 1950s and 1960s – and which had seemed in the early 1970s about to take over Hollywood itself via Altman, Scorsese, Coppola and Malick – fell out of favour with audiences and critics. In metropolitan centres around the world, art-house cinemas and film clubs began to close. The new action blockbuster 'cinema of sensation' arrived with Spielberg and Lucas, *Jaws* (1975) and *Star Wars* (1977), and it was with this type of film (and its distribution and marketing strategies) that Hollywood reconquered the world. Popular Hollywood cinema generated its own version of postmodernism, notably Ridley Scott's *Blade Runner* (1982), which due to its themes of identity and the questioning of authenticity, its stylistic impurity referencing as pastiche multiple genres and its vision of hybrid globalized culture and retro-futurism, was commonly described as postmodernist in knowing contrast to the 'pure' stylistic and conceptual modernism of Kubrick's *2001: A Space Odyssey* (1968).[7] By the end of the 1970s modernist cinema such as that of Bergman and Antonioni and the existentialist investigation into the loss of meaning was routinely criticized as too slow, too obscure and too pretentious. Postmodernist film at its most overtly antagonistic to the preceding modernist cinema emerged in France with Jean-Jacques Beineix (*Diva*, 1981), Luc Besson (*Subway*, 1985) and the *Cinéma du Look*. In Britain the self-reflexive art film of Peter Greenaway (*The Draughtsman's Contract*, 1982) and Derek Jarman (*Caravaggio*, 1986) though often politically radical (anti-Thatcherite) epitomized the ludic, stylistically heterogeneous and anti-realist aesthetic of postmodernism. Postmodernist film found its best-known auteur in Spain with Pedro Almodóvar (*Women on the Edge of a Nervous Breakdown*, 1988), and various currents of cinematic postmodernism spread throughout 'world cinema' including Japan: Takeshi Kitano (*Sonatine*, 1993); Hong Kong: Wong Kar-wei (*Chungking Express*, 1994); and China: Zhang Yimou (*Raise the Red Lantern*, 1994).

In America the uptight 'art film' became the looser 'indie film' displaying an ironic self-reflexive tone and references to popular culture and kitsch. The films of Jim Jarmusch, Hal Hartley and David Lynch exemplified the turn towards stylistic pastiche and the mobilization of genre tropes as an intertextual pleasure in itself. In discussions of postmodernism, Lynch films, especially *Blue Velvet* (1986), were and still are invariably singled out as examples of how postmodern stylistics could express the sensibility of the period in its giddy superficiality while also signalling what those stylistics might be repressing, the traumatic and obscene real that lies just beneath the surface of late-twentieth-century postmodern culture and just behind the kitsch façade. The aesthetic logic of postmodern indie film was confirmed by the ubiquity in the 1990s of cult cinema and the trash film. If Greenberg had counterposed modernism to kitsch, postmodernism (especially in film) reversed the binary and happily embraced kitsch. The cinephile was no longer the lover of modernist art film but the cult fan of trash sub-genres.

Cinematic postmodernism culminated with the merging of the Hollywood blockbuster 'cinema of sensation' with the loose ironic aesthetic of the indie film centring on genre pastiche and the obsessive referencing of other films (rather than reality). This convergence occurred during the 1990s in the films of Quentin Tarantino (*Reservoir Dogs*, 1992, *Pulp Fiction*, 1994) and the extraordinary popular and critical impact of these films around the world seemed to confirm the definitive triumph of cinematic postmodernism.

Realism, modernism and postmodernism

Modernism in the novel and in film is essentially a realism, but one which engages with the limits and failures of preceding realist aesthetic modes – and realism is constantly reinventing itself as an engagement with the limits and failings of formalism and the modernist aesthetic. Within this schema it may therefore be legitimate to posit the triad *realism, modernism and postmodernism* as different facets of an ongoing aesthetic response to the condition of capitalist modernity. In which case it might now seem less strange to consider how, out of the postmodernism of the late twentieth century, a contemporary or millennial cinematic modernism emerged. The standard argument is as follows: exasperation at the dominance of the hyper-kinetic action blockbuster on the one hand and the exhaustion of the postmodern art film of ironic pastiche on the other generated a desire (and a cinephile nostalgia) for the heyday of postwar modernist art cinema. A reaction occurred in the 1990s against the dominant cinema of the time – mainstream and art – and the reaction was 'over-determined' by a process of negation: that is to say, the new cinematic modernism generated its stylistics by opposing point for point the stylistics of the dominant (blockbuster) mainstream and (postmodern) art films of the period.

- In reaction against the hyper-*kinetic* action film, the new cinematic modernism would be *slow* and *static*.

- In reaction against digital special effects (CGI) saturated films, the new cinematic modernism would be realist and respect the ontological integrity of the photographic image.
- Against the *immersive* cinema of *sensation*, the new cinematic modernism would be *distanced* and *contemplative*.
- Against the contemporary *quality drama* and well-made heritage film (recalling Truffaut's diatribe against the French 'cinema of quality' in the 1950s), the new cinematic modernism would be *de-dramatized* and *loosely plotted*.
- Against the aesthetic of the luxurious glamour, the sexy 'look' and advertisement/pop video sheen of 1980s postmodernist film and its privileging of chic *style*, the new cinematic modernism would deploy an *anti-style*, an austere updating of neorealism and a minimalist mise-en-scène.
- Against the sensibility of ironic pastiche characteristic of postmodern film during the era of triumphant neoliberalism and the 'end of history', the new cinematic modernism would be *serious* – a representation of existentialist doubt and alienation afflicting the individual amid the multiple existential crises of contemporary capitalism.

However, cinematic modernism which mechanically negates postmodernist film or consciously negates contemporary popular film by trying to revive the postwar modernist art film as a kind of 'retro genre' tends to be unconvincing, giving rise to an unintentionally parodic cinematic modernism of shallow mannerism. Contemporary cinematic modernism at its best doesn't reject or side-step postmodernism but instead passes through postmodernism, incorporating its ironic modes *in sublimated form*.

Chantal Akerman

Chantal Akerman is a key figure in the recent history of cinema in that she represents an almost unique point of connection between (European) postwar cinematic modernism of the 1960s and (American) experimental film of the 1970s, between (American) indie film of the 1980s and the new cinematic modernism of the 1990s. She also represents the assimilation of postmodernism into contemporary cinematic modernism.

Akerman both directed and starred in her 1968 debut short *Saute ma ville* playing a young woman arranging her kitchen in an apparently consumerist frenzy only for it to turn out that she is actually arranging her suicide in the gas

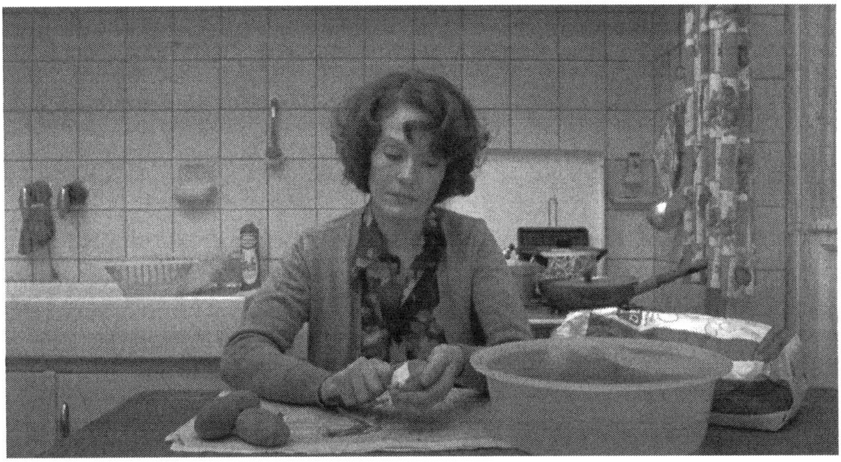

Figure 14 *Jeanne Dielman, 23, quai du Commerce, 1080 Bruxelles* (1975), Chantal Akerman.
A portrait of a housewife's daily chores: in this case peeling potatoes. But as with the scene of Maria the maid performing kitchen chores in *Umberto D*, in cinematic modernism this use of real-time minimalist realism has the function of implying dramatic undercurrents through repression, a suspenseful repression which will 'return' in explosive violence. As Jeanne (Delphine Seyrig) laboriously peels the potatoes, her mind is slowly unravelling in ways which will lead to murder.

cooker. Unusually for a young Godardian filmmaker, Akerman (at the age of twenty-one) then went to live in New York where she became enamoured of the experimental film scene – especially Warhol, Michael Snow and Yvonne Rainer. The influence of American minimalism on *Hotel Monterey* (1972) is clear, the silent 'documentary' film mostly consisting of fixed-frame long-duration shots of spaces within the hotel such as the foyer, corridors, elevators and skyline views from the hotel roof. Occasionally hotel guests and staff will enter the frame. *News from Home* (1977) is a similar minimalist exercise consisting of long-take shots of various street locations in downtown New York overlaid with a soundtrack of Akerman reading letters she had received from her mother. *Jeanne Dielman, 23, Quai du Commerce, 1080 Bruxelles* (1975) is a meticulous and rigorous presentation of a housewife performing her household chores, while also conducting prostitution from home. The hyper-realism of *Jeanne Dielman* is anything but typically documentary, being instead rendered through the extreme formalism of 'minimalist' static long takes (Figure 14). Like an early *nouveau roman* novel, the objective attention to the everyday is a kind of repression of steadily increasing hysteria leading to breakdown and murder.[8] Everyday reality is also defamiliarized by having the glamorous art-house star Delphine Seyrig play the dowdy housewife doing the household chores – Marguerite Duras used a similar defamiliarization strategy by casting Jeanne Moreau and Lucia Bosé as the two women performing everyday chores in a domestic space in *Natalie Granger* (1972). Leaving to one side all the readings that can and have been made of *Jeanne Dielman*, the pertinent point here is that the film (and Akerman herself) represents a rare for its time encounter between European art-house and American experimental film (Akerman rather than Godard fulfilling the role assigned by Wollen's 'two avant-gardes') and this combination of previously estranged aesthetics has become one of the most recognizable features of contemporary cinematic modernism, not least in its propensity for the static long take. In addition, it is Akerman films such as *Je Tu Il Elle* (*I You He She* 1974) and especially *Toute une nuit* (*All Night Long*, 1982) and *J'ai faim, j'ai froid*, (*I'm Hungry, I'm Cold*, 1984) that introduce the deadpan style, loose narrative and cool realism with an ironic twist, into an American alternative cinema previously dominated by structuralist film. If *Jeanne Dielman* and *Les Rendez-vous d'Anna* (1978) can be considered as prefiguring contemporary cinematic modernism, particularly in its 'slow cinema' variation, then *Je Tu Il Elle* and *Toute une nuit* might together be the godmother of American indie from Jarmusch through to the 'mumblecore' of the early 2000s (Andrew Bujalski having studied under Chantal Akerman in the 1990s).

American indie film: Modernist or postmodernist?

The idea that modernism and postmodernism, in film, should be seen as interrelated rather than crudely oppositional might help to explain why certain strands of contemporary cinematic modernism developed out of the postmodern 'independent' American cinema of the 1980s and 1990s. The obvious example of such a figure of continuity or overlap between modernist art film and postmodern indie film is Jim Jarmusch. But first, the curious case of David Lynch.

David Lynch

Dressed in black designer suits and cultivating a Warholian persona combining knowing irony and faux-naivete, David Lynch embodied the style of postmodernism and his films were – and are – generally seen as epitomizing postmodernism. If Lynch's breakthrough film *Eraserhead* (1977) had initially been located by critics as belonging to some ill-defined post-punk 'underground' sub-genre, the critical and commercial success of *Blue Velvet* (1986) and its pervasive influence on 1980s culture can be seen as confirming the arrival of cinematic postmodernism: an art film which rendered the preceding modernist art film tradition *passé*, calling into question the very category of 'art film' and completely reconfiguring the Greenbergian distinction between art and kitsch. *Blue Velvet* embraced dialogue constituted by banal cliché, a knowing superficiality of characterization and character psychology, pop-cultural references, trash genres and tropes, and embraced kitsch both comically and seriously. *Blue Velvet* was almost instantly recognized as the quintessential example of this new cinematic postmodernism primarily because everything in the film (character, plot, mise-en-scène) is filtered through a self-reflexive, ironic sensibility of pastiche. According to Jameson's influential reading, a film like *Blue Velvet* is not exactly 'parody', it is not satirizing or critiquing anything specific, its retro tropes are not consistent with a single time or place, instead the film is governed by a 'pastiche' style: cinematic and broader pop-cultural references circulate as a 'play of signifiers' with no signified but with an ironic detachment facilitating a fetishistic pleasure in the more or less arbitrary deployment of such signifiers.[9] This was especially evident in the fact that *Blue Velvet* appeared to be set in the contemporary America of the 1980s yet was filled with retro stylings referring to a self-consciously mythical postwar America (of the late 1950s and early 1960s): the present is mediated by the tropes of nostalgia. 'Retro' as a free-floating signifier (without a particular or consistent referent in an actual past) came to be seen as a primary distinguishing mark of cinematic postmodernism.

However, it should be remembered that Lynch considers himself to be part of the surrealist tradition and happily attests to the influence of classic surrealist cinema on his work (Bunuel/Dali, Rene Clair, Duchamp, Man Ray et al.). Surrealism was a major modernist movement, albeit an idiosyncratic modernist movement from the point of view of a Greenberg or an Adorno. The one set of cultural references that Lynch does not pastiche is surrealism itself, which is another way of saying that Lynch really does believe in the unconscious, in erotic and sado-masochistic fetishism, and he believes in the Freudian uncanniness of home (in Lynch's case, the apparently idyllic home of small-town America). Most of all, he believes in the existence of the dark traumatic and obscene 'real' that lies just behind the façade of everyday life and its contrived and fragile normality.[10]

From this point of view, *Blue Velvet* and Lynch's subsequent films do not mark the 'disappearance of nothingness' (as Kovács describes the key characteristic of cinematic postmodernism).[11] Nothingness, the void and the traumatic real remain at the heart of Lynch's films, and as such they are as existentialist as Antonioni's films and as much the product of an all-consuming anxiety or dread as the films of Bergman. In other words, Lynch's cinema does not so much oppose the modernist art film as assimilate the modernist art film into the 'ironic' sensibility and stylistic register of pastiche commonly identified with postmodernism of the 1980s and 1990s.

After the original *Twin Peaks* series (1990–1) Lynch's work met with diminishing critical and commercial returns, passing out of fashion. That his films should not be reduced to the 1980s 'moment' of postmodernism has nevertheless been confirmed by the success of *Mulholland Drive* (2001), a 'comeback' film of sorts and arguably his most surrealist film to date and also one recognizably related to the films of Bunuel's 1960s art-house heyday, to some of the surrealist-influenced Eastern European modernist art cinema of the 1960s, and to that strand of the French New Wave (Resnais, Rivette, Duras and especially Robbe-Grillet) influenced by the *nouveau roman* – films such as *Last Year at Marienbad* (1961) and *L'Immortelle* (1962) with their mise-en-abyme narrative structures, proliferation of unreliable narrative perspectives and contradictory plot-lines which cannot be resolved. Lynch's deployment of pastiche and kitsch in *Blue Velvet* and *Mulholland Drive* should not distract from the way in which these films are in dialogue not only with vintage surrealist film but with the postwar modernist art film, both in terms of Lynch's experimentation with narrative form and in terms of his abiding interest in the angst produced by the encounter with a repressed obscene and violent trauma, an anxiety which he sees, in an almost Kafkaesque way, as characterizing the psychology of modernity.[12]

Jim Jarmusch

In the 1970s American indie cinema was still synonymous with American experimental 'underground' film, following in the diverse lineages of experimental film auteurs like Stan Brakhage, Maya Deren, Kenneth Anger, Jonas Mekas, Hollis Frampton, Andy Warhol and Jack Smith. Within this tradition there had been a degree of overlap between expressionism (abstract or otherwise), surrealism, camp kitsch and durational minimalism. By the 1970s a self-conscious Greenbergian avant-garde modernism had achieved a degree of aesthetic/ideological hegemony over the experimental scene, centring on the materiality of the medium (modifying the film print or the filmic apparatus) and a tendency towards extreme abstraction. Despite its residual elements of expressionism, surrealism and hyper-realism, Michael Snow's *Wavelength* (1967), structured by a forty-five-minute fixed-camera zoom across a room in an apartment (in which several events including a murder appear to have occurred), retrospectively emerged as a key film in its assimilation of both the durational minimalist film modes associated with Warhol and the abstract anti-narrative film associated with Brakhage, a combination of modes which in turn generated an extreme formalism in the guise of the 'structuralist' cinema of Hollis Frampton, Ernie Gehr and their fellow-travellers. Structuralist film shared with the earlier underground film a degree of antipathy towards the mainstream modernist cinema of Antonioni, Bergman and even Godard, and positioned itself as related not to the critical discourse of cinema but to developments in painting, sculpture, performance art and the installation. Above all, structuralist cinema defined itself as non- or anti-narrative. Notwithstanding the merits of individual structuralist films and filmmakers, the structuralist movement came to represent, for many, a sterile conceptualist formalism and structuralist film and its successors have mostly left the cinema altogether for the more conducive environment of the gallery. However, the static minimalism typical of structuralist film has, largely by way of Chantal Akerman, been assimilated back into narrative art-house film to become a readily identifiable influence on both American indie film and contemporary cinematic modernism.

Although sometimes relegated to the status of an apprentice work, Jim Jarmusch's *Permanent Vacation* (1980) turned out to be of seminal importance. Allie, the protagonist, is a young hipster kid who plays old Charlie Parker vinyl singles on a retro record player and some of his acquaintances are post-punk hipsters of the CBGB ilk, but the film itself is not an exercise in 'cool' – it is a loose episodic neorealist type narrative in which an existentialist loner wanders through a disorientating decaying downtown Manhattan cityscape searching for meaning, an odyssey interrupted by more or less random unresolved encounters with eccentric characters who, like the city itself, seem to be down on their luck, frazzled, psychologically broken. Pitched somewhere between Rossellini and the early films of Wenders via Akerman, *Permanent Vacation* tracks a Deleuzian wandering through unmapped ruins, revealing a set of fundamental dislocations, spatial and temporal, concrete and psychological.

Filmed in bleached-out grainy black-and-white stock and largely in long takes without reverse angle point-of-view shots, Jarmusch's breakthrough film *Stranger than Paradise* (1984) deploys minimalist mise-en-scène, real locations (a few very basic rooms and streets), minimalist dialogue and a minimalist plot, all of which explicitly declares both an art-house and an 'underground' cinematic aesthetic – both aesthetics having become increasingly rare by 1984. The story, such as it is, consists of New York hipster losers Willie and Eddie looking after newly arrived relative Eva from Hungary who is en route to an aunt in Cleveland. Willie (played by John Lurie) makes little effort to communicate with his unwelcome guest but predictably becomes enamoured, as does Eddie, and they all end up in snowy Cleveland with Aunt Lotte. The trio escape to the sunshine of Florida and the film ends with a farcical mix-up when Eva fails to catch her plane back to Hungary and Eddie accidently ends up on the plane instead.

The impact of *Stranger than Paradise* on subsequent American indie film, through to Tarantino, lay primarily in its deadpan acting style, droll dialogue and incessant retro pop-cultural references. Unlike *Permanent Vacation*, it is possible to see not merely the hipster characters but *Stranger than Paradise* – the film itself, its aesthetic, dialogue and plot (and with it the director's own vision) – as evincing a would-be 'urban cool' sensibility different to its immediate influences such as Wenders's *Kings of the Road* (1976) and Akerman's *Je Tu Il Elle* (1974).[13] Nevertheless, Jarmusch differed from many postmodernists in that he was clearly not intending to relegate the European existentialist art film or its American equivalents (Cassavetes) to the dustbin of cinema history. If anything the opposite. In 1984 existentialist modernism couldn't be 'revived' but it could be updated if mediated by the self-reflexivity and detached irony associated with postmodernism. A problem for Jarmusch (and much American indie cinema) is that the sensibilty of droll irony proved too successful. Jarmusch's own subsequent career is instructive in that the majority of his films are relatively light romantic hipster cult-film fare and only occasionally has he been able to harness the ironic sensibility to a serious intent.

Stranger than Paradise attempts to redeem the European modernist art film of Antonioni and Wenders by filtering the tropes of art-house cinema, existentialist angst and ennui, through the self-reflexive tropes of hipster irony and pop-cultural kitsch; that is to say, to redeem cinematic modernism through the sensibility of its supposed nemesis: postmodernism. *Stranger than Paradise* is widely regarded as inaugurating the new wave of American indie film, a film which rescued American alternative cinema from the cul-de-sac of the structuralist avant-garde and returned it to the loose and romantic narrative register of neo-Bazinian realism in the tradition of the French and German New Waves.[14] Jarmusch took film back out of the gallery and loft and returned it to the cinema (preferably flea-bitten), away from reference points in conceptual art and back to cinematic reference points: not only the Hollywood genre film, the B-movie, the road movie, film noir but also the European modernist cinema of Antonioni, Rohmer, Wenders and, above all, Chantal Akerman.[15]

The return of cinematic modernism

In the 1980s and 1990s the influence of a new current of cinematic modernism became evident in films across several national cinema cultures, beginning with the Taiwan New Cinema (Hou Hsiao-hsien) and the New Iranian Cinema (Abbas Kiarostami). Cinematic modernism of a recognizable kind was also discernible in Russia (Alexander Sokurov), Hungary (Bela Tarr) and China (Jia Zhangke). By the late 1990s, contemporary modernist films of the 'neo-Bazinian aesthetic' type discussed in this book had become ubiquitous on the international film festival circuit and the 'world cinema' market – DVD and home cinema replacing the art-house cinema as the prime site of distribution and screening. These films were usually marketed as a new national cinema (Taiwanese, Iranian, Chinese, Romanian, Argentinian etc.), closely modelled on the example of the new waves from the postwar era of modernist film. These contemporary modernist films were also marketed in terms of auteur cinema, the cult/brand of the director, again closely modelled on the example of the auteur cinema of postwar modernist film. In the 2000s contemporary cinematic modernism has been, arguably, the dominant aesthetic in international art film, certainly as regards critical reception and prestigious festival prizes, and had an influence on everything from American indie mumblecore to the emerging brave new world of 'quality' cinematic drama made for television and various digital streaming platforms.

What did the national contexts in which cinematic modernism returned have in common? They tended to be national contexts far from the serene 'end of history', they tended to be national contexts in which history was, in fact, taking an unpredictable turn: the traumatic turn to capitalism in China and the collapse of communism and even more traumatic turn to capitalism in Russia and certain countries within the former Eastern Bloc. Taiwan and Iran are two countries that in very different ways found themselves caught between a collapsing dictatorship and a colonial or neo-colonial past, tensions between extreme liberalism and extreme conservatism, and an intensified relationship to the emerging end-of-century global 'New World Order'. Taiwan and Iran represent national contexts in which the contradictions of post-Cold

War globalization – economic, political, military *and cultural* – first became apparent, long before the generalized crisis of neoliberalism and globalization in the twenty-first century as manifested in the far-reaching consequences of the 2008 financial crash.

Taiwan New Cinema

As is seemingly the case with every national film movement and 'new wave', there has been a contentious debate about what – and who – exactly constitutes the Taiwan New Cinema. Leaving the arcane debates to one side (important though they may be), it is clear that from the perspective of 'world cinema', its festivals and institutions, and from the perspective of the critical discourse on modern art cinema, there is a consensus that a wave of remarkable films and directors emerged in Taiwan in the 1980s, a 'wave' which carries the convenient identifying label of 'Taiwan New Cinema'. This wave had an enormous initial local impact but had run into difficulties in Taiwan itself by the early 1990s. However, the influence of Taiwan New Cinema on the international art film continued to grow and develop as did the careers of its leading *auteurs* Hou Hsiao-hsien and Edward Yang.

The Taiwan New Cinema provided an early example of the now familiar narrative of the supposed rise and fall of each national wave via co-option into 'transnational' film production, distribution and reception. The exhaustion of a national new wave cinema is usually formulated as a capitulation of haughty *auteurs* either to exoticization of the national for the international market or to the homogeneity of a festival film 'international style'. In both cases this sell-out or dilution of the authentically national is accompanied by a rejection by local audiences of the new wave, its films being designated – derided – as largely for foreign consumption.

From the point of view of this book the main interest is not in the authenticity of 'national culture' but precisely in the aesthetics of this international style and how it mediates the 'particular' of a national context and the 'universal' of contemporary art cinema – with the assumption that, in the relative autonomy of its aesthetic, the contemporary modernist art film retains a relationship to a more fundamental 'universal', namely a sensibility of generalized existential crisis and anxiety, reflecting or metonymically 'standing in' for an otherwise unrepresentable Lukácsian totality (i.e. 'the crisis of late capitalism in the age of globalisation'). At a more immediate level, the main interest is in how the Taiwan New Cinema provided a template for the neo-Bazinian aesthetic that so much subsequent international art film would follow, the international style that this book is referring to as contemporary cinematic modernism.

Why Taiwan?

The question of national identity and ethnicity is particularly fraught in Taiwan. 'Native Taiwanese' might refer to the various aboriginal inhabitants or to successive waves of Chinese, mostly Han, arriving from the mainland over the centuries. Added to which Taiwan has been subjected to colonization by Portugal, Spain, the Netherlands and Japan – raising the obvious issue of whether the Han Chinese population have been colonizers or colonized (or both). The twentieth century began with occupation by Japan in 1900 lasting until 1945. Among its other Imperial adventures, Japan also occupied Korea and, in the 1930s, Manchuria and then China as a whole, an occupation contested by Chiang Kai-shek's nationalist Kuomintang (KMT) government and Mao's Communist Party. As well as the fight with Japan and various Chinese warlords, the KMT and communists were engaged in a long-running civil war with each other. Following Japan's defeat in the Pacific War, Mao's communists took Beijing and declared a People's Republic on 1 October 1949. The defeated KMT performed a hurried retreat to their stronghold in Taiwan, accompanied by a huge Han migration, the apparent plan being to consolidate and regroup in order to fight another day (rather as Mao had done in the 1935 communist retreat to Yan'an mythologized as the Long March). In the context of the messy end of the Pacific War and the incipient Cold War, Taiwan was backed and defended militarily by America as a bulwark against Asian communism.

In the 1945–9 period, therefore, the liberation of Taiwan from Japanese occupation took the form of coming under the domination of a nationalist Chinese dictatorship representing the influx of Han Chinese and backed by US interests. The consolidation of KMT rule on the island was violent – essentially the imposition of a totalitarian state under the personality cult of Chiang Kai-shek enforced through imprisonment, torture, execution and massacre of opponents by the new regime. Although martial law continued right through the postwar era, only being officially lifted in 1987, Taiwan had to an extent settled by the 1960s, at least compared to the tumultuous events on the Chinese mainland accompanying the Cultural Revolution, and the island enjoyed an 'economic miracle' driven by American economic links. By the 1980s Taiwan shared with Japan and South Korea an East Asian version of the consumer society and pop culture (including film) derived from 'Americanization' as both something imposed and something appropriated. These forms of popular culture also interacted with similar cultural currents in Hong Kong and Singapore.

With the passing of Mao and Chang Kai-shek and the rapprochement between China and the United States, Taiwan's political position that the government in Taipei was merely in temporary exile and remained the only legitimate government of all China became increasingly untenable. In the early 1980s the Taipei government conceded the momentous but inevitable acknowledgement that Taiwan had no hope of recovering mainland China. The now 'reformist' governments in Beijing and Taipei began to establish a pragmatic 'normalization' of relations between the 'two Chinas'. Liberalization in Taiwan did not produce anything as traumatic as the 1989 Tiananmen Square events on the mainland, but it did release a vibrant period of political reform and cultural interrogation of what actually constitutes Taiwan and Taiwanese identity. It also unleashed an interrogation of nationalist ideology and the long-repressed history as to how Taiwan under Chiang Kai-shek came into being in the late 1940s.

In other words, despite (or because of) its 'economic miracle', Taiwan in the 1980s was marked by a fervent cultural and political liberalization movement, investigating the fundamentals of national identity and how that nation had come into existence. Two of the main cultural movements investigating what might constitute a modern Taiwanese identity were the Homeland Literary Movement and the Taiwan New Cinema – the literary and film movements being closely linked. The Taiwan New Cinema is usually dated to the anthology films *In Our Time* (1982), co-directed by Edward Yang, Tao Te-chen, Ko I-cheng and Chang Yi, and *The Sandwich Man* (1983), co-directed by Hou Hsiao-hsien, Zeng Zhuang-xing and Wang Jen. These were low-budget films produced by the state-owned Central Motion Picture Company but, unlike standard Taiwanese film, these films displayed a neorealist influence, casting non-professional actors and following an unconventional loosely plotted narrative structure.

Hou Hsiao-hsien

Hou Hsiao-hsien (whose family had been part of the Han influx of 1948) initially made his name as a director in Taiwan by working within the commercial mainstream, making 'romcoms' featuring teen idols of a kind derived from the Japanese popular cinema of the time. His first films as director portray a contrast between the superficiality of the urban and the authenticity of the rural, the latter characterized by family life in close-knit village communities set among lush green and fertile scenic landscapes, a peaceful idyllic land denoting the authentic Taiwanese identity.

The commercial 'youth film' staple proved to be adaptable to the Taiwan New Cinema, which tended to involve coming-of-age stories: gangs, fights, sexual awakening, discord between the adolescent wish for freedom and excitement and the strictures of conservative parents, and Hou Hsiao-hsien moved seamlessly but radically from the commercial romantic comedy *Cute Girl* (1980) to his first major international art-house breakthrough *The Boys from Fengkuei* (1983). An exciting and accessible youth film of gangs, violence, romance and adolescent angst, already discernible in *The Boys of Fengkuei* are features corresponding to what would become typical features of the neo-Bazinian strand of contemporary cinematic modernism:

- neorealist mise-en-scène
- naturalistic acting
- de-dramatization
- long take
- fixed view/static image – into which actors and action enter and depart the frame
- discontinuities of sound and image
- elliptical editing
- elliptical narrative (and episodic narrative structure)
- critical social realism combined with an aesthetic formalism

By the mid-1980s the Taiwan New Cinema's pop-cultural obsession with the youthful alienation of generations growing up in the 1960s, 1970s and 1980s began to encroach on more politically sensitive periods, namely the youthful alienation of the immediate postwar generation growing up in the 1940s and 1950s, an historical context which couldn't help but refer to the traumatic circumstances through which modern Taiwan came into existence.

The landmark Taiwan New Cinema film dealing with the events and repressed history surrounding the birth of modern Taiwan is Hou's *City of Sadness* (1989). This film is about the 1940s but the making and release of the film itself was facilitated by its own historical context of the late 1980s: the beginning of a shift towards political reform and social liberalization accompanied by the opening up of debate over Taiwanese history and the long-repressed trauma concerning the events of the 1940s. The film portrays a family living through the violence of the end of Japanese occupation, attempting to negotiate the demands of political radicals, criminal gangs and militias (sometimes representing different ethnic communities), living through the events leading to the consolidation of KMT rule and the massacre of 28 February 1947 in Taipei, when an estimated 30,000 people were killed. This massacre and the events surrounding it had been a taboo subject, reference to which had been strictly censored until the lifting of martial law in 1987. The screening of *City of Sadness* in Taiwan was in effect the lifting of the taboo on discussing the February 1947 massacre, and the film occasioned mass interest and intense debate.

City of Sadness was distributed on the international festival circuit, where it won multiple prizes, including a prestigious Golden Lion award at the 1989 Venice Film Festival. This international prestige protected the film from censorship or repression back home and transferred some of its prestige to Taiwan itself – legitimacy to the new reforms, liberalization and democratization; legitimacy to the idea of Taiwan as a modern nation embracing freedom, in stark contrast to the stalling of reform and reversion to totalitarianism on mainland China as manifested in the 1989 Tiananmen Square massacre.

City of Sadness deploys to an extreme formalist degree all the features of cinematic modernism listed earlier, including (notwithstanding moments of explosive violence) de-dramatization – important events are presented obliquely, action often occurs off-screen and the overall pace of the film is stately. In *The Story of Film* Mark Cousins sees Hou as repudiating the kinetic cinema of the 1980s (Hollywood, Hong Kong) and developing a kind of cinematic modernism that is 'classicist', a cinema of formal rigour and balance, in this case indebted to Mizoguchi and, especially, Ozu. In his discussion of *City of Sadness* Cousins writes:

> The film lasts 158 minutes and contains only 222 cuts, meaning that the average shot length is an astonishing forty-three seconds, longer even than those of Mizoguchi in Japan in the 1930s. [. . .] Hou's film is a meditative longing for the past and, as he said, 'A screen holding a long-shot [i.e., long take] has a certain kind of tension.' [. . .] Hou does not refer to the issue of narrative suspense or dread. Instead, the tension in his films lies in their ability to contain such complex portraits of rural Taiwan in the 1950s and 1960s in such rigorous, minimal formal structures. The dread is that the structure will collapse. [. . .] In Hou's spare conception of cinema, there is only one way to film a place. Or, rather, since these are films about remembering, places and visual memories of them are the same thing.[16]

Cousins stresses the static minimalist formalism of *City of Sadness* (and Hou's subsequent films), which places Hou in the lineage of Ozu rather than Mizoguchi, the influence of Ozu being something Hou has frequently acknowledged, most explicitly in the 2003 Japan-set film *Café Lumière*, a complex homage to Ozu.

Ozu and cinematic modernism

Ozu became a conspicuous influence on recent cinematic modernism in a way he wasn't to postwar modernists in the 1950s and 1960s, when he was largely unknown outside Japan and was generally reviled by the young directors of the Japanese New Wave. At the time of his death in 1963 Ozu was regarded as a conservative mainstream director (although appreciated as a highly original auteur by non-Japanese observers like Donald Richie). In a similar fashion to Hitchcock, Ozu's reputation and influence has increased inexorably over the last few decades, long outstripping the reputations of the Japanese modernist auteurs against whom he was once unfavourably judged. Like Ozu a commercial mainstream director, Mizoguchi had been discovered by the French critics in the 1950s and recast as a proto-modernist auteur largely because of his use of long fluid tracking shots, often as part of an elaborately choreographed long-take sequence shot, which by the 1960s accorded with the deployment of the long-take sequence shot in the films of Antonioni and Jancsó (and many others). By contrast the international reception of Ozu, when it arrived in the 1970s and 1980s, was in terms of de-dramatization, narrative ellipses, stylized 'artificial' acting (anti-psychological Bressonian 'model' acting), an everyday domestic mise-en-scène, static fixed-camera shots, the dead-time still-life 'pillow' shots of mundane objects, buildings and empty spaces, and the low camera angle (often characterized as looking from a tatami-mat seated position). Also much discussed has been Ozu's frontal positioning of his actors, especially when speaking, addressing with an eye-line looking not quite at but just past the camera, creating an unusual shot/reverse shot schema which has been thought to modify the 'suturing' of viewers into a scene of dialogue and into a film as a whole. In short, Ozu is considered to have created an alternative to Hollywood codes of continuity, especially in editing. Ozu's reception within the critical discourse of cinematic modernism was influenced by the example of Bresson and gave primacy to the perceived austere rigour of Ozu's aesthetic. As far as narrative content is concerned, it is difficult to imagine two directors more different, but what Ozu and Bresson share is a stylistically similar kind of rigorous *static* formalism.

Two sides of the neo-Bazinian aesthetic

The strand of contemporary cinematic modernism identifying with a 'neo-Bazinian aesthetic' is split into two contrasting yet overlapping strands, both developing out of Rossellini: the 'static' strand represented by Bresson and the 'fluid' strand represented by Antonioni.[17] The critical reception of Ozu and Mizoguchi outside Japan can be contextualized in part by this split: Ozu aligned with the static (Bresson) and Mizoguchi aligned with the fluid (Antonioni). In Taiwan New Cinema, Hou's *City of Sadness* is aligned with Ozu, while Edward Yang's *Terrorizers* (1986) is aligned with Antonioni. Both strands – static fixed-camera long take and fluid long-take sequence shot – can be minimalist, both can deploy de-dramatization and many of the other characteristic techniques of cinematic modernism, but what is of note is that in the postwar modernist film the two linked strands split completely and with the French *nouvelle vague* dispersed into a multiplicity of styles. In contrast, in contemporary cinematic modernism these two strands remain closely linked and, together, represent two sides of a single predominant aesthetic.

In a rerun of old debates over Antonioni, contemporary cinematic modernism is often accused of aestheticizing politics (as opposed to politicizing aesthetics). In the case of *City of Sadness* and the events of Taiwan 1947, a critical argument might be that the obliqueness and 'difficulty' of the contemporary cinematic modernism aesthetic creates an obscurantism which helps such a film avoid provoking or outraging the public (or governments) and indeed, despite its international awards and international critical acclaim, *City of Sadness* remains a 'difficult' film, arguably Hou's most challenging film. A more positive argument would be that *City of Sadness* provides an early example of what will characterize the 'return' to cinematic modernism in films ranging from Bela Tarr's *Sátántangó* (1994) to Jia Zhangke's *Platform* (2000): the representation of complex traumatic (and taboo) events necessitates an aesthetic of detachment, distancing and ellipsis (sublimation of traumatic material) and a recourse to the serious reflective existentialist sensibility of postwar modernist film.

In Taiwan the reception of *City of Sadness* represented a high-water mark for the Taiwan New Cinema, the result of the timing of its release in the middle of the cultural liberalization movements, but thereafter the aesthetic of cinematic modernism appears to have been an obstacle to local mainstream audiences, given that the appeal of the Taiwan New Cinema waned at the end of the 1980s. Internationally, however, the Taiwan New Cinema (marketed as a still continuing 'new wave') went from strength to strength as both Hou and Yang enjoyed a sustained run of critically lauded films. Of particular relevance to the development of an international cinematic modernist style is Edward Yang's *Terrorizers*, a film which, as mentioned earlier in contrast to *City of Sadness*, moves away from neorealism towards the overt cinematic modernism of Antonioni and a formalist cinema of urban ennui and alienation. In the wake of the continued international success of Hou and Yang (in Yang's case tragically curtailed by his death in 2007) a 'second wave' emerged during the 1990s, including mainstream director Ang Lee and Malaysian-Taiwanese director Tsai Ming-liang, the latter representing a radical extension of the stylistics associated with Taiwan New Cinema. Tsai's international breakthrough film *Vive L'Amour* (1994) recreates Taipei in the image of Antonioni's Rome, in which an economic miracle has pushed socio-economic hardship to the margins but replaced it with a floating social strata experiencing a very modern precarious rootless existence marked by atomization and an incapacity to sustain social (or sexual) relationships. Strangers, two men and one woman, occupy an apartment waiting to be sold (the woman works for a property agency). They fleetingly encounter each other in the apartment, constituting a peculiar and barely acknowledged ménage à trois, culminating with the woman making love to the young man while, unknown to the couple, the other man masturbates under the creaking bed – he is furtively in love with the young man. The film ends with the woman walking to an empty park, sitting on a bench and crying – captured by a fixed-camera long take lasting more than seven minutes.

New Iranian Cinema

The American-backed coup of 1953 installed the autocratic rule of the pro-Western Shah (Mohammad Reza Pahlavi), a reign combining selective social liberalization and a cultural renaissance across the arts with extreme brutality and political repression, a set of contradictions which ultimately led to the Islamic revolution of 1979 and the establishment of an Islamic Republic deploying draconian repression both political and cultural. The 'Westernizing' cultural liberalization of the Shah's rule had to an extent facilitated the Iranian New Wave, which emerged and attracted some international attention in the 1960s and early 1970s. The films of the Iranian New Wave were characterized by a poetic take on the neorealism which remained a strong tendency in cinema of 'developing nations' well into the 1970s. The internationally best-known films of the New Wave included *The House Is Black* (Forough Farrokhzad, 1963), *Mud-Brick and Mirror* (Abrahim Golestan, 1965) and *The Cow* (Darius Mehrjui, 1969).

The austere, de-dramatized, minimalist films of Sohrab Shahid Saless *A Simple Event* (1973) and *Still Life* (1974) are especially notable in prefiguring many of the stylistic features that would become associated with Kiarostami and the Iranian films of the 1990s.

With the establishing of the Islamic Republic in 1979 almost all cinemas were closed down and films banned, both art film and popular film being seen as too Westernized, too decadent and too un-Islamic. During the Iran–Iraq War (1980–8) the Iranian film industry was revived with a view to producing wartime propaganda and very quickly a kind of neorealism re-emerged albeit in the guise of propaganda film, the best-known example being Amir Naderi's *The Runner* (1985). After this period of cultural isolation, a new or 'second wave' of Iranian films started appearing at international film festivals, apparently encouraged by tentative liberalization undertaken by certain factions in the post-Khomeini leadership. In the late 1980s Iranian films began to attract critical acclaim, initially in France, before going on to have a huge impact internationally, including some cross-over to mainstream audiences. Films such as *Close Up* (1990), *Through the Olive Trees* (1994) and *Taste of Cherry* by Abbas Kiarostami (1997); *Salaam Cinema* (1994) and *A Moment of Innocence* (1996) by Mohsen Makhmalbaf; *The Apple* (1998) by Samira Makhmalbaf; *The Mirror* (1997), *The Circle* (2000) and *Crimson Gold* (2003) by Jafar Panahi are just a few of the most acclaimed films from the second Iranian New Wave which peaked in the 1990s and became known as the 'New Iranian Cinema'. These films combined a basic neorealist style (Rossellini) with an ascetic and challenging formalism (Bresson) including elliptical narrative, downgrading of plot, de-dramatized acting, non-professional actors and the serial repetition of shots and, even, scenes. This combination of realism and formalism is then further complicated by an unstable integration of documentary elements with fictive elements – both documentary and fictive scenes being staged and, often, restaged more than once within a film – generating proliferating mise-en-abyme effects, in which it becomes unclear what is 'real' or documentary, and what is staged and fictive. The resulting aesthetic has made Iranian film the quintessential example of how a development of the neo-Bazinian aesthetic came to constitute a contemporary cinematic modernism.

The New Iranian Cinema has been prone to attacks from within Iran and from the Iranian diaspora accusing the films of ignoring the demands of Iranian audiences and instead presenting a very narrow perspective of Iran and its culture, a perspective which caters to the demands of a contemporary festival film 'international style'. More seriously for the filmmakers, despite international critical and popular success, the films still frequently run into difficulties with censorship at home and Iranian cinema remains vulnerable to changes of political direction within the regime, conservative elements in the Islamic leadership seeing Iranian art cinema and its international prestige as a dangerous thing. It remains a complicated situation: Abbas Kiarostami eventually turned to working abroad; Mohsen Makhmalbaf and his filmmaking family, including daughter Samira, moved into exile in Paris; and Jafar Panahi has had to work under varying degrees of house arrest in Tehran.

Given its recent historical context, two overlapping perspectives on Iranian cinema emerge. First, that Iranian cinema was essentially 'frozen' during the aftermath of the Islamic revolution and, in conditions of cultural isolation, variations on neorealism continued to be the default aesthetic for Iranian art cinema, whereas elsewhere postmodern stylistics or new realisms, derived from classical Hollywood rather than neorealism, became dominant. In other words, a distinctive cinema developed in Iran according to an 'internal' evolutionary logic precisely because of its isolation.[18] The second perspective is that while the Islamic revolution created an obvious interruption, there is an underlying continuity in Iranian cinema, to the extent that the Iranian New Wave is often seen as one phenomenon divided into a 'First', 'Second' and even 'Third' Wave. Either way, there is a critical consensus that the 1990s New Iranian Cinema was not a throwback to neorealism oblivious of recent trends in world cinema but a radical development, parallel to the new cinema emerging in Taiwan and refining the neo-Bazinian aesthetic that would come to inform contemporary cinematic modernism as an international style.

7

Contemporary cinematic modernism

Currents and controversies

Although most of the independent art-house cinemas that once thrived in metropolitan centres and university towns have closed, cinephilia has not, despite the anxieties of Susan Sontag and others, died but instead taken on a new generational aspect, driven by the proliferation of film studies as an academic subject in universities around the globe and by the access to films and new modes of reception enabled by DVD.[1] With the advent of digital streaming, through which almost every surviving film ever made becomes available online at the touch of a button, access to the history of cinema is becoming ever more freely available, backed up by myriad internet film sites, some more authoritative and informative than others, alongside an explosion of film blogs with their cultish tendencies. In other words, cinephilia and levels of 'cine-literacy' have probably never been higher than in the twenty-first century and never been more international in scope.

The idea that 'cinema' itself is constituted by films with particular kinds of artistic value remains potent. The debate over 'cinema' as an aesthetic, rather than merely a medium, flared up once again in 2019 when Martin Scorsese, bemoaning how the market dominance of the current Hollywood superhero franchises squeezes out other kinds of film from theatrical distribution, let slip the view that the superhero movies (and related fare) might not actually be 'cinema' at all but belong to some other tradition such as the theme park (to which might be added: video game, graphic novel or perhaps a twenty-first-century version of the 'cinema of attractions' from the pre-narrative cinema of the early 1900s).[2] Predictably the controversy went viral via the internet and amid the ensuing controversy Francis Ford Coppola weighed in declaring that the Marvel superhero films are 'despicable' and definitely *not* 'cinema'.[3] This controversy overlapped with an equally vexed debate over whether 'cinema' (including that informed by cinematic modernism) has migrated over to its old nemesis television, initially by way of the 'quality drama' Netflix series format, via digital streaming onto home cinema platforms.

As the Scorsese controversy shows, the idea of 'cinema' as an art and as an aesthetic is alive and well, if under constant pressure, and films which are considered to be part of the ongoing history and critical construct of 'cinema' continue to be made. In Hollywood, many 'art' filmmakers today can be identified within a genealogy of cinematic postmodernism – Quentin Tarantino, the Coen brothers, Wes Anderson and Sophia Coppola – while the majority of successful contemporary directors, from David Fincher, Kathryn Bigelow and Paul Thomas Anderson to Christopher Nolan, work their way through different genres and styles in ways which lie outside of any clear distinction between overarching conceptions of modernism and postmodernism – although when contemporary directors declare their influences and submit favourite film and filmmaker lists, their preferences are more often than not closely aligned with the auteur canon which originated with Bazin and *Cahiers du cinéma*, the new waves and postwar cinematic modernism.[4]

Despite, or perhaps because of, the relentless rise of the action blockbuster, of CGI special effects and superhero franchises, the 'neo-Bazinian aesthetic' deployed by the Taiwan and Iranian new waves that gained international recognition in the 1990s became a template for a global counter-cinema in the twenty-first century. This counter-cinema set itself against the dominant commercial cinemas of Hollywood, Bollywood, Hong Kong and elsewhere by deploying an austere realist aesthetic influenced by Italian neorealism combined with a self-reflexive formalist aesthetic. This particular configuration of neorealism and formalism is what this book has defined as 'contemporary cinematic modernism' and situated as belonging to a lineage that goes back to the postwar modernist film and its new waves. This book has further argued that while the postwar new waves diversified into several distinct aesthetic strands, contemporary cinematic modernism has tended to remain within a realist 'neo-Bazinian aesthetic', albeit often tending towards either the ascetic static formalism of Bresson and Ozu or the fluid sequence shot aesthete formalism of Antonioni and Tarkovsky.

Cinematic modernism has become a truly international style, often marketed as a 'new wave' emerging from a national cinema (Taiwanese, Iranian, Chinese, Romanian, Argentinian) and promoted through the auteur 'brand' of a director. The established canon of directors and notable films is too large to be listed here, suffice to say that representative auteurs of what this book is defining as contemporary cinematic modernism would include Hou Hsiao-hsien, Edward

Yang, Tsai Ming-liang, Apichatpong Weerasethakul, Lee Chang-dong, Jia Zhangke, Abbas Kiarostami, Mohsen and Samira Makhmalbaf, Jafar Panahi, Alexander Sokurov, Béla Tarr, Nuri Bilge Ceylan, Pedro Costa, Lucrecia Martel, Lisandro Alonso, Lav Diaz and Angela Schanelec – to name only a few of the most prominent directors. The next and final chapter, Chapter 8, will give readings of particular films by some of these prominent directors, while this chapter will attempt to provide context in the form of an overview of key indicative currents, tendencies and debates.

Currents of contemporary cinematic modernism

The Berlin School

The 'Berlin School' label designating a movement and aesthetic became attached to a group of young German film students attending the Berlin Film School (Deutsche Film und Fernsehakademie Berlin) in the 1990s where they were mentored by, among others, veteran radical filmmaker Harun Farocki. A network quickly developed linking up the Berlin group with young filmmakers in Munich and Vienna. As usual with film 'wave' labels there has been controversy over which directors belong to the Berlin School and over whether such a school or group actually exists. However, it is reasonably well established that a new generation of German filmmakers rejected the relatively mainstream wave of German 'history' films which had some national and international success in the early twenty-first century, films such as *Downfall* (2004), *The Lives of Others* (2006), *Goodbye, Lenin!* (2003) and *The Baader-Meinhof Complex* (2008). Regarding these 'cinema of consensus' films as exploiting stereotypes of German history, the Berlin School filmmakers instead looked back to the New German Cinema of the 1970s, especially Fassbinder, and the postwar European films of Rossellini, Bresson and Antonioni. In other words, they set about developing what this book is referring to as cinematic modernism in an updated neo-Bazinian aesthetic mode. The features of this aesthetic refashioned by Berlin School directors will be familiar: elliptical narratives, blocking viewer identification with central characters, slow pacing and dead-time duration, austere or minimalist mise-en-scène and de-dramatized long takes, whether static fixed-camera shots or fluid sequence shots.

The three core directors of the Berlin School were Christian Petzold, Thomas Arslan and Angela Schanelec. The larger network came to include Christoph

Hochhäusler, Ulrich Köhler, Benjamin Heisenberg, Henner Winckler, Maren Ade and Valeska Grisebach. The group produced their own journal *Revolver* and connected up with sympathetic directors internationally: Béla Tarr, Abbas Kiarostami, Jia Zhangke, Tsai Ming-liang and Jessica Hausner. The group also issued some radical declarations, notably Ulrich Köhler's 2009 'Why I Don't Make Political Films':

> If art is political then it is so in exactly this manner: it resists its appropriation for daily political and social concerns. Its strength lies in its autonomy.[5]

This statement sums up the group's ethos, not to make manipulative political message films but to make films with an aesthetic which challenges the viewer, generates a critical consciousness and resists appropriation by any major ideological formation. This revives a standard post-1968 strategy (Godard's old line: 'we don't make political films, we make films politically') and indeed goes back to the debates of the Frankfurt School in the 1930s. It is a position which resembles the arguments of Adorno (and Greenberg) that modernist aesthetics enable art to become autonomous (especially from the rest of the culture industry) and it is precisely in as far as art achieves aesthetic autonomy that it is 'political', that it stands in critical relation to society. The Berlin School films do not generally address political events head-on but instead portray a sensibility (often angst or alienation) in characters set against a contemporary socio-economic background. The films document a 'history' of the present not the past and the kind of history usually considered unrepresentable in film, not a dramatic event but a context such as the new finance capitalism, or immigration and racism, or the changing German identity since reunification.

The early Berlin School films attracted some attention in France but were not particularly successful in Germany and were vehemently condemned for undermining the German film industry, its commercial prospects and its international reputation, the main criticism being that the Berlin directors were making passé films, taking German cinema back to the post-1968 cinema of alienation. One prominent critic claimed after watching the premiere of Petzhold's *Gespenster* (*Ghosts* 2005) that he felt as if 'they had locked me up again in the hell of the German *Autorenfilm* [auteur films] of the 1970s, in which the protagonists remain meaningfully silent and each character functions as a metaphor for existential thrownness'.[6]

Marco Abel begins his detailed 2013 chronicle *The Counter-Cinema of the Berlin School* with the following concise summary:

> If one wanted a film-historical shorthand description for the films of the Berlin School, one could do worse than to start by considering how they tend to pursue an aesthetics of reduction reminiscent of the films by Robert Bresson, Michelangelo Antonioni, Michael Haneke, or the Dardenne Brothers, as well as second generation directors of the French New Wave such as Maurice Pialat, Jean Eustache, and Philippe Garrel, although a more contemporary filmmaker such as Thai-born director Apichatpong Weerasthakul has also left his mark (the ending of Köhler's third feature, *Schlafkrankheit* [*Sleeping Sickness*, 2011] seemingly evokes a film such as *Loong Boonmee raleuk chat* [*Uncle Boonmee who can recall his past lives*, 2010]). Many, though not all, Berlin School films are dominated by long takes, long shots, clinically precise framing, a certain deliberateness of pacing, sparse usage of extradiegetic music, poetic use of diegetic sound, and, frequently, the reliance on unknown or even nonprofessional actors who appear to be chosen for who they are rather than for whom they could be. In so doing, films such as *Milchwald* (Hochhäusler, *This Very Moment*, 2003) and Arslen's *Aus der Ferne* (*From Far Away*, 2006) sharpen the viewer's attention while effortlessly creating undramatic tensions. And cumulatively, these cinematic aspects stress the characters' spatiotemporal existence – the fact that unlike the films belonging to the 'cinema of consensus' cycle, these films unmistakably take place in a specific time and place: in the here and now of unified Germany.[7]

Abel locates the Berlin School firmly in a genealogy of postwar modernism – Bresson, Antonioni – but stresses the Bazinian 'realist' aspect of this modernism as reclaimed by the 1970s French post-new wave directors and the German New Cinema. Abel proceeds to connect up the Berlin School to the broader contemporary cinematic modernism in a second book, *The Berlin School and Its Global Contexts: A Transnational Art Cinema*, which presents a series of essays, each reading a Berlin School director alongside a contemporary international director: Abbas Kiarostami, Béla Tarr, Nuri Bilge Ceylan, Kelly Reichardt, Apichatpong Weerasethakul, Lisandro Alonso and Lucretia Martel – a familiar list, all aligned with cinematic modernism as a contemporary international style.[8]

Ulrich Köhler's *Bungalow* (2002) is about an unlikable young man on military service, Paul, who for no apparent reason decides not to rejoin his regiment and instead retreats to a bungalow (owned by his absent parents) where he does very little apart from irritate his brother (visiting with a girlfriend). *Bungalow* differs from the typical contemporary social realist film of Ken Loach or Dardenne brothers in that no motivation, psychology or social context is given other than a generalized alienation and sense of an impasse. The film also differs from social realist cinema in containing a number of bravura formalist shots, notably the beginning: a three-minute sequence shot in which a group of soldiers enter a Burger King, and one figure (who will only later be revealed as the protagonist of the film) gradually separates himself off from them and stays behind when they leave to return to their military trucks. This opening scene is mirrored in the final scene of the film in which Paul is apparently arrested for desertion and taken away by the military police, but the scene is filmed as a lengthy sequence shot, mostly filmed in long shot, Paul disappearing among the distant indistinguishable military personnel in the road outside the bungalow. The viewer scans and tries to 'read' the image, but, as in Antonioni's famous closing sequence shots, the meaning is left open as to what is actually happening: Does Paul's disappearance from the image signify his arrest or escape or something else?

It would be wrong to overstate the formalism of Berlin School films. Most of the films are grounded either in a standard (social) realism or in genre tropes. Petzhold's breakthrough film *Gespenster*, which so upset critics in 2002, is actually a fairly straightforward story of juvenile delinquency in a tradition going back to Truffaut's *400 Blows* and beyond, albeit *Gespenster* centres on girls rather than boys and incorporates contemporary concerns with child abuse and child abduction. Petzhold's strategy is to take old texts, old films and popular genres, and rework them to defamiliarize the political present. This is not the playful subversion or mixing and matching of genre and intertexts associated with postmodernism but a rigorous and respectful reworking of cinematic intertexts and genre tropes for a given political purpose. As such Petzhold's films are informed by the legacy of cinematic modernism, even if his films have gradually moved away from formalist aesthetics.

Barack Obama listed Petzold's *Transit* as one of his favourite films of 2019, further evidence perhaps that the Berlin School has turned out to be decidedly more mainstream as regards cinematic form than it might initially have appeared to both its detractors and its advocates.[9] The strength and the accessibility of the films which have emerged from the Berlin School was confirmed by Marin Ade's 2016 'comedy-drama' *Toni Erdmann* winning the FIPRESCI award at Cannes, an Oscar nomination for best foreign-language film at the Academy Awards and being polled by critics as the best film of 2016 in *Cahiers du cinéma*, *Sight & Sound* and *Film Comment*. That the Berlin School has been one of the more interesting cinematic 'waves' of the twenty-first century is clear, but the degree to which its directors and its films correspond to the cinematic modernism with which this book is concerned may be limited, with one obvious exception: Angela Schanelec.

From the outset Angela Schanelec was the most formally radical of the original Berlin School filmmakers and she has remained so, developing her signature style without compromise in a run of critically acclaimed films: *Passing Summer* (2001), *Marseille* (2004), *Afternoon* (2007), *Orly* (2010), *The Dreamed Path* (2016) and *I Was at Home, But* (2019). Schanelec's aesthetic can be summed up as 'elliptical'. She is not making avant-garde films, she is making recognizably modernist films: realistic narratives, stories, characters, in realistic settings (real locations), but the causal links between events that would constitute a plot are with-held, similarly spatial relations – the layout of a room or a street – are often obscured by compressed tightly framed shots and partial or blocked camera views which don't provide enough information for a viewer of the film to orientate their perspective of a given space. Elliptical edits often jump from one place to another. In *Marseille* the location jumps abruptly from Marseille to another place, Berlin, and then back to Marseille. Elliptical edits can also mark an abrupt shift forward in time – an hour or a day or years (in *The Dreamed Path* the central cut seems to cover several years) – the viewer only retrospectively reconstructing the temporal schema of a film. In addition Schanelec, despite the prevalence of conversations between characters in her films, has (like Chantal Akerman) abandoned 'shot/reverse shot' editing, further adding to the discontinuity of time and space and the instability of perspective. Almost uniquely in contemporary cinematic modernism, Schanelec's films foreground fragmentation and discontinuity, an almost Godardian return to the investigation of radical montage.

American indie cinema: Mumblecore to neo-neo realism

The label 'American indie cinema' has come to stand for a particular style as much as it might or might not refer to films which are actually produced independently of major studios or media platforms. The label, as presently understood, rejected the American experimental/avant-garde tradition of Brakhage and Mekas, instead embracing the realist/modernist example of Cassavetes and can be traced back to Jim Jarmusch's films of the 1980s, the label generally indicating a droll deadpan humour, a mixing up of 'high' (modernist) and 'low' (pulp trash) cinematic modes, constant cinematic intertextuality (borrowing from and referencing other films), pop-cultural references, self-consciously 'cool' romantic posturing, beatnik/punk/hipster attitude and a sensibility of ironic detachment: irony as a kind of autonomous aesthetic rather than having a satirical (socio-political) object of critique. Given these characteristics, American indie was therefore considered a key example of cinematic postmodernism, a view which appeared to be confirmed by the commercial and critical success of such films in the 1990s, culminating in phenomenal impact of *Reservoir Dogs* and *Pulp Fiction*, Tarantino being an idiosyncratic product of American indie and sharing many of its traits.

However, as discussed in the previous chapter, Jim Jarmusch's first two films, *Permanent Vacation* and *Stranger than Paradise*, look back to Italian neorealism and the French and German New Waves: realist locations and mise-en-scène, a casual improvised ambience and an existentialist sensibility of romantic alienation. The heyday of cinematic modernism (Rossellini, Antonioni, Bresson) was not rejected but was now only accessible through the mediation of reflexive irony. Such a level of mediation was already present in Godard and especially Fassbinder, but now even that brand of modernist irony became itself a retro object of ironic detachment. Yet any tendency towards parody and pastiche in American indie cinema was countered by a genuine desire to get out into the streets and into the apartments, with minimal crew and minimal script, to make realist films of social observation, mostly about the social and sexual codes and rituals of contemporary life as experienced by a young contemporary urban milieu, the obvious models being Rohmer and early Wenders.

Richard Linklater

One of the defining films of American indie, Richard Linklater's *Slacker* (1990) – clearly influenced by Chantal Akerman's *Toute une nuit* (*All Night Long* 1982) – is a chain of vignettes about (mostly) young people in Austin, Texas; more or less random short scenes which combine to provide a cumulative portrait of the 1990s Generation X. The film is both a kind of genuine contemporary neorealism and yet a droll parody of indie neorealism.

Linklater's ambivalence towards the heritage of cinematic modernism is explicit in *Waking Life* (2001). Ostensibly a remake of *Slacker*, it is structured by a similar chain of realist scenes recording characters in and around Austin engaged in conversation in everyday locations. In the conversations, the topics of which begin with Sartre and end with Kierkegaard, the idea of dreaming or 'lucid dreaming' keeps cropping up, along with its inevitable tag: How do I know when I'm dreaming? Do I spend my life in a daydream state interrupted by brief epiphanic moments 'awake' or vice versa? Basically *Waking Life* is asking the archetypal existentialist questions: How do I know I am alive? What does it mean to be truly ('authentically') living? I might be physically alive but is my life unreal? Am I living this life as if I were dead?

These are questions closely associated not only with postwar cinematic modernism (Antonioni, Bergman) and also with Bazin and Kracauer, for both of whom the issue of cinematic realism was inextricably bound up with questions concerning the nature of existence (how real is cinematic reality? is pro-filmic reality itself representational?) and existence as marked by time, by mortality: What is the temporal status of the present and presence – the reality – 'captured' on film? Is this past 'ontological' reality and these perhaps long-dead people – actors – on the screen 'mummified' (Bazin) or 'redeemed' (Kracauer)? Does cinema provide the possibility of a kind of immortality or merely a virtual ghostly afterlife? For Bazin the uncanny aspect of cinematic reality provides a clue to the uncanny 'virtual' temporal dimension of lived mortal existence.

Of course the postmodern conceit of *Waking Life* is that the film is animated, its increasingly anguished interrogation of reality is rendered via the completely unnaturalistic means of highly stylized animation. The film was staged and acted out and then the live footage was overlaid by animators using a contemporary digital version of the 'rotoscoping' technique.[10] The result is an animated approximation of the 'real' and 'live' footage. Although it initially seems that reality and real actors have become unreal cartoon characters, Linklater's intention is not to mock or parody but to defamiliarize cinematic realism in order to throw into relief its uncanny aspects. This intention is made amusingly explicit in a scene in which the unnamed protagonist (played by Wiley Wiggins) in his animated form enters a film theatre to watch a film entitled 'The Holy Moment' and finds himself watching and listening to a cartoon character on the animated screen within the screen, the character being Caveh Zahedi (the director of controversial 'real-life' autofictional films) in animated form and who proceeds to expound a version of Bazin's theory of cinematic realism. Bazin, according to Zahedi, thought that cinema can capture and redeem the essence of the lived moment – the 'holy moment' – the essential reality that is lost in the numbed flow of real life. In short, the idea familiar from Joyce, Proust, Woolf and early-twentieth-century literary modernism, that art redeems life by retrieving in aesthetic form its epiphanic moments or, to use Woolf's term, its 'moments of being'. The joke in *Waking Life* being that this declaration of belief in the holy reality of cinema is expounded by a real person who has been turned into an utterly unreal cartoon character in an animation film.

Mumblecore

At first the micro-budget 'DIY Indie' filmmaking movement – inevitably better remembered now as 'mumblecore' – appeared to be a kind of response to the

Dogme 95 manifesto which endorsed handheld camera filming of reality in its immediacy (real location and lighting) and forbid post-production. But the mostly European (Danish) Dogme filmmakers used 'anti-aesthetic' realist means to film set-up contrivances in the form of performative situations in the postmodern manner, the resulting 'hyper-realism' being a reflexive encounter with the 1990s explosion of docu-drama and 'reality television' and also, as Lars Von Trier's subsequent career confirmed, a critical encounter with modernist realism (Bergman, Dreyer, even Brecht). Mumblecore by contrast was a standard 'back to basics' return to the French New Wave and the spontaneous documentation of a generational milieu and its romantic ennui by way of improvisation upon loose narrative threads and low-key characterization. The contemporary significance of mumblecore lay in its non-parodic reworking of realist tropes and its foregrounding of dialogue, of naturalistic conversation rather than dramatic action. The mumblecore aesthetic is generally attributed to the influence of Eric Rohmer and John Cassavetes, but all the rudiments have been present in American indie since the 1980s, since Jarmusch's *Stranger than Paradise* and Linklater's *Slacker*.

The mumblecore strand of American indie is usually dated back to 2002 and Andrew Bujalski's directorial debut, *Funny Ha Ha*. Bujalski had studied film at Harvard with Chantal Akerman as a supervisor. Akerman therefore emerges again as a point of contact between the American independent cinema and the European, having in the 1970s represented a rare encounter of the European modernist cinema with the American experimental scene, then going on to influence Jarmusch and the American indie cinema of the 1980s, and now acting as a guiding spirit for the DIY mumblecore group in the 2000s. As with American indie of the 1980s and 1990s, the Akerman films influencing the DIY Indie of the 2000s are not so much the extreme formalist *Jeanne Dielman* as the looser digressive films *Je, Tu, Il, Elle* (1974) and *Toute une nuit* (*All Night Long* 1982). The mumblecore group came together at the 2005 South by Southwest Festival in Austin, which screened several related films including Bujalski's second film, *Mutual Appreciation* (2005). The idea of a mumblecore 'wave' was consolidated by a 2007 season at the IFC Center in New York, titled 'The New Talkies: Generation D.I.Y' and which screened ten films considered as part of a movement. The season featured *Hannah Takes the Stairs* (Joe Swanberg 2007) starring Greta Gerwig, who then acted in and co-wrote the comedy-drama *Francis Ha* (Noah Baumbach 2012), a film which marked the dispersal of the mumblecore movement into the mainstream, Gerwig going on to become a critically and commercially successful director with *Lady Bird* (2017) and *Little*

Women (2019), films which in different ways reflect a common strategy to make films informed by a contemporary feminist perspective.

The mumblecore films have been criticized as self-indulgent and narrow in their focus on white middle-class urban twenty-somethings – part of an already passé hipster milieu – mumbling interminably about themselves, without the charm or coherence (however misguided) of Rohmer's talkative young protagonists. However, like the Berlin School films – and Bujalski linked up with the Berlin filmmakers as kindred spirits – the mumblecore films capture something of the emerging anxieties and insecurities of the millennial generation as the realities of the gig work economy, extortionate rents and house prices and 24/7 social media became evident in the lead up to the 2008 financial crash.

Neo-neo realism

Alongside mumblecore, another strand of American indie film in the 2000s turned, apparently without any residual postmodern irony, to the example of Italian neorealism and a simplified version of the Bazinian aesthetic. This wave attracted attention with the success of Ramin Bahrani's first three films *Man Push Cart* (2005), *Chop Shop* (2007) and *Goodbye Solo* (2008). Roger Ebert praised *Man Push Cart*, a contemporary reworking of *Bicycle Thieves*, as a return to the authentic values – 'the very soul' no less – of neorealism:

> *Man Push Cart* was filmed in Manhattan by an American born in Iran and an American born in Pakistan, and embodies the very soul of Italian neo-realism. Free of contrived melodrama and phony suspense, it ennobles the hard work by which its hero earns his daily bread. He owns a stainless steel bagel wagon, which he pushes through the lonely pre-dawn streets. He sells bagels and sweet rolls and juice and coffee and many customers call him by his first name although they would never think to ask his last one. [. . .] Ramin Bahrani, the writer-director, shot his film on a shoestring, in less than three weeks. He often used a concealed camera, shooting what was really happening. There's a scene of unforced spontaneity when Ahmad offers to sell some bootleg videos. The two guys he pitches say they know where they can get bootlegs, two for eight bucks, in Brooklyn. The two guys did not know they were in a movie. [. . .] Ahmad's cart is stolen, and therefore his livelihood. We get a glimpse backstage of how the vending cart economy operates. What can he do without a cart and a way to replace it? He will, we understand, keep pushing, if not the cart, then something. 'Man Push Cart' as a title encapsulates human survival at a most fundamental economic level.[11]

Ebert went on to acclaim Bahrani as the best new director of the decade, praising *Goodbye Solo* despite the fact that the film was in part a homage to Kiarostami's *Taste of Cherry*, a film which Ebert had denounced as 'excruciatingly boring', 'the emperor's new clothes' and later listed as one of his 'most hated films of all time'.[12]

Like Roger Ebert, A. O. Scott in the *New York Times* endorsed realist films like Bahrani's, arguing that Hollywood-dominated American cinema had never allowed neorealism to develop but, with the 2008 financial crash and new ethnic/migrant social formations (and new inexpensive digital means of production), American indie cinema was at last in a position to access the unpretentious humanism and authentic social realism for which Italian neorealism remains the template. Using Bahrani and Kelly Reichardt as his main examples, Scott dubbed this realist turn in American indie cinema 'neo-neo realism'.[13] Richard Brody in the *New Yorker* immediately responded to Scott, criticizing the contemporary American neo-neo realist films as having the limitations of neorealism: its sentimentality, naïve naturalism and fetishization of the social. Brody argued that Rossellini (unlike De Sica) had overcome the limitations of neorealism in *Journey to Italy* through recourse to a modernist formalist aesthetic, rendering the psychological complexity of the alienated individual and in doing so had provided a bridge to the cinematic modernism of Antonioni and Fellini.[14]

Although the polemics were framed in opposing ideological terms, Ebert, Scott and Brody actually all share and privilege a humanism of the individual. Nevertheless, the polemics over neo-neo realism generated a debate about cinematic aesthetics which, unusually, attracted widespread attention: Ebert seeing the new realist films as an accessible and authentic counter to the obscurantist 'festival films' in the formalist-realist international style represented by Kiarostami; Scott arguing that neo-neo realism was somewhere in the middle, both social realist and reflecting the new formalist/existentialist international style (contemporary cinematic modernism); Brody regarding neo-neo realism as a throwback to superficial social realism, sentimental virtue-signalling 'message films' of limited aesthetic or psychological interest. The Scott and Brody polemic was part of a much broader debate which developed in two directions, either opposing or conflating neo-neo realism with the international style of cinematic modernism in its minimalist, contemplative and 'slow cinema' variant. The debate soon degenerated into a more general critical backlash against the ascetic international style, whether realist or modernist.

The confusion behind these polemics became evident with the scandal and success surrounding Kelly Reichardt's third film *Wendy and Lucy* (2008), the story of a young woman (played by Michelle Williams) en route to work in Alaska, who suddenly falls into homelessness in Oregon after a car breakdown and after being caught stealing dogfood from a supermarket for her only companion, Lucy the dog. Lucy is impounded, leaving Wendy without money, without a home, without transport and without a companion. The film's release coincided with the 2008 financial crash and was viewed as a representation of the new downward mobility, Wendy being an extreme example of the 'precariat' generation, always only a few steps away from falling through the cracks in the social and economic system, down into poverty and its associated ills.

Reichardt's debut film *River of Grass* (1994) had been a fairly typical 'postmodern' American indie film, a parodic noir anti-road movie about a would-be romantic outsider couple on a killing spree. By contrast *Wendy and Lucy* appeared to be 'straight' contemporary social realism informed by neorealism, with an obvious nod to De Sica's *Umberto D.* A. O. Scott praised *Wendy and Lucy* as one of the defining neo-neo realist films, while J. Hoberman praised the film in similar terms in the *Village Voice*:

> Spare, actor-driven, socially aware, and open-ended, *Wendy and Lucy* has obvious affinities to Italian neorealism. Reichardt has choreographed one of the most stripped-down existential quests since Vittorio De Sica sent his unemployed worker wandering through the streets of Rome searching for his purloined bicycle, and as heartbreaking a dog story as De Sica's *Umberto D.*[15]

But Hoberman is also careful to praise the unsettling ambiguity of the film and to declare it 'modest but cosmic' in its understated range and resonance. Richard Brody on the other hand, in a *New Yorker* review polemically titled 'Against *Wendy and Lucy*', denounced the film in his familiar terms: first dismissing De Sica for not having superseded neorealism as Rossellini had, and then denouncing *Wendy and Lucy* as both too social realist and too mannerist in its minimalism, a 'calculated blank':

> *Wendy and Lucy* is a work of self-conscious manipulation, in which Reichardt filters out the cinema's subjectivity and personalism in order to intensify the viewer's sympathy with a cipher. The ostensible objectivity of Reichardt's meticulous naturalism is a device that she uses to portray a sliver of physical reality as the whole truth; her rejection of psychology as well as of cultural context plays false and reeks of demagogy.[16]

Brody goes on to say that Reichardt's film projects a 'pseudo-universal neutrality', is 'message mongering', doesn't show Wendy's 'unfolding inner life' and his diatribe concludes in loaded but vague terms that Reichardt's film doesn't offer 'ambiguities and complexities' and that therefore the film is not endowed with the 'enduring mysteries of art'.

For its advocates *Wendy and Lucy* is a film that goes beyond neo-neo realism and in its low-key formalism (too easily labelled 'minimalist' or 'slow') achieves a complex poetic register, enabling the film to capture the 'inner life', the sensibility, not necessarily of its protagonist but of its historical moment: a vulnerable young woman caught in the growing web of a very contemporary socio-economic precariousness with all its attendant risks and dangers. To its detractors *Wendy and Lucy* is guilty of being a reductive social realist film *and* an obscurantist piece of minimalist slow cinema.

Whither Jean-Luc Godard?

After a comeback of sorts in the late 1970s and early 1980s – *Sauve qui peut (la vie)/(Every Man for Himself/Slow Motion*, 1980), *Passion* (1982) – and a brief flurry of controversy over *Hail Mary* (1985), Godard's post-new wave films fell into a prolonged neglect. Regarded as incoherent and incomprehensible, by the late 1980s few of his films were even considered worthy of a release outside of France. Although Godard himself is fiercely loyal to the specificity of the film theatre and the large screen, the development of home viewing platforms (particularly DVD) facilitating repeat viewing and close analysis has been responsible for a rehabilitation of 'late' Godard and the acclaim granted to *Eloge de l'amour* (*In Praise of Love*, 2001) and *Notre Musique* (2004). It has belatedly become apparent to critics and a sizeable international audience that Godard's films are not incoherent but constructed with extremely dense layers of montage. The appreciation of late Godard has been helped by the success of *Histoire(s) du cinéma* (1988–98) which, aside from its provocative story of cinema, provides clear insights into the way Godard has continued to elaborate his theory and practice of montage.

From his earliest films Godard embraced montage to a degree that constituted a veritable Oedipal rebellion against Bazin. When Godard did use the long take, as in the thirty-minute take of Bardot and Piccoli arguing in their apartment in *Le Mépris* (*Contempt*, 1963), it was both a self-conscious formalist exercise (proto-structuralist) and a parody of the long-take aesthetic. Since the early 1980s and *Passion*, Godard has been developing montage which generates correspondences of image across a film as a whole, rather than to the images immediately juxtaposed. This is standard modernist practice. In *Ulysses* Joyce has almost every word carry allusions, symbolism or a *leitmotif* function which relate to other words or phrases hundreds of pages earlier or later in the text. Montage in late Godard produces relationships between almost every image within a film and sometimes from one film to another: a particular shot of blue sky, white cloud or waves on the shore; part of a body or a gesture; an intertextual image or shot. Such cross-referencing also occurs on the soundtrack through the repetition of certain fragments of speech or music or the sound of gulls crying, a dog barking. Variations on Godardian montage can be widely seen in advertising and music video, and arguably can also be discerned in the hyper-kinetic fast cutting style of recent action films such as the *Bourne* series, though without Godard's extreme 'serial' or 'mosaic' patterning, redolent of certain 'parametric' styles of montage associated with postwar cinematic modernism. By contrast contemporary art cinema remains militantly anti-parametric montage, preferring the Bazinian option of integral durations and montage immanent to the long take. There are, however, exceptions, including Angela Schanelec as mentioned earlier and directors like Mike Figgis and Jonathan Glazer as discussed below.

Three British directors: Mike Figgis, Jonathan Glazer and Joanna Hogg

Mike Figgis

Although in terms of sensibility associated with postmodern cinema of the 1990s, Mike Figgis remains an avowed Godard fan, and his *Hotel* (2001), with its large starry ensemble cast playing a film crew holed up in a Venice hotel, attempting to rehearse and shoot a Dogme version of Webster's *The Duchess of Malfi*, is reminiscent of late Godard films like *Passion*, *Detective* and *King Lear* in its set-up and 'estranged' Brechtian performance modes (and default recourse to sexual fetishism). The cast of *Hotel* improvised most of their scenes and lines in Venice with little or no idea of what the final film was supposed to be, Figgis extracting and constructing *Hotel* from the improvised material in the editing process after shooting had finished. The 'unsteady steadicam' digital camerawork jumps back and forth between multiple storylines and, as in late Godard, almost every image is then treated (e.g. colour saturation or filtering, or different types of image framing including multiple variations on the split-screen). This overload of image treatment is not particularly integrated with the storylines, *Hotel* sometimes resembling a guide to the then-new digital in-camera and post-production special effects.

More successful critically and commercially than *Hotel*, cult favourite *Timecode* (2000) manages to be both Godardian and Bazinian.[17] Filmed on location off Sunset Boulevard, *Timecode* sets up four distinct but carefully interlinked storylines revolving around a chaotic Hollywood film production office. Each part of the ensemble cast developed their storyline through improvisation and then, unlike in *Hotel*, acted out a whole narrative strand in one continuous take. The eventual film consists of four continuous ninety-three-minute takes, digitally filmed simultaneously by four cameramen. When shown in theatres the screen is divided into quadrants, each quadrant showing one of the complete takes. The viewer watches all four storylines but the sound mix (and dialogue) features one narrative and then another, so the viewer tends to focus primarily on one narrative strand at a time, while still being aware of how the other three narratives are progressing. Figgis has performed different live 'mixes' of the film at special showings and on the original DVD it was possible for viewers to perform their own audio mix of the four storyline screens. If *Hotel* was marked by Godardian fragmentation and discontinuity, *Timecode* – despite the split into four screens – accentuates the continuous; the simultaneity of the four uncut takes generating a real-time tension, a foregrounding of the present continuous. *Timecode* obviously owes a lot to the experimental cinema of the 1960s, particularly Warhol's split-screen *Chelsea Girls* (1966) which used complete reel continuous takes to be projected in random orders. The split-screen technique, albeit without any aleatory component, briefly made its way into the mainstream in the late 1960s in films such as *The Thomas Crown Affair* (Norman Jewison 1968) as well as music films such as *Woodstock* (Michael Wadleigh 1970). *Timecode* is both Godardian (montage of the four juxtaposed screens, quadrants or image tracks) and anti-Godardian, that is to say Bazinian, in that *Timecode* presents four continuous sequence shots, all occurring in the same real-time ninety-three minutes, maintaining the same integrity of real time and real space across four simultaneous interrelated narratives.[18] As Mike Figgis told Richard Williams in *The Guardian*:

> Editing is a huge series of gimmicks with which we've all become overfamiliar. [. . .] The marriage between editing and plot has got to such an extent now that the audience is hooked on this constant adrenalin delivery. [. . .] I've been struggling the last couple of years to find different narrative forms. This film [*Timecode*] is delivering constantly the idea that you might be missing something, so you can't afford to go and take a piss or take your eyes off the screen. People who watch it seem far more alert, whether they like it or not, because of the degree of attention required to watch the film.[19]

Timecode, like Sokurov's equally celebrated ninety-six-minute single take *Russian Ark* (2002), is filmed digitally, which many critics argue alters the 'cinematic' integrity of the long take (particularly regarding possibilities for post-production). Figgis retains a 'postmodern' ironic humour – *Timecode* gives a parodic nod to vintage minimalist experimental cinema in its opening sequence and throughout to the Altmanesque ensemble cast multi-narrative form, and the film ends with a young woman filmmaker, Ana, presenting a spurious film theory-laden pitch to the production company commissioning meeting:

> Montage has created a fake reality . . . my film goes beyond the paradigm of collage, of montage. Eisenstein and Vertov were influenced by Russian formalism with its theory of estrangement, the estrangement of the image in a poem, in cinema the isolation of the image, the isolated take . . . capitalism has absorbed these innovations . . . [digital] technology is demanding new sensations, my film will be an unmade film, one continuous take, in real time . . . imagine four cameras in sync, each of these cameras will follow one character, the characters are going to meet with each other, creating the plot of the story.[20]

This is a comically reflexive pitch for *Timecode* itself, the film we have been watching, couched in Bazinian terms – one continuous take, loosely digressive narratives and so on, but the meeting ends with a tragi-comic shooting incident and Ana filming the company mogul (played by Stellan Skarsgård) as he lies slowly bleeding and dying after being gunned down.

If Godard remains an exception in recent art cinema in foregrounding montage rather than the long-take sequence shot, the 'serial' or 'mosaic' editing style developed by Resnais and Robbe-Grillet in films such as *Hiroshima mon amour* (1959), *Last Year at Marienbad* (1961), *Muriel* (1963) and *l'Immortelle* (1963) is even rarer. This style enjoyed a vogue in the 1960s, particularly in Eastern European film, as a means of representing the (modernist) stream of consciousness, often with 'flash' cuts for fleeting memories and fantasies, and briefly entered the mainstream as a kaleidoscopic editing stylistics evoking the psychedelic experience. The only director who took this up this kind of editing as a signature style was Nic Roeg in his run of classic films from *Performance* (1968) through to *Bad Timing* (1980). An updated variation on the Roeg style ('psychic montage' as discussed in Chapter 4) can be discerned in the films of Jonathan Glazer.

Jonathan Glazer

Jonathan Glazer's debut film *Sexy Beast* (2000) tapped into a millennial vogue in mainstream British cinema for the 'geezer' (London) gangster genre. In its basic characterization, dialogue and plot *Sexy Beast* adheres to the genre stereotypes, with a happily retired gangster (Ray Winstone) on the Costa Del Sol being lured back by Don (Ben Kingsley), a psychotic gang member, to England for one last heist. However, images from the narrative sections belonging to sun-drenched Spain appear in the grey London sections and vice versa. Similarly, images relating to key events, the heist itself or the killing of psychotic Don, occur intermittently in different narrative contexts. There are also dream sequences and outlandishly surreal images. In other words, *Sexy Beast* updates the mosaic montage technique in its 'psychedelic' manner, traceable back to 1960s gangster films such as *Point Blank* (Boorman 1967) and *Performance* (Roeg and Cammell 1968), complete with flash cuts and subliminal edits.

Under the Skin (2013) is a striking example of a thoroughly contemporary film deploying, perhaps even 'subverting', stylistic and thematic elements associated with postwar cinematic modernism, Glazer claiming to be inspired by a standard modernist auteur canon: Fassbinder, Pasolini and Bresson.[21] *Under the Skin* is a hybrid of contemporary genre tropes drawn from science fiction, horror and, in its finale, woman-in-peril thriller. The film is also loaded with very current subtexts concerning identity, gender and race.[22] The basic story is of an alien who takes the form of a woman (played by Scarlett Johansson) and who encounters various humans, mostly men interested in her sexually, who then die in a surreal scenario of absorption into the void, presented as passing down and through into a liquid mirror, a scenario which can be interpreted any number of ways, for example as men passing into the void of sexuality/femininity as a mirror of deluded masculine desire. Similarly reminiscent of *Orphée*, the bodies of the alien's victims are dispatched at the hands of an alien accomplice in the form of a Cocteauesque 'angel of death' motorcyclist.

Like *The Man Who Fell to Earth* (Roeg 1976), *Under the Skin* is less interested in the alien than in seeing the human world from the alien's perspective, seeing 'under the skin' of mundane everyday reality, behind its familiarity, in order to render that everyday reality strange. It is not so much the visitor from another planet who is alien but the human world which is alien from the visitor's perspective. Much of the film consists of the alien, calling herself 'Laura', driving around Glasgow and the Scottish Highlands in a commandeered white van, looking at the world around her from the van and occasionally venturing out into that world: a Glasgow street, a shopping mall and department store, a nightclub techno rave, a highland restaurant. Laura observes the world through her windscreen with a range of deadpan expressions closer to Mr Badii in *Taste of Cherry* than Travis Bickle in *Taxi Driver*, and it is up to each viewer to interpret each expression. This means that viewers not only are likely to project their own

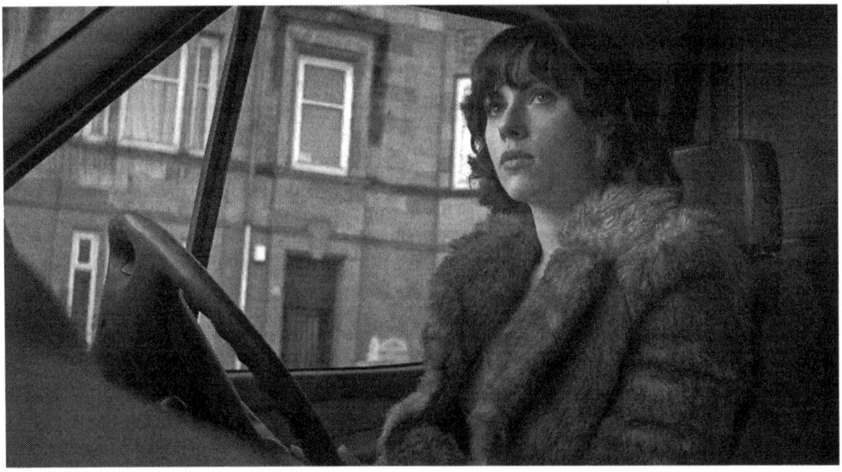

Figure 15 *Under the Skin* (2014), Jonathan Glazer.
In an obvious reversal of the cinematic norm, a young woman drives around the city, cruising, picking up men, voyeuristically looking at the world and its people from the safety of the bubble of her vehicle. Laura (Scarlett Johansson) observes the world through her windscreen with an inscrutable gaze, a gaze which becomes the object of the obsessive gaze of the camera (and viewer) from every angle, in this case from an uncertain position below the driving wheel and looking up and across at the young woman's eyes.

conscious and unconscious fantasies, fears and prejudices onto Laura (as figure of the alien, the other) but are also likely, through her, to project their own interpretations onto the people, situations and objects she sees (this space for interpretation extends to the ideological subtexts of the film). The 'minimalism' of expression in Johansson's acting in this role is combined with a minimalism of script. The original *Under the Skin* novel (Michel Faber 2000) and early screenplays had more elaborate plot, characterization, dialogue and backstory, but Glazer gradually removed these layers, eliminating almost all background context and dialogue until he was left with a bare-bones episodic narrative, allowing for improvisation in each scene. As such *Under the Skin* contains some of the formal features of ascetic minimalist cinematic modernism. For scenes of people in Glasgow streets, Glazer uses jumpy fast cutting in the style of French New Wave street scene montage, reserving static long takes for shots of Laura sitting in her van staring out at nothing in particular, inviting the viewer to scan and read Laura/Johansson's face and eyes in a vain attempt to fathom her inscrutable gaze (Figure 15).

Aside from the minimalist elliptical narrative and deadpan acting, the aspect of *Under the Skin* that has garnered most critical attention is its use of verité modes of cinematic realism, especially given the film's unrealistic science fiction genre trappings. According to Glazer and his producer James Wilson, large parts of the film originated in Johansson driving the van each day with ten concealed surveillance cameras in the van filming whatever incidents happened on the drive, Johansson improvising her reactions to and (banal) dialogue with strangers she encountered, as Glazer and Wilson recounted to *The Guardian*:

> For life to feel real, he [Glazer] decided, they needed real life. Extras shouldn't just be non-professional actors, but people who didn't even know they were being filmed, caught on hidden cameras when she pulled up at the roadsides of Glasgow. (Glazer and crew were concealed in the back.) She was hardly ever rumbled; who expects to be accosted by Johansson on their way to the Asda in Govan? She was, Glazer says, 'Devoted. Unflinching.' And as she chose where to drive next, Glazer – as with most directors, used to being in control – gladly gave up his film to the random.
>
> 'There were times I said to Jim [Wilson], Let's just dump the last two-thirds of the script and stay in the van. Because I loved the idea of leaving the door open to reality. The surprises. The treasure.'
>
> There is more to *Under the Skin* than the van. Besides the abstract social realism is a skeletal story, heartbreak, horror, extraordinary sweetness. But if the goal was to make the humdrum lurchingly strange, it worked. As Johansson totters through a Glasgow shopping centre, passing between Clinton Cards and H. Samuel, the human environment looks so unshakably weird. [. . .] Wilson pleaded with him [Glazer] to book conventional extras, have a scripted Plan B. Wilson explains: 'I was saying: "What if Scarlett drives all day and nothing happens? What if there are no happy accidents?" But Jon was insistent. And he was right.'[23]

Like Bowie's alien in *The Man Who Fell to Earth*, Scarlett Johansson in *Under the Skin* begins by looking at this strange human world with an objective neutral gaze before gradually becoming more human physically, emotionally, psychologically and becoming more empathetic and therefore more vulnerable. And as with Bowie's alien Newton, for Johansson's Laura the process of humanization is largely figured as sexualization, a kind of contamination by human sexuality. Johansson spends the first half of the film as a cruising predator of men, subverting cinematic gender stereotypes, but ends the film as a woman-in-peril victim – the alien becomes human by 'becoming a woman' in a pastiche of de Beauvoir (a process defined in the last part of the film by genitalia, sexual intercourse, rape and death), integrated into a 'heteronormativity' that will result in her annihilation.

Such ideological interpretations of *Under the Skin* in terms of early-twenty-first-century gender (and racial) politics are legitimate – the film sets up an allegorical register in order to generate such resonances and the film deploys certain Cronenbergian body-horror tropes to figure the 'monstrous other' of both masculine and feminine sexuality. Yet such readings can be reductive and miss the primary aim of the film to present not a particular monstrous other but otherness itself. Glazer says that he is not a fan of sci-fi, he dismisses *Star Wars* and its ubiquitous contemporary ilk, predictably aligning *Under the Skin* with Tarkovsky and Kubrick and, like their forays into science fiction, *Under the Skin* foregrounds ideas and images which are intended to remain unfathomable:

> [T]he science fiction that I've loved has been the science fiction that somehow remains inscrutable. 'Solaris' (1972) I am thinking of, '2001: A Space Odyssey' of course. Something remains unfathomable or inscrutable about the ideas. Not inscrutable, but just philosophical. [. . .] I think I have a genuine interest in form, and in the form of film, and in the opportunity in the medium of film. Film is a kind of offshoot of theater, filmed theater. That doesn't interest me enough. I'm more closely connected to silent movies and the power of images and how images somehow bypass the intellect and we view them at a deeper level.[24]

As in almost all modernist aesthetics, primacy is afforded to ellipsis and the image. Ellipsis – the partial yet radical erasure of narrative causality – is a precondition for creating images with the degree of autonomy required to both facilitate interpretation and yet indefinitely defer narrative and interpretative closure.

Under the Skin is an example of a contemporary film which acknowledges current stylistic trends and mainstream genres and modes – science fiction, horror, thriller – while also being informed by classical postwar cinematic modernism (self-reflexive formalism) and the neo-Bazinian aesthetic, including the use of 'documentary' source material for the representation of reality within fictive narrative-based modes. *Under the Skin* marks the assimilation of contemporary cinematic modernism into a broader hybrid category of contemporary cinema in which realism and non-realist genre modes interact.

Joanna Hogg

In the 1980s heyday of postmodernism, British cinema enjoyed a modest revival in its international standing due to directors such as Peter Greenaway, Derek Jarman and Sally Potter and their quintessentially postmodern films including *The Draughtsman's Contract* (1982), *Caravaggio* (1986) and *Orlando* (1992) respectively. In the twenty-first century directors like Peter Strickland continue to work out of this lineage and its tendency towards intertextual and genre pastiche in radically new ways, while other directors such as Lynne Ramsay, Steve McQueen and Jonathan Glazer seem more inclined to reconnect with a cinematic modernism which assimilates postmodern stylistics to varying degrees. In such a context Joanna Hogg stands out as an anomaly in British cinema by self-identifying uncompromisingly with the aesthetics of a 'pure' cinematic modernism. Aside from her own work as a director, Hogg has been a driving force behind the A Nos Amours collective, named in homage to the 1983 Pialat film and dedicated to screening classic or rare films by Bresson, Tarkovsky, Rivette, Bergman, Duras, Béla Tarr, Kiarostami, Tsai Ming-liang – a veritable roll-call of modernist auteurs, postwar *and* contemporary. The collective's most ambitious project has been what purported to be the world's first complete Chantal Akerman retrospective, held at different venues across London over a period of three years.

The traditional strengths of British cinema have been social realism and literary adaptation 'heritage' or period/costume drama film, the latter often unfairly maligned as a redundant 'cinema of quality' (in Truffaut's pejorative sense). Hogg's films initially confused critics because they appeared to be social realist but were set in an upper-middle-class social milieu more indicative of 'heritage' cinema. The upper-middle classes if they appear in films by Ken Loach or Mike Leigh are invariably cast as derided caricatures, yet this social strata has increased rather than declined in importance with regard to the sociology of the contemporary city, most evidently in relation to both gentrification and the precariat, and needs to be properly represented in contemporary cinema. Hogg's decision to focus on this class strata is explained with self-deprecating humour in *The Souvenir* (2019) in which the autobiographically based middle-class protagonist Julie is a young student at film school. For her graduation project Julie is attempting to make a worthy film about the struggles of a working-class single mother in Sunderland. It is obvious that Julie knows nothing of the life she is filming and that the project is ethically dubious if not outright exploitative. The implication being that it would be far more credible – and useful – if Julie made films about lives in the upper-middle-class social world she actually has experience of.

Hogg spent most of her early career as a director making gritty social realist drama for British television, including many episodes for prime-time BBC series such *Casualty* and *EastEnders*. In complete reaction against her television work, Hogg embraced the tradition and aesthetics of cinematic modernism in order to represent – with empathy but not uncritically – the culture, psychology and sensibility of the London and Home Counties upper-middle class, a social milieu which provides a point of access to a broader representation of twenty-first-century social structures and mores. This strategy resembles the transition in postwar Italian cinema from neorealists taking the working class as their subject to the later films of Antonioni and Fellini which took the middle-class beneficiaries of the 'economic miracle' as their subject. In a diagnosis similar to that in Antonioni and Fellini's films, the upper-middle classes in Hogg's first two feature films *Unrelated* (2007) and *Archipelago* (2010) are portrayed as afflicted by an alienation resulting from chilly emotional repression and family dysfunction. *Exhibition* (2013) portrays a sophisticated socially progressive couple – both artists – living in a beautifully designed modernist house, which not only acts as a protective cocoon against an often hostile urban world outside on the London street but also incubates the tensions within the couple's relationship. *Exhibition* is filmed in a way largely determined by the house and its interiors: geometric shapes, clean framing lines – verticals, horizontals and diagonals – and most strikingly the glass surfaces which form much of the exterior of the house, surfaces from which reflections proliferate, creating a constant play not just of light but of image. *The Souvenir* (2019) has a more sharply delineated narrative and more precisely drawn characterizations manifesting a nuanced and sometimes deceptive clash of class cultures. Unlike the preceding films *The Souvenir* is set in the past, in the 1980s, but aside from the occasional piece of music, hairstyle and item of clothing, the film eschews 1980s retro cliché. The film is experienced in its 'present', not as something safely consigned to a past cultural moment. Although Hogg's earlier films had a repressed quality which always seemed about to – and sometimes did – explode into visceral conflict or implode into despair, *The Souvenir* calls the repressive veneer into question from the beginning with its central narrative of the futility of disavowal in relation to heroin addiction. *The Souvenir* picked up a 'film of the year' position in practically every critic's poll of 2019. Having initially alienated audiences and critics with her object of study, the contemporary British upper-middle class, and alienated some still further with her stylistic debts to Antonioni, Rohmer and Pialat, Joanna Hogg's cinematic modernism has opened up unexpected new possibilities for contemporary British film.

Controversies in contemporary cinematic modernism: Slow cinema, transcendental style, modernist pastiche

Slow cinema

Various labels have been used: 'minimalist', a term going back to the experimental cinema of the 1960s; 'contemplative', a term favoured by partisans of this type of film; but 'slow cinema' is the label that has stuck, partly (as is often the case) because the label is readily deployed by those critics who denigrate this type of cinema and what it supposedly represents with regard to various cultural and ideological anxieties of the day. A 'slow food' movement emerged in Italy in the 1980s, reasserting the value of slow preparation, slow cooking and slow eating in opposition to a rapidly expanding fast food and ready meal culture. In the twenty-first century the general perception is that the pace of life has accelerated dramatically, partly because of the advent of 24/7 social media, and there have been many 'slow' and 'calm' lifestyle movements in various spheres purporting to resist the relentless speed of modern life. In cinema 'slow' has occupied a tangible position of resistance because of the conspicuous dominance of fast action special effects driven blockbuster film in mainstream cinema.

Veteran *Positif* critic Michel Ciment is credited as having first attributed slowness to a kind of cinematic international style as it emerged as something identifiable on the film festival circuit. Jonathan Romney in *Sight and Sound*, although an advocate of the films themselves, began applying the label in a somewhat wry fashion in various film reviews. Matthew Flanagan attempted to theorize and provide a genealogy for the types of film associated with 'slow cinema' in his 2008 paper 'Towards an Aesthetic of Slow in Contemporary Cinema', while an inaugural 'As Slow As Possible' film and media festival was held in Newcastle in 2012. Slow cinema was attacked in a 2010 *Sight and Sound* editorial by Nick James, sparking a heated debate over whether this type of film had degenerated into empty mannerism.[25] Less subtle controversies occurred elsewhere, particularly in the United States, mostly reruns of the old 'entertainment versus art' or 'Hollywood versus Europe' debates about film from the 1960s when such diatribes were peppered with obligatory attacks on Antonioni, Bergman and European art cinema.[26]

In recent years a number of academic books have been published on slow cinema, but Flanagan's paper remains the most concise introduction:

> In defiant opposition to the quickening of pace in mainstream American cinema, a distinctive narrative form devoted to stillness and contemplation has emerged in the work of a growing number of filmmakers over the last two decades. Most widely exhibited on the festival circuit, this 'cinema of slowness' (as categorised by Michel Ciment in 2003) has begun to signify a unique type of reflective art where form and temporality are never less than emphatically present, and a diminution of pace serves to displace the dominant momentum of narrative causality. The most distinctive active practitioners of such a style might be thought to comprise, in loose chronological order, Philippe Garrel,

> Chantal Akerman, Theo Angelopoulos, Abbas Kiarostami, Béla Tarr, Aleksandr Sokurov, Hou Hsiao-hsien, Tsai Ming-liang, Sharunas Bartas, Pedro Costa, Jia Zhangke, Apichatpong Weerasethakul, Lisandro Alonso, Carlos Reygadas, Gus Van Sant and Albert Serra.[27]

As will be evident from Flanagan's list of filmmakers, there is an overlap between slow cinema and what this book is attempting to delineate as contemporary cinematic modernism. Or to put it more precisely, 'slow cinema' is a critical discourse about one strand of the broader category of cinematic modernism. Flanagan is alert to this, referring to an 'aesthetic of slow', which to a greater or lesser degree informs various contemporary films rather than designating an exclusive category or label 'slow cinema'. He then goes on to relate the 'aesthetic of slow' to how Bazinian conceptions of cinematic realism tend to lead towards the long take, away from montage, and the influence of this tendency on postwar modernist film. Flanagan notes that the narrative ambiguity and de-dramatization characteristic of contemporary slow cinema is also a more or less conscious borrowing from modernist film, singling out the Deleuzian trope of a narrative digression in which a figure walks through a disorientating cityscape or landscape (itself a borrowing from the modernist novel: *Ulysses*, *Mrs Dalloway*, *Revolving Lights* and Benjamin's reading of the flâneur):

> This form of de-dramatisation has its roots in European modernist cinema of the 1950s and 1960s, where emotional restraint began to suppress dramatic incident and the themes of alienation, isolation and boredom usurped the weight of familiar conflict. An aesthetic of slow exaggerates this tendency toward de-dramatisation, draining emotional distance and narrative obfuscation even further by extending the stretches of temps mort and subordinating non-events to extended duration within the shot. One direct factor of influence stems from the modernist introduction of a 'cinema of walking', the lineage of which can most likely be traced from Rossellini's *Viaggio in Italia* (1953) to Antonioni's *L'Avventura* (1960) by way of Varda's *La Pointe Courte* (1954) and Resnais' *Hiroshima mon amour* (1959).

As Flanagan suggests, formal 'restraint' is generally intended to increase not lessen emotional impact and many viewers would argue that the much imitated steadicam mobile tracking shots of figures walking in Béla Tarr's films, especially *Sátántangó*, do not mark de-dramatization or even slowness, but are shots of agitated movement and carry an intense often ominous emotional and narrative charge. This points to a more general issue, that the category of slow cinema tends to focus on a few surface techniques rather than the underlying meanings and effects generated by those techniques in particular films. An opposition is set up between the (cult) stylistics of slow and (mainstream) viewer resistance in the form of boredom and incomprehension. Similar debates occurred a century ago over the modernist novel – Joyce, Woolf, Richardson, Proust – which typically consisted of elliptically juxtaposed long-duration scenes or episodes described in minute detail but without dramatic action or events. These novels were regularly denounced as lacking interest in action, plot or characterization. Postwar, such debates were repeated with Alain Robbe-Grillet, Nathalie Sarraute, Michel Butor and the *nouveau roman* and again with Beckettian drama – *Waiting for Godot* – and the hostile reception to Pinter's early plays like *The Birthday Party* which, before they became intelligible to audiences, seemed slow, boring and meaningless.

Faced with the impasse of subjective responses to the aesthetic of slowness and their relativity – one person's boredom is another person's excitement and one person's slow might be another person's fast – Flanagan takes a Bordwellian turn to empiricism, towards stopwatch-in-hand number crunching of statistics governing ASLs – average shot lengths. The statistics don't clarify the aesthetic value of a given film, but the concern with ASLs does raise questions which takes us back to the divide in cinematic modernism between the Bazinian long take and Eisensteinian montage.

Montage, the time-image and fast cinema

In the early 2000s David Bordwell noted a new default style emerging in mainstream cinema, what he called 'intensified continuity':

> Camera movement has increased, yielding relentless tracks and pans seemingly unmotivated by the logic of plot, staging or performance. The sustained medium (or medium-long) two-shot has been replaced by close framings and single shots, thus enabling editors to manipulate the temporal progression of events far more readily. Intensified continuity has transformed a cinema of efficacy into a cinema of acceleration.[28]

What Bordwell labels 'intensified continuity' arguably designates its opposite: discontinuity, what Matthew Flanagan describes as 'visuals segregated by cuts that serve to fragment rather than unify'. Although numerous mainstream action films have adopted variations on 'intensified continuity', the films that have come to exemplify this style are the *Bourne* series, particularly the three films in the franchise directed by Paul Greengrass: *The Bourne Supremacy* (2004), *The Bourne Ultimatum* (2007) and *Jason Bourne* (2016). The films concern an amnesiac secret CIA operative/assassin (played by Matt Damon) trying to find out who he is and why he is on the run and from whom. *The Bourne Ultimatum* (2007) generates an average shot length of just under 2 seconds, compared to an average shot length of 151.4 seconds in Béla Tarr's *Sátántangó*.[29] Clearly there is a self-conscious diametric opposition in average shot length between contemporary action cinema and slow cinema, but in the same way that the slow variant of cinematic modernism should not be reduced to the long take, contemporary action cinema should not be reduced to fast cutting. There needs to be some contextualization in terms of the aesthetic of both types of film and the purpose of a given aesthetic.

In Bazinian terms the purpose of the long take is not necessarily to slow down the pace of a film, but to allow for montage *within* the sequence shot (and within depth of field), to allow events of varying degrees of significance to unfold within the ostensible temporal integrity of the long take, to allow 'reality' to reveal itself within the aesthetic form. Because Deleuze seems to make a distinction between the (Hollywood) action film as all but synonymous with the 'movement-image' and the modernist film (postwar European art film), with its de-dramatization and downgrading of 'action', as all but synonymous with the 'time-image', there is an assumption that modernist film, particularly in its 'slow' variants, embodies the time-image and that the long take constitutes the cinematic image of Bergsonian duration. But it could be that the time-image also emerges in accelerated serial/mosaic montage of the early Resnais type (*Muriel*, 1963) or in late Godard (*Passion*, 1982), and it would now appear that the widely perceived rapidly accelerating speed of life in the twenty-first century is generating new aesthetic forms to represent new temporal flows.

Paul Greengrass made his reputation directing radical social realist documentaries for British television, a figure somewhere between Ken Loach, David Garnett and Nick Broomfield, with strong roots in the cinema-verité movement. Greengrass was brought in to take over directing the *Bourne* films in order to bring a 'direct cinema' style to the franchise and, according to Bordwell:

> Greengrass claims that his creative choices [for the *Bourne* films] were influenced by the cinema-verité documentary school and cites as well *The Battle of Algiers*, which helped popularize the handheld look in the 1960s.[30]

Jerky handheld camerawork has been used since the 1960s to evoke a documentary immediacy and urgency *as an aesthetic effect*. Or, in the case of the 1990s Dogme films, for *faux*-verité parodic effect. It now seems to have lost its documentary referent, transcended its parodic register and become an aesthetic designating kinetic energy, speed *and a fragmented unknowable reality*. The *Bourne* films are exemplary in this regard because they create an elliptical narrative form, something usually associated with cinematic modernism, and do so by combining several techniques in a contemporary manner: very short shot lengths and a variety of framings (sometimes jerky, sometimes 'wobbly') which present fractured partial images of characters and actions within disorientating spaces. Together these techniques have created an aesthetic of accelerated fragmentation and discontinuity. If slow cinema supposedly bores and sends some viewers to sleep, it has been widely reported that some viewers find the *Bourne* films incomprehensible and the jerky visuals nauseating or headache-inducing. Bordwell concludes:

> So *Ultimatum* raises the stakes by applying the run-and-gun style in a more thoroughgoing way. Everything is dialled up a notch. The flashbacks are more expressionistic than those of *Supremacy*: instead of dark hallucinations we get blinding, bleached-out glimpses of torture and execution, in staggered and smeared stop-frames. The conversation scenes are bumpier and more disjointed; the cat-and-mouse trailings are more disorienting, with jerky zooms and distracted framings; the full-bore action scenes are even more elliptical and defocused. It's as if the visual texture of *Supremacy's* tunnel chase has become the touchstone for the whole [*Ultimatum*] movie.[31]

As discussed previously, András Bálint Kovács in *Screening Modernism* elaborates a complex taxonomy of modernist film, which can be reduced to four broad categories: naturalist (Rossellini), minimalist (Bresson), theatrical (Rivette) and ornamental (Fellini); and two basic archetypes of form: continuous (Antonioni) and fragmented (Godard).[32] 'Slow cinema' would mostly correspond to a modernist-informed convergence of the naturalist, minimalist and continuous categories, while the use of handheld camera work, jerky (what Bordwell calls 'unsteady steadicam') or otherwise, and close framing is ubiquitous in 'realist' films, mainstream and art, whether 'continuous' or 'discontinuous', especially since the advent of digital video filming – a recent striking example of the new 'intensified' digital aesthetic in neo-Bazinian realist film would be Hu Bo's *An Elephant Sitting Still* (2018). 'Slow cinema' is therefore but one strand of contemporary cinematic modernism and a brief consideration of directors as different as Abbas Kiarostami, Béla Tarr, Jia Zhangke and Angela Schanelec would suggest how reductive the 'slow cinema' label can be in describing a contemporary realism defamiliarized by modernist formalist features and incorporating a range of responses to the idea of the time-image.

Transcendental style in film revisited

> *What began as a four-second shot of a passing train in Ozu grows to eight minutes of meandering cows in Béla Tarr.*
>
> – Paul Schrader[33]

Paul Schrader wrote *Transcendental Style in Film* in 1971 when he was a young film student at UCLA film school and working as a budding film critic for the *Los Angeles Free Press*. Having only recently left behind an upbringing in a Calvinist religious community, Schrader had been unusually alert to the fact that a certain type of film dealt with issues of redemption, salvation and matters of the spirit at the level of content, and that cinema at an aesthetic level could itself be an experience of the otherness associated with religious ritual and revelation.[34] Inspired by a couple of Susan Sontag essays on Bresson, Schrader developed an idea that in film the encounter of a realism of the mundane everyday with rigorous stylistic formalism often denoted an attempt to access this spiritual or transcendental experience, the common formal features being austere camerawork and mise-en-scène, non-expressive acting and low-key but formalistic editing, features producing overall effects of objectivity, neutrality, de-dramatization, silence, slowness and stasis.[35] Schrader explained this idea of a universal 'transcendental style' with reference to three directors from different cultural backgrounds and different film industries: Ozu, Bresson and Dreyer.

Transcendental Style in Film was widely read despite being entirely at odds with film theory of the time and it has remained an influential text, while Schrader went on to success as screenwriter of *Taxi Driver* and as director of *American Gigolo*, *Mishima* and many other films. With the advent of contemporary cinematic modernism, especially in its slow cinema variant, his book has taken on an obvious resonance, and for its 2018 reissue Schrader has written a much-discussed new introduction 'Rethinking Transcendental Style'. Initially it appears that he now considers what he had thought in 1971 was a transcendental style specific to a handful of directors was actually one strand of a much broader movement, that of a modern and 'mature' cinema which emerged after the war with Welles's *Citizen Kane* but more importantly with Rossellini and neorealism and which went on to take many forms in the art-house and new wave film of the 1950s, 1960s and 1970s. This is of course the Bazinian story of the emergence of modern cinema and Schrader acknowledges the continued centrality of Bazin to his own thinking, but after he wrote the original book in 1971 two things happened:

> What Happened? Gilles Deleuze happened. So did Andrei Tarkovsky.[36]

According to Schrader, Bazin's story of the two ages of cinema is clarified by Deleuze's theory of the shift from cinema of the movement-image to cinema of the time-image, the 'transcendental style' being but one manifestation of this broader shift.

> World War II dates the rough demarcation of a shift, more in Europe than America, from movement-image to time-image. Screen movement still occurred, of course, but it was increasingly 'subordinated to time'. What does this mean? It means that a film edit is determined not by action on the screen but by a creative desire to associate images over time. Man exits one room, enters another – that's movement-image editing. Man exits one room, shot of trees in the wind, shot of train passing – that's time-image editing. Man exits one room, the screen lingers on the empty door. That's time-image editing. Deleuze calls this the 'non-rational cut.' The non-rational cut breaks the sensorimotor logic. Deleuze first sees this in the deep-focus films of Welles but, for practical purposes, it comes to the fore in walking/wandering films like Rossellini's *Voyage in Italy* (1954), Antonioni's *L'Avventura* (1960), Resnais's *Hiroshima Mon Amour* (1959) and *Last Year at Marienbad* (1961). This time-image reached first full expression in the films of Yasujiro Ozu. 'The vase in *Late Spring* (1949),' writes Deleuze, 'is interposed between the daughter's half-smile and her tears. . . . This is time, time itself . . . a direct time-image which gives change unchanging form.'[37]

Schrader notes that Deleuze begins *Cinema II* with a discussion of the same four-minute sequence of Maria the maid doing her chores in the kitchen in *Umberto D* which Bazin had discussed as a key example of the modern film in *What Is Cinema?* eighteen years earlier.[38] However, Schrader goes on to argue, Deleuze's concept of the time-image modifies Bazin in crucial ways and the emergence of the time-image in Rossellini and De Sica, *Journey to Italy* and *Umberto D*, combined with the formalism of Bresson, leads to a long process of development through which the time-image reaches its culmination in the films of Tarkovsky:

> Tarkovsky rejected the Soviet school of montage in favour of André Bazin's 'ontology of the photographic image' and Bazin's advocacy of the Italian neorealists. Bazin felt that with the invention of moving photographs, the age-old artistic desire to represent reality had reached its apotheosis. Cinema was 'as complete an imitation as possible of the outer world.' Sergei Eisenstein felt that the power of cinema was in its ability to orchestrate reality. Bazin said it was just the opposite: the power of cinema was not to manipulate reality. Neorealism revealed 'the aesthetic implicit in cinema.' 'Neorealism knows only immanence,'

> said Bazin. 'It is from appearance only.' For Bazin the long take favored by the neorealists enabled spectators to choose what they wanted to see rather than what had been dictated by montage.
>
> Tarkovsky embraced Bazin. Then he turned neorealism on its head. Bazin had written, 'The photographic image is the object itself. The object freed from the conditions of time and space that govern it. Viewed from this perspective, the cinema is objectivity in time. Now, for the first time, *the image of things is in the image of their duration*' [Schrader's italics]. Of the duration of the Eskimo waiting for the seal in Flaherty's *Nanook of the North* (1922), Bazin said, 'The length of the hunt is the very substance of the image, its true object.' But for Tarkovsky duration was more than mere waiting. It was Henri Bergson's '*durée*', duration, time itself, the vital force governing and meditating on all organic life.
>
> Tarkovsky stands in a line of documentary observers of life. Also in the line are contemplative stylists Ophüls, Mizoguchi, Rossellini, Resnais, Dreyer, Bergman, Ozu, Bresson. What exactly makes him so special?
>
> Here's what I think is the difference: Ozu, Bresson, Dreyer, Mizoguchi, De Sica and the rest used film time to create an emotional or intellectual or spiritual effect. Tarkovsky used film techniques to study time. For Tarkovsky time was not a means to a goal. It was the goal.[39]

Schrader's account can be summarized as follows: Bazin argues that cinema has arrived at a new image of 'revealed' reality, Deleuze then argues that Bazin's image of reality is saturated with the image of time; the image of temporal duration takes precedence over any other reality in the image. Notwithstanding the spiritual and existential content in his films, Tarkovsky represents the apogee of this process by which aesthetic form comes to be 'over-determined' by the time-image. The time-image primarily represents itself – time and duration, not a spiritual transcendence. Tarkovsky was doing and representing lots of other things (not least spiritual transcendence), but it is his representation of time that made him the 'fulcrum' (Schrader's term) of the cinema of the time-image. Schrader argues that it was inevitable that cinema of the time-image would arrive – and probably end – with 'slow cinema', a cinema which is wholly defined by its relationship to, and representation of, temporal duration.

Schrader reviews the various strands of contemporary art film and proposes three main categories: *the surveillance camera film*, which has developed out of Bazinian neorealism and documentary cinema verité and in which a film more or less objectively and obsessively records or interrogates a given reality; *the art gallery film*, in the lineage of minimalist experimental film and now aligned with the aesthetic of the gallery installation rather than cinema; *the mandala*, the contemplative and meditative film. Schrader's point is that all three of these tendencies converge around the aesthetics of slow cinema: primacy of image (over dialogue and sound) and autonomy of individual image, visual flatness, long take, static camera, dead-time/*temps mort*, slow pacing, repetition (of shots and motifs), non-dramatic acting; or to put it more starkly, the aesthetics of minimalism and slowness.

This book has argued that the contemporary art film converges around an aesthetic of cinematic modernism that is relatively narrow (compared to the cinematic modernism of the 1960s) and is rooted in a neo-Bazinian aesthetic and the Deleuzian time-image, that is to say an aesthetic engaged with reality and time (and the otherness of both), but this book has also argued that this aesthetic can't be reduced to one particular characteristic such as slow pacing or the foregrounding of duration for its own sake. The time-image may involve multiple differing temporal flows and might even involve 'fast cinema'. And are so-called 'dead-time' shots actually emptied of meaning and emotion? As Deleuze and Schrader suggest, viewers are often reduced to a flood of tears by the shot of the vase from *Late Spring*, not because of the beauty of the vase, but because the vase, though not exactly symbolic, embodies displaced emotion bound up with the relationship between the father and daughter and the theme of the stages and cycles of life, the passing of time and intimations of mortality.

Very few contemporary directors identify with the label 'slow cinema' or see slowness as anything other than a means to a greater aesthetic or thematic end. Films like *Taste of Cherry*, *Sátántangó*, *Colossal Youth* and *Still Life* all have themes concerning society, social groups and aspects of the 'human condition' in its particulars and its universals and all have complex narratives and narrative structures and strong characterizations. The best of these films are only slow to viewers not accustomed to the cinematic conventions being utilized. For viewers who are conversant with the conventions of contemporary cinematic modernism, *Taste of Cherry* and *Sátántangó* are not slow but very concentrated and intense. The scene of the little girl Estike killing and burying her cat and then killing herself in *Sátántangó* may deploy long takes and foreground extended duration, but it must rank as one of the most dramatic and intense scenes in recent cinema and functions as part of the complex interlocking narrative – and temporal – structure of *Sátántangó*. Even the infamous meandering cows in the eight-minute prologue of *Sátántangó* are not just any cows but cows carrying thematic and satirical resonances and foreshadowing crucial aspects of the plot.

Schrader appears to conclude that modern cinema, the cinema of the time-image, leads to and ends in slow cinema. However, a more sceptical reading of 'Rethinking Transcendental Style' suggests that Schrader may be constructing a straw-man argument in order to justify, not revise, the thesis of his original 1971 book. First, it will be recalled that for Schrader a truly spiritual transcendental style – Bresson, Dreyer, Ozu – is austere and ascetic and effaces itself. By contrast in Tarkovsky the sublimity of style and form is exhibited in every shot. Schrader's 'transcendental' directors are noted for their fixed or static shots, Tarkovsky is noted for the fluid long-take sequence shot. Tarkovsky's films wear their religious and spiritual thematic garb too explicitly and clumsily because, according to Schrader, they do not aim at a universal transcendental style but are instead an expression of Tarkovsky's selfhood. Even 'cinematic time' is, in Tarkovsky, a means of (narcissistic) personal expression:

> A transcendental guide or guru or film director self-effacingly seeks to escort the respondent to another level of consciousness, a Wholly Other world. The transcendental film director is a 'spirit guide'. Tarkovsky was more interested in passing through the portal himself than he was in escorting his viewer.[40]

Tarkovsky represents, for Schrader, as for Kovács in *Screening Modernism*, the end of postwar modernist cinema, but an unfortunate one. Worse still, slow cinema has returned to this cul-de-sac and, in a futile attempt to revive Tarkovsky's cinema of the time-image and its stylistics, has reduced it to a set of formulaic mannerisms. This subtext to Schrader's account becomes clear when he admits to his sympathy with the common complaints against slow cinema: it is boring, an indulgence in ennui, it goes against the very essence of cinema which is action and empathy, slow cinema is 'passive-aggressive' towards the long-suffering viewer.[41] To which he adds that whereas Bresson, Dreyer and Ozu developed their authentic hard-won transcendental style within the commercial and profane world of cinema as a mass medium, slow cinema only exists on the film festival circuit and in the art gallery, reliant on patronage, not a ticket-buying audience in a cinema.[42]

Schrader's ultimately negative account of slow cinema reflects a common critical opinion that the contemporary art film has reached an impasse and that slow cinema is a symptom of that impasse. When an art form reaches such an impasse the next stage is usually critical negation in the form of self-reflexive pastiche modes. In contemporary cinematic modernism this negation is represented in very different ways by the films of Pedro Costa and Albert Serra.

Contemporary cinematic modernism: The uses of pastiche

If the neo-Bazinian international style of cinematic modernism is to survive, it will likely do so via a further self-reflexive twist, one which inevitably involves an irony about its own aesthetic and in which reality ceases to be something found and revealed and once again becomes something self-consciously performative and mediated by pastiche cinematic genre modes: Fassbinder rather than Bresson. Two directors represent this option by which contemporary cinematic modernism might evolve beyond the impasse of slow or contemplative cinema mannerism.

Although both Pedro Costa and Albert Serra are self-styled 'punk' provocateurs and both have been associated with slow cinema minimalism, they have completely different sensibilities. Costa is engaged in an avowedly serious attempt to represent a contemporary social milieu at the ethnic and class margins of a modern European neoliberal economy, while Serra is engaged in darkly comic or absurdist pastiche in the form of fantastical recreations and reconfigurations of historical narratives. What they share is an embrace of digital video as a means of filming cheaply with few time constraints and filming unobtrusively, recording 'reality' with little intervention. The style of shooting may resemble that of documentary but both Costa and Serra set up scenarios, dialogue and characterization as the raw material to be filmed, that is to say 'reality' is initially 'staged' to a greater or lesser extent, and then the films are constructed in the editing process out of the hours of raw footage. The staging and the editing are dictated primarily (and in the classic modernist fashion) by the search for *images* intuitively felt by the directors to have originality and depth, images both precisely determinate and yet with an indeterminacy facilitating ongoing interpretation on the part of the 'active' not 'passive' viewer, to use the terms privileged by modernism. These images are carried by the form of long static takes respecting the integrity of real-time durations and are structured by elliptically juxtaposed narrative episodes.

Costa and Serra both deploy stylistic pastiche. They construct images which 'quote' films and paintings with regard to framing, angle of perspective, body posture and gesture, facial expression and – notably – play of light. Costa draws heavily from silent film, German expressionism and classical Hollywood horror stylistics (Tourneur) in the staging and lighting of his images. Another connection between Costa and Serra is that for all the references to classical and modernist directors, their main influence might be the 'documentary/theatrical' wing of 1960s American experimental cinema – distinct from the abstract, structuralist wing – such as the films of Andy Warhol/Paul Morrissey in which minimalistic theatrical scenarios are staged in real locations with 'real' people, often non-professional actors turned 'Factory Superstars', and then the camera is pointed at the action and whatever happens (or doesn't happen) is filmed until the reel runs out. The result resembles a documentary 'direct cinema' recording of a role-play event in which the lines of documentary reality and the theatrical or cinematic cross and converge. The new digital technologies allow filmmakers like Costa and Serra to film as much and as surreptitiously as they want, without the intrusive awkwardness of Warhol and Morrissey with their bulky apparatus of cameras and microphones, cables and leads, but the aesthetic which emerges has a family resemblance. In Warhol a camp or trash self-reflexivity emerges from the encounter of an objective documentary realist mode with staged theatricality. Neither Costa nor Serra is aligned with camp or a trash aesthetic (although Serra comes close) but, as with Warhol, it is the collision between a documentary impulse and theatricality which produces a new kind of critical realism[43].

Pedro Costa

Pedro Costa's debut feature *O Sangue* (*Blood* 1989) has an elliptical narrative concerning three youngsters (two brothers and a girlfriend) trying to continue normal life after the death of the brothers' father while they unravel a web of debts, deceit and criminality in the family legacy. Filmed in stylish black and white, *O Sangue* is full of elegantly staged and executed shots, many of them carrying an echo of particular shots from films of classical Hollywood melodrama, horror and noir, although the overall ambience is closer to the haunting menacing quality of gothic than noir, close to the surreal nightmarish quality of *Night of the Hunter* (Charles Laughton 1955). The retro style and its sheen, along with the pastiche intertextual 'quoting' of other films, made *O Sangue* feel like a superior example of a 1980s postmodern 'cinema of quality'.

The equally well-received follow-up *Casa de Lava* (1994) complicated things somewhat. Inspired by Jacques Tourneur's *I Walked with a Zombie* (1943), the film tells the story of a nurse caring for a migrant labourer injured in a work-place accident in Lisbon and now in a coma. The young nurse accompanies the comatose body of the man back to his home in the former Portuguese colony of Cape Verde. Apart from the skeleton of the story – a black man in coma as the 'zombie' and the white woman as his uncomprehending nurse – the film doesn't owe that much to Tourneur or horror, being shot not in gothic chiaroscuro but in bright colour in sun-blanched landscapes and Costa resists an explicit zombie angle, whether as horror motif or as allegory of (black) colonial subjects struck down into paralysis by (white) colonialism. Instead Costa prefers to follow various narrative digressions involving characters from both the Cape Verdean community and the Portuguese colonials who have washed up on Cape Verde and don't seem able to leave, including Edith, the central white 'local' character, who came in the 1960s searching for her lover, a political prisoner held in fascist dictator Salazar's prison camp on Cape Verde. The lover is long dead but Edith has never left. Costa is less interested in revealing and analysing the tangled web of political histories than in tracking the effects of these histories. Not an allegory of colonialism as paralysis but, for all the characters in the film, existential limbo as a fact of life.

When filming on *Casa Lava* finished, members of the Cape Verde community involved in the film gave Costa letters to take with him back to Lisbon, to deliver to migrant relatives working there. Costa found most of the letters were for migrants living in the small ramshackle Fontainhas shanty town in Lisbon, an area populated by African migrants from the former Portuguese colonies alongside the Lisbon junkie 'underclass'. Costa befriended some members of this underclass and for *Ossos* (*Bones* 1999) cast them as themselves-playing-themselves-as-characters in a loosely fictional narrative of a mother trying to sell her child. The film therefore navigated the well-worn blurred line between documentary and fiction with 'reality' or 'truth' immanent not in the documentary 'real' but in the 'imaginary' produced by the collision between documentary and fictive modes. *Ossos* was a critical and commercial success but Costa was afflicted by doubts, aesthetic and ethical, about invading and filming the Fontainhas inhabitants in the conventional way, with a large film crew and imposing a fictional narrative upon the reality of the inhabitants' lives. He then befriended a heroin addict, Vanda Duarte, and took to visiting her and her fellow addicts in their rooms. Filming alone with a digital camera, improvising lighting set-ups with whatever came to hand, Costa stayed with Vanda and her circle for several hours each day, over many weeks, filming their conversations and drug routines in static long takes.

A kind of ethnological practice – with the junkie subculture as its object of study – developed with all the usual vexed issues: Does the direct cinema 'fly-on-the-wall' approach capture the objective reality of what is being filmed? Or does the filmmaker's presence influence and distort the reality being filmed? These issues have been debated since Flaherty's *Nanook of the North*, but *In Vanda's Room* (2000) poses these issues in an acute way because the events being filmed are taking place in a limited space, in a room and Costa is in the room, with his camera and apparently not partaking in the drug taking.

There is another connection here with the 1960s American experimental cinema of Warhol/Morrissey and films like *Chelsea Girls* (1966), but Andy Warhol's non-judgemental verité objectivity in filming junkie life purported to be apolitical, blank, whereas Costa is non-judgemental about what he is filming but politically conscious and extremely aware of the politics of class, gender and race. Liberated by low-cost digital filmmaking, Costa filmed whatever was happening on a particular day, the 'found' or 'pro-filmic' reality, but like Flaherty he also set up narrative ideas incorporating the pro-filmic events and (unlike Warhol) would film these scenarios multiple times; over several months Costa accumulated a vast amount of filmed material, much of it therefore resembling multiple takes. This mass of footage could then be edited in a relatively conventional way – selecting the strongest takes, the strongest performances, the strongest images, and reconstructed to create a loosely 'narrative' film.

Costa had experienced an epiphany about what kind of film to make and how to make it. This led him to reject the art-house 'cinema of quality' but *In Vanda's Room* was a challenging and uncomfortable film for the viewer – a three-hour minimalist film of static long takes rendering the life of a heroin addict in an underclass milieu – and unsurprisingly the film was decidedly unpopular with audiences. Costa gained confidence in his methodology by filming a documentary on Jean-Marie Straub and Daniele Huillet *Where Lies Your Hidden Smile?* (2001). Since the 1960s Straub and Huillet have sustained their uncompromising aesthetic based on quotation and intertextuality and combining de-dramatization with theatrical staging, elliptical fictive narrative with documentary, all in the service of a Brechtian critical distancing. Inspired by the example of Straub and Huillet, Costa returned to the Fontainhas shanty town, again spending months staying with selected members of community, again combining documentary footage with staged scenarios and dialogue. Costa filmed in rooms and back alleys, hundreds of hours of footage were shot and then assembled into an elliptical narrative in the editing room, the result being the epic *Colossal Youth* (2006).[44] This film again featured members of the Lisbon junkie underclass, including Vanda, but featured more of the migrant Cape Verdean community, many of whom had worked in the construction industry on major prestigious building projects (the premise of *Casa de Lava*), but were now left without work, old or disabled by work-related injuries and illness, left to waste away in the netherworld of Fontainhas.

The central character, Ventura, a stately looking Cape Verdean is cast by Costa as a kind of village elder with a shamanic aura and the film follows Ventura on his perambulations around Fontainhas, visiting the residents of his realm, dispensing enigmatic wisdom and repeatedly reciting from memory an affecting love letter in which a man addresses his distant beloved with his dreams and his hopes of giving her 'a hundred thousand cigarettes, dresses, a car'. The letter represents the futile dreams of migrant construction workers in Lisbon pining for the loves they left back in Cape Verde, but it first appeared in *Casa de Lava* as the letter of a Portuguese political prisoner in Salazar's prison camp in Cape Verde and, in fact, the lines of the letter are largely taken by Costa from an actual letter written by surrealist poet Robert Desnos in the 1940s from a Nazi concentration camp just prior to his death. The poetic letter is real but not real – a composite put together by Costa and put to different purposes in more than one film. The status and function of this letter corresponds to Costa's cinematic approach: an abject reality is filtered through a poetic cinematic aesthetic consisting of a composite of visual 'quotations' from silent film era expressionism, classical Hollywood and postwar modernist film, alongside 'quotations' from Flemish painting (Figure 16). This aesthetic stages effects rather than causes (Costa is not interested in the particular case history of a political prisoner, migrant worker or heroin addict) and lends autonomy to the effects, universalizing romantic longing, despair, frustration, loneliness, melancholy, and this universalizing in turn works the other way: humanizing and individualizing those who might otherwise be defined and dismissed as just another anonymous migrant worker or junkie.[45]

As Costa was filming *Colossal Youth* the Fontainhas slum was being demolished and the residents dispersed around Lisbon to newly built flats in blocks on distant estates. Costa incorporates this transition into his film, contrasting the organic quality of the slum with the antiseptic white walls of the new apartments, the implication being that for all its degradation, and notwithstanding Costa portraying Fontainhas as a Hades populated by the undead in limbo, the slum was an authentic community, preferable to the social atomization of the new estates. It is this 'romantic' message projected by Costa the middle-class outsider that emerges from *Colossal Youth*, despite his giving primacy to the autonomy of images in an attempt to foreclose just such romanticism, such banal socio-political messaging. Accusations of exploitation, exoticization and nihilistic romanticism are almost inevitable given that Costa is constructing films out of the poverty and misery of his subjects. To take just one example, Ventura was not in actuality regarded by the Fontainhas residents as a wise elder, he was instead known as an alcoholic with a serious mental health condition. His nobility, his status as a 'colossus' of the community, is

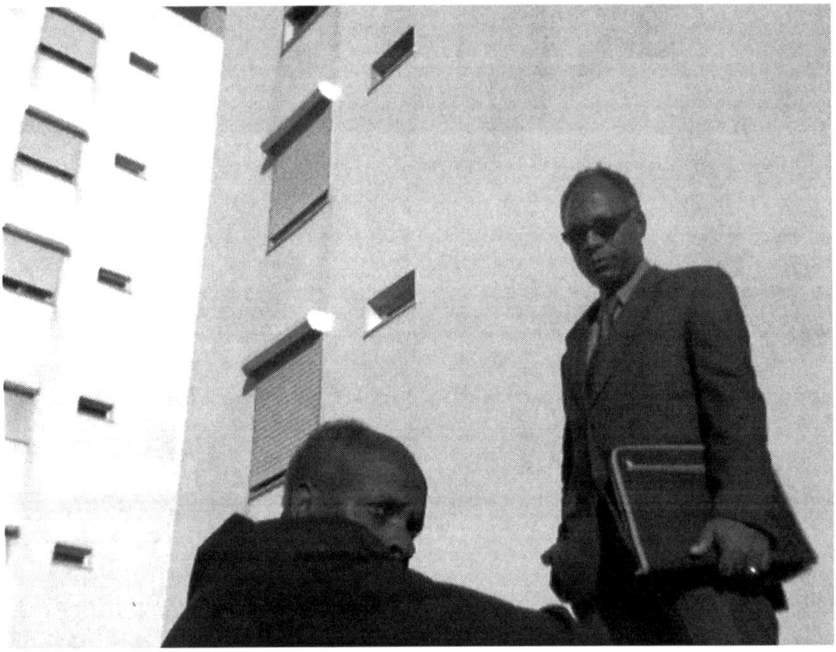

Figure 16 *Colossal Youth* (2006), Pedro Costa.
An abject reality is filtered through a poetic cinematic aesthetic consisting of a composite of visual 'quotations' from silent film era expressionism, classical Hollywood and postwar modernist film. Filmed from a low expressionist angle, Ventura stares into space, looked down upon (in every sense) by the official overseeing his rehousing into the anonymous white tower blocks which dominate the figures and dominate the image; the minimalist white modernist architecture is designed to look antiseptic, to resist contamination by modernity's underclass.

created by Costa the filmmaker, although it might be argued that his aura in the film sublimates an acknowledgement of his actual vulnerability. But perhaps the problem of reductive messaging and allegorization is a bigger concern: Is *Colossal Youth* an existentialist film concerning old age and the failure of youth and its unrealistic dreams? Or is *Colossal Youth* 'about' Portuguese colonialism, about the failure of the 1974 revolution, about the failings of neoliberalism in the 1980s and 1990s? Is *Colossal Youth* about racism or about liberal white guilt? Or are these films a critique of the leftist's 'bourgeois' antipathy for the 'underclass'? And so on. Costa's desire to avoid any further accusation of such platitudinous messaging might explain why, after *Colossal Youth*, in subsequent Fontainhas films *Horse Money* (2014) and *Vitalena Varela* (2019) the elliptical nature of the narratives is further accentuated – time, place and narrative causality are unstable as is characterization – the films as a whole becoming surreal and ghostly, an unreliable memory of a recurring nightmare, the meaning of which remains open to each viewer and the collective unconscious. *Horse Money*, featuring a now elderly and infirm Ventura, deals with the (non)relationship between black Cape Verdean migrants and the white Portuguese revolution of 1974 by replaying certain incidents from 1974 as a ghost play, repressed memories which 'return' as symptoms of denial, characters as the undead caught in a limbo of history from which they struggle to awake: migrant construction workers, revolutionary students and army soldiers are all equally immobilized, like Ventura, in the madness of a petrified afterlife. Any stirring of the Portuguese political unconscious raises the question '*whose* unconscious?' to which the film would appear to answer a collective 'ours', but this unconscious or afterlife is represented as a nightmare Foucauldian institution in which blacks and whites still occupy different positions of power.

In his essay 'Pedro Costa's Politics' (2009) Jacques Rancière takes a pessimistic view, arguing that art can no longer analyse, evaluate or judge, it can no longer intervene in the world on behalf of the oppressed, art can only – and Rancière credits Costa as being the first filmmaker to fully understand and accept this – provide, through a defamiliarizing stylization deploying cinematic intertextuality, quotation and non-ironic pastiche, an aesthetic space for representation in which the 'invisible' experience of the oppressed might become discernible:

> Cinema cannot be the equivalent of the love letter or the music of the poor. It can no longer be the art that simply gives back to the humble the palpable riches of their world. It should consent to being merely the surface on which the experience of those relegated to the margins of economic circuits and social pathways seeks to be ciphered in new forms.[46]

Albert Serra

Albert Serra has been a conspicuous presence on the film festival circuit over the last decade with a punk shtick and channelling the provocateur spirit of Fassbinder. Long takes, long shots, static camera, elliptical narrative, de-dramatization – initially Serra seemed to be yet another purveyor of the slow cinema aesthetic. *Honor of the Knights* (*Honor de Cavalleria* 2006) – featuring two non-professional actors playing Don Quixote and Sancho Panza wandering the hills of Catalonia with only oblique references to Cervantes's text – established Serra's modus operandi: select an interesting landscape and a small group of (non-professional) actors chosen in the manner of Fellini or Pasolini for the way their physical character or bodily presence interacts with the landscape and then, by way of the skeleton narrative of a well-known historical text, allow the cast to role-play their characters within the landscape in episodic scenes loosely derived from the text.

Although these episodes are artfully filmed by Serra's accomplished camera crew, the hours of footage shot in digital video merely provide source material for the editing process. Like most films, Serra's films are 'created' in the editing process, however it would be truer to say that in a Serra film the source material is 'mediated' by the editing process. This is not Eisensteinian or Godardian montage but closer to Rossellini: in the editing process Serra is searching for particular images (usually in the form of an extended scene or episode) which the director intuitively feels have a resonance or power in themselves. These image-scenes are then juxtaposed with other extended image-scenes with a similar relative autonomy in terms of their resonance or strength, but the juxtapositions or order of image-scenes are determined by the residual structure of the original narrative or text.

Where does the resonance, power or strength of an image reside? What Serra is looking for are those image-scenes which teeter on the edge between the recreated historical past (of the narrative) and the present in which the film is being shot, between extreme naturalism (real non-professional actors in real time in a real landscape) and extreme theatricality (the actors are both playing 'themselves' and playing their characters in the narrative) and, it might be added, between the comic and the serious and, often, between the sacred and the profane. Serra sets up a project in which these opposites or contradictions flourish in the making of the film, and the work of editing is to reveal and select those image-scenes in which the contradictions are simultaneously most evident and yet reconciled within the overall aesthetic of the film – and only a few image-scenes contain both these qualities at the same time. Editing is a kind of filtering process, filtering out the 'weak' images and then structuring the whole film around these 'strong' image-scenes. The resulting aesthetic of a Serra film is dream-like; both the 'reality' of the shooting, actors and location and the diegetic reality of the narrative – in this case of Cervantes's *Don Quixote* – is seen and experienced by the viewer of *Honor of the Knights* as if through the uncanny unreality of a dream.

The method in Serra's madness becomes evident in *The Lord Has Worked Wonders in Me/El Senyor ha fet en mi meravelles* (2011), a film about the making of *Honor of the Knights*, but a 'making of' documentary in which the lines between the opposites outlined in the previous paragraph become even more blurred. The banal documentary footage of the actors and film crew in their hotel or on location talking, eating, sleeping, arguing, complaining – and occasionally in character and acting – rather than undermining the mysterious quality of *Honor of the Knights*, itself becomes reintegrated into Serra's aesthetic approach to the *Don Quixote* mythos and starts to take on a would-be visionary otherness. It may be that *The Lord Has Worked Wonders in Me* is the 'final' film in which the heterogeneous material arrives at its definitive form and *Honor of the Knights* merely an early iteration.

Serra's most critically acclaimed film *Birdsong* (*El cant dels ocells* 2008) pushes the slow aesthetic to its limit with its beautifully graded black-and-white cinematography, minimalist lack of story and a lack of drama exemplified by a now notorious eleven-minute long take of the three main characters walking across a desert-scape into long shot, going up a distant sand dune and disappearing over the horizon – only for their heads to bob up on the horizon again and after a confused consultation apparently deciding to walk back the way they came (Figure 17). This scene probably did seem calculated to exasperate audiences back in 2008, but it is not one long take in real time, the scene is subtly

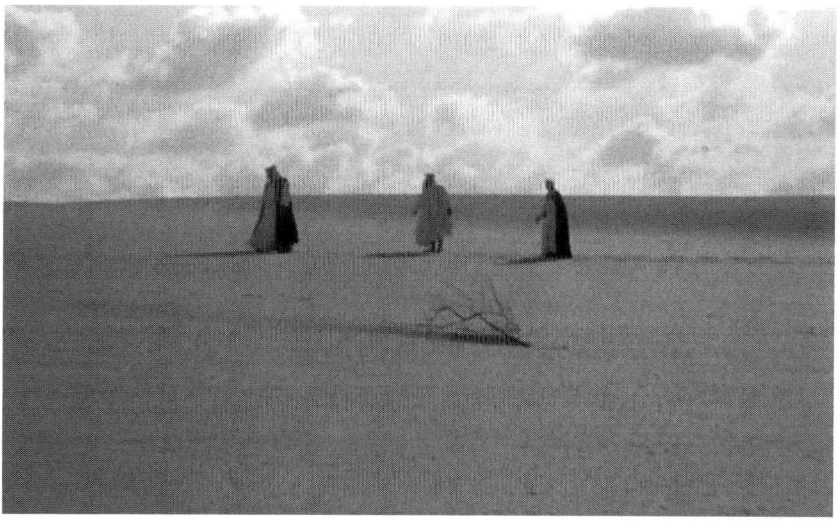

Figure 17 *Birdsong* (2008), Albert Serra.
An eleven-minute take of three characters (the Magi) walking across a desert-scape. But as the camera perspective changes so does the angle of the dramatic horizon and a play of horizontal lines develops, as does the shifting relationship of the figures to passing objects like the tree branch and the strange shifts in light and shadow, elements which when combined evoke an image of the sublime – the sacred, even – within the mode of pastiche.

edited, the camera perspective changes and there is actually a lot happening in the scene both at a narrative level (where are the three figures going? what are they doing?) and visually/cinematically (the 'sublime' landscape and its play of horizontal and vertical lines, the transition of the figures into ever more distant long shot, the strange 'sublime' shifts in light and shadow).

Birdsong has a story, one of the most fundamental, the story of the three Magi making their way to Bethlehem to acknowledge the birth of Christ. The story is stripped to its essentials, with a focus on the three Magi, played by non-professional actors (from Serra's regular troupe), each chosen for their endearingly eccentric physical and personal presence. The three figures are seen arguing about directions, sleeping among bushes, frolicking in the sea (their bodies shot from underneath by an underwater camera) and walking through the spectacular if austere volcanic Icelandic landscape representing the 'North' and eventually arriving in the 'South' of Palestine 2,000 years ago (a few choice landscapes in Tenerife acting as an evocative stand-in). Guided by a charming young angel, the Magi are greeted at the humble site of the new-born child by an unassuming Mary and Joseph (the latter played by an American film critic).

The story is told with beauty, pathos and humility, closer to Pasolini's *Gospel According to St Matthew* than anything by Bunuel, yet the film is steeped in irony, sometimes comically so: the three wise men are bumbling innocents and the scene of Christ's birth – a crumbling hovel – is denuded of any aura as are Mary and Joseph, but as in Rossellini's *St Francis* the absurdity of the believers does not demystify but respects the mystery of faith in its very stupidity. The only way Christianity can be represented today is through a knowing *but non-satirical* irony at its absurdity. Substituting 'cinema' for 'Christianity' provides a clue as to Serra's emblematic status for contemporary cinematic modernism. Serra loudly denounces almost all commercial film of a Hollywood action-drama type and 'quality' art-house film equally. His canon is fairly predictable – Fassbinder, Pasolini, Bresson, Dreyer – and his films are consciously related to a distinct recent strand of cinematic modernism – Lisandro Alonso, Lav Diaz, Ben Rivers – but Serra senses the impasse that contemporary cinematic modernism has reached and, in a move which resembles that of Fassbinder and Pasolini in the 1970s, Serra's films suggest that the only way the modernist aesthetic and its representation of existential alienation and the tragedy of the contemporary can be sustained today is through a knowing irony at the absurdity of its modes of representation. To be clear, this is not so much the postwar cliché of the 'absurdity of existence' but rather an acknowledgement of the 'mannerist' absurdity of existentialist or modernist aesthetic modes (Bergman, Antonioni, Tarkovsky, but also Tarr, Sokurov, even

Costa) and their inadequacy as means to represent a sensibility reflective of the proliferating catastrophes of the twenty-first century.[47]

Serra may be the first of the contemporary directors from the realist/slow/minimalist neo-Bazinian aesthetic strand to embrace an absurdist theatricality, but he won't be the last. The absurdist artificiality, apparent nihilism and turn to the 'theatrical' in Serra, as with Fassbinder, may incorporate modes of ironic pastiche but – so far – works as a strategic manoeuvre necessary to sustaining a recognizably modernist engagement with alienation and transcendence, with the abject and the sublime.

Adorno, Foucault and many other thinkers in the tradition of critical theory have proposed variations on a (questionable) thesis that the European Enlightenment of the 'long eighteenth century' marks the beginning of modernity and marks the point where scientific rationality and instrumental reason, in conjunction with the emergence of capitalism, took precedence over 'organic' social and cultural life. The privileging of reason and economic/technological progress was always likely to produce an intolerance of what became classified as irrationality, and therefore an intolerance of otherness. Although Enlightenment reason posited ideas of freedom and democracy, it actually produced the antithesis: the subjection of the other (racism), colonialism and finally genocidal totalitarianism. Serra's recent films purport to be an engagement with the Foucauldian version of the above thesis, the films being set in a painterly eighteenth century in which the spirits of eros and libertarianism fight it out with puritanism, instrumental reason and the death drive.

In *Story of My Death* (*Història de la meva mort* 2013) Casanova enjoys the benefits of being an epicurean aristocrat making his way through an eighteenth-century pastoral idyll enjoying the hospitality of rural life, mostly erotic and always heterosexual, before meeting a violent end at the hands of Dracula, a character who has strayed in prematurely from the nineteenth century, the supposed age of repression, in which good old-fashioned sexual perversity has become bound up with biopolitics, power, violence and death. Casanova represents life lived in its enjoyable quotidian banality. Dracula represents a bloodless insatiable vampiric death drive appropriate to the insatiability of capital accumulation. However, any expectations that *Story of My Death* will present a Brechtian interrogation of the Enlightenment are likely to be disappointed. The staging of an encounter between Casanova and Dracula is presumably intended to undermine any pretension to historical seriousness, Serra's interest lying elsewhere, but where?

Rossellini's *The Rise to Power of Louis XIV* (1966) presented in rigorous objective detail the deathbed scene of Cardinal Mazarin and the workings and rituals of the court as power shifted to the young King. Serra's *The Death of Louis XIV* (2016) focuses in rigorous objective detail on the deathbed scene of the now old king but gives us little in the way of insight into the broader workings of power. There must be a suspicion that the historical inquiry is merely a backdrop for Serra's real interest which, as the two film titles *Story of My Death* and *The Death of Louis XIV* suggest, is in mortality: what it is to be alive, to be dying and to be dead. This interest in mortality centres on the immediacy of presence as the signifier of what it is to be authentically alive but which in the cinema of the time-image has an uncanny relationship with memory and absence: when we are watching the immediacy of presence in film we are simultaneously watching something now past, absent, dead; something mummified, according to Bazin and Kracauer, and awaiting redemption in the consciousness of the viewer.

The casting of a 73-year-old Jean-Pierre Léaud as the dying king in *The Death of Louis XIV* confirms that Serra is tormented by the process of bodily decay. The flesh that was once a site of sensuous pleasure becomes a site of pain and degeneration. What is the relationship between this physical process of death and the extinguishing of identity, of what used to be called the soul? The king was supposed to have two bodies, the body of a man and the symbolic body of a king. Jean-Pierre Léaud regarded *The Death of Louis XIV* as being primarily about his own death. As someone captured by Truffaut on film as a child acting out being a child in *The 400 Blows* (1959) and as someone who has acted out each stage of his life on film, it makes sense that his own death should be filmed, necessarily in advance of the real event, as something acted out. Like the king, the actor also has two bodies, the body of an actor and the body of an acted role, a character, but in Serra's film it is the real decaying body of Léaud which acts out the symbolic death not only of Louis XIV but of the famous film actor Jean-Pierre Léaud – with all the obvious connotations for the passing of the *nouvelle vague* and cinematic modernism.

8

Contemporary cinematic modernism

An international style – commentaries on ten contemporary films

Fredric Jameson argues that it is a common condition of the contemporary world that almost every country perceives itself to be subject to alien forces beyond its control, namely the markets of globalized finance capitalism, hence in reaction the proliferation of populist and fundamentalist nationalisms.[1] This perception first made itself felt in the 1980s in relation to nations with a particularly unstable relationship with the emerging 'new world order' and, from the point of view of culture and the arts, the question arose of how to represent the complex interaction between national cultural tradition and an emerging global culture: How to resist a step back to a reactionary national(ist) culture and instead embrace internationalism while at the same time resisting the homogeneous globalized commercial culture, long characterized in terms of 'Americanization'? This quandary was especially evident in cinema where Hollywood and its global influence has long provided the textbook example of the workings of 'cultural imperialism', yet the heritage film celebrating and self-exoticizing a national culture is equally suspect. It was in such countries at the sharp edge of globalization that an international style informed by cinematic modernism developed not only as a counter to the dominance of Hollywood but also as a counter to the idea of an 'authentic' national cinema. So although contemporary modernist cinema, like its postwar precursor, is invariably marketed in terms of national new waves and auteurs, it is notable how far these films embrace the international style of cinematic modernism and its sources (Rossellini, Bresson, Ozu, Antonioni, Tarkovsky) as a means of resisting the mainstream culture of globalization and also of resisting any aesthetic redolent of an essentializing national culture. While contemporary politics tends to favour the location of identity in difference, cinematic modernism retains a characteristically modernist preference for the cosmopolitan and the international, a residual utopian preference for the particular within the universal rather than the privileging of the particular in itself.

What follows is a snapshot of what is now three decades of contemporary cinematic modernism as an international style, as represented by ten of the best-known directors and their most significant films.

Alexander Sokurov

As a student at the VJIK film school in Moscow in the 1970s Alexander Sokurov was mentored by Tarkovsky prior to the latter's exile from the Soviet Union. Sokurov's early films, mostly experimental documentaries, met the not unusual Soviet fate of being made but then having their release blocked for obscure ideological reasons. His first major feature film *Days of the Eclipse* (1988) did get an international release and attracted much attention, including an enthusiastic essay by Fredric Jameson in *The Geopolitical Aesthetic*. Writing in 1992 Jameson saw *Days of the Eclipse* in terms of how modernist cinema had given way to postmodernism and magic realism, but in retrospect the film stands as the reverse: an early example of how 'postmodern' elements became assimilated into the newly emerging international style of contemporary cinematic modernism. This was confirmed by the ascetic trilogy Sokurov made in difficult conditions during and immediately after the collapse of the Soviet Union: *The Second Circle* (1990), *Stone* (1992) and *Whispering Pages* (1993).[2] The films are shot in a degraded washed-out black and white, with use of anamorphic lenses to produce distortions of space and of physical features, especially bodies and faces, but more importantly, distortions in the perspective of the viewer, introducing a further layer of ambiguity or opaqueness to the already unstable images, which take on the aura of spectral images. The trilogy moves from the dark realism of the contemporary, a young man trying to organize the burial of his father in *Second Circle*, to the strange surrealism of *Stone* in which a young night watchman at the Chekhov museum is visited one night by a ghost, dream or hallucination of Chekhov. In this timeless zone of night the awkward encounter between present and past only confirms the impossibility of meaningful communication between the living and dead. The third film of the trilogy, *Whispering Pages*, completes the journey into the abyss: a young man drifts through a surreal, sinister and frequently threatening netherworld, a city of not quite – yet – dead souls. The film appears to be set in the past, but is also a nightmare premonition of the future – the present in which the film was made – that of the collapsing Soviet society as dreamt, perhaps, by Dostoyevsky from the depths of his own abyss in the nineteenth century.

Days of the Eclipse (1988)

Malyanov, a young idealistic Russian medic, accepts a posting to a poor, remote town in Turkmenistan (the town where Sokurov spent his teenage years) at the outer limits of the disintegrating Soviet Union. Mostly Muslim, the town is a mix of nationalities, some of whom ended up in this region as a legacy of the forced migrations of the Stalin years and, although Malyanov is accepted by the locals as a doctor, as a Russian he will always be the alien, a representative of the colonizer. In his ramshackle office and in the constant stultifying heat, Malyanov treats his patients and works on a thesis proposing that religious faith appears to help a community resist mental and physical ill-health.

Days of the Eclipse was, like *Solaris* and *Stalker*, loosely based on a science fiction story and like the Tarkovsky films has attracted a variety of allegorical readings. Was it an allegory of the hopes of the glasnost era or an allegory of the failure of Gorbachev's reforms, an allegory of the decay and stagnation of the last days of the Soviet Union? Malyanov's daily life is interrupted by a series of strange and surreal episodes. A Russian neighbour, an old communist, commits suicide; another neighbour has a large snake which keeps escaping and getting into Malyanov's office; a lobster in aspic is mysteriously delivered; a soldier on the run from his regiment takes Malyanov hostage, leaves and is hunted down and shot by the military, presumably by his former comrades; a strange 'cosmic' child arrives with a mysterious ailment and is cared for by Malyanov until his guardian suddenly turns up to collect him. The house of Malyanov's closest friend Vecherovsky, a Crimean Tartar, develops an inexplicable black growth on a wall, a veritable Lacanian-Hitchcockian stain or irruption of the real.[3]

The narrative of *Days of the Eclipse* consists of episodes with little or no causal links and few narrative transitions. Much of the film is shot in filtered yellow and sepia hues interspersed with scenes shot in degraded 'documentary' black and white, and in fact a number of scenes of the town, its festivities and its sanatorium, are actual documentary footage cut into the fictional narrative. Notwithstanding its languid long takes, the film is structured by ellipses, by abrupt shifts of film stock and colour filters, and by the juxtaposition of fiction and documentary. *Days of the Eclipse* is therefore experienced by the viewer in the archetypal fashion of the modernist artwork as a mosaic or collage of fragments generating an ambivalence of interpretation and resisting 'closure' of meaning. In this respect, Sokurov's film is reminiscent of Tarkovsky's *Mirror*, perhaps the definitive 'mosaic' film. In both *Days of the Eclipse* and *Mirror*, at a formal level, an aesthetic tension between continuity and discontinuity manifests historical/political contradictions, but whereas such contradictions in *Mirror* are still negotiated by the fluidity of the sequence shot mediating the fluidity of the spatial and the temporal (as personal memory and as a historical event), in *Days of the Eclipse* the dialectic is at a standstill and produces an impasse, an existential limbo in which memory is suspended or rather sublimated into a present continuous resembling stasis. The only dynamic is an intermittent one drawn from random, inexplicable *external* events. Fredric Jameson sees this intrusion of the external event, whether a suicide, an AWOL soldier, an uncanny child – or a UFO/alien intervention – as reflecting the reality of the stagnation of the Soviet Union, in which hope and fear reside in the anticipation of intervention from an alien force outside the system, from that other planet known as capitalism.[4]

Béla Tarr

Béla Tarr started out making idiosyncratic social realist films in the 1970s while studying at the Béla Balázs Studios in Budapest. *Macbeth* (1982) and *Almanac of Fall* (1984) saw Tarr experimenting with a more eclectic stylization in colour, camera angles and shot length, an eclecticism which was stripped away when Tarr arrived at his signature style with *Damnation* (1988): black-and-white cinematography and lengthy elaborately choreographed sequence shots reminiscent of Tarr's countryman Miklós Jancsó from the heyday of 1960s modernist film. Tarr combines a gritty realism with an extreme formalist aestheticization in the service of narratives concerning the relationship between political betrayal and existentialist angst at the level of both individual and collective, the particular and the universal. *Damnation*'s main character Karrer schemes to obtain the objects of his obsessive desire, sexual and financial, both of which depend on achieving a degree of power within his small world, a stagnant backwater that is inexorably sliding into endemic corruption. Karrer's schemes fail, and he turns into a police informer. Even this is not the end. In a Tarr film there is always a further layer of degeneration in which to fall, and Karrer is eventually reduced to the bestial, reduced to the level of the stray dogs scavenging for scraps in the detritus of a decaying social system. *Sátántangó* (1994), in which the inhabitants of a rundown communal farm are promised better times only to be swindled and betrayed, is Tarr's most acclaimed film and is discussed in the following section. A powerful and sadly prescient film about a town descending into nationalistic mob rule,

Werckmeister Harmonies (2000) flagged up the danger of Tarr's style becoming mannerism and risked aestheticizing, beautifying even, its disturbing subject matter. The film also teetered on the brink of crude allegory. Tarr responded to this impasse with opposing strategies. *The Man from London* (2007) rigorously eliminates any possible allegorical significance. The film is an exercise in pure form, a Simenon story evacuated of any suspense or tension, a thriller with the thrills expunged, leaving just the empty skeleton of the noir thriller form. *The Turin Horse* (2011), on the other hand, is a pure existentialist Beckettian allegory: a man and his daughter sleeping, dressing, undressing, eating potatoes and caring for a sick horse as the wind rages outside their home.

Sátántangó (1994)

The seven-hour *Sátántangó* is divided into three parts, and each part is divided into a few chapters, which are themselves divided into just a few scenes. *Sátántangó* therefore takes the episodic structure to an extreme, each episode being juxtaposed elliptically but achieving overlapping or interlocking narrative and temporal effects.

Sátántangó tells the story of a collapsed communal farm and the dispersal of its inhabitants as (mis)directed by a messianic political opportunist (and police spy) Irimiás. Tarr has called Krasznahorkai's original novel a satire, and it is possible to see the storyline as an allegory of how the old collective farms in Hungary were broken up as communism collapsed. For non-Hungarians, the satirical allegory seems pertinent to the experience of much of the former Eastern Bloc, particularly Russia, in the 1990s, where the population was misled and robbed on an unimaginable scale by the combined chicanery of political demagogues, opportunists from the old regime, capitalist entrepreneurs and gangsters. However, Tarr's aesthetic transcends the simplifications of satire in order to achieve something closer to what Tarr considers the truth. This is evident in the oblique and contradictory representations of the agitator Irimiás (Jeremiah: prophet of doom). He is introduced, along with his amusingly sceptical sidekick Petrina, as a weak lowlife itinerant being pressured by a police chief to turn into an informer. We next see him in a bar threatening to blow up everyone he despises and telling Petrina how much the residents of the farm village disgust him. Then he becomes the messianic agitator mesmerizing the villagers with his speechifying, his vision of a utopian future and his elegiac words following the suicide of the little girl, Estike. We even see him fall to his knees in a mystic rapture at the sight of fog, much to Petrina's exasperation. We last hear of Irimiás by way of two police functionaries typing up his poetic but savage observations on each of the villagers into regular informer reports. From these contradictory views of Irimiás the picture emerges of a man who is not just a money-grabbing fraudster but someone who really is an idealistic prophet, a violent nihilist terrorist and a police informer – he is all these things and really believes himself to be all these things – and his collaborators, Petrina and the boy Sanyi, also believe it of him. Moreover, the viewer of the film can empathize with Irimiás's public idealistic speechifying and private violent disgust at the state of the world, while being fully aware of the shallowness of his obscurantist rhetoric. The viewer is therefore put in the position of having some empathy with Irimiás while at the same time recoiling from his ruthless manipulation and exploitation of his victims. Instead of safely identifying with a satire we are placed in the position of becoming uneasily complicit with the reversals of guilt and horror, compassion and disgust, which we are watching. And the truth is that most political leaders, especially the 'messiahs', have this quality of believing in their own lies, of being extreme idealists and extreme cynics at the same time – part saint, part shyster, or as Tarr remarks in an interview, most messiahs are also police spies.[5]

If Irimiás is not quite the caricature villain of a satire, it is also the case that there are no caricature innocents in *Sátántangó*. All the characters are selfish and gross yet treated with a mixture of disgust and sympathy by the film. It is therefore apposite that the most obviously innocent character, the little girl Estike, performs the most shocking and gruesome act in the film – her torturing and poisoning of a cat. Yet this scene too remains morally ambivalent because it is retrospectively complicated by Estike's idealistic attitude towards her own imminent death and her wish to join the angels.

The complexity of moral meaning in *Sátántangó* is supported by an elliptical narrative structure and Tarr's aesthetic formalism. The infamous 'cows prologue' being an obvious example. The eight-minute opening scene of *Sátántangó* begins with a static shot, medium height and at medium distance, geometrically framed by the angles of farm buildings. A herd of cows emerges from one of the buildings into the muddy yard, the camera slowly panning as the cows disperse and one cow breaks away to move directly towards the camera. The cows regroup and begin to move off together down a street through the village. The camera pans and then moves left into a steady horizontal tracking shot which parallels the movement and direction of the cows, although the cows are absent from the image, obscured by farm buildings – the tracking shot is therefore mostly of decrepit walls and the backs of buildings. Eventually the cows come back into view, grouped in a village square, and the tracking shot halts. A long-held static shot shows the cows exiting the square, heading into a field. After the last cow leaves the frame the camera doesn't follow the cows but remains fixed on the now empty square, a now 'empty' image.

An eight-minute sequence shot of cows is a peculiar way to begin a film, and the viewer can't assign definitive narrative meaning to the scene. It is an ostensibly indeterminate image, a recording in integral duration of a real event: cows leaving a shed and moving through a field out into a lane. But this reality is carefully staged in terms of squalid ambience, including the sounds of an ominous electronic hum overlaid with the mooing of the animals. And the cows' activity is made to appear curiously choreographed by the way the scene is shot, giving rise to a mood of sinister pathos, which sets the tone for the subsequent film (the film is loosely centred around a plot concerning a struggle for money derived from the sale of the cattle). In addition, the image of a herd of cows has an oblique symbolic function, prefiguring the herd-like behaviour of the villagers, the main characters in the film.

The characteristic Tarr sequence shot that most impresses viewers of *Sátántangó* is the Steadicam shot, from the rear or front, of people walking (Figures 18 and 19). These lengthy shots in which the camera follows the shoulders and backs of figures striding along streets or muddy tracks exceed any narrative function. They are shots of bodies moving in duration, foregrounding

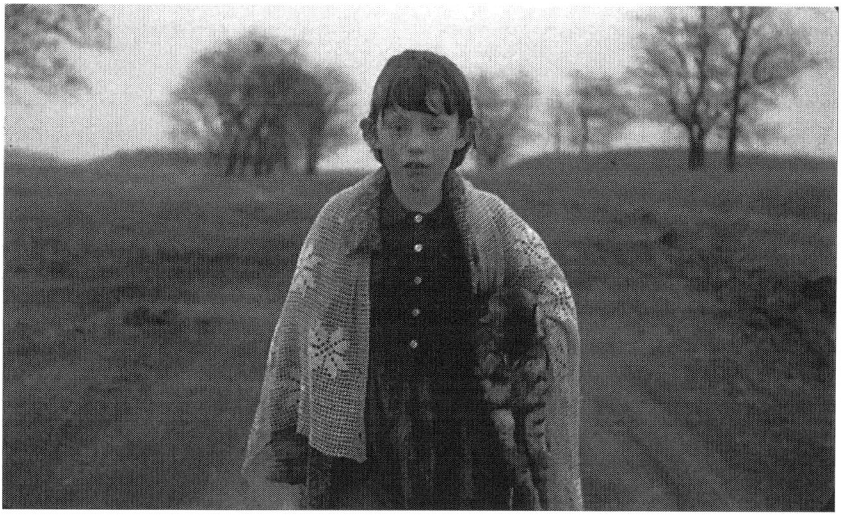

Figure 18 *Sátántangó* (1994), Béla Tarr.
The little girl Estike, betrayed by everyone and having poisoned her cat, walks – holding the dead cat – inexorably towards her own willed death, suicide, through which she and her cat will join the angels, a death which will be cruelly exploited by the false messiah/police informer Irimiás. Béla Tarr's *Sátántangó* is famous for its lengthy Steadicam 'walking shots', variations of which became a ubiquitous feature of films informed by contemporary cinematic modernism. Sometimes characters walking are filmed in profile, but more commonly from behind or, as in this case, from the front, the character staring directly into the camera, at the viewer.

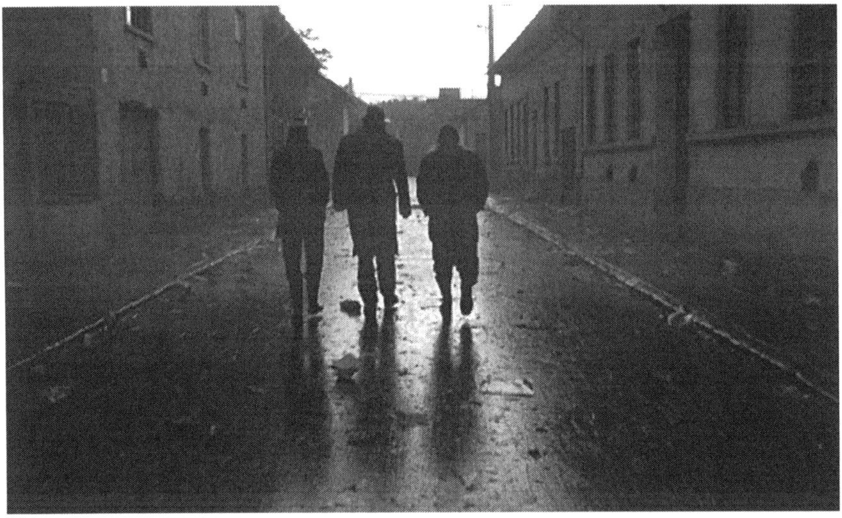

Figure 19 *Sátántangó* (1994), Béla Tarr.
A lengthy 'walking shot' of the shadowy conspirators: Irimiás (centre), Petrina (right) and young Sanyi (left), filmed from behind as they stride through dark deserted streets. The walking shots described by Deleuze as a feature of postwar cinematic modernism referred to casual strolling and aimless wandering through ruined or dislocated spaces in the films of Rossellini and Antonioni. In Tarr's films, however, the walking shot is an expression of the inexorable, whether that be of a blind Schopenhauerian will or a movement driven towards some abject stand-in for fate or destiny.

stride, posture and grim determination. These images may also represent an almost behaviourist view of characters locked into automated movements, determined by other forces; there is a sense that the movement itself is something inexorable. These shots often last for three or four minutes in the scenes of Irimiás and Petrina walking through the paper-strewn streets to and from the police headquarters and, joined by the boy Sanyi, along rain-swept country lanes towards the village. At certain points, the camera moves ahead of the walkers, replacing them with its own momentum and showing the road, the fields, the trees and the distant horizon. It is as if the camera is tracking the figures' journey through the landscape without them; they are absent from the image of their own movement.

Another Tarr speciality, the extended zoom, is perhaps less striking in *Sátántangó* than in *Damnation*, but there are a number of examples, such as when the villagers, having left their farm, bed down to sleep for the first night at the Manor, the utopian commune promised by Irimiás. As darkness fills the screen and characters' voices declare their hope in the future and the need to trust each other, the camera very slowly zooms in a straight line out of the room

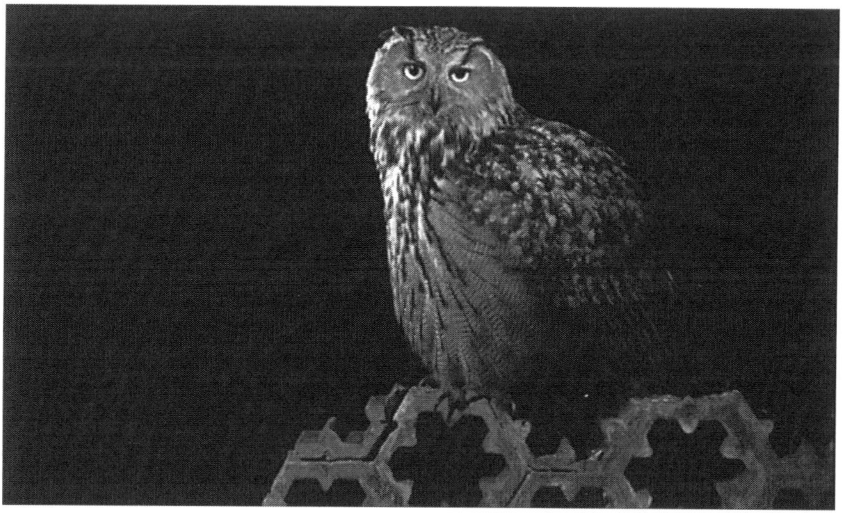

Figure 20 *Sátántangó* (1994), Béla Tarr.
What characterizes Béla Tarr's trademark extended sequence shots, often incorporating elaborate zooms, is that the viewer can rarely predict where the shot is going, what objects it will take in on its arc and on what object it will finally rest. In a latter episode from *Sátántangó*, a lengthy sequence shot begins in the refuge house where the villagers are holed up and travels through the rooms of the house, over the sleeping villagers (and their voiced dreams), travels along the corridors of the house and slowly zooms towards a lighted window and, finally, on to a sustained close-up of an owl. Although Tarr's sequence shots are unpredictable, there is something inexorable about their slow steady progress, particularly in the slow final zoom-in.

and down a passage way, through a broken wall to a luminous light outside which, as the zoom completes its course into a close-up, is revealed to be an owl (Figure 20). A close-up of the owl is held, capturing the intense eyes and swivelling of the head. The image then fades to black followed by a lengthy sequence shot, an elaborate overhead crane shot of the sleeping villagers, circling above them while a voiceover narrates their anxious dreams. The power of the owl image is directly related to the substantial time it has taken to be revealed, the 'real-time' of the zoom. But what does this unexpected image encountered at the end of the zoom mean? The owl's eyes may manifest surveillance – that of the never sleeping unconscious or the ever-watching expressionless unreadable eyes of power. Yet the precise meaning of the owl image, like *Sátántangó* as a whole, remains mysterious. Out of its concrete particularity *Sátántangó* achieves an open universality to the extent that finally the film is delivering a universal message: the world as a whole (global capitalism) is a failed project and yet the dream of a revolutionary overthrow of capitalism is a self-deceiving fantasy.

Abbas Kiarostami

Abbas Kiarostami achieved international recognition in the 1990s with 'The Koker Trilogy': *Where Is the Friend's Home?* (1987), *And Life Goes On* (1992) and *Through the Olive Trees* (1994) and the 'documentary re-enactment' collaboration with Mohsen Makhmalbaf, *Close-Up* (1990). Kiarostami acknowledged the influence of Rossellini's films, particularly *Journey to Italy* and *Germany Year Zero*, on his own aesthetic, and his first major international award was, appropriately enough, the *Prix Rossellini* at Cannes 1992. He was awarded the *Palme d'Or* in 1997 for *Taste of Cherry*. Following his final Iranian feature film *The Wind Will Carry Us* (1999) Kiarostami, perhaps sensing that his aesthetic risked becoming mannerism, turned to overtly documentary filmmaking alongside minimalist experiments in the direction of the gallery installation aesthetic. Before his untimely death in 2016 Kiarostami had returned to fiction feature films with the international productions of *Certified Copy* (2010) – a homage to Rossellini's *Journey to Italy* and postwar European modernist film of the Antonioni type – and the Japan-set *Like Someone in Love* (2012), both of which met with a mixed critical response.

Taste of Cherry has been selected for commentary here not only because it is one of Kiarostami's most celebrated films but because of its combination of naturalism and formalism and its subject matter: alienation as an existentialist issue. In both its form and content therefore, *Taste of Cherry* represents an explicit link between postwar modernist film and contemporary cinematic modernism.

Taste of Cherry (1997)

The film begins with a middle-class man, Mr Badii, driving around Tehran, looking at day labourers and asking them if they would like to earn some money by doing a job for him. His discretion or embarrassment about the job generates a suspicion that he may be 'cruising', looking at young men out of a sexual interest. One labourer tells Mr Badii, 'Go away or I'll smash your face in.' A young Kurdish soldier agrees to a lift and, after some small talk about army life and the ritual of regimental marching, Badii takes him to a tree on a hillside outside Tehran and explains the job: he wants to end his life and has dug a grave by this tree. He will lie down in this grave tonight, take an overdose and needs someone to come at dawn, check if he is dead and, if so, cover him over with several spadesful of earth. In other words, Badii wants somebody to bury him. Upon finishing this explanation and offering money up front, the frightened young soldier jumps out of the car

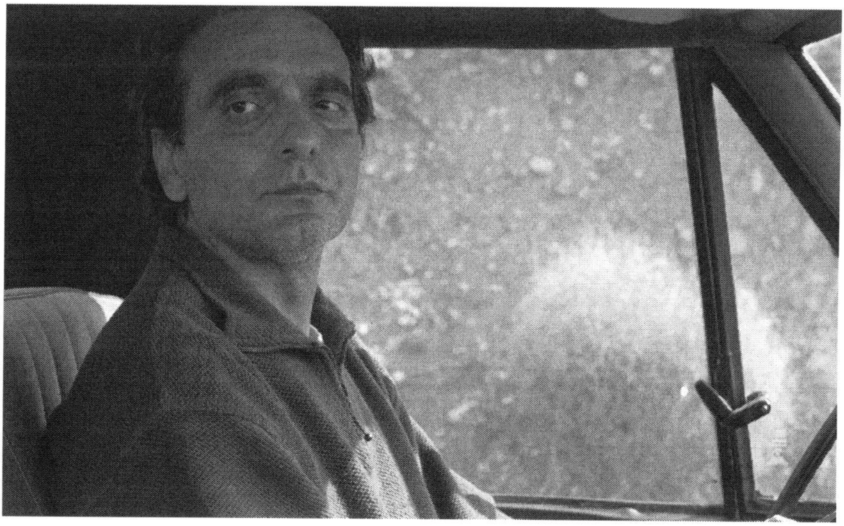

Figure 21 *Taste of Cherry* (1997), Abbas Kiarostami.
Entire Kiarostami's films are constructed around the motif of 'protagonist in a car', filmed from inside the vehicle, from behind or in front of the driver or from next to the driver, in profile. A particular feature of *Taste of Cherry* are repeated shots of Mr Badii looking past the camera/viewer out of the car window to the world outside, scrutinizing the world yet unable to grasp or engage with it, a voyeurism of exasperated distance – as if he will never leave the bubble of isolation that is his car, any more than he will ever leave the bubble of futility in which his life is trapped.

and runs off, down the hill and back to his army base. Mr Badii then picks up a young Afghan seminarian and makes the same strange request. A long debate ensues, the seminarian declaring it to be un-Islamic to kill anyone, including oneself, Badii arguing that it is an Islamic duty to help others in desperate need. Exasperated, Badii says that if he had wanted a theological discussion he would have sought out an experienced cleric, not a trainee seminarian.

Much of *Taste of Cherry* consists of Badii in his car driving round and round the outskirts of north Tehran, around an industrial quarry area, encountering various poor labourers or migrants, most of whom treat him with great courtesy, but he is too narrowly focused on the quest to end his life to respond in kind. As in many of his other films, Kiarostami creates his trademark formalist minimalism through the limitations of locating almost all the action within a moving car (Figure 21). When Badii is alone and driving, the camera is placed behind him, an over-the-shoulder shot, or placed as a point-of-view shot from Badii himself through the windscreen as he drives, or sometimes placed looking at him in profile as if from the empty seat next to him. *Taste of Cherry* provides perhaps the best examples of Kiarostami's characteristic long shots, usually from above, of the car as it follows the zig-zag course of the road as it snakes up or down a hillside or round a valley. During these overhead long shots of the car on the road, the audio of the conversation between Mr Badii and his passenger continues; we hear the discussion in the car while watching from afar the car follow its course. This creates a strange juxtaposition; on the audio we hear the conversation close up, as if in the car, but visually we watch the car from a distance.

The conversation with the seminarian seems to impress upon Badii the impossibility of finding anyone to bury him after his suicide and the fundamental outlandishness of his request. Arriving once more in the industrial quarry – a veritable circle of hell – he gets out of the car and watches trucks unload rocks and gravel and a conveyor belt carrying stones to be smashed: noise and dust everywhere. He sits, eyes closed, a dark night of the soul in the blinding midday light. In the middle of this unreal nightmarish scene, strange shadows are cast in the walls of dust, out of which a workman appears:

'Hey mister, move your car and go, what are you doing here? This is no place to sit, you can't sleep here. If you want cement go to the office. Are you sick? Do you want some tea?'[6]

Mr Badii looks at the workman with forlorn eyes and gets up and returns wearily to his car. What follows is probably the most striking elliptical cut in the film, a cut to a long shot of the car zig-zagging its way up and down the hillside roads; for several minutes we will view the car as it makes its progress away from the quarry and back to Tehran, but while watching the long shot of the car we hear a new conversation going on in the car, a very one-sided conversation, a passenger talking to Badii as he drives. Kiarostami withholds any view of the passenger and any information about who the new passenger is. As viewers and listeners we have to let the episode unfold in its duration and peculiar mystery. Gradually the long shots of the car following the zig-zag road give way to a conventional shot/reverse shot sequence of the passenger, an older man, telling a story to Badii who doesn't speak, but listens with interest:

'I'd decided to kill myself. I got up, left my wife sleeping and left the house and drove to a tree plantation. I chose a tree and tried to throw a rope over the branch, but it wouldn't catch. I tried climbing the tree and tied the rope but felt something soft. It was a cherry, a mulberry. Mulberries are deliciously sweet, so I ate one. It was so succulent. I ate a second and then a third. Suddenly I noticed the sun rising above the mountaintop and the beautiful green scenery. I saw children on their early morning way to school. They stopped to look at me.

I got home, my wife was still sleeping. She woke up and had a mulberry!

I left to kill myself and I came back with Mulberries!

My dear man, you need to change your outlook – be optimistic! Be positive! You are in your prime!

Please take a left.'

[Mr Badii smiles sceptically.]

Accounts of the film often assume that this is the 'meaning' of the film: that the suicidal Mr Badii realizes that the taste of cherry – life's little fleeting pleasures – is what makes life worth living. In fact, Badii remains silent as he drives, following his passenger's directions, merely offering an occasional smile as the man carries on talking. The car arrives at its destination, the Tehran Natural History Museum where the passenger works. Badii makes him promise to keep his word and come to bury him tomorrow morning:

'Now please take the money. Remember you have given your word. I'll see you at six tomorrow morning – or rather you'll see me at six!'

This is Badii's little dark joke. By this point viewers are piecing together the narrative since the elliptical cut at the quarry: sunk in the deepest misery, realizing the impossibility of getting anyone to bury him after his suicide, Badii had driven away from the quarry and then picked up another man needing a lift, a middle-aged (Turkish?) man called Mr Bagheri, who teaches at the Natural History Museum (as a taxidermist?) and who talked about a sick child in his family. So, grasping the unexpected opportunity, Badii had asked the man to perform the burial task in return for a lump sum of money for the child's medication and treatment. Like the previous passengers, this man had tried to get Badii to give up the idea of suicide but had at least understood, telling of his own failed suicide attempt, the story of the taste of cherry.

Does Mr Badii have his own taste of a cherry moment? In the grounds of the Natural History Museum he looks up as an aeroplane leaves its stream across the sky. He sees children walking around the well-kept grounds. A fantastic view of Tehran below. A cat walks along the wall. No. There are no second thoughts (Figures 22 and 23). Cut to a long-distance 'surveillance' shot of an understandably agitated Badii in his flat, putting on his jacket and turning out the lights. Cut to countryside late at night. An archetypal Kiarostami long shot following the car, a

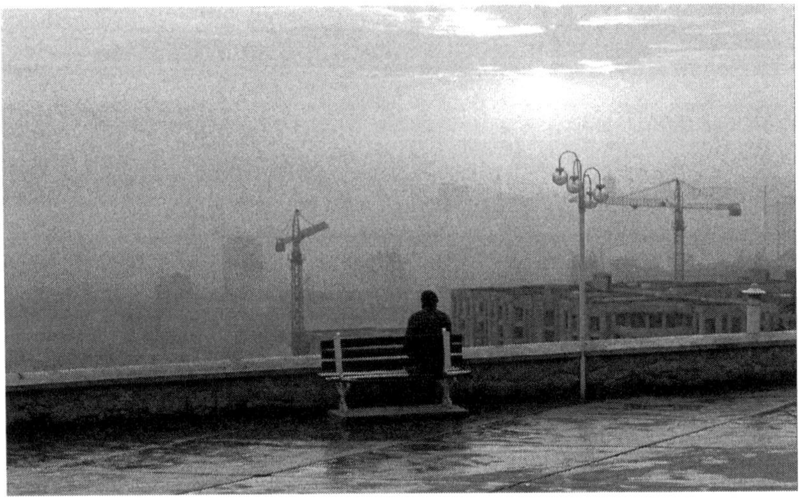

Figure 22 *Taste of Cherry* (1997), Abbas Kiarostami.
Filmed in a static long shot from behind, a lonely abject figure, Mr Badii, sits on a seat staring down at the bustling city of Tehran, with all its cranes and construction sites, reduced to a vague shapeless yellowish void below onto which Mr Badii projects his own nothingness. Or, now resigned to his suicide this very evening, perhaps Mr Badii looks down from his platform of lofty isolation at Tehran as the world of life from which he is about to depart and from which he is already excluded.

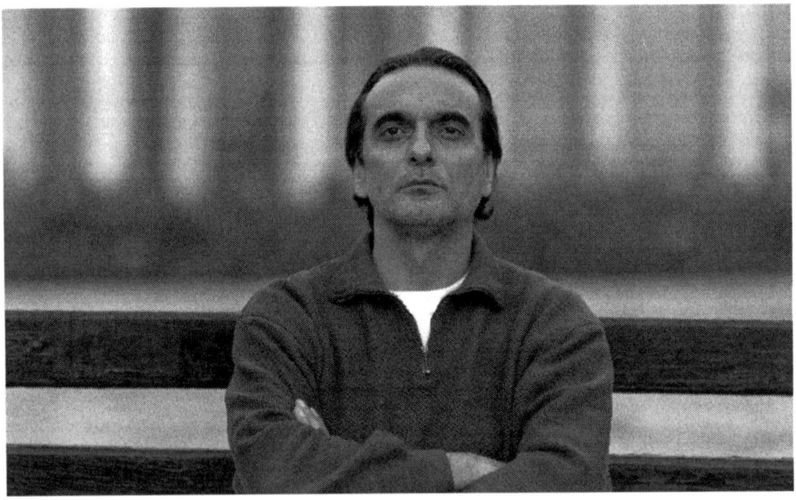

Figure 23 *Taste of Cherry* (1997), Abbas Kiarostami.
Kiarostami cuts to a frontal close-up of Mr Badii sitting on the seat, confirming that his gaze is not focused on its object (Tehran) but is instead a stare without an object, a stare which sees too intensely and therefore sees nothing. The unsettling paradox being that the close-up positions Mr Badii as staring directly at the viewer, thus rendering the viewer an object of nothingness.

taxi, as it makes its way along the zig-zag bends in the road. Long shot of the tree on the hillside which marks the burial hole. Headlights make strange shapes on the tree, and Badii gets out of the taxi and sits by the tree smoking a cigarette, the lights of Tehran twinkling below. Filmed from behind in middle distance, he turns his face in response to a flash of lightning and we see the taxi disappearing down the bends in the road in the valley below. Badii stands up, stubs out the cigarette with his foot and steps down to the grave, throws down his bag and goes towards the hole by the tree. Cut to Badii in his grave – close-up of his face, eyes wide open with intensity, looking at the sky, the moon shining through streaming black clouds. The sound of thunder. Fade to black. A flash of lightning lights up Badii's face with eyes open. Black out, strange animal sounds. A little flash of light in the blackness: Badii with his eyes closed. Screen completely blacked out. Sounds of thunder and rain.

Kiarostami exemplifies the neo-Bazinian aesthetic, but the ambiguity of this climactic death scene of Badii lying in his dug-out grave owes as much to modernist montage as to the long take. We have a sequence of short sharply juxtaposed images, incorporating something approaching subliminal flash cuts of Badii's face, ending with a long blacked-out screen. This montage sequence is accompanied by an almost indecipherable soundtrack of thunder, rain and ambient sounds, including the hum of traffic and the barking of dogs in the distance. The montage can be read in several ways. The most obvious reading would be: Badii lays down in his dug grave and takes his pills, he stares at the sky in the last moments of life and his eyes then close as death takes hold. The blacked-out screen equals death. Alternatively, it is possible to read the sequence as: Badii falls asleep and then wakes up and clambers out of the grave. Or do the barely audible sounds during the blacked-out screen represent Mr Bagheri arriving to find Mr Badii dead, asleep or awake?

Or perhaps, as with much modernist art, we should experience the images and their juxtaposition in their rich indeterminacy and not try to impose a single fixed reading. This is what Susan Sontag argued in 'Against Interpretation', an essay written in 1961 as a response to the *nouveau roman* and films like *Last Year at Marienbad* and *The Silence* and an essay that now reads like a 'how to' guide for watching contemporary films informed by cinematic modernism.[7] Death normally signifies a definitive closure in narrative as in life but, if the 'death' scene of *Taste of Cherry* is 'open', it is opened still further by the controversial coda.[8]

The morning light comes up

We seem to be still on the hillside, with Tehran below in the distance

The film stock has switched from celluloid to grainy blurry video

Cut to a shot a troop of soldiers running along chanting 'Hup two three' (or equivalent in Persian), resembling a scene early in the film, following the conversation Mr Badii had with the young soldier, about the strange rituals of army life

A man walking along carrying a large film camera, he meets another member of the film crew

The film crew relaxing between takes.

The actor who plays Mr Badii enters the frame and walks up to Kiarostami and shares a cigarette

A sound-man with microphone crouches in bushes

Cut to a long shot of soldiers marching. The soldiers reach the road behind a tree – the tree by the grave?

Kiarostami says over his walkie-talkie:

'That's enough, you hear? Tell your men to stay near the tree to rest. The shoot is over. We're here for a sound take.'

(Kiarostami seems to want an audio-only take of the soldiers marching, not another visual take of them marching past the 'suicide tree' which might be too obvious an image with which to end the film).

Becoming audible on the (extra-diegetic) soundtrack is some jazz, a New Orleans funeral march tune? (It is a recording from the 1920s of Louis Armstrong playing 'St James Infirmary').

Shot of soldiers on hillside, some of them look back at the camera, some joking around, enjoying this break from barracks (we assume they are non-actor soldiers, rather than actors playing soldiers).

Slightly out of focus shots of members of the film crew scattered about the hillside.

Last shot of Kiarostami and two of the film crew recording the sound.

Blacked-out screen. Louis Armstrong continues to play on soundtrack. The closing credits come up.[9]

This coda is not only shot on digital video, obviously a very different picture quality to the preceding film, but also 'roughly' shot and edited in a casual documentary verité style contrasting with the rigorous formalism of the preceding film. What is the relationship between this coda and the preceding film? At a basic level it is a Brechtian 'demystification' device, showing us the crew and actors who produced the film: don't worry, Mr Badii isn't really dead, he was just an actor who is now sharing a cigarette with the director! Perhaps the coda is the true 'taste of cherry' moment – after the grim suicide of Badii in the film, the coda provides us with a picture of 'life goes on' in the magical banality of the everyday. Badii the fictional character may have resisted the consolation of the taste of cherry, but the film itself and we the viewers do access and accept the consolation of existence in its fleeting everyday presence as manifested in the coda.

But does the coda merely present an idiosyncratic 'happy ever after' resolution? The strange thing about the actual experience of watching *Taste of Cherry* is that the film, including Badii's death, seems acutely real while the coda seems unreal, dream-like. The juxtaposition of celluloid with video adds to the uncanny quality of the coda. Instead of 'life goes on' it is as if in the coda we are watching images of the afterlife. Anyone who has had the misfortune to have experienced a protracted coma (or clinical 'near death') will be familiar with how on recovering consciousness the intensity of the world coming back into the senses can intermittently break: the images of life suddenly seeming unreal compared to the vivid hallucinatory world of the coma. And there is something of this in *Taste of Cherry*. The coda seems haunted or marked by death or, at the very least, marked by the fragility of existence. At which point we should remember that this is a film about suicide, about a man whose life has become a living death. This is why the story of the cherries had no impact on Badii – if one's life is already a living death then happiness, pleasure, memories, far from consoling actually make things worse because the self is alienated from such enjoyment, the inability to enjoy the delicious taste of cherries simply reinforces how meaningless such pleasures have become.

There is no correct reading of the coda or *Taste of Cherry* as a whole. Each viewer will shift between different interpretations depending on personal experience, sensibility and mood. The intensity of the film is dependent upon this slippage between different, sometimes opposing, interpretations. Ambiguity and indeterminacy are not in themselves aesthetically 'advanced' or politically 'progressive', but they become a crucial feature of cinematic modernism because they correspond to the multiplicity of perspectives in a film like *Taste of Cherry* and are integral to its openness of meaning. The purpose of withholding or delaying information is therefore not to tease the viewer but to facilitate the viewer's participation in constructing the narrative and, as importantly, creating spaces or openings for each viewer's subjective identifications.

The most obvious information gap in *Taste of Cherry* concerns the reason why Badii wants to end his life. There has been criticism that this absence of a 'suicide backstory' means that the character of Badii lacks the necessary motivation, and therefore the viewer cannot sympathize, a problem accentuated by Badii's self-absorbed rude behaviour to others. He is not a sympathetic character. This is wholly misguided criticism. As Badii tells Mr Beghari, the type of pain he is experiencing is impossible to communicate and makes it difficult for him to interact with others, makes him insensitive to the pain he might be causing others. Our sympathy for the extreme nature of his torment is activated precisely because the reasons for his depression are not revealed. His depression is beyond this or that 'motivation'. His condition is absolute. Which is why the taste of cherry would provide no solace. *Taste of Cherry* and its coda are therefore open to largely unconscious identifications on the part of the viewer. This is probably why, despite being generally considered to be one of the greatest films of recent times, *Taste of Cherry* has also elicited some bizarrely negative responses: perhaps the film is *too close*, perhaps it reveals aspects of the viewer that would prefer to remain disavowed?[10]

The modernist form of *Taste of Cherry* also makes it open to various allegorical readings. Laura Mulvey notes that Kiarostami's own reading tended, along Bazinian lines, towards seeing the film as some kind of allegory for cinema's relationship to death and its ability to 'embalm' the past, including the life and vision of the director. Mulvey sees a significance to the Louis Armstrong instrumental on the soundtrack to the coda and credits, in that it refers to an old blues song:

> While the theme of death demands finality, an ending in the manner of Hitchcock, Kiarostami ends the film more in the spirit of Rossellini and *Journey to Italy*, where, after its formal end, the film casually indicates that life goes on. However, Louis Armstrong's 'St James' Infirmary' plays on the sound-track accompanying the coda sequence. The song simply, in two verses, tells of a man who finds his lover laid out dead in the morgue and who then visualizes his own death.[11]

From this perspective, the coda suggests that Kiarostami, having laid to rest his main character Badii, now envisions his own death and the death of cinema (celluloid to video). If Badii's is the first death, then Kiarostami's final instruction: 'the shoot is over' presents us with the second death.

Tsai Ming-Liang

Some of Tsai Ming-liang's films address poverty and homelessness: *I Don't Want to Sleep Alone* (2006) is structured around a kind of fantasy in which three more or less homeless characters, two men and one woman, sleep together on a found mattress, while *Stray Dogs* (2013) tells the story of a family brought down to underclass homelessness by the alcoholism of the husband. Yet Tsai's realism is not so much gritty as fleshy; he is the chronicler of bodily intimacy. Sleeping, washing, bathing, eating, urinating, fellatio, masturbating – the most intimate parts and functions and dysfunctionality of the body become an object of care, something shared, in which nursing a damaged body becomes indistinguishable from making love to a desired body. Notwithstanding this realist level to his films, Tsai Ming-liang is aligned with the shift away from neorealism towards Antonioni-informed cinematic modernism, a shift evident in the attention to beautifully composed formalist images and choreographed (but static) long takes and also in the shift of focus towards the alienation and ennui of the urban middle class, albeit in Tsai's films often a precariat strata of that class.

In terms of their 'queer' sensibility, however, Tsai's films are different from most modernists, whether postwar or contemporary, although his films could obviously be placed within a 'queer modernist' lineage going back to Fassbinder and Pasolini. As well as portraying bodily intimacy in a way not seen before, Tsai also presents graphic sexuality in a non-judgemental way: no desire is perverse, or rather the supposedly perverse is simply the normal. For example, in *The Wayward Cloud* (2005) the portrayal of youthful urban ennui is intercut with the making of a pornographic 'film within the film'. *The Wayward Cloud* begins with 'watermelon sex' and ends with a long-take blow job. The film also includes some camp musical numbers. Tsai manages to combine Antonioni at his most seriously modernist – urban alienation! – with Pasolini at his most camp.

Tsai's trademark static long take reaches its apogee in *Stray Dogs*, which draws towards its inconclusive conclusion with a fifteen-minute fixed-camera long take of the alcoholic husband (regular Tsai muse Lee Kang-sheng) and his wife staring at a mural in an abandoned building. If *Vive L'Amour* (1994) established the rudiments of Tsai's aesthetic out of Antonioni's modernism and *Goodbye, Dragon Inn* (2003) represented the self-reflexive peak of that aesthetic, then *Stray Dogs* suggests that the aesthetic has reached a limit point beyond which cinema ends and the gallery art installation beckons. As Tony Rayns commented:

> *Stray Dogs* is in fact unlike Tsai's nine previous features in one crucial respect: it does away almost completely with continuity editing. Most of its scenes are single shots, and there's no causal link between one and the next. Some shots are so realist that they could have been taken with a hidden camera. Others are so stylized that they might well represent dreams. [. . .] The backstory, if there ever was one, has been suppressed.[12]

Goodbye, Dragon Inn (2003)

Goodbye, Dragon Inn begins with the dramatic opening credits sequence from the classic martial arts movie *Dragon Inn* (King Hu 1967) and a glorious colour scene with the emperor getting out of his carriage. We then see the big screen from a series of angles, a series of different seat positions within a large movie theatre in which every seat is filled: a cinema apparently full of life. We are watching a 1967 film within a 2003 film and, apart from a brief coda, the whole of Tsai's *Goodbye, Dragon Inn* will be enclosed within the screening and running time of King Hu's *Dragon Inn*. The main soundtrack of Tsai's film is the dialogue, music and sound-effects from King Hu's film. After the opening, Tsai's film cuts to the entrance of the Fu Ho Grand Theatre in Taipei on a rainy evening. From a little street opposite, a young man (later revealed as Japanese) steps out and crosses over to look at the posters outside the cinema. The young man walks into the cinema, passes a woman in the ticket office, enters the auditorium, takes his seat and settles into watching *Dragon Inn*. Whereas in the prologue the cinema was full, now it is almost empty; the only other spectator we initially see is a little child who turns out to be accompanied by an old man (this is autobiographical, as a child Tsai was taken to grand movie theatres in Kuching, Malaysia, every day by his grandfather and saw *Dragon Inn* around the age of ten).

The rest of the film consists of the young Japanese man moving around the auditorium and encountering a small shifting band of strange fellow spectators, while the 1967 King Hu movie plays on the big screen. At various points the young man finds himself sitting near a middle-aged man in a leather jacket and a vamp-like woman who might be a prostitute and who the Japanese man takes to be a ghost. These persons have a tendency to suddenly disappear and reappear, sometimes sitting a few rows away and then directly behind the young man and then abruptly appearing sitting in the seat next to him. Why do these spectators sit so closely together when the rest of the seats in the theatre are empty? Why do they spend so much time looking furtively at each other rather than at the screen? In one extended scene, the young Japanese man gets up from his seat and moves down a few rows to sit next to an impassive older man, ostensibly to ask for a light for his cigarette. The young man stares at the face and neck of the older man, who ignores him, staring straight ahead at the big screen, despite the young man almost clambering over him. Eventually the young man gives up and walks off in a huff, the impassive older man conceding a slight glance at the departing figure.

These scenes in the theatre are intercut with scenes in which the young Japanese man leaves the auditorium to wander around the back corridors of the cinema building, while the woman we saw at the beginning of the film in the ticket office (played by Tsai regular Chen Hsiang-chyi) makes similar circuits of the building with a slowness accentuated by a heavy limp. She is usherette and cleaner as well as working in the ticket office. In one lengthy episode the young man, while wandering the labyrinthine corridors, encounters various men passing each other in increasingly tight doorways and darkened passages. The Japanese man stops next to a handsome young man, who is smoking, and points to his cigarette. The other man pulls out a lighter, they stare at each other, the Japanese man gets closer and closer to the smoking man, as if he wants to kiss him – he touches him – then the smoking man unexpectedly speaks, the first dialogue in the film:

'Do you know this theatre is haunted? This theatre is haunted. Ghosts.'[13]

The young man blurts out 'I'm Japanese', to which the other man replies 'Sayonara' as he turns and walks off down the corridor, leaving the young man staring after him in a long-held static shot, a typical Tsai Ming-laing 'dead-time' shot.

Goodbye, Dragon Inn contains a particularly (in)famous scene. It begins with the usherette in the gentleman's washroom, cleaning out the toilets with her bucket and mop – she checks each cubicle and pulls the chain in each – but one cubicle is occupied so she leaves it. As she departs the occupied cubicle door opens slightly. There is then a long-held shot from above looking down at an angle at the row of urinals (with the row of cubicles behind). The young Japanese man, our protagonist, is standing at his urinal. Another man stands at the urinal to his right, smoking. Another comes in and stands at the urinal to the young man's left (Figure 24). They all stand and stare impassively ahead at the wall. Then the occupied cubicle behind the three standing figures opens and a man comes out and exits after washing his hands in a washbasin. Then we see a hand come out of the cubicle and close the door. The three men sense this going on behind them but carry on standing at their urinals impassively,

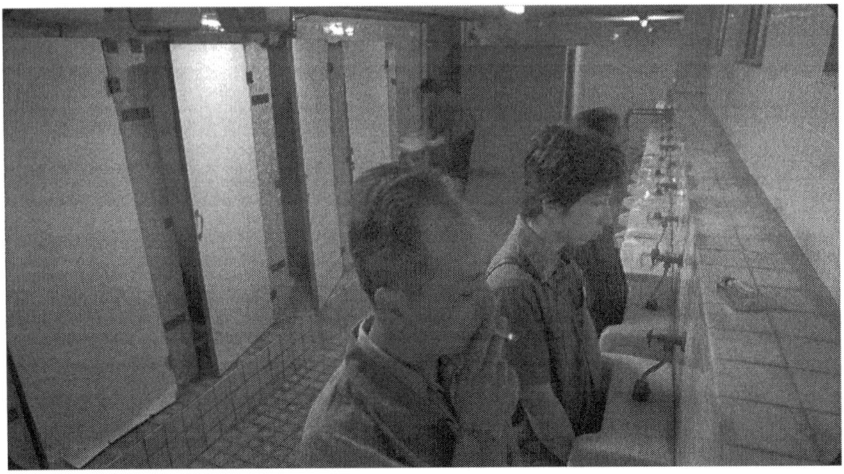

Figure 24 *Goodbye, Dragon Inn*, Tsai Ming-Liang.
Looking down at an angle from above at a row of urinals (with a row of cubicles behind). The scene lasts several minutes and is the epitome of fixed-camera long take slow cinema. Almost nothing happens apart from three men standing at their urinals for an absurdly long period of time. Yet the way the entrances and exits from the toilets are choreographed, along with the fact that there is no dialogue, gives the scene the deadpan comedic intensity of a slapstick scene from Chaplin or Keaton, yet the comedic register might better be described as 'queer deadpan', a kind of knowing but non-ironic sublimation of camp.

one still smoking, all three looking ahead at the wall, not behind at whatever is going on in the cubicle. This is clearly turning into an elaborate comic scene. Another person enters and appears to come between the young man and the smoking man, in fact he has just come in to collect his pack of cigarettes left on the shelf in front of urinals, a droll red-herring. The scene lasts several minutes and is the epitome of fixed-camera long take slow cinema. Almost nothing happens apart from three men standing at their urinals. Yet the way the entrances and exits from the toilets are choreographed, along with the mysterious events in the occupied cubicle, give the scene the comedic intensity of an action-packed slapstick scene from Chaplin or Keaton; *Goodbye, Dragon Inn* is full of visual gags and sharp comic timing, sometimes feeling as much a homage to silent-era cinema as to *wuxia*. That the comedic aspect of *Goodbye, Dragon Inn* is akin to that of a silent film is obvious in that there is no dialogue in the 'urinals scene' and virtually no dialogue in the whole film, apart from the dialogue, music and sound of the 1967 *Dragon Inn* film, the soundtrack of which is heard directly in the auditorium or heard distantly in the background in the scenes outside the auditorium.

Although *Goodbye, Dragon Inn* represented a landmark in the development of Tsai's minimalist static long-take aesthetic, the film enjoys some little jokes at the expense of other styles, including shot/reverse shot montage in a scene where the usherette is peeping out from the side of stage up at the big screen, gazing at the face of the heroine of King Hu's film; the faces of usherette and star look at each other back and forth in series of fast cuts, the face of the usherette bathed in ecstatic spots of light from big screen, from the image of the star.

As the screening of *Dragon Inn* draws to a close and the final credits come up, there would appear to be only three people left in the auditorium, the old man with the little boy and a middle-aged man in a leather jacket. There is a close-up of the man in a leather jacket smiling at the screen, looking intently and then a tear appears in one eye and then the other. This spectator is played by Shih Chun, the King Hu regular and star of *Dragon Inn*, while the old man with the child is played by Miao Tien, another star of the original film. Shih Chun and Miao Tien bump into each other coming out of the theatre foyer and exchange the film's second and last piece of dialogue:

'I haven't seen a movie in a long time.'
'No one goes to the movies anymore, and no one remembers us anymore.'[14]

Back in the auditorium, the usherette puts on the house lights and checks that everyone has gone. She exits the frame but Tsai Ming-liang continues to hold a fixed-camera long take, several minutes in total, of the theatre, as if to say: this is the place of cinema and this is how it looks when the film is over, this is how it looks completely devoid of an audience. When the lights come up perhaps even the ghosts depart.

In another sub-plot the usherette hankers after the elusive projectionist and has spent the duration of the film trying to see him. The hitherto invisible projectionist finally appears (a belated appearance for Lee Kang-sheng) and he finds a bun the woman has left for him, he then closes the cinema, lowers the shutters and rides off on his motorcycle, watched by the woman who has stayed behind nearby to catch a glimpse of him. With everyone gone, the music from an old 1960s Chinese pop song comes up over the closing images of the empty rainy streets outside the cinema:

'So much of the past
Lingers in my heart.
Half is bitter

Half is sweet.

Year after year

I can't let go,

Can't let go,

Can't let go.

I'll remember with longing forever.'[15]

Goodbye, Dragon Inn sets up at least three broad explicit layers of meaning. First, it is a film about the activity of going to a cinema and watching a film. It is a film in which we watch people watching a film. It is also a film about the other activities which occur in a cinema – looking at the posters outside, paying for a ticket at the box office, entering the darkened auditorium, finding a seat, drinking and eating and disturbing other spectators, visiting the lavatories. It is a film about the people who work in a cinema, the usherette and the projectionist and the additional work they have to do – who cleans the lavatories in a cinema? And it is a film about the movie theatre itself as a unique type of building, a strange architectural and social space.

Second, the film sets up a relationship between the film we are watching, Tsai's *Goodbye, Dragon Inn*, and the original King Hu martial arts film *Dragon Inn*. Throughout Tsai's film it is King Hu's film that provides the soundtrack. The basic idea here is that in 1967 King Hu's film played to huge sell-out audiences, while in 2003 only a handful of people are watching that same film. The film and the actors in the film are now forlorn Bazinian ghosts who only come alive when the 'mummified' film is unwrapped, revived and screened. But, if so few people come to watch it, can it really be said to come alive again? With so few people to view and appreciate it, does *Dragon Inn* now belong in a ghostly limbo, endlessly repeating itself in cinematic purgatory to no one? In 1967 this magnificent large movie theatre was filled with people every night. Now it is a rundown building, which only attracts a pitifully small number of people. And perhaps it is not only the golden age of the martial arts film, or the heyday of this particular cinema building which belong to the past, perhaps it is also cinema as a mass entertainment medium or art form which is in terminal decline.

Thirdly, a film is an erotic voyeuristic medium, and a cinema as a building or social space may have its own erotics. The young Japanese man and his furtive encounters in different spaces of the theatre building obviously carry connotations of gay cruising with all its rites and rituals, its confusions, frustrations and absurdities. This is not just symbolic but may have its own nostalgic subtext because certain movie theatres, like this one in Taipei, were actual sites for gay cruising.[16]

Goodbye, Dragon Inn may be less an exercise in poignant nostalgia for the golden age of the *wuxia* film than an example of contemporary cinematic modernism's ambivalent nostalgia for the golden age of postwar cinematic modernism, a kind of film which purportedly no longer has an audience or a home (which for Tsai may mean leaving the cinema and finding a new home in the gallery). More importantly, *Goodbye, Dragon Inn* sets up an encounter between the labyrinthine space of the movie theatre and the way the cinematic gaze engages with the uncanny world of the film and its characters/actors on the big screen. It then reconfigures this encounter, this gaze, this otherness, as analogous to an experience of desire, in this case gay desire within the practice of cruising. And so an elegy for cinema becomes interwoven with an elegy for a mode of gay desire which was in many ways specific to a particular space and historical context. From this perspective Tsai's *Goodbye, Dragon Inn* redeems King Hu's *Dragon Inn* and forestalls the actual death of cinema and/or cinematic modernism through the exercise of a droll – some might say 'queer' – nostalgia for its golden age and in doing so redeems a lost history, lost moments, of gay desire.

Angela Schanelec

Angela Schanelec's films, like those of her Berlin School peers, mostly deal with intense family tensions or alienated, often female, protagonists trying to find a place in life. These tensions and this pervasive alienation are obliquely linked to the pressured unreality of post-economic miracle neoliberal capitalism in Germany and a dazed limbo into which, according to these filmmakers, Germany entered after reunification. In other words, Schanelec follows in the cinematic modernist tradition of Antonioni in foregrounding individual alienation and psychological breakdown as an implied symptom of broader social, economic and political dysfunction.

This is a cinema of existential alienation, it is a realist cinema, it is a cinema of de-dramatized Bressonian acting, it is a cinema of the static long take, of minimalism, a cinema of duration and the time image, and it might be considered an example of slow cinema (Schanelec's 2001 film *Passing Summer* has the German title *Mein langsames Leben*, which translates winningly as 'My Slow Life'). However, in the actual experience of watching a Schanelec film such as *Marseille* (2004), it is the sense of fragmentation, a radical fracturing of narrative structure, along with a fracturing between and within images (including a propensity for frames within frames) that predominates over the sense of integral slow duration. Despite her use of static long takes for key scenes, Schanelec's aesthetic is one of density, discontinuity and elliptical montage.

Marseille (2004)

Sophie, a young woman from Berlin, is exchanging flats for a couple of weeks with a young woman, Zelda, from Marseille. They swap keys but Sophie finds the flat in Marseille almost empty, as if no one has been living there. It later transpires that Zelda never arrived or stayed at the flat in Berlin. Sophie meets a young car mechanic, Pierre, and they have a couple of dates and presumably have a brief relationship although, if so, this is not actually shown in the film. Sophie returns to Berlin, and the story abruptly shifts to the household of Hanna, an actress, her partner Ivan, a photographer, and their little boy, Anton. Sophie child-minds Anton when Hanna and Ivan are at work, and there are suggestions that Sophie has unrequited feelings for Ivan, but she is essentially an outsider in the household. Feeling that she might have been more at home in Marseille than Berlin, Sophie decides to return to Marseille for a longer period, but upon coming out of Marseille railway station she is caught up in a violent street incident. The film ends with Sophie giving her report of the incident to the French police.

Sophie is a photographer and spends her time wandering nondescript parts of a city – this is why she has come to Marseille – taking pictures of backstreets, traffic junctions, little shopping malls and uninteresting buildings (Figures 25 and 26). She has an eye for peripheral urban sites that are hidden in plain view. By finding the right angle (in every sense) for a shot, she attempts in her pictures to capture the 'presence' of these spaces as something mundane, to capture the quality of ordinariness, yet at the same time to defamiliarize these sites and the very idea of the 'ordinary'. In a gently comic comment on the sinister privatization of public space, Sophie is prevented from taking pictures in a shopping centre by a burly security guard who even feels the need to call up reinforcements. Are Sophie's photographs realist? Are they purely aesthetic images? Or do the photographs have some other meaning(s)? These questions, of course, can also be applied to Schanelec's film.

As might be expected from being mentored by tutors like Harun Farocki, the original generation of Berlin School directors in the late 1980s and early 1990s

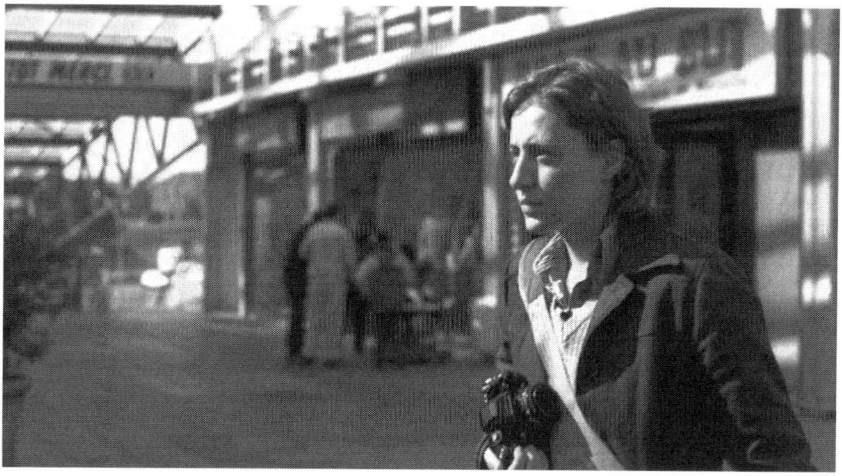

Figure 25 *Marseille* (2004), Angela Schanelec.
Sophie is a photographer and spends her time wandering nondescript parts of Marseille, taking pictures of backstreets, traffic junctions, little shopping malls. Walking through a bland shopping mall Sophie is in focus, in sunlight, walking purposefully with her camera, looking straight ahead for the right shot ignoring, in the background and out of focus, a group of youths (from an ethnic 'other') fooling around, perhaps menacingly.

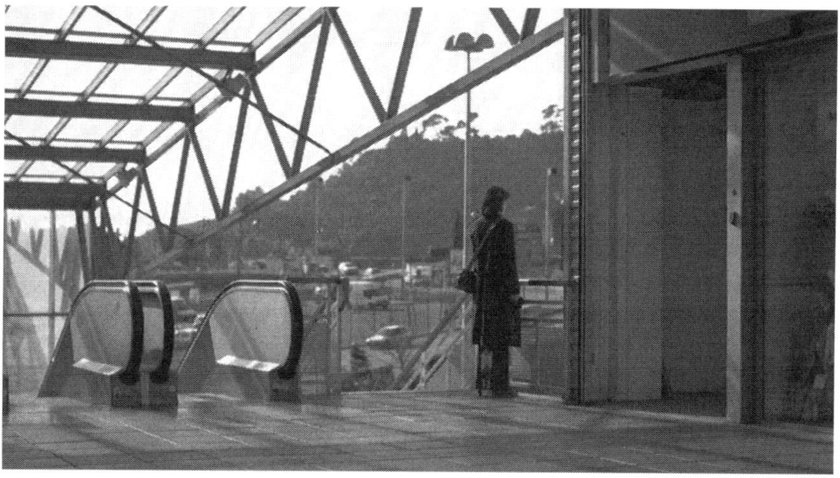

Figure 26 *Marseille* (2004), Angela Schanelec.
The sublime banality of the urban modern. Schanelec replicates Sophie's activity as a photographer by a decentred framing of Sophie herself in long shot as a marginal anonymous presence, back to camera, standing and looking out from the most mundane spot in the mundane shopping mall. In a comic comment on the sinister privatization of public space, Sophie is about to be threatened with arrest by burly security guards for attempting to take photographs from this utterly innocuous spot in the mall.

were schooled intensively in Bresson, Godard and Antonioni, Schanelec being part of a small group that spent weeks in close analysis of Antonioni's *The Passenger*.[17] Like the protagonist Locke (Jack Nicholson) in Antonioni's 1975 film, Sophie is a passenger drifting between two places, Berlin and Marseille, and two identities, the taking on of a new identity triggered by the erasing of another person's identity – the vanished Zelda in Marseille – and Sophie also has a desire, however diffidently expressed, to usurp Hanna's position as wife and mother to Ivan and Anton respectively in Berlin. In other ways Sophie is closer to the Maria Schneider character in *The Passenger*, a character without an identity who seemingly drifts around Europe and tellingly has no name and is cast simply as 'the girl'.

The destabilization of identity and characterization in a Schanelec film is related to the most striking feature of her work: the fragmentation of narrative. Antonioni set an example for this in the way a film such as *L'avventura* might start with one apparent protagonist and storyline and then gradually or abruptly shifts focus to another protagonist and different storyline. More generally Antonioni films move back and forth between thriller, romantic and quest genres, usually shifting into an 'investigation' plot structure, but one in which the investigation dissipates, remains unresolved and shifts back into an equally unresolved romance mode. Despite Antonioni's experimentation with episodic narrative form, his films retain a formal continuity underpinned by the prevalence of long-take sequence shot durations. Schanelec may share Antonioni's themes, but her approach to storytelling is closer to Godard in its overt fracturing of narrative. *Marseille* is an extreme example in that the film is divided into three distinct parts. Part 1 is the story of Sophie in Marseille. Part 2 is Sophie's return to Berlin, but at this point the film shifts its focus to Hanna and Ivan and relegates Sophie to a peripheral role. This part of the film is further subdivided in that we see a lengthy scene of professional photographer Ivan at work taking portraits of women workers in a factory (a scene in which both Hanna and Sophie are absent) and a lengthy scene of professional actress Hanna on a theatre stage rehearsing her role in a Strindberg adaptation (a scene in which Ivan and Sophie are absent). The third part of *Marseille* consists of Sophie at a police station giving a witness statement about a robbery. Although it is possible to discern thematic connections and common (visual) motifs which link these distinct parts and sections of the film, the crucial point is that they are *supposed* to be distinct, semi-autonomous narrative units. Schanelec has stated in a number of interviews that this was one purpose in this film: to experiment in radical switches from one storyline to another and in which a character central to one section would be marginal or absent in another.

The most audacious part of *Marseille* is the third. Schanelec had been demonized, particularly by German critics, for making 'slow cinema' in which 'nothing happens'. In the final part of *Marseille* there is an extraordinary violent action sequence: on coming out of Marseille Station Sophie is accosted by a masked man in a red jumpsuit who has just committed a major crime (robbed a bank?). He points a gun at Sophie and orders her to strip and to put on his jumpsuit so that the police will follow and arrest her while he makes his getaway. She thought she was about to die and realized that she really wanted to live and at that moment the man waived her away and ran off. The conceit is that none of this is actually shown in the film, instead the whole dramatic episode is simply told, haltingly, by Sophie to the police; the dramatic action sequence is rendered as pure narration, a story told to listeners. Filming someone telling a story can be 'cinematic', can be in itself an interesting action sequence as the viewer listens to the voice and watches each expression come and go on the face of the person telling a story. Bergman did this in *Persona* in the scene where the nurse (Bibi Anderson) is drunk and tells of an erotic escapade from her past to her silent watchful patient (Liv Ullman). Godard brings out both the erotic and the psychoanalytic associations of storytelling in the pornographic story told at the beginning of *Weekend*. In *Marseille* there is no eroticism, only a slowly dawning trauma as, in the very act of telling the story, Sophie starts to process the incident she has just experienced. A fixed camera catches Sophie's face at an angle and from slightly above throughout the take. Schanelec often uses this kind of very precise angle and perspective for close-ups, redolent of expressionist film or film noir. Towards the end of the witness statement the policeman asks Sophie a question:

'You are a photographer? What do you photograph? Is the question so difficult?'

[long silence]

'Streets'[18]

After giving this answer Sophie's face disintegrates into tears, an obvious climactic point to end the film, reminiscent of the seven-minute static long take of the female protagonist crying, which closed Tsai Ming-liang's *Vive L'Amour* (1994). But Schanelec leaves things more open by adding two coda scenes. In the first, Sophie, in a yellow dress given to her by police, walks nonchalantly along the street to the German Embassy: to get help to leave or stay in Marseille? We don't know. The final scene of *Marseille* is filmed in long shot in a couple of long takes. The long shot is a particular trait of the Berlin School and Schanelec uses it for a closing scene of holidaymakers on the Marseille beach in late afternoon, which shifts via a dissolve to the beach at dusk, the lights of the resort area glimmering in the background and, amid the now considerably thinned out clusters of people, the viewer recognizes the figure of Sophie in the distance, walking along the beach, the sea lapping at her feet, diminishing as she walks further and further away from the camera (which remains fixed throughout) until, in vintage Antonioni style, she becomes an anonymous dot and then vanishes from our view.

Jia Zhangke

The influence of neorealism was evident in the first post-Mao era Chinese film to attract international attention *Yellow Earth* (1984), directed by Chen Kaige with cinematography by Zhang Yimou and telling the undramatic story (in austere 'minimalist' images rather than dialogue) of a communist cultural worker in the countryside collecting songs and trying to help a poverty-stricken illiterate peasant family, especially the downtrodden daughter of the family, living in an unrelentingly hostile landscape. The film inaugurated the 'fifth generation' of Chinese filmmakers, Chen Kaige and Zhang Yimou finding success in China and internationally but quickly moving into mainstream genre filmmaking. *Yellow Earth* had a life-changing impact on the young Jia Zhangke and, like other directors of the 'sixth generation', his filmmaking is in part an attempt to further develop the neorealist aesthetic of *Yellow Earth* in line with the development of cinematic modernism out of neorealism in postwar Italian film. In the booklet essay accompanying the British DVD of *Still Life* Chris Berry remarks:

> Writing in *The Village Voice*, Anthony Kauffmann describes Jia Zhangke as 'cinema's foremost poet of globalization' (8 January 2008). Of course, he's right. And Jia uses the long-shot long take realism he learnt about reading André Bazin and watching Italian neorealism while studying at the Beijing Film Academy to document China's transformation, albeit with breathtakingly beautiful imagery.[19]

'Bazinian poetry of globalization' would be a succinct formulation of a central idea running through this book, that since the early 1990s certain directors around the world have used an international style, poetic realist yet formalist, with a lineage going back to Bazin and to Rossellini and Antonioni and postwar cinematic modernism, in order to chart processes of national transformation, whether economic miracles or political catastrophes (often both at the same time) within the context of the era of globalization. The same DVD booklet for

Still Life includes an essay by Jia Zhangke himself in which he writes about his time at the Beijing Film Academy, about how during a relative ideological thaw in the late 1990s it was cinema rather than literature that brought previously forbidden international ideas and critical thinking to his generation in China:

> Literary and philosophical concepts such as 'stream of consciousness' or 'alienation' were, to a very large extent, introduced to China by way of the discussion of Western films. To Chinese intellectuals, works like Alain Resnais' *Last Year at Marienbad* or Antonioni's *Red Desert* served as their introductory course to Western arts. Words such as 'Godard', 'jump cut', 'Rive Gauche', or 'Fassbinder' began to creep into their writings.[20]

These films brought a new range of images to a culture that had long been suffering from what Jia calls 'image deprivation', and he notes that his generation suddenly gained access to banned films in the 1990s through rapid advances in the technology of DVD and through networks of pirate DVD production and distribution:

> Before the easy availability of pirate DVDs, it was hard to imagine how an ordinary citizen could access Godard's *Breathless* or Tarkovsky's *Mirror*.[21]

As this background suggests, Jia Zhangke's own films are informed by the traditions of postwar European cinematic modernism and are a good example of how these influences are not imitated but assimilated and transformed within a new cultural context.

Jia's films have been marked by a combination of verité documentary modes with (cinematic) genre tropes, including gangster/film noir, and reflexive theatrical elements. The combination of neorealism and an almost Brechtian theatrical mode is particularly evident in *Platform* (2000), a film about a young theatre troupe from the 1960s in transition from Cultural Revolution agit-prop workers into the post-Maoist period and the turn to capitalism. The film focuses on the everyday life of its protagonists rather than momentous historical events, and the story is told via de-dramatized, often static long takes, and in episodes structured by radical ellipses. The staging of theatrical scenes by the acting troupe adds a further level of reflexivity to the representation of realism in the film, making *Platform* a distant relation to Angelopoulos's *The Travelling Players* (1975) with its acting troupe staging its banal play through different key moments in the traumatic history of war-time Greece.

Jia Zhangke's later films (mostly shot digitally) have been set in contemporary China and reflect in acutely critical fashion the dramatic changes China has undergone since the initial market-driven reforms of the 1980s: the economic miracle, the increasing political authoritarianism of Communist Party rule since the 1989 Tiananmen Square massacre and China's entry into a world economy dominated by 'globalization' and 'neoliberalism'. *Unknown Pleasures* (2002) concerns alienated youth, the central characters being a disaffected teenage couple who maintain their cool pose while getting increasingly lost in the aimlessness of their lives, mirrored by the increasing aimlessness of the narrative. *Unknown Pleasures*, like most of Jia's films from *Xiao Wu* (*Pickpocket* 1997) through to *Ash Is Purest White* (2018), to a greater or lesser degree, adapts the genre tropes of the gangster film, so ubiquitous in world cinema since the 1990s. In Jia's films the gangster motif refers not just to actual gangsters outside the law but to institutionalized gangsterism as an integral part of the current hybrid communist/capitalist system.

Jia's films bear witness to Antonioni-like alienation and ennui as symptoms of an economic miracle which harbours a dysfunctional society riven with corruption and violence. However, in Jia Zhangke's films the alienation is felt mainly by the disaffected young or dislocated workers, rather than a modern Chinese equivalent to Antonioni's Italian upper-middle classes, although *Still Life* does include the nouveau riche in its representation of class and uses Antonioni-like stylistics to do so.

Still Life (2006)

The location of *Still Life* is the Three Gorges on the Yangtse River, one of the most scenic sites in China, depicted in countless paintings and poems down the centuries. However, this site of classical natural beauty has become a modern industrial site of construction and demolition, a site full of dust, noise and rubble. It is the time of the Three Gorges Dam, a project begun in 1994 and completed in 2015. Although the benefits of the dam in terms of energy generation should be huge, the project required the flooding of many towns and villages. Jia Zhangke first visited the area in 2005 and was shocked at the scale of destruction and the dislocation of so many communities. What particularly interested Jia was the idea that the state of flux in which China finds itself is manifested in the mobility of its people, huge flows of internal migration as people leave moribund regions and travel to development zones in search of work. Such mobility leads to a breakdown of old ties of family and kinship. In his director's statement accompanying the film Jia says:

> *Still Life* was shot in the old town of Fengjie. Great changes have come to this place due to the construction of the Three Gorges hydro project: countless families

> who lived there for many generations had to relocate to other cities. Fengjie's old town, which had a 2000-year history, was torn down and submerged forever. I entered this condemned city with my camera and I witnessed demolitions and explosions. In the roaring noise and fluttering dust, I gradually felt that life really could blossom in brilliant colours even in a place with such desperation.[22]

While pulling no punches, the film wears its political and historical baggage lightly, Jia foregrounding the actual conditions in Fengjie – the incessant noise, the rubble, the concrete ruins, the heat and the dust – and then allowing the characters, storylines and, above all, the images to take on a life and sometimes surreal logic of their own, rather than adhering to a programmatic political message.

The film sets up two parallel narratives, which in typical modernist fashion seem designed to eventually converge without ever quite doing so. The first narrative features a middle-aged man, Han Sanming, from Shanxi province, who has come to Fengjie in search of his wife and daughter. He hasn't seen them for ten years. While waiting for contact to be made with his wife, he moves into a hostel and takes work on one of the city's numerous demolition sites. The second narrative features a young woman, Shen Hong, also from Shanxi province, who has come to Fengjie in search of her husband, who she hasn't seen for two years. The film has a three-part narrative structure: the first part is Sanming's story, the second part switches to Shen Hong's story and the third and final part switches back to Sanming's story. Despite the obvious parallels between the two storylines, the two characters and their narratives remain unconnected. The film is elliptical in the relationship between the two narratives, the three parts and in the relationship between each extended scene. A scene can occur in a different time and place to its preceding scene, the shift between scenes occurring in the cut between scenes, the shift in temporal and spatial markers not being represented for the viewer. In an early scene in *Still Life* Sanming goes to a jetty by the river, walks on to a boat and meets an oldish man who is cooking. Sanming asks about 'Missy Ma'.

> The cook says, 'Let's go on deck'
> A number of people are on deck. Because of the heat and humidity, everyone is in vest and shorts. Everyone has mobile phones. Everyone is smoking. Two men eating bowls of noodles look at Sanming suspiciously.
> The cook: 'Missy Ma not here – she's down river'
> Sanming: 'Where's my kid?'
> The cook: 'You're the uncle, you should know. This is our first meeting. We must never talk about past again. Police decide.'

> One of the men suddenly jumps up and kicks Sanming, shouting, 'Fuck you, fuck you'.
> Sanming: 'I came all this way to see my daughter'
> Another man scowls: 'If you make trouble you go in the river'
> This dialogue is followed by a fixed camera long take of the men on the deck of the boat.
> Sanming offers a drink from a bottle of countryside liqueur, which he has brought from Shanxi.
> The cook: 'I don't want it'
> The camera shifts to a pan of a huge industrial transportation ship going past.[23]

In an abrupt shift, the next scene will be of Sanming working on a demolition site, a strange scene in which men in silver body-insulation suits and helmets, looking like spaceman from an alien planet, tanks on back, are spraying the demolition site with disinfectant. The viewer at this point in the film has little idea of who Sanming is, who 'Missy Ma' is and no idea about the other characters or what they are talking about. What the viewer has experienced is the noise, dust, heat, confusion and chaos. From the beginning of the film the viewer has also experienced a palpable sense of aggression underlying each scene. The viewer will have gathered that Sanming is from a distant province and is treated as a country bumpkin and subjected to violence and exploitation. The scene on the boat is riven with a chaotic atmosphere and an ambience of suspicion and barely concealed threat. But the precise meaning of the dialogue exchange on the boat remains unclear. The viewer may have a sense that Sanming is searching for his wife and daughter but the background to this story and the significance of the cook in the story is only revealed gradually towards the end of the film.

Between parts one and two of the film there is an ellipsis and a link: weird things are happening in the sky and what appears to be an unidentified flying object shoots around the gorge. Initially, this seems to be the object of Sanming's gaze, but it turns out to be the object of the gaze of an unknown young woman; in other words, the transition from part one to part two takes place within a transfer of the gaze, of point of view, from Sanming to Shen Hong. There follows a series of scenes in which the young woman – an outsider – wanders around sites in various states of demolition, places defamiliarized by her stranger's gaze. She also witnesses the results of a violent altercation between residents and gangster-types employed by the local 'boss'. It slowly becomes evident that she is trying to contact her husband and that her husband may be this boss-figure called Mr Bin.

She meets a surveyor who works for Bin, and he agrees to try and help her contact her husband, but this sets up an unpredictable series of narrative

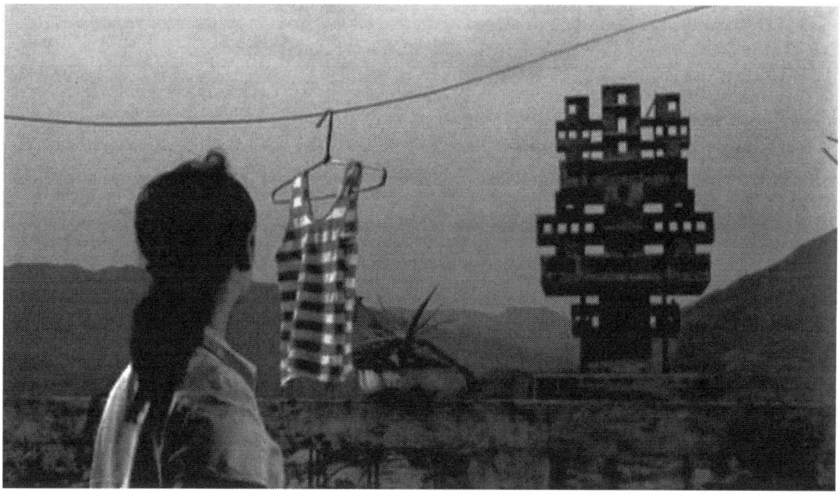

Figure 27 *Still Life* (2006), Jia Zhangke.
Perhaps the strangest 'still life' composition in the film: a woman, Shen Hong (Zhao Tao), filmed from behind, gazes out at a blue-striped T-shirt on a wire washing line and, beyond, a bizarre edifice. Later, smoke will start to come out of the base of the edifice and the whole structure will launch off like a rocket into the sky.

digressions. The young woman goes back to the surveyor's apartment. Are they going to have an affair? Nearby is a strange large edifice. Some children are playing around the structure. The surveyor cooks the young woman a meal; the strange structure is visible through the windows in his flat. She says that she hasn't seen her husband for two years and then suggests that her husband now has a new mistress: 'You men are always shielding each other.' The surveyor protests his innocence. She starts to cry. Shen Hong washes her blouse, which she then puts on a washing line out the back of the flat. As she does this she gazes at the strange edifice (Figure 27). Smoke starts to come out of the base of the edifice and the whole structure launches off like a rocket into the sky! Cut to another time and place, and the surveyor telling Shen Hong that he has 'found the man she is looking for'. The man, Mr Bin, arrives and is a smartly dressed 'boss' figure, whether a private entrepreneur or party bureaucrat. Surprisingly she walks away, but he tells her to get in a car. Cut to a scene by the side of a lake or reservoir where nouveau riche couples are dancing to an old Chinese pop tune. The dialogue between Shen Hong and Bin is minimal and fragmented:

'What's going on? Is there something wrong at home? Don't be angry with me – it's hard for me too'.

As Bin says this, he puts out a hand and they fall into an embrace. They dance to the music, holding on to each other, apparently reconciled, at least for a moment, then she suddenly breaks off and says:

'I have something to tell you – I'm in love with someone else'.

'Who?'

'Do you really care? He's waiting for me – we are going to Shanghai'.

'Sounds good!'

Presumably Mr Bin, her husband, is being sarcastic, but he looks mystified rather than upset.

She says:

'Let's divorce. I'm leaving, so please sign the divorce papers when you have time'.

With this closing statement she walks off.

He shrugs and walks off in a different direction.[24]

In its stylization, its faltering dialogue and its presentation of a couple's failure to connect, this scene has been especially reminiscent of Antonioni: the demand for love and the inability to feel love; the supposed 'modern' difficulty of empathy and authentic communication. In this highly stylized second part of the film, the young middle-class woman Shen Hong is played with originality by actress Zhao Tao, but in a role that might well be channelling the spirit of Monica Vitti and her distracted Deleuzian wanderings. Cut to the young woman Shen Hong on a boat. Old television newsreel images of Mao and Deng respectively visiting the Three Gorges. Cut to our original protagonist, Sanming, looking at boats in the harbour, including the boat on which our second protagonist, Shen Hong, is departing. The transition from part two to part three of the film is again transferred from one protagonist and storyline to the other via a gaze, by an act of looking.

The third and final part of *Still Life* does fill in some of the information required to make sense of the storyline of Sanming, his wife 'Missy Ma' and his daughter, and is mostly filmed in a gritty realist style, but it continues to be structured by ellipses and punctuated by surreal images, including a sudden shot of a tower block exploding and falling down and, right at the end of the film, just before the closing credits, a strange scene in which a man is walking a tightrope between two tall buildings.

The overall effect of ellipses in *Still Life* is to erase causal links between events, allowing the viewer to focus instead on the flow of images while periodically reinterpreting the events in order to reconstruct possible storylines. This reconstruction of a storyline with its sub-plots can only really occur at the end of the film when all the different scenes have been presented and even then the resolution of the film at the level of story is unlikely to provide narrative closure, there will still be many 'open' elements for the viewer to consider long after the film is over. What might have been a predictable social realist film with obvious targets becomes something much richer, in which a moral evaluation of the characters and a political analysis of the situation at the Three Gorges is not given by the film but must be drawn in different ways by each viewer from the vivid but conflicting representations of that situation.

Lucrecia Martel

Lucrecia Martel's films can be viewed from a number of perspectives: as part of the latest 'wave' of New Argentine Cinema or as representing a regional sensibility, that of the Salta province in north-west Argentina. Alternatively, Martel's films can be seen as reflecting Argentinian class politics, reflecting especially the recent period of post-dictatorship neoliberalism, increasingly extreme levels of class inequality and social/class differences as manifested in ethnic inequalities and racism which, in turn, leads to an acknowledgement of long neglected issues of colonialism. Martel's films can also be seen as expressions of feminism and a critique of patriarchy. More generally, the approach to issues of gender and sexuality in Martel's films corresponds to contemporary queer theory and politics. Put simply, Martel's cinema reflects a very contemporary configuration of concerns with gender, class, race and colonialism.

These concerns were evident in Martel's first two films, *The Swamp* (*La ciénaga*, 2001) and *The Holy Girl* (*La niña santa*, 2004), both of which portrayed febrile if often repressed sexuality amid a dysfunctional middle-class patriarchal social milieu. Martel's fourth and most recent film, *Zama* (2017), is an historical drama about a Spanish colonial functionary in eighteenth-century Argentina, frustrated by the demands of his superiors and then falling into the hands of rebels and indigenous tribesmen. *Zama* has been widely praised as being a kind of 'deconstruction' of the period or historical heritage drama, representing Argentina's colonial past as an oblique and fragmented fever dream or nightmare, tapping into a collective unconscious filled with memories of trauma and guilt still repressed, still not properly processed.[25] Martel's third feature film *The Headless Woman* (*La Mujer sin Cabeza* 2008) with its motifs of amnesia and guilt could be read as having an allegorical dimension referring to a middle-class disavowal of the military dictatorship period and its associated atrocities.

This subtext to the film may be more evident to Argentinian viewers.[26] From a non-Argentinian perspective such an allegorical register seems contrived, the film being much more pertinent as a portrayal of class, race and gender issues in the present. Aside from its ideological resonances, *The Headless Woman* sees the director embracing the international style of cinematic modernism and this is the primary focus of the following reading.

The Headless Woman (2008)

The Headless Woman begins with three boys and their dog running, jumping and laughing along the grassy bank of a main road, barely stopping to let a bus go by before running across the road, down into an empty canal beside the road and up onto grassy waste grounds, where two boys hide from the other. One boy hides by climbing the scaffolding of a roadside advertising hoarding.

This has been a highly kinetic opening to the film, both in the lively running and playing around of the three boys and in the fast cutting and camera work pursuing the boys. There are some additional things to note about this opening. The boys are in their early teens, indigenous, and we will later find out that they come from the poor area outside the main town, part of a class that work in various service capacities to the middle-class citizens of (white) European extraction. At one point it seems like one boy with his dog has been left behind in the canal next to the road, after the other boys run off to hide. There is a strange almost subliminal flash-edit, the image of a smirking face with a cut lip observing the boy(s) through long grass. Does this face belong to one of the hiding boys or someone else?

Cut to a striking image: two women at weird angles divided by diagonal lines of light and shade. The image is a reflection seen in the glass of a car window, the shapes and textures produced by the play of light. It is a gathering of women in a car park, collecting children to be driven home. Children put their sticky hands on the car door window of a vehicle belonging to an elegant blonde middle-aged woman. This scene is notable for the almost abstract imagery: close-ups of eyes, mouths and parts of the body, an extreme fragmentation of image and sound, the latter being snatches of the women's bizarre conversation about turtles interspersed with children's voices.

Cut to the blonde woman – Veronica ('Vero') – driving her car, listening to an old pop song on the car radio, her mobile phone rings and as she stretches out to her bag to retrieve the phone the car experiences a bump underneath, Vero being thrown about in her seat and knocking her head. She stops the car, stunned. She considers getting out of the car to investigate and thinks about looking back to see what object her car might have hit. She does neither and instead puts on her dark glasses and drives on. As the car pulls away from the scene, the outline of a child's sticky hands becomes visible on the car door window and, through the back window of the car, the body of a large dog lying in the road is very briefly glimpsed. This seems to be our – the viewer's – image rather than Vero looking back or looking in her rear-view mirror. After driving a bit further, she takes off her dark glasses, turns off the radio, stops the car and gets out. The camera remains fixed at an angle focused on the steering wheel, but through the car window, in the periphery of the image, we see parts of Vero's body as she walks up and down in an agitated state. Drops of rain begin to fall on the windscreen and the glimpses of Vero outside the car quickly become blurred by streams of rain running down the glass.

Cut to a black screen. The opening credits come up: *La Mujer sin Cabeza/The Headless Woman.*

The whole film continues in the same style as its prologue: elliptical narrative and fragmented images. Immediately after the opening credits a distracted Vero visits a hospital to have her head wound dressed and X-rayed. The nurses, who are mostly indigenous, think they recognize Vero as the sister of a doctor at the hospital (the doctor is Vero's brother Marcelo). Vero books into a hotel and gets a long sleep, and then, as she goes downstairs in search of a cup of tea, a group of middle-aged men enters, one of whom happens to be a close family friend called Juan. He takes Vero to her room and, as he tries to settle her down, she draws him into a passionate embrace on the bed, and they make love. He drives her home. Vero runs upstairs, locks the door and takes a shower in her clothes. But in the next scene she is in her underwear and her husband, Marcos, is lying on the bed in a pair of swimming trunks (a present from her) – have they just had sex?

The main part of the film tracks Vero, over a few days, attempting to resume her normal everyday life: going to work, visiting relatives, attending social occasions, chatting with friends and so on. Numbed and disconnected, Vero performs normality, *pretending to be herself* while the people around her try to support her performance. But, traumatized and suffering from amnesia, is she still herself? Towards the end of the film Vero dyes her hair from blonde to black, perhaps signalling, among other things, that she is no longer the same person. She becomes convinced that her car ran over not a dog but one of the young boys seen at the beginning of the film, and suddenly one night she confesses to her husband: 'I killed someone on the road.' They drive in the dark back to the stretch of road where the accident took place. He insists that it was a dog in the road, but she refuses to confirm this with her own eyes. The three men – the husband Marcos, Vero's doctor brother Marcelo and the close family friend Juan, who is in the judiciary (and who had sex with Vero in the hotel on the evening of the accident) – convene at the husband's request to deal with 'the situation'.[27] Together they are able to check with the police and hospitals and say they can find no record of any young boy being killed over the weekend in question. They insist to Vero that her car knocked into a wild dog and that she has nothing to feel worried or guilty about. 'Nothing happened', they repeatedly insist.

However, Vero discovers that a young boy is missing at a garden store out by the indigenous quarter near the road where the accident took place and that the canal next to the road is filling up because something, perhaps a body, is blocking the main drain. This sets Vero on her own investigation. She visits the hospital she went to on the night of the accident but they have no records of her admission. At the hotel she went to on the night of the accident the receptionist can find no record of Vero having stayed. The film ends with a party scene and all the main characters dancing to 1970s disco, Demis Roussos singing 'Mammy Blue'. Is Vero now 'normal', reintegrated into her bourgeois milieu and social set? Has she regained her mind? Is she no longer the 'headless woman'?

The foregoing synopsis of the film's storyline can only be reconstructed after watching the film two or three times. Like a number of contemporary films informed by cinematic modernism, *The Headless Woman* is a 'puzzle film' designed to remain unresolved, the ambiguity and lack of a singular truth or explanation being a key intentional characteristic of this type of film.

At a narrative level an obvious point of reference is Antonioni, whose first feature film *Chronicle of a Love Affair* (1950) was structured by a plot in which a young couple are unsure if they bear responsibility for the fatal accident of a friend. Some years later an investigation into the accident is reopened and the couple are forced to act as if they were guilty of murder. Their relationship and their lives become determined by an event of uncertain status: Was it an accident or was it a murder? This device of the uncertain or undecidable event became central to Antonioni's 'deconstruction' of the thriller plot. In *L'avventura* (1960) the plot is generated by the mysterious disappearance of a young woman from a boat: Has she swum away and survived or did she drown and if so was it suicide? The main couple in the film investigate the disappearance of their friend but their relationship is determined by guilt over an event the status of which is never resolved. At the centre of *Blow Up* (1966) is a similarly uncertain and unresolved event, a murder which may or may not have happened, a dead body the image of which may or may not have been caught on a photograph. *The Headless Woman* uses this device, the whole film is determined by an event of uncertain status: Vero's car bumped into something, was it a dog or a young boy or both? Or was it just a bump in the road? Has she killed someone? Or is it the case that, as her husband keeps telling her, 'nothing happened'?

The Antonioni film to which *The Headless Woman* has most often been compared is *Red Desert*, not a puzzle film as such but a film in which a middle-class woman in the midst of a breakdown becomes increasingly disconnected from her marriage, family and social life.[28] Pasolini argued that *Red Desert* was the epitome of modernity in film because of its use of the 'free indirect subjective', in which every detail in every image – every line, colour, shape – is carefully composed to reflect the 'alienation' of the neurotic protagonist, but in aligning 'objective' images with the 'subjectivity' of the protagonist, the film itself becomes an expression of alienation. In *Red Desert* Antonioni famously painted grass and trees a particular shade of green to fit in with the colour scheme of the film, and Pasolini sees this as evidence that the film is no longer merely representing a character's point of view but the 'objective' world of the film, manifesting the 'subjective' vision of its neurotic bourgeois modernist director, Antonioni (formalism being a symptom rather than a critical expression of alienation).[29]

The Headless Woman may be critical of its protagonist, this cold and not especially likeable bourgeois woman, but the composed nature of every detail in every image, along with the fragmentation of the film, is aligned with yet exceeds the point of view of Vero. What Pasolini calls neurotic formalism and delirious aestheticism therefore manifests the perspective or sensibility of the film as a whole. The film is already elliptical and fragmented in the way it films the three boys playing at the beginning of the film *before* Vero has appeared and, in fact, Martel has said in interviews that in *The Headless Woman* she *completely* eschews 'subjective' shots from a character's point of view, which adds a further layer of formalist objectivity or 'alienation' to the overall experience of watching the film.[30]

In *Screening Modernism* András Bálint Kovács designates Antonioni as belonging to a cinematic modernism of continuity, not discontinuity, as adhering to the primacy of the long-take sequence shot.[31] *The Headless Woman*, however, adheres to the primacy of discontinuity. Martel favours fast cutting, each scene begins and ends *in media res* – there are few if any 'establishing shots' – and the relationship between one scene and the next is temporally and spatially uncertain, and uncertain in terms of relationships of causality between narrative events. The individual images are fragmented, divided up by horizontal, vertical and diagonal lines of doors, walls, windows; frames within frames, reflections within reflections. Many images contain body parts with, as befits the film's title, lots of heads decapitated by the frame. Like many films informed by contemporary cinematic modernism, Martel favours cropped close-ups of heads in focus with backgrounds (including other figures) out of focus, often reduced to blurred abstract blobs.

Considering the 'puzzle film' in connection with extreme fragmentation of narrative and image brings us closer to Resnais's *Muriel* (1963) than Antonioni's *Red Desert*. Like María Ornetto's Vero in *The Headless Woman*, Delphine Seyrig's character Hélène moves with a pained smile through the welter of elliptical images in *Muriel* in a state of barely repressed agitation triggered by events of unknown and unresolved status, such as the true identity of her (fascist?) lover and her son's involvement in the torture of an Algerian girl while on military service. This combination of undecidable event, elliptical montage and fragmentation of image creates an overall effect of intense unease and lends itself to paranoia: Is discontinuity and fragmentation concealing a traumatic event or secret truth which we could access if only we could put the fragments together in the correct way? Truffaut praised *Muriel* as a tribute to Hitchcock, and Martel has acknowledged the influence on *The Headless Woman* of *Vertigo* in the characterization of Kim Novak's destabilized identity as Madeleine/Judy and in the uncertainty over the main events, the deaths/suicides, which may or may not be what they seem.[32]

Paranoia in *The Headless Woman* is signalled towards the end of the film in various indications that the three men – Vero's husband, brother and her sometime lover – have been engaged in covering up the car accident. Have they been removing evidence that after the accident Vero went to a hospital and had X-rays? Or that she stayed at a hotel? Or that the car was badly damaged? If so, this conspiracy is the opposite of a 'gaslighting' plot: the three men are not trying to drive Vero mad or make her believe she is guilty of killing someone, instead their conspiracy would be to convince Vero that she is *not* mad, that she did not kill a boy in a car accident and, indeed, that 'nothing happened'. But is making a woman who is undergoing a mental breakdown believe that she is *not* undergoing a breakdown itself a dubious exercise? As in *Red Desert* and *Muriel*, there is in *The Headless Woman* a strong sense that a woman's justifiable and rational alienation from her role and position is being denied and disavowed by a patriarchal conspiracy which, through its unique power (access to hospitals, police records, etc.), can force the reintegration of a woman back into the normality which is the very source of her abnormal behaviour.

Lisandro Alonso

Argentinian filmmaker Lisandro Alonso's debut film *La libertad* (2001) tracked the life of a young lumberman, Misael, living in almost total isolation in lush woodlands. Through the cycle of seasons and climate, Misael's daily life is recorded: cutting down trees, chopping wood and going to a village to sell the wood and buy provisions. The film also tracks his daily routines: cooking, eating, sleeping, even dreaming. Titling the film 'Freedom' implies allegorical baggage that the film actually resists, yet neither is the film an exercise in pure documentary. The anthropological gaze of the film is offset by a stripped-back aestheticization of the image that belongs to cinematic modernism, initially resembling a Bressonian formalism in its deadpan de-dramatization and eschewal of story, plot, psychology and anything approaching personal expressivity. *La libertad* turned out to be influential, creating a template for a distinctive strand of contemporary cinematic modernism, films which document the life of an isolated outsider amid nature and raw climate and at the margins of civilization and globalization, albeit with connections of radio and phone or connections to the digital world (these outsiders are not self-consciously anti-modernity or anti-technology).[33]

Alonso's second film, *Los Muertos* (2004), is similar in setting and style to its predecessor but introduces more narrative momentum, tracking a man, Vargas, as he is released from prison after serving a long sentence and as he journeys through jungle and upstream in a boat to a remote swampland where his grown-up daughter lives in an impoverished settlement. The man is taciturn, *Los Muertos* containing as little dialogue as *La libertad*, but the protagonist here does have a psychological profile: he is a loner because the weight of prison and his crime hangs heavy – the film begins with a short visceral prologue scene in which two boys are brutally murdered. The film has a quest narrative arc – Vargas trying to find his way to his daughter – however most of the film consists of Vargas carrying out necessary chores like cooking, eating and washing, as he makes his way up river, although these chores include activities which may be less familiar to the average viewer, such as catching, slaughtering and skinning a goat. Much of this activity is filmed in real-time long takes in an observational documentary mode but within what is overall an aestheticized, poetic, formalist style. As with his first film, Alonso's title here seems too overwrought for the film itself: Who are the dead? Is Vargas the dead?

In 2008 Alonso achieved an international breakthrough with *Liverpool*, another film about a taciturn loner on a journey through inhospitable terrain – in this case snow and freezing temperatures contrasting with the humid heat of the jungle in *Los Muertos* – and this journey is again back to a home and family which might prove to be strange and unwelcoming. Alonso's cinematic style has been seen as the epitome of minimalist slow cinema, but this is misleading, his films belong to the lineage of Rossellini in being primarily experiments in narrative form, the 'deconstruction' of story, plot and characterization, rather than the foregrounding of duration per se.

Liverpool (2008)

Liverpool begins on a large industrial container ship. The camera follows a straggly long-haired man wearing a red jumpsuit and white T-shirt as he wanders the vessel and then returns to his cabin where he smokes and takes regular swigs from a bottle of vodka. In a fixed-camera long take the man talks to the captain on the ship's bridge, asking to be dropped off at a port en route to the ship's destination. The man, now identified as 'Farrel', says he needs to see his mother for the first time in years. Farrel disembarks, walking off down the quay in the snowy slush amid the flashing lights of a port area.

Apart from the virtual lack of dialogue and long(ish) takes, the most notable aspect of the film is the sharp elliptical cutting, one scene cutting into another scene in media res, with little or no indication of the transition, of what happened between the two scenes or how much time has passed. Much of the film consists of striking images and abrupt shifts of scene without any explanatory context; the viewer has little idea of what is going on other than that Farrel is on a journey, a quest of some kind. In one scene Farrel is in a café eating some bread and pasta. He looks furtive, distracted. He drinks some beer, gets up and exits the frame. Cut to the backs of two women in skimpy clothing – a disco with hostesses. Farrel sits at the bar with bottles of beer looking at the women. This scene lasts little more than a minute. Cut to a hangover Farrel in the back of a derelict bus where he has found shelter to sleep. He wakes up, lights a cigarette and swigs from a bottle of vodka: Is he an alcoholic or just cold and trying to keep warm? Cut to a shot of seagulls and then Farrel with a red shoulder bag (a Liverpool football club merchandising duffle bag) walking through a container park and entering a transit hut in which a woman watches television and two men play cards. Farrel helps himself to coffee and waits. Cut to a young woman getting into the front of a truck while Farrel climbs onto the open back, loaded with logs. The journey by truck reveals the austere beauty of the passing landscape: ground covered in snow, yellow and brown-leaved trees, long panning shots of trees dusted with snow, mountains in the background. Cut to Farrel getting out of the truck and trudging off, across a snow-covered football pitch where he goes up to a goal post and scrapes it, maybe looking for a message scratched onto the goal post from his youth?

Finally Farrel arrives at his destination, a little settlement with a few huts, cabins and cottages dotted about. He goes into a dingy canteen; a few other customers at the benches give him a pensive look. The canteen owner Torres serves Farrel some bread and a plate of stew or soup, along with some wine, while in the kitchen a radio exchange can be heard discussing how many roads in the area are now blocked with snow. A teenage girl comes and stands in front of Farrel staring at him. The owner comes out of the kitchen and gives her a pot of food which she takes away. This extended scene is followed by another series of elliptical cuts: Farrel spying through the window of a cabin at the girl from the canteen talking to someone. Lights go out. Blackness. Cut to the bright light of the next morning, and Farrel passed out or dead in a frozen derelict outhouse. Cut to the canteen man Torres and an older man carrying a stiff frozen Farrel into a cottage where they lay him down on a bed. They light up a wood stove. After Torres departs, the older man mutters some fragments of dialogue to the unconscious body of Farrel on the bed:

'Why have you come back here? You left just after Analía was born. No-one here knows you know. Even your mother – she's sick – she doesn't know you. You left me one heck of a legacy. I know you can hear me.'[34]

Cut to the teenage girl, Analía, wearing a red jacket and playing with rabbits. A little later she is sitting in her cabin drawing a heart when a now recovered Farrel comes in and tries to engage her in conversation. 'Will you give me money?' she replies. He goes into a red-painted room, two beds, his bedridden mother looks up and smiles. They talk briefly, but she has dementia and it is not clear whether she does or does not recognize her son. Analía again asks him for money, 'Here' he says, giving her all the money from his wallet, 'and don't let anyone take it from you'. She puts her jacket on and goes out. He picks up a photograph from the shelf and puts it in his bag and leaves. Cut to outside: Farrel runs after Analía and tells her not to give away her money, and he gives her something else, a little trinket of some kind? He then trudges off across the fields, a rather beautiful snowy landscape in the sunshine. A fixed-camera long take records him slowly disappearing into the distance, receding, getting smaller and smaller, finally he becomes a black dot against the white snowy field and then vanishes completely from view (Figure 28).

Farrel, the protagonist of the film, has disappeared from the film, presumably returning to the port to rejoin his ship. The film still has at least a third of its

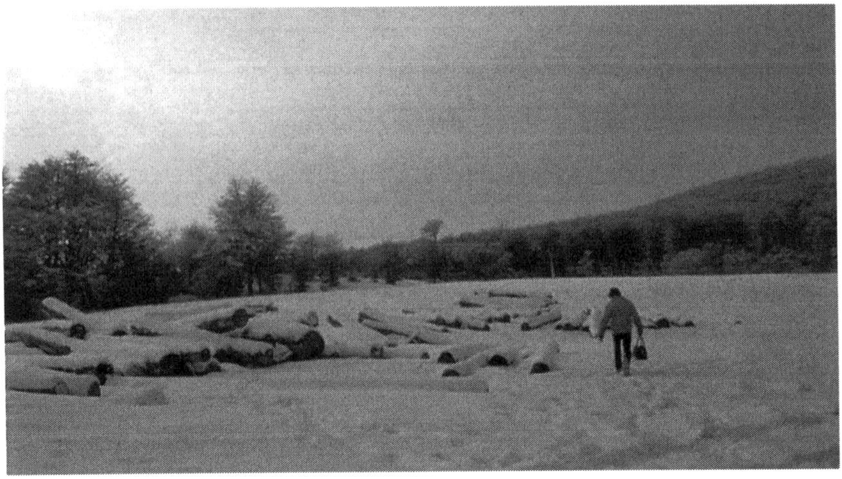

Figure 28 *Liverpool* (2008), Lisandro Alonso.
Farrel trudges off across the fields, a rather beautiful snowy landscape in the fading sunshine. A fixed-camera long take records him slowly disappearing into the distance, receding, getting smaller and smaller, finally he becomes a black dot against the white snowy field and then vanishes completely from view. Farrel, in a way not uncommon in cinematic modernism, has disappeared from the film in which he was the ostensible protagonist, a film which still has a third of its running time remaining.

running time to go and much of this is taken up with scenes of Analía's routine: visiting a saw-mill and a barn, looking after sheep, helping with the trapping of foxes, and in the evening collecting her food pot from the canteen which she takes back to her cabin to feed Farrel's bedridden mother. The viewer learns that the inhabitants of the settlement are thankful that Farrel has left as quickly as he came. Analía is what her community would describe as a 'simpleton', an innocent, but she is also sexualized, being probably the only teenage girl in the community. The viewer also learns what it was Farrel gave Analía as he left. In the final scene of the film, in a close-up shot, Analía leans against a post outside the barn and takes something from her pocket – the trinket Farrel gave her – it is a keyring which says 'Liverpool' (as in the football club). The camera focuses on her hands, her fingers turning the Liverpool keyring over and over. A 'rosebud' moment? The screen goes black. End of film.

As with his previous films, *Liverpool* is shaped by the conditions and landscapes of an isolated part of the world, in this case the harsh freezing conditions of one of the islands in the archipelago of Tierra del Fuego on the southernmost tip of South America. Although the storyline is similar to that of *Los Muertos* – a loner making a journey to a home and daughter – Alonso seems to have developed a more elaborate script with background context and psychological motivation for the main characters, possibly involving incest, prostitution, alcoholism, abuse of some sort, trauma, revenge – in short, a complex plot. In the making of the film or in the editing, however, Alonso has, in the typical manner of cinematic modernism, privileged the images and scenes in themselves, as autonomous from any plot. Or, put another way, the film as an assemblage of carefully composed images has been extracted from the script, erasing most of the narrative detail and only retaining the residual structure of the original story.

What does become evident by the end of the film is that Analía is Farrel's daughter and that he abandoned her in circumstances unknown years ago, leaving her without prospects or money in the care of his mother. Now his mother is bedridden and increasingly incapacitated by dementia, the still teenage and 'simple' Analía must act as her carer, the tiny local community supporting the pair in various ways, although the film also hints that Analía is vulnerable to sexual exploitation by some men within that same community. These elements of a skeletal storyline add to the intensity of the film but any attempt to explain the film by reimposing the original story derived from interviews with Alonso would be an injustice to the fragile beauty and disturbing undertow of the film, and Alonso himself prefers to see the gaps or questions in the final film as left open: What traumatic event happened all those years ago? Does the mother recognize Farrel? Does Analía realize that Farrel is her father? Who was her mother? Will Farrel make it back to his ship?

The film's closing scene of Analía's hands toying with the Liverpool football club keyring is moving because of our, and maybe her, uncertainty at the end of the film as to whether she acknowledges Farrel as her father and what significance can be attributed to this tacky keyring. The arbitrary parting gift withholds its secrets but generates uneasy interpretation, as does the film.

Lee Chang-dong

South Korean cinema has long been notable for its vibrant and eclectic genre cinema, but particularly relevant to the arguments of this book is the critical recognition and international audience reaction that has greeted the latest film by Lee Chang-dong, *Burning* (2018), a film which is consciously situated within the genealogy of cinematic modernism, both postwar and contemporary.

Lee's fifth film *Poetry* (2010) confirmed his international reputation as an art-house auteur, winning major awards at Cannes and elsewhere. In the film an elderly woman called Yang Mi-ja (played by Yoon Jeong-hee) experiences the onset of Alzheimer's disease while looking after her adolescent grandson and trying to deal with a series of complicated family affairs. *Poetry* presented viewers with a radically unresolved ending: when police arrive at Yang Mi-ja's home to arrest her grandson for involvement in the rape of a girl, it is unclear if Yang Mi-ja understands what is happening and why her grandson is being arrested or indeed whether it was Yang Mi-ja herself who informed the police about her grandson. The mysterious quality of consciousness associated with Alzheimer's, the shifts in and out of lucidity and the struggle for moments of clarity that can only ever be fleetingly grasped, become symptomatic of the fluidity of identity and morality in contemporary Korea, indicative of an opaque reality that can no longer be 'processed' by the individual. Although various elements in the narrative of *Poetry* suggest that at some level Yang Mi-ja has been deeply affected by knowledge of the girl's rape and is uneasy at attempts to cover up the crime, the ending remains intentionally undecidable and for each viewer this ambiguous ending will destabilize interpretations of the whole preceding narrative, as Lee explains:

> I left the answer up to the audience. I pictured the film to have much space, as poems do. Blanks that the audiences could fill in. In that sense it can be seen as an 'open' film. The conclusion will be in the audience's mind.[35]

Burning (2018) continues Lee's interest in elliptical, ambiguous narratives and 'open' film, while proving accessible to mainstream audiences.

Burning (2018)

Jong-su is a young aspiring novelist at a loose end, currently having to look after his father's farm, the father having been arrested for a violent altercation. Jong-su runs into Hae-mi, an old childhood friend from the Paju countryside, although he barely remembers her. Over a drink in a bar she tells him about the 'Great Hunger' dance of the Kalahari Bushmen, a dance which expresses not physical starvation but existential questions: Who am I? What is the meaning of this life? Jong-su goes back to Hae-mi's apartment, they have sex, and she asks him to feed her cat while she is away on a trip to Kenya. While Hae-mi is away Jong-su visits the apartment, tries unsuccessfully to locate and feed the cat (who may or may not be an imaginary cat) and, recalling his original sexual encounter with Hae-mi, masturbates in her room.

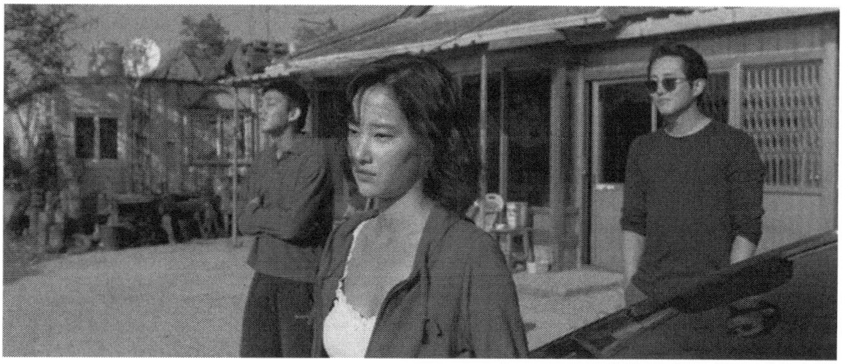

Figure 29 *Burning* (2018), Lee Chang-dong.
David Bordwell sees a predominant stylistic technique of cinematic modernism as being the 'planimetric image', the flat frontal shot of a character or row of characters 'in tableau' staring at or towards the camera/viewer (see cover image of this book). In the image the three characters, Jong-su, Hae-mi and Ben, are now standing, more separated and have changed positions relative to each other in the yard, though not in the perspective of the image, and the formalism of the preceding planimetric image is still evident in the arrangement in profile of the figures in this composition.

Jong-su meets Hae-mi at the airport when she returns from Nairobi, but she is with a fellow Korean traveller, Ben. A strange ménage à trois develops in a succession of episodes in which Jong-su, Hae-mi and Ben meet up. Some of these episodes take place in Seoul, in upmarket coffee shops and restaurants or at Ben's luxury modern apartment in the Gangnam district, but a lengthy central scene occurs in the countryside at Jong-su's farm, where the three sit outside the house as evening falls, drinking wine and smoking cannabis: Ben confesses to a pyromaniac compulsion to burn down dilapidated greenhouses, Hae-mi becomes nostalgic for her childhood in the Paju countryside and Jong-su wonders why Ben is so rich and sophisticated and so apparently amoral (Figure 29).[36] As the scene becomes increasingly intense, Hae-mi suddenly gets up and strips off most of her clothes to perform a sensual jazz dance which gradually turns into the 'Great Hunger' dance, her ecstasy turning to tears under the perplexed, awed and desiring gaze of the two men. Is she a free spirit or unhinged? Hae-mi's dance ends when she collapses and exits the frame, leaving the camera to slowly pan across the background countryside scenery, capturing the lights of cars on a nearby highway and, behind the highway, the border – the long take continuing to pan the hills and mountains of North Korea in the distance. After this episode the narrative takes a drastic turn when Hae-mi suddenly disappears and Jong-su starts to suspect that Ben may have killed her. The film therefore has a tantalizing thriller plot, but the appeal of *Burning* lies in its enigmatic quality, quite a lot happens but the meaning of what happens remains unclear. In other words, the film adheres to a modernist privileging of ambiguity.

Early on in *Burning* Jong-su tells Ben that his favourite writer is William Faulkner and much later in the film Ben, having taken up the recommendation, is encountered reading Faulkner in a coffee shop. Faulkner is an example of a (modernist) novelist who often takes story and plot forms and then 'scrambles' them structurally so that the temporal and causal relations between events become unclear and fragmented, and then further scrambles the storylines by having the same events recounted by different characters – that is to say, the story is told from multiple (unreliable) perspectives.[37] The purpose of this fragmenting of narrative form and perspective is to resist narrative closure and the imposition of one meaning or truth and to facilitate instead the ongoing interpretative activity of each reader. In *Burning* the destabilizing of narrative coherence is largely due to the uncertain status of many scenes which might be dreams, fantasies or memories, or may even be scenes imagined by Jong-su as scenes in the novel which he is trying to write throughout the film. The tendency of the three main characters to tell stories which, especially in Hae-mi's case, may or may not be true, adds to a fundamental unreliability of narrative perspective.

A cinematic modernism analogous to modernist novels such as those of Faulkner arrived with *Citizen Kane*, a film that takes an apparently straightforward linear narrative (the story of a very public man's life) and scrambles the causal links between events and gives us multiple contradictory and unreliable perspectives. Who was Charles Foster Kane? We will never know; his true identity will always remain a mystery, a matter of conjecture. *Citizen Kane* is sometimes called, unflatteringly perhaps, 'the first puzzle movie' (*Burning* is certainly a 'puzzle movie'), and at a basic level the epithet refers to the main ambiguity of the film, which is that the rosebud story might be the secret that reveals the truth and meaning of Kane's life or that the rosebud story might be an irrelevant detail that explains nothing in Kane's life. The viewer is forever caught between interpreting the rosebud story as providing narrative closure or interpreting the rosebud story as just another detail in a fragmented narrative that will always remain open.

Burning assumes the fluidity of modern identities, the (a)morality of modern cosmopolitan relationships, and sexuality as physical function and perverse desire, an explicit attention to sex which has become associated with Korean cinema via the films of Hong Sang-soo and others. For Lee Chang-dong, the question of identity is bound up with the trauma of Korea's twentieth century: colonization by Japan, the civil war, occupation by the United States, the ongoing split between North and South Korea and the succession of dictatorships and repressions in the South. Since the establishment of democracy in 1987, problems of political corruption, violence and repression have continued alongside an 'economic miracle'. For Lee, the history and legacy of war, occupation and dictatorship is important and it resonates throughout *Burning* in oblique but powerful ways, not least in the fact that North Korean propaganda broadcasting across the border zone can be heard at Jong-su's house, which is not far from the border, something that Ben finds highly amusing. However, Lee's main focus is on how the 'success' of the economic miracle throws into relief the inequalities of Korean society and brings to light the contemporary problems associated with atomized identity in a competitive materialist consumer society. Lee sees contemporary identity as marked by a generalized existential alienation, but an alienation which takes particular concrete forms, primarily as issues of class, sexual and gender identity and the symptoms of which include ennui, compulsive behaviour, lack of empathy and outbursts of repressed violence.

The problem of Korean identity is therefore not only a symptom of the violent split between North and South Korea but, in the South, an endemic sense of alienation produced by both the long-standing class structure and the new contemporary consumerist ideology. Or put another way, the economic miracle has shaken up and reconfigured the class struggle, and it turns out that the abiding spirit of *Burning* is not Faulkner but F. Scott Fitzgerald. As Jong-su says to Hae-mi on the balcony of Ben's luxury Gangnam apartment:

> 'Why is Ben so rich? Where does he get his money? Where does he come from? He is like Gatsby. Korea is full of Gatsbys now.'[38]

In his films of the early 1960s Antonioni saw the Italian economic miracle as having stripped people of their 'authentic' identities, producing a void, coated in narcissism and neurosis, where once there had been an identity. Lee Chang-dong offers a similar diagnosis: Koreans have lost their identity and so they struggle to fill the void left behind, struggle to know who they are, where they have come from and what they might be. But, as with *L'avventura* or *The Great Gatsby*, the diagnosis proposed by *Burning* is less important in itself than its function of providing a specific social grounding for the ambiguity of the narrative. For Roland Barthes, in his 'letter to Antonioni', the crucial thing is the sustained gaze that captures the 'being there' or presence of a place or time, mood or ambience, as experienced by an individual sensibility.[39] Rather than overtly presenting a 'social diagnosis', it is through the filtering of subjective particularity that social context is accessed, and this filter, in the case of Antonioni and Lee Chang-dong, is the formalist aesthetic of cinematic modernism.[40] As Barthes addresses Antonioni:

> It is because you are an artist that your work is open to the Modern. Many people take the Modern to be a standard to be raised in battle against the old world and its compromised values; but for you the Modern is not the static term of a facile opposition; the Modern is on the contrary an active difficulty in following the changes of Time, not just at the level of grand History but at that of the little History of which each of us is individually the measure.[41]

Contrary to many reviews, *Burning* is not simply 'about' the Korean class system or the crisis of masculinity, or the split between country and city or the split between North and South Korea. None of these issues is the definitive meaning to which the film can be reduced. Instead 'grand History' is manifested through the mysterious 'little History' of individual sensibility, a mystery or otherness that denotes the 'active difficulty' of understanding the changes wrought by the modern. By representing this 'active difficulty' of the modern, Lee Chang-dong succeeds in representing the 'little histories' of his young characters in *Burning*. His main character, Jong-su, however, is not so successful in his artistic endeavour, confessing to Ben towards the end of the film that he has abandoned writing his novel. Why? 'Because life is a complete mystery to me.'

Hu Bo

Hu Bo's acclaimed 2018 film *An Elephant Sitting Still* shows that contemporary cinematic modernism informed by a neo-Bazinian aesthetic might yet reinvent itself for the third decade of the twenty-first century. The significance of *An Elephant Sitting Still* is that – in 2018 – it successfully combines both gritty social realism/neorealism and highly aestheticized formalism (complete with accompanying existential angst) and does so in a new and very contemporary way, transcending its influences, whether Bresson and Antonioni or Jia Zhangke and Béla Tarr.

Hu Bo graduated from the Beijing Film Academy in 2014 with a degree in directing and received mentoring from Béla Tarr (who became a strong supporter), going on to direct three well-received short films, and writing fiction, including two novels.[42] Hu finished *An Elephant Sitting Still* in late 2017 shortly before his suicide at the age of twenty-nine, so the numerous prizes and awards picked up by *An Elephant Sitting Still* in 2018–19 were granted posthumously. It can only be speculated how far any depressive state afflicting Hu Bo at the time of his death may have affected his film. *An Elephant Sitting* can be criticized as one-dimensional in its miserabilism and one-sided in its negative portrayal of China's 'economic miracle', as making Jia Zhangke's films seem almost optimistic by comparison. A certain immaturity might be discerned when the characters turn to overt nihilistic philosophizing: 'the world is disgusting', 'everybody sucks', 'you think some other place will be different but it never is', 'life is a wasteland' and so on. The other side of this nihilism is an occasional lapse into the sentimental, for example in old man Wang Jin's loving relationship with his little grand-daughter and the film's sympathy with his nostalgia for China's Maoist past. That *An Elephant Sitting Still* was a debut feature film is perhaps responsible for a few of the less convincing plot contrivances. Nonetheless, any flaws in the film are outweighed by its rigour, even in its presentation of all-encompassing existential angst. The film therefore deserves to be viewed in its own terms and context, cinematic and social, rather than as the director's personal expression of some unknown private crisis.

An Elephant Sitting Still (2018)

An Elephant Sitting Still is framed by a reference to its title, beginning with a prologue: a series of short shots introducing the four main characters interspersed with close-ups of snow-covered ground, while a voiceover explains the strange story of an elephant in a zoo in the northern Chinese city of Manzhouli. The elephant sits in an enclosure, never getting up, perhaps people have been stabbing at it with forks or maybe the elephant enjoys just sitting there, ignoring or oblivious to the world and everyone in it. Then the opening credits come up. The film ends four hours later with an off-screen haunting drone over the closing images, presumably the sound of the elephant letting out a primal cry of angst, or maybe a cry of resistance? Then the final credits come up. In between the opening and closing scenes, the four main characters in the film recount this story, and by the latter stages of the film the protagonists are escaping from their respective situations and their city, by heading to a real or fantasy Manzhouli and its elephant, begging the question of whether they wish to escape into oblivion or to resist.

An Elephant Sitting Still is filmed on video by Steadicam, the dominant shot being a close-up, a close-cropped tight framing of a character's face from the front or at a side-angle in profile or moving around the head. The camera is highly mobile and constantly moving in and around its immediate objects, usually faces and heads, giving the film a claustrophobic feeling of repressed energy always threatening to explode. A typical shot throughout the film is from behind a character, just over the shoulder, in a kind of point-of-view shot with the object

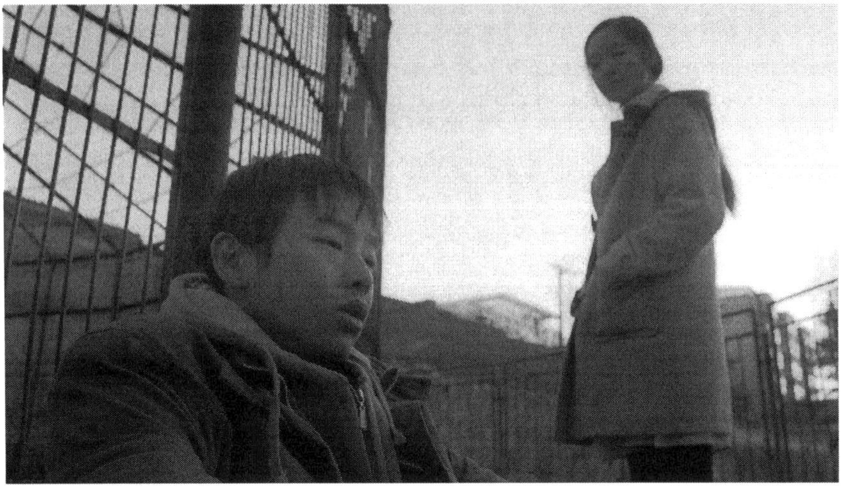

Figure 30 *An Elephant Sitting Still* (2018), Hu Bo.
Contemporary cinematic modernism has a penchant for having the foreground in clear focus and the background blurred, and Hu Bo composes many variations on this. In this figure, Wei, shot from a low angle, sits staring into space while his girlfriend Huang, slightly out of focus, looks down at him with a gaze and posture engaged yet estranged, she is unsure whether to stay or go.

out of focus, Hu Bo having a penchant characteristic of contemporary cinematic modernism for having the foreground in clear focus and the background blurred (Figure 30). The camera work rarely crosses over into the jerky 'unsteadicam' style and, despite a number of static long takes and 'dead-time' long-held shots after a character has left the frame, the film in its busy camera work and highly concentrated elliptical editing rarely feels like 'slow cinema'.

In classic modernist fashion *An Elephant Sitting Still* takes place over the course of one single day, and in equally classic modernist fashion the events of the day are presented in a mosaic form: a series of distinct or relatively autonomous episodes, often extended scenes, which follow an interlocking structure in relation to time, place and storyline. Only gradually do the four main characters and the four main storylines emerge from the assemblage of scenes, only gradually does the viewer begin to fit the scenes together and only gradually does the viewer realize that these events are all taking place in one place in one day and that the storylines are gradually converging.

The four main protagonists live in cramped apartments in anonymous blocks in a large unnamed industrial city. Schoolboy Wei Bu is on the run after pushing the school bully down the stairs after an argument about a mobile phone. The bully's gangster brother Yu Cheng and his gang are looking for Wei Bu, seeking to avenge this dishonour to the family and the gang. Wei Bu's classmate Huang Ling is trying to get away from her dysfunctional mother. She is also on the run because a video is circulating around the school on social media of her in a compromising position with the school vice-principal with whom she has been having an affair. Also living in a cramped apartment is pensioner Wang Jin, veteran of the Maoist era, now battling with neighbours and local hoodlums while his own family tries to expel him from their shared flat by putting him in a nursing home. The fourth protagonist turns out to be none other than Yu Cheng, the gangster brother who is looking for Wei Bu to have him beaten up. Yu Cheng is something of a reluctant gangster and has his own problems: in the daringly complex elliptical opening sequence of the film his best friend jumps off a tower block balcony to his death after walking in on Yu Cheng making love to his wife. Later Yu Cheng will remark that it was his best friend who told him about the elephant in Manzhouli.

The storylines summarized in the previous paragraph become considerably more convoluted as the film progresses, and the connections and overlaps between the storylines can only be pieced together by the viewer retrospectively. The script is rigorous in that almost every scene or episode, no matter how much of a sub-plot or digression it might initially seem, eventually becomes integrated into the story as a whole. The overall effect of these multiple plot developments is to complicate the moral perspective: all of the characters are trying but failing to do the right thing in a situation, a world, in which there is no right thing. And when a character does the wrong thing, as they frequently do, there is usually a reason or context which explains why they are doing the wrong thing, yet without necessarily providing justification for the immoral act. The difference between right and wrong is not simply a matter of moral abstractions; it leads each of the four protagonists into acts of violence. This is true for the seventeen-year-old schoolgirl Huang Ling who abuses her long-suffering single mother verbally and, after her affair with her school vice-principal is exposed in a school 'group chat', she attacks the vice-principal's wife with a baseball bat. The pensioner Wang Lin, being driven out of his home, having no money and losing his beloved dog, resembles a psychopathic Umberto D., being prone to extreme violence and on one occasion smashing Yu Cheng's thugs around the head with a snooker cue. Nevertheless, Wang Lin is the nearest thing in the film to a good character in the sense of consistently making good moral choices, and it is therefore striking that he is a proud ex-soldier, a veteran of Mao's People's Army, that he is of an older generation – the grandfathers – for which director Hu Bo and his generation might have been expected to have an antipathy. In contrast, the generation of the fathers is condemned. For example, Wei Bu's father, an ex-policeman, is presented in the film as abusive and corrupt.

The most interesting and complex character in the film is small-time gangster Yu Cheng. He spends the film trying to find Wei Bu in order to avenge the attack on his brother, the school bully, yet admits that his brother was a 'worthless piece of trash' and ends up advising Wei Bu on his love life and then setting him free to make his journey to Manzhouli to see the elephant. Yet Yu Cheng frequently behaves appallingly, trying to blame the suicide of his best friend not on himself but on the wife for sleeping with him and later blaming an ex-lover on the grounds that if she hadn't rejected him he wouldn't have had to sleep with his best friend's wife! Yu Cheng is a gangster and a thug who believes that the whole world is rotten and that 'everyone sucks', yet in the course of the film it seems that he is genuinely trying to fathom out and untangle the webs of corruption, violence and nihilism in which he is caught. In what might be the climactic moment of the whole film, Yu Cheng suddenly takes out his phone and rings the mother of his best friend and admits that he was there in the apartment and saw her son jump to his death, thereby finally admitting his responsibility, his guilt, for sleeping with the wife of his best friend and causing the suicide.

Towards the end of the film Yu Cheng is shot in farcical circumstances and is the one character of the four protagonists who does not make it to Manzhouli, but it is his actions that are responsible for allowing the other three to make the journey and to see the elephant.

Appendix

Contemporary cinematic modernism: 100 films (in chronological order)[1]

1. *Terrorizers/Kǒngbù Fènz* (1986) Edward Yang
2. *Where Is the Friend's Home?/Khane-ye dust kojast* (1987) Abbas Kiarostami
3. *The Day of the Eclipse/Dni zatmeniya* (1988) Alexander Sokurov
4. *Damnation/Kárhozat* (1988) Béla Tarr
5. *A City of Sadness/*Bēiqíng Chéngsh (1989) Hou Hsiao-hsien
6. *Close Up/Klūzāp, nemā-ye nazdīk* (1990) Abbas Kiarostami
7. *The Second Circle/Krug vtoroy* (1990) Alexander Sokurov
8. *Quince Tree Sun* (1992) Victor Erice
9. *Life and Nothing More/Zendegi va digar hich* (1992) Abbas Kiarostami
10. *The Stone/Kamen* (1992) Alexander Sokurov
11. *Vive l'amore* (1994) Tsai Ming-liang
12. *Casa De Lava* (1994) Pedro Costa
13. *Sátántangó* (1994) Béla Tarr
14. *Whispering Pages/Tikhiye stranitsy* (1994) Alexander Sokurov
15. *Fate/Verhängnis* (1994) Fred Kelemen
16. *Through the Olive Trees/Zīr-e Derakhtān-e Zeytūn* (1994) Abbas Kiarostami
17. *Salaam Cinema* (1995) Mohsen Makhmalbaf
18. *Few of Us/Mūsų nedaug* (1996) Šarūnas Bartas
19. *Goodbye South, Goodbye/Nánguó zàijiàn, nánguó* (1996) Hou Hsiao-hsien
20. *A Moment of Innocence/Nūn o goldūn* (1996) Mohsen Makhmalbaf
21. *Taste of Cherry/Ta'm-e gīlās . . .* (1997) Abbas Kiarostami
22. *The Mirror/Ayneh* (1997) Jafar Panahi
23. *The River* (1997) Tsai Ming-liang
24. *The Apple* (1998) Samira Makhmalbaf
25. *The Wind Will Carry Us/Bād mā rā khāhad bord* (1999) Abbas Kiarostami
26. *Ratcatcher* (1999) Lynne Ramsay
27. *Werckmeister Harmonies* (2000) Béla Tarr
28. *Platform/Zhàntái* (2000) Jia Zhangke

29. *Mysterious Object at Noon/Dokfa nai meuman* (2000) Apichatpong Weerasethakul
30. *Blackboards/Takhté siah* (2000) Samira Makhmalbaf
31. *Timecode* (2000) Mike Figgis
32. *Freedom/Laisvė* (2000) Šarūnas Bartas
33. *The State I'm In/Die innere Sicherheit* (2000) Christian Petzhold
34. *Passing Summer/Mein langsames Leben* (2001) Angela Schanelec
35. *La libertad* (2001) Lisandro Alonso
36. *Eureka* (2001) Shinji Aoyama
37. *Distant/Uzak* (2002) Nuri Bilge Ceylan
38. *Russian Ark/Russkiy kovcheg* (2002) Alexander Sokurov
39. *Unknown Pleasures/Rèn xiāo yáo* (2002) Jia Zhangke
40. *Bungalow* (2002) Ulrich Köhler
41. *Morvern Callar* (2002) Lynne Ramsay
42. *Waiting for Happiness/Heremakono* (2002) Abderrahmane Sissako
43. *Ten* (2002) Abbas Kiarostami
44. *The Deserted Station /Istgah-e Matrouk* (2002) Alireza Raisian
45. *Crimson Gold/Tala-ye Sorkh* (2003) Jafar Panahi
46. *Goodbye Dragon Inn/Bú sàn* (2003) Tsai Ming-Liang
47. *At Five in the Afternoon* (2003) Samira Makhmalbaf
48. *Elephant* (2003) Gus Van Sant
49. *West of the Tracks* (2003) Wang Bing
50. *Marseille* (2004) Angela Schanelec
51. *The World/Shìjiè* (2004) Jia Zhangke
52. *Regular Lovers/Les Amants réguliers* (2004) Philippe Garrel
53. *Evolution of a Filipino Family/Ebolusyon ng Isang Pamilyang Pilipino* (2004) Lav Diaz
54. *Los Muertos* (2004) Lisandro Alonso
55. *Café Lumière/Kōhī Jikō* (2005) Hou Hsiao-Hsien
56. *The Wayward Cloud/Tiānbiān yī duǒ yún* (2005) Tsai Ming-Liang
57. *Kinetta* (2005) Yorgos Lanthimos
58. *The Death of Mr. Lăzărescu* (2005) Cristi Puiu
59. *Still Life/Sānxiá hǎorén* (2006) Jia Zhangke
60. *Climates/İklimler* (2006) Nuri Bilge Ceylan
61. *Syndromes and a Century/Sæng ṣ̄atawǎat* (2006) Apichatpong Weerasethakul
62. *Colossal Youth/Juventude em Marcha* (2006) Pedro Costa
63. *Honour of the Knights Quixotic/Honor de cavalleria* (2006) Albert Serra
64. *I Don't Want To Sleep Alone/Hēiyǎnquān* (2006) Tsai Ming-Liang

65. *Windows on Monday/Montag kommen die fenster* (2006) Ulrich Köhler
66. *Bamako* (2006) Abderrahmane Sissako
67. *Fallen/Krišana* (2006) Fred Kelemen
68. *Afternoon/Nachmittag* (2007) Angela Schanelec
69. *Four Months, Three Weeks and Two Days/4 luni, 3 săptămâni și 2 zile* (2007) Christian Mungiu
70. *Silent Light* (2007) Carlos Reygadas
71. *Liverpool* (2008) Lisandro Alonso
72. *Wendy & Lucy* (2008) Kelly Reichardt
73. *The Headless Woman/La mujer sin cabeza* (2008) Lucrecia Martel
74. *Birdsong/El cant dels ocells* (2008) Albert Serra
75. *Melancholia* (2008) Lav Diaz
76. *Orly* (2010) Angela Schanelec
77. *Morgen* (2010) Marian Crișan
78. *Poetry* (2010) Lee Chang-dong
79. *Certified Copy* (2010) Abbas Kiarostami
80. *The Turin Horse* (2011) Béla Tarr
81. *Le Quattro Volte* (2010) Michelangelo Frammartino
82. *This Is Not a Film/In film nist* (2011) Jafar Panahi
83. *Two Years at Sea* (2011) Ben Rivers
84. *Jealousy* (2013) Philippe Garrel
85. *Stray Dogs* (2013) Tsai Ming-Liang
86. *A Touch of Sin/tiān zhùdìng* (2013) Jia Zhangke
87. *Story of My Death/Història de la meva mort* (2013) Albert Serra
88. *Under the Skin* (2013) Jonathan Glazer
89. *Exhibition* (2014) Joanna Hogg
90. *Timbuktu* (2014) Abderrahmane Sissako
91. *From What Is Before/Mula sa Kung Ano ang Noon* (2014) Lav Diaz
92. *Horse Money/Cavalo Dinheiro* (2014) Pedro Costa
93. *Jauja* (2014) Lisandro Alonso
94. *No Home Movie* (2015) Chantal Akerman
95. *Cemetery of Splendour/Rak Ti Khon Kaen* (2015) Apichatpong Weerasethakul
96. *Sieranevada* (2016) Cristi Puiu
97. *The Dreamed Path/Der Traumhafte Weg* (2016) Angela Schanelec
98. *Zama* (2017) Lucrecia Martel
99. *Burning* (2018) Lee Chang-dong
100. *An Elephant Sitting Still/Dà Xiàng Xídì Érzuò* (2018) Hu Bo

Selected Filmography[1]

8½
Director: Federico Fellini
Italy 1963

The 400 Blows
Les Quatre cents coups (original title)
Director: François Truffaut
France 1959

2001: A Space Odyssey
Director: Stanley Kubrick
USA / UK 1968

Accident
Director: Joseph Losey
UK 1963

A Corner in Wheat
Director: D.W. Griffith
USA 1909

A Moment of Innocence
نون و گلدون / *Nūn o Goldūn* (original title)
Director: Mohsen Makhmalbaf
Iran 1995

À nos amours
To Our Loves (alternate title)
Director: Maurice Pialat
France 1983

Alice in the Cities
Alice In Den Städten (original title)
Director: Wim Wenders
Germany 1974

An Elephant Sitting Still
大象席地而坐 / *Da xiang xi di er zuo* (original title)
Director: Hu Bo
China 2018

Antonio das Mortes
Director: Glauber Rocha
Brazil 1969

The Apple
سيب / *Sib* (original title)
Director: Samira Makhmalbaf
Iran 1997

Birdsong
El cant dels ocells (original title)
Director: Albert Serra
Spain 2008

Black Girl
La noire de… (original title)
Director: Ousmane Sembène
Senegal, France, 1966

The Boys from Fengkuei
風櫃來的人 / *Feng Guilai De Ren* (original title)
Director: Hou Hsiao-Hsien
Taiwan 1983 (Release)

Bungalow
Director: Ulrich Köhler
Germany 2002

Burning
Beoning (original title)
버닝 (original title)
Director: Lee Chang-dong
South Korea 2018

The Cabinet of Dr. Caligari
Das Cabinet des Dr. Caligari (original title)
Director: Robert Wiene
Germany 1919

Chess Fever
Шахматная горячка / *Chakhmatnaia Goriatchka* (original title)
Director: Vsevolod I. Pudovkin
USSR 1925

Chinese Roulette
Chinesisches Roulette (original title)
Germany 1976
Director: Rainer Werner Fassbinder

Citizen Kane
Director: Orson Welles
USA 1941

A City of Sadness
悲情城市 / *Beiqing chengshi* (original title)
Director: Hou Hsiao-Hsien
Taiwan 1989

Climates
Iklimler (original title)
Director: Nuri Bilge Ceylan
Turkey 2006

Colossal Youth
Juventude Em Marcha (original title))
Director: Pedro Costa
Portugal 2006 (Copyright)

The Colour of Pomegranates
Sayat nova (original title)
Director: Sergei Paradjanov
USSR 1968

The Confrontation
Fényes Szelek (original title)
Director: Miklós Jancsó
Hungary 1968

Contempt
Le Mépris (original title)
Director: Jean-Luc Godard
France 1963

Cronaca di un amore (original title)
Chronicle of a Love Affair
Story of a Love Affair
Director: Michelangelo Antonioni
Italy 1950

Damnation
Kárhozat (original title)
Director: Béla Tarr
Hungary 1988

Days of the Eclipse
Дни затмения / Dni Zatmenija (original title)
Director: Aleksandr Sokurov
USSR 1988

Distant
Uzak (original title)
Director: Nuri Bilge Ceylan
Turkey 2003

Du Coté d'Orouët
Director: Jacques Rozier
France 1971 (Release)

Earth
Земля / Zemlya (original title)
Director: Alexander Dovzhenko
USSR / Ukraine 1930

Éloge de l'amour
In Praise of Love (alternate title)
Director: Jean-Luc Godard
France 2001

Entr'acte
Director: René Clair
France 1924

Eros Plus Massacre
エロス+虐殺 / *Erosu purasu gyakusatsu* (original title)
Eros + Gyakustatsu (alternative title)
Director: Yoshishige Yoshida
Japan 1969

Exhibition
Director: Joanna Hogg
UK 2013

Faces
USA 1968
Director: John Cassavetes

Fata Morgana
Director: Werner Herzog
Germany 1971

Freedom
Laisvė (original title)
Director: Šarūnas Bartas
Lithuania 2000

Goodbye, Dragon Inn
Bu San (original title)
Director: Tsai Ming-liang
Taiwan 2003

The Headless Woman
La Mujer sin Cabeza (original title)
Director: Lucrecia Martel
Argentina 2008

Honor de Cavalleria
Honor of the Knights
Director: Albert Serra
Spain 2006

Horse Money
Cavalo dinheiro (original title)
Director: Pedro Costa
Portugal 2014

Humanity and Paper Balloons
人情紙風船 / *Ninjō Kami Fūsen* (original title)
Director: Sadao Yamanaka
Japan 1937

Ivan the Terrible
Иван Грозный / Ivan Grozni (original title)
Director: Sergei Eisenstein
USSR 1945

Je Tu Il Elle
I... You... He... She (alternative title)
Director: Chantal Akerman
Belgium 1974

Jeanne Dielman 23, Quai du Commerce, 1080 Bruxelles (original title)
Jeanne Dielman (alternative title)
Director: Chantal Akerman
Belgium 1975

Journey to Italy
Viaggio in Italia (original title)
Voyage in Italy (alternative title)
Director: Roberto Rossellini
Italy 1954

Knife in the Water
Nóż w wodzie (original title)
Director: Roman Polanski
Poland 1962

L'amour fou
Director: Jacques Rivette
France 1968

L' Atalante
Directed by: Jean Vigo
France 1934

L' avventura
Director: Michelangelo Antonioni
Italy 1960

L' eclisse
The Eclipse (alternative title)
Director: Michelangelo Antonioni
Italy 1962

L'Immortelle
Director: Alain Robbe-Grillet
France 1962

La Collectionneuse
The Collector (alternative title)
Director: Eric Rohmer
France 1966

La Dolce Vita
Director: Federico Fellini
Italy 1960

La Libertad
Director: Lisandro Alonso
Argentina 2001

La Notte
Director: Michelangelo Antonioni
Italy 1961

La Pointe Courte
Director: Agnès Varda
France 1954

Le Gai Savoir (original title)
The Joy of Learning (alternative title)
Director: Jean-Luc Godard
France 1968

Les Rendez-vous d'Anna
The Meetings of Anna (alternative title)
Director: Chantal Akerman
Belgium 1978

Los Muertos
Director: Lisandro Alonso
Argentina 2004

Los Olvidados
Director: Luis Buñuel
Mexico 1950

Last Year at Marienbad
L' Année dernière à Marienbad (original title)
Director: Alain Resnais
France 1961

Late Chrysanthemums
晩菊 / *Bangiku* (original title)
Director: Mikio Naruse
Japan 1954

Late Spring
晩春 / *Banshun* (original title)
Director: Yasujirō Ozu
Japan 1949

The Life of Oharu
西鶴一代女 / *Saikaku Ichidai Onna* (original title)
Director: Kenji Mizoguchi
Japan, 1952

Liverpool
Director: Lisandro Alonso
Argentina 2008

The Lodger
The Lodger A Story of the London Fog (original title)
Director: Alfred Hitchcock
UK 1926

Love is Colder than Death
Liebe ist Kälter als der Tod (original title)
Director: Rainer Werner Fassbinder
Germany 1969

Loves of a Blonde
Lásky jedné plavovlásky (original title)
Director: Milos Forman
Czechoslovakia 1965

Loving
Director: Stan Brakhage
USA 1957

Man Push Cart
Director: Ramin Bahrani
USA 2005

Man with a Movie Camera
Chelovek s kinoapparatom (original title)
Человек с киноаппаратом (original title)
Director: Dziga Vertov
USSR 1929

Marseille
Director: Angela Schanelec
Germany 2004

Meshes of the Afternoon
Director: Maya Deren
USA 1943

Metropolis
Director: Fritz Lang
Germany 1927

Mirror
Зеркало / Zerkalo (original title)
Director: Andrei Tarkovsky
USSR 1974

The Mirror
آینه / *Ayneh* (original title)
Director: Jafar Panahi
Iran 1997

Modern Times
Director: Charlie Chaplin
USA 1936

Muriel
Muriel ou Le Temps d'un retour (original title)
Director: Alain Resnais
France 1963

The Musketeers of Pig Alley
Director: D.W. Griffith
USA 1912

My Night with Maud
Ma nuit chez Maud (original title)
Director: Eric Rohmer
France 1969 (Release)

Nathalie Granger
Director: Marguerite Duras
France 1972

Night and Fog in Japan
日本の夜と霧 / *Nihon no Yoru to Kiri* (original title)
Director: Nagisa Oshima
Japan 1960

Not Reconciled
Nicht versöhnt oder Es hilft nur Gewalt, wo Gewalt herrscht (original title)
Director: Jean-Marie Straub
Germany 1965 (Release)

One Week
Director: Buster Keaton with Eddie Cline
USA 1920

Orly
Director: Angela Schanelec
Germany 2010

Orphée
Director: Jean Cocteau
France 1950

Out 1
Out 1- Noli Me Tangere (alternative title)
Director: Jacques Rivette
France 1970

Paisà
Paisan (alternative title)
Director: Roberto Rossellini
Italy 1946

Paris nous appartient
Paris Belongs to Us (alternative title)
Director: Jacques Rivette
France 1961

The Passenger
Professione: reporter (original title)
Director: Michelangelo Antonioni
Italy 1974

Passion
Passion Amour / Travail (original title)
Director: Jean-Luc Godard
Switzerland / France 1982

The Passion of Joan of Arc
La Passion de Jeanne d'Arc (original title)
Director: Carl Dreyer
France / Denmark 1927

Pather Panchali
Director: Satyajit Ray
India / West Bengal 1955

Performance
Directors: Nicolas Roeg and Donald Cammell
UK 1968 / 1970

Permanent Vacation
Director: Jim Jarmusch
USA 1980

Persona
Director: Ingmar Bergman
Sweden 1966

Pickpocket
Director: Robert Bresson
France 1959

Platform
站台 / *Zhàntái* (original title)
Director: Jia Zhangke
China 2000

Poetry
시 / 詩 / *Si* (original title)
Lee Chang-dong
South Korea 2010

Point Blank
Director: John Boorman
USA 1967

The Quince Tree Sun
El sol del membrillo (original title)
Director: Víctor Erice
Spain 1992

Rashomon
羅生門 (original title)
Director: Akira Kurosawa
Japan 1950

Reconstruction
Anaparastasi (original title)
Director: Theo Angelopoulos
Greece 1970

Red Desert
Il deserto rosso (original title)
Director: Michelangelo Antonioni
Italy 1964

Riddles of the Sphinx
UK 1977
Direction: Laura Mulvey and Peter Wollen

The Round-Up
Szegénylegények (original title)
Director: Miklós Jancsó
Hungary 1966

Salaam Cinema
Salam cinéma (original title)
Director: Mohsen Makhmalbaf
Iran 1995

Sátántangó
Director: Béla Tarr
Hungary 1994

The Second Circle (1990)
Krug vtori (original title)
Director: Aleksandr Sokurov
USSR 1990

The Silence
Tystnaden (original title)
Director: Ingmar Bergman
Sweden 1963

Sisters of the Gion
祇園の姉妹 / *Gion no kyodai* (original title)
Director: Kenji Mizoguchi
Japan 1936

Solaris
Солярис (original title)
Director: Andrei Tarkovsky
USSR 1972

Soleil Ô
Director: Med Hondo
Mauritania / France 1970

The Spirit of the Beehive
El espíritu de la colmena (original title)
Director: Víctor Erice
Spain 1973

Steamboat Willie
Director: Walt Disney
USA 1928

Still Life
三峡好人 / *Sānxiá Hǎorén* (original title)
Director: Jia Zhang-ke
China 2006

The Story of My Death
Història de la meva mort (original title)
Director: Albert Serra
Spain 2013

Stranger than Paradise
Director: Jim Jarmusch
USA 1982

Strike
Стачка / Stachka (original title)
Director: Sergei M. Eisenstein
USSR 1925

Stromboli
Stromboli, Terra Di Dio (original title)
Stromboli, Land of God (alternative title)
Director: Roberto Rossellini
Italy 1950

Syndromes and a Century
Sǣng ṣ̄atawǎat (original title)
Director: Apichatpong Weerasethakul
Thailand 2006

Taste of Cherry
طعم گیلاس / *Ta'm-e gīlās...*(original title)
Director: Abbas Kiarostami
Iran 1997

The Terrorizers
恐怖分子 / *Kongbu Fenzi* (original title)
Director: Edward Yang
Taiwan 1986

Theorem
Teorema (original title)
Director: Pier Paolo Pasolini
Italy 1968

This Is Not a Film
این فیلم نیست / *In film nist* (original title)
Director: Jafar Panahi
Iran 2011 (Copyright)

Through the Olive Trees
زیر درختان زیتون / *Zīr-e Derakhtān-e Zeytūn* (original title)
Director: Abbas Kiarostami
Iran 1994

Timecode
Director: Mike Figgis
UK / USA

Touch of Evil
Director: Orson Welles
USA 1958

Touki Bouki
The Journey of the Hyena (alternative title)
Director: Djibril Diop Mambéty
Senegal 1973

The Travelling Players
O Thiassos (original title)
Director: Theo Angelopoulos
Greece 1975

Umberto D.
Director: Vittorio De Sica
Italy 1952

Un Chien Andalou
An Andalusian Dog (alternative title)
Director: Luis Buñuel with Salvador Dalí
Spain / France 1928

Under the Skin
Directed by: Jonathan Glazer
UK 2013

Unknown Pleasures
任逍遥 / *Rèn xiāo yáo*
Director: Jia Zhangke
China 2002

Vertigo
Director: Alfred Hitchcock
USA 1958

Vive L'Amour
爱情万岁 / *Aiqing Wansui* (original title)
Director: Tsai Ming-liang
Taiwan 1994

Waiting for Happiness
Heremakono / في انتظار السعادة (original title)
Director: Abderrahmane Sissako
Mauritania 2002

Walkabout
Director: Nicolas Roeg
UK / Australia 1970

Weekend
Week End (original title)
Director: Jean-Luc Godard
France 1967

Wendy and Lucy
Director: Kelly Reichardt
USA 2008

Werckmeister Harmonies
Werckmeister Harmóniák (original title)
Director: Béla Tarr Co-director: Ágnes Hranitzky
Hungary 2000

Where Is the Friend's Home?
خانه دوست کجاست / *Khane-ye dust kojast* (original title)
Where is My Friend's House? (alternative title)
Director: Abbas Kiarostami
Iran 1987

Wild Strawberries
Smultronstället (original title)
Director: Ingmar Bergman
Sweden 1957

Work
Director: Charles Chaplin [Essanay Studio]
USA 1915

Yeelen
Director: Souleymane Cissé
Mali 1987

Yellow Earth
黄土地 / *Huáng tǔdì* (original title)
Director: Chen Kaige
China 1984

Zéro de conduit
Zero for Conduct (alternative title)
Director: Jean Vigo
France 1933

Notes

Introduction

1 Siegfried Kracauer, *Theory of Film: The Redemption of Physical Reality*, originally published 1960 by Oxford University Press (Princeton: Princeton University, 1997), p. 60.
2 Richard Schickel, *D. W. Griffith: An American Life* (New York: Simon & Schuster, 1984), p. 603.
3 Kracauer, *Theory of Film*, Preface, p. l.
4 Ibid., p. 303.
5 Ibid., Preface, p. xlix (his initial reference here appears to be a comment by Germaine Dulac); p. 31.
6 Kracauer, *Theory of Film*, p. 27.
7 Ibid., p. 20.
8 In the last two decades there has been much discussion and specialist research on various aspects of modernism within the different academic fields of film, literary and art studies, and 'modernist studies' is an international academic field in itself. This book is informed by this research but is not primarily intended as an intervention into current specialist debates within film studies. The aim is rather to construct a broader historical and interdisciplinary narrative as a context in which to chart the relationship between modernism and a particular cinematic aesthetic.
9 Kracauer, *Theory of Film*, Preface, p. li.

Chapter 1

1 Mark Cousins, *The Story of Film* (London: Pavilion, 2004). Cousins's book is the current standard popular history of film and has subsequently been turned into an acclaimed television series and DVD box-set. The three chapters on cinematic modernism are titled as follows: Chapter 6, 'The Swollen Story (1953-1959): Rage and Symbolism in 1950s Filmmaking – Widescreen, International Melodrama and New Early-Modernist Directors'; Chapter 7, 'The Exploded Story (1959-1969): The Breakdown of Romantic Cinema and the Coming of Modernism – A Series of New Waves Transform Innovative Filmmaking on Every Continent'; Chapter 8, 'Freedom and Want See (1969-1979): Political Cinema around the Globe and the

Rise of the Blockbuster in America' (this chapter includes a section entitled 'Beyond the New Waves: Political Modernism' pp. 368–77).

2 András Bálint Kovács, *Screening Modernism: European Art Cinema 1950–1980* (Chicago: University of Chicago Press, 2007); D. N. Rodowick, *The Crisis of Political Modernism: Criticism and Ideology in Contemporary Film Theory* (Urbana: University of Illinois Press, 1994); Sam Rohdie, *Film Modernism* (Manchester: Manchester University Press, 2015); see also *Masterpieces of Modernist Cinema*, edited by Ted Perry (Bloomington: Indiana University Press, 2006). Taking a different approach, Perry's collection constructs a canon ranging from silent film to the contemporary and including avant-garde / experimental filmmakers such as Deren, Brakhage, Warhol and Gehr alongside modernists like Vertov, Resnais and Bresson. This book will follow the implications of Bazin's approach in arguing for a distinction between cinematic modernism and avant-garde film.

3 A relatively early book outlining a broad contemporary conception of cinematic modernism (albeit with a Nietzschean slant): John Orr, *Cinema and Modernity* (Cambridge: Polity/Blackwell, 1993). See also: John Orr, *Romantics and Modernists in British Cinema* (Edinburgh: Edinburgh University Press, 2010). For an in-depth 'continental' philosophical reading of canonical postwar cinematic modernism (Antonioni, Bergman, Godard, Resnais), see: Hamish Ford, *Post-War Modernist Cinema and Philosophy: Confronting Negativity and Time* (New York: Palgrave Macmillan, 2012).

4 Laura Marcus, *The Tenth Muse: Writing about Cinema in the Modernist Period* (Oxford: Oxford University Press, 2007).

5 David Trotter, *Cinema and Modernism* (London: Blackwell, 2007). Although his main focus is on Griffith and Chaplin, Trotter does attend to the relationship between literary modernism and 'art' or 'modernist' film directors, namely Eisenstein and Gance.

6 Marshall Berman, *All That Is Solid Melts Into Air: The Experience of Modernity* (London: Verso, 1983); T.J. Clark, *Farewell to an Idea: Episodes from a History of Modernism* (New Haven: Yale University Press, 2001); Fredric Jameson, *A Singular Modernity: Essay on the Ontology of the Present* (London: Verso, 2002); Fredric Jameson, *The Modernist Papers* (London: Verso, 2007); Raymond Williams, *The Politics of Modernism* (London: Verso, 1989).

7 For a concise but comprehensive critical account of the various usages of the term 'modernism' in the arts over the last century see Vincent Sherry, 'Introduction', to *The Cambridge History of Modernism*, edited by Vincent Sherry (Cambridge: Cambridge University Press, 2017), pp. 1–26.

8 Virginia Woolf, 'Character in Fiction', in Virginia Woolf, *Selected Essays*, edited by David Bradshaw (Oxford, 2008), p. 38. This essay, published in the T. S. Eliot edited *Criterion* in July 1924, was republished by Hogarth later in October 1924, confusingly taking the title of an earlier related piece, 'Mr Bennett and Mrs Brown'.

9 Clive Bell, 'The Aesthetic Hypothesis' [1914], in *Modern Art and Modernism: A Critical Anthology*, edited by Francis Frascina and Charles Harrison (London: Harper and Row, The Open University, 1982), p. 68.

10 'Let no one imagine that representation is bad in itself; a realistic form may be as significant, in its place, as part of the design, as an abstract.' Bell, 'The Aesthetic Hypothesis', p. 72.

11 Roger Fry, 'An Essay in Aesthetics' [1909], in *Modern Art and Modernism: A Critical Anthology*, edited by Francis Frascina and Charles Harrison (London: The Open University, 1982), p. 80 [first published in *New Quarterly*, 1909].

12 Ibid., p. 80.

13 Ibid.

14 Ibid., p. 86.

15 Clive Bell, 'The Debt to Cézanne' [1914], in *Modern Art and Modernism: A Critical Anthology*, edited by Francis Frascina and Charles Harrison (London: Harper and Row, The Open University, 1982), pp. 76–7.

16 In 1948 Barnett Newman writes: 'We are reasserting man's natural desire for the exalted, for a concern with our relationship to the absolute emotions.' Barnett Newman, 'The Sublime Is Now', *Tiger's Eye* vol.1 Dec.1948, cited by Donald Judd 'Barnett Newman' [November 1964], in *Modern Art and Modernism: A Critical Anthology*, p. 131. Despite Clement Greenberg and Michael Fried's attempts to divest abstract form of its quasi-religious baggage, the most famous monument to postwar American abstract painting would be the Rothko Chapel in Houston, opened in 1971.

17 Clement Greenberg, 'Modernist Painting' (1965), in *Modern Art and Modernism: A Critical Anthology*, p. 5 [original source: *Art and Literature* no.4, spring 1965, pp. 193–201].

18 'The self-criticism of Modernism grows out of but is not the same thing as the criticism of the Enlightenment. The Enlightenment criticized from the outside, the way criticism in its more accepted sense does; Modernism criticizes from the inside, through the procedures themselves of that which is being criticized. It seems natural that this new kind of criticism should have appeared first in philosophy, which is critical by definition, but as the nineteenth century wore on it made itself felt in many other fields. A more rational justification had begun to be demanded of every formal social activity, and Kantian self-criticism was called on eventually to meet and interpret this demand in areas that lay far from philosophy.' Clement Greenberg, 'Modernist Painting' [1965], p. 5.

19 Barthes distinguishes between *texte lisible* and *texte scriptible*, in *S/Z* and *The Pleasure of the Text*.

20 In many ways Greenberg and Barthes are replaying the debates of Adorno, Benjamin, Marcuse, Brecht and Lukács from the 1930s about the degree to which modern art should be 'realist' and the degree to which it should be 'formalist',

what was the right balance for each art medium and for each work? The Frankfurt School debates were themselves echoing the arguments of T. S. Eliot, Ezra Pound, Wyndham Lewis, James Joyce, Virginia Woolf and other modernists from the early twentieth century. For the Frankfurt School, as for Lukács and Brecht, the question was also: What constitutes 'realism' in relation to the abstract (social) totality of a given society or system? See, *Aesthetics and Politics* (London New Left Books, 1977).

21 The essay 'Modernisms' is in three parts, which appeared individually in *Encounter* and *The New Statesman* and is sometimes known by its first part 'Discrimination of Modernisms'. The essay as a whole, dated '1965–1966', was published as chapter 1 'The Modern' in Frank Kermode, *Continuities* (London: Routledge, 1968). Books under review include Stephen Spender, *The Struggle of the Modern* (1963); Cyril Connolly, *The Modern Movement, 100 Key Books from England, France and America, 1880–1950* (1965); *The Modern Tradition*, edited by Richard Ellman and Charles Feidelson (1965).

22 For example, *A Survey of Modernist Poetry* by Laura Riding and Robert Graves [1927].

23 Kermode resigned in May 1967 as editor of *Encounter*. Editors Kermode and Spender both denied knowledge of CIA patronage and resigned when they found out, however, both were widely accused of political naïveté.

24 Kermode, 'Modernisms', *Continuities*, 'schisms' p. vii and 'Flaubert' p. 2.

25 Serge Daney, 'La période non légendaire des *Cahiers* (pour préparer le cinquantième anniversaire)', *L'Exercise a été profitable, Monsieur* (Paris: P.O.L., 1993), cited in Dudley Andrew, *What Cinema Is!* (Wiley-Blackwell, 2010), p. 5.

26 Cited by Hugh Grey in 'Introduction', *What Is Cinema* volume 1, p. 5.

27 André Bazin, *What Is Cinema?* Volume 1 [1967], essays selected and translated by Hugh Gray, (Berkeley: University of California Press, 2004); André Bazin, *What Is Cinema?* Volume 2 [1971] essays selected and translated by Hugh Gray (Berkeley: University of California Press, 2005).

28 Dudley Andrew, 'Foreword to 2004 Edition', Bazin, *What Is Cinema?*.

29 Rudolf Arnheim, 'Melancholy Unshaped', *The Journal of Aesthetics and Art Criticism* 21, no. 3 (Spring, 1963), pp. 291–7 retrieved 20 July 2019 at https://www.jstor.org/stable/427438.

30 Recollection of Soma Morgenstern, cited by Miriam Hansen, Introduction p. xiv, Siegried Kracauer, *Theory of Film: The Redemption of Physical Reality*, originally published in 1960 by Oxford University Press (Princeton: Princeton University, 1997).

31 Ibid., p. 306.

32 Jacques Rancière, *The Intervals of Cinema*, 'Preface', translated by John Howe (London: Verso, 2014), p. 3.

33 'Stromboli', *Variety*, 31 December 1949, accessed 11 November 2019 at https://variety.com/1949/film/reviews/stromboli-1200416587/.

34 Of the 'neo-Hollywood' directors, Cavell developed a particular interest in the films of his one-time philosophy student and fellow Heideggerian Terrence Malick, which he discusses in the 1979 preface, Stanley Cavell, *The World Viewed* [1971], enlarged edition (Cambridge, MA: Harvard University Press, 1979), pp. xiv–xv.

35 In the original book Cavell relies on assumptions concerning the ontology of the photographic image drawn from Bazin (and Panofsky) but critical reactions to the book necessitated a subsequent 1973 paper 'More of the World Viewed' published in the 1979 reprint of *The World Viewed*. In the essay Cavell responds at length to the 'obvious objections': that the photographic and cinematic image is staged, composed and edited and therefore has no relationship of immediacy to unmediated pro-filmic 'reality' and so on.

36 *The World Viewed*, p. 41. Cavell is citing from Baudelaire, *The Painter of Modern Life* (1859).

37 *The World Viewed*, p. 103.

38 Ibid., pp. 122–3.

39 Ibid., p. 159.

40 Ibid., p. 25. Cavell refers in his 1979 postscript to his assumption of the relationship between the cinematic image and reality as 'mythological', a myth of 'revelation', of 'immaculate conception', Ibid., p. 184.

41 Ibid., p. 122.

42 Cavell goes on to give his reverie a Heideggerian twist: 'I am not asking for more stream-of-consciousness. Stream-of-consciousness does not show the absence of words as the time of action unwinds; it floats the time of action in order to give space for words. I am asking for the ground of consciousness, upon which I cannot but move', Ibid., p. 148.

43 Miriam Bratu Hansen, *Cinema and Experience* (London: University of California Press, 2012), p. 271.

44 Ibid., p. 6. Hansen gives the Lukács reference as: Georg Lukács, *Theory of the Novel* (1920) (Cambridge, MA: MIT Press, 1971), p. 41. Of course, the lapsarian discourse on modernity and the decline of civilization long predates the First World War but was intensified by the war and associated events in its aftermath.

45 Hansen, *Cinema and Experience*, p. 6.

46 Hansen prefers the title 'The Work of Art in the Age of Technical Reproducibility', see Hansen, *Cinema and Experience*, p. xv.

47 Hansen, *Cinema and Experience*, pp. 99–100. Hansen breaks up the quotation, so the quotation here is taken from Zohn's translation: 'The Work of Art in the Age of Mechanical Reproduction, xii', Walter Benjamin, *Illuminations*, translated by Harry Zohn, edited by Hannah Arendt (London: Fontana, 1992), p. 227.

48 Hansen, *Cinema and Experience*, p. 166. See Adorno to Benjamin, 18 March 1936, translated by Harry Zohn, in *Aesthetics and Politics*, p. 123.

49 Ibid., pp. 207–8. See Adorno to Benjamin, 18 March 1936, *Aesthetics and Politics*, p. 123.

50 Adorno to Benjamin, 18 March 1936, *Aesthetics and Politics*, pp. 123–4.

51 Hansen, *Cinema and Experience*, p. 207.

52 Ibid., p. 209. Adorno, 'Transparencies on Film' (1966), translated by Thomas Y. Levin, *New German Critique* 24–25 (Fall-Winter 1981–1982), pp. 199–205. In her 'Introduction' essay to this translation Hansen also discusses Adorno's scattered references to film in *Dialectic of Enlightenment*, *Aesthetic Theory* and elsewhere. Miriam Hansen, 'Introduction to Adorno, "Transparencies on Film" (1966)', *New German Critique* 24–5 (Fall-Winter 1981–2), pp. 186–98.

53 Adorno, 'Transparencies on Film', p. 202.

54 Ibid., p. 201; Hansen, *Cinema and Experience*, p. 223. Hansen adds the following parenthetical note to her quote from Adorno's 'Transparencies on Film': (TF 201; FT 355; translation slightly altered). The reader might notice that Adorno's scene of dreamy subjectivity here resembles Cavell's *nouvelle vague* style epiphanic romantic scene, discussed earlier.

55 Hansen, *Cinema and Experience*, p. 254.

56 Ibid., p. 254.

57 Ibid., p. 276, with quotation references to Kracauer, *Theory of Film*, pp. 255, 268–70, 272.

58 Hansen, *Cinema and Experience*, p. 159. Hansen is quoting from Benjamin's 'Reply to Oscar A. H. Schmitz' (1927); much of this passage later found its way into 'The Work of Art in the Age of Mechanical Reproduction', section xiii.

59 Hansen, *Cinema and Experience*, pp. 270–1. See Kracauer, *Theory of Film*, pp. 238–9, 257.

60 Miriam Bratu Hansen, 'The Mass Production of the Senses: Classical Cinema as Vernacular Modernism', *Modernism/Modernity* 6, no. 2 (1999), p. 60.

61 For 'classical' film, see David Bordwell, Janet Staiger and Kristin Thompson, *The Classical Hollywood Cinema: Film Style and Mode of Production to 1960* (London: Routledge, 1988). For the location of an 'other' to classical Hollywood in early cinema and 1930s Japanese film, see Noël Burch, *Life to Those Shadows* (Berkeley: University of California Press, 1990) and *To the Distant Observer* (Berkeley: University of California Press, 1981). See also Tom Gunning, 'The Cinema of Attraction: Early Film, Its Spectator and the Avant-Garde', *Wide Angle* 8, no. 3–4 (1986): 63–70. Debate over the terms 'classical' and 'modernity' within film studies has been fraught. For a polemical overview, see Tom Gunning, 'Modernity and Cinema: A Culture of Shocks and Flows', in *Cinema and Modernity*, edited by Murray Pomerance (New Brunswick: Rutgers University Press, 2006), pp. 297–315.

62 Hansen, 'Mass Production of the Senses', p. 65.

63 Ibid., p. 60.

64 'But I do think that, whether we like it or not, American movies of the classical period offered something like the first global vernacular. If this vernacular had a transnational and translatable resonance, it was not just because of its optimal mobilization of biologically hardwired structures and universal narrative templates but, more important, because it played a key role in mediating competing cultural discourses on modernity and modernization, because it articulated, multiplied, and globalized a particular historical experience.' Hansen, 'Mass Production of the Senses', p. 68.

65 Or: Antonioni yes, Welles probably, Chaplin probably not, Mickey Mouse no.

66 *Variety* 22 October 2019, 'Directors vs. Marvel: A Breakdown of the Criticism' by, Jordan Moreau, at https://variety.com/2019/film/news/directors-vs-marvel-breakdown-everything-you-need-to-know-1203379604/. This controversy will be discussed further in Chapter 7.

67 The problem is prefigured in Tarkovsky's own career. In the Russian films like *Mirror*, even *Stalker*, auratic effects emerge out of the 'opaque singularity' and 'otherness' of reality in its everyday and material forms – and its historical forms – whereas the late films made in exile *Nostalgia* and *Sacrifice* abandon the 'otherness' of concrete reality and contrive the otherness of the aura directly; consequently the auratic effects become ersatz, empty mannerism.

Chapter 2

1 Raymond Williams, 'Theatre as a Political Forum', *The Politics of Modernism* (London: Verso, 1989), pp. 84/85.

2 Ibid., pp. 85–6.

3 It is possible to see Chekhov's plays as precursors of the Bazinian aesthetic that will become prominent in postwar modernist film, and Chekhov is a conspicuous influence on contemporary cinematic modernism. Nuri Bilge Ceylan says that Chekhov stories have influenced all his screenplays: 'Actually in all my films I believe there is an element of Chekhov, because Chekhov wrote so many stories. He had stories about almost every situation, and I love them very much. So maybe he's influenced the way I look at life. Life follows Chekhov for me, in a way. After reading Chekhov, you begin to see the same kind of situations in life. And in the scriptwriting stage, I remember the stories somehow.' Ceylan, interviewed by Geoff Andrew onstage at BFI Southbank, 'Nuri Bilge Ceylan', *The Guardian* 6 February 2009, retrieved 17 September 2018 at https://www.theguardian.com/film/2009/feb/06/nuri-bilge-ceylan-interview-transcript.

4 Ezra Pound, 'A Few Don'ts By An Imagiste', *Poetry* (March 1913), quoted from *Imagist Poetry*, introduced and edited by Peter Jones (London: Penguin, 1972). The three imagist anthologies included poems by Ezra Pound, Hilda Doolittle (H. D.),

Richard Aldington, F. S. Flint, D. H. Lawrence, James Joyce, Ford Madox Ford, Amy Lowell, Marianne Moore and William Carlos Williams.

5 These rules are a selection from M. S. Flint, 'Imagisme', *Poetry* (March 1913); Ezra Pound, 'A Few Don'ts By An Imagiste', *Poetry* (March 1913); 'Preface to *Some Imagist Poets* 1915' and are quoted from *Imagist Poetry*, introduced and edited by Peter Jones (London: Penguin, 1972).

6 Vachel Lindsay, *The Art Of The Moving Picture* (1915), Denver Art Association reprint 1922, accessed 11 June 2019 at The Project Gutenberg Online (eBook #130292004), https://www.gutenberg.org/files/13029/13029-h/13029-h.htm. Munsterberg's *The Photoplay: A psychological study* was published in 1916 a year after Lindsay's book.

7 Laura Marcus, *The Tenth Muse: Writing about Cinema in the Modernist Period* (Oxford: Oxford University Press, 2007), pp. 188–9.

8 Laura Marcus points out that this interest in hieroglyphics can be traced back to American Transcendentalism, Emerson, Whitman and Poe, and also features not only in Pound and Eisenstein but in early film theorist Rocciotto Canudo and also in Kracauer and Adorno. Marcus, *The Tenth Muse*, pp. 191–2.

9 *Imagist Poetry*, p.95.

10 Sergei Eisenstein, 'The Cinematographic Principle and the Ideogram' (1929), in *Film Form: Essays in Film Theory*, edited and translated by Jay Leda (New York: Harcourt, 1949), pp. 31–2. The original essay appeared in Russian in 1929 and has a somewhat different translation as '1929: Beyond the Shot', in *The Eisenstein Reader*, edited and translated by Richard Taylor and William Powell (London: British Film Institute, 1998), p. 84.

11 'An "Image" is that which presents an intellectual and emotional complex in an instant of time. I use the term "complex" rather in the technical sense employed by the newer psychologists [. . .] It is the presentation of such a "complex" instantaneously which gives that sense of sudden liberation; that sense of freedom from time limits and space limits; that sense of sudden growth, which we experience in the presence of the greatest works of art.' Ezra Pound, 'A Few Don'ts by an Imagiste' originally in *Poetry: A Magazine of Verse*, March 1913, p. 200.

12 This is a recurring issue in cinematic modernism. A concrete socio-political ground is required for a narrative yet the lasting political resonance of films by Antonioni, Tarkovsky and Tarr rarely lies in their immediate political/philosophical 'message'.

13 Stein's experimentation is at the level of syntax rather than the word: innovative syntax being a relatively common feature of the modernist novel. Subversion at a linguistic level in writing and speech was associated with Dada and futurist provocations, but in the 1920s took on a more programmatic aspect through the Paris-based journal *transition* and its editor Eugene Jolas (and the extracts from and explications of *Finnegans Wake* carried by the journal). The 'Revolution of the

Word' manifesto appeared in *transition* 16–17 June 1929. Such concerns of course remain a key aspect of avant-garde poetry into the postwar period.

14 Marcus, *The Tenth Muse*. Marcus deals in depth with Wells's and Woolf's writings on cinema.

15 This marks a difference between much expressionist and (Soviet) montage film and the postwar neo-Bazinian cinematic modernism. Although ellipsis in postwar cinematic modernism becomes more radical in terms of eliding causality, events and time, it is presented as contingent, resembling in certain respects Paul Rotha's account of the dissolve in silent film: 'A dissolve is never harsh or exciting. Its mood is smooth and harmonious to the eye, involving a slow rhythm. It causes an instantaneous mental dissolve in the mind of the spectator. This has been very well described as the momentary condensation of a train of thought into another that has yet to serve its purpose. The aim of the dissolve is to associate the old with the new in the mind of the audience.' Paul Rotha, *The Film Till Now* [1930], p. 249, cited by Marcus, *The Tenth Muse*, p. 371.

16 In her 1926 essay 'Cinema' Woolf praises the ability of film to present images of a reality 'as they are when we are not there'. Virginia Woolf, 'The Cinema', *Selected Essays* (Oxford: Oxford University Press, 2008), p. 172.

17 May Sinclair, 'The Novels of Dorothy Richardson', *The Egoist* 5, no. 4 (April 1918), p. 58. Available online at the Modernism Journals Project at https://modjourn.org/issue/bdr522839/# [p. 10]. A major cultural figure of the day, May Sinclair was a successful novelist over a long period and wrote a modernist novel *Mary Olivier: A Life* (1919) using the stream-of-consciousness method. Sinclair refers to the common early complaint against *Pilgrimage* that it has no beginning, middle or end, which can't help but bring to mind that when faced with a similar accusation Godard quipped 'a film should have a beginning, a middle and an end, but not necessarily in that order'. The famous aphorism has been traced to a discussion at the 1966 Cannes festival as reported by Ken Tynan, *The Observer*, 22 May 1966, Weekend Review: Verdict on Cannes by Kenneth Tynan, Quote Page 24, Column 8, London, England (Newspapers_com); background at https://quoteinvestigator.com/2020/01/04/middle/.

18 Ivone Margulies, *Nothing Happens: Chantal Akerman's Hyperrealist Everyday* (Durham: Duke University Press, 1994). In every respect Sinclair could have used this title for her essay '*Pilgrimage*: Nothing Happens: Dorothy Richardson's Hyperrealist Everyday'. *Le Monde*'s claim in 1975 that Akerman had made 'the first masterpiece of the feminine in the history of the cinema' recalls Virginia Woolf's assertion that Richardson had invented 'the psychological sentence of the feminine gender'. Virginia Woolf, review of *Revolving Lights* in *The Nation and the Athenaeum*, 19 May 1923. For *Le Monde* on Akerman, see https://www.bbc.com/culture/article/20181030-how-chantal-akermans-modernist-masterpiece-changed-cinema.

19 Sinclair, 'The Novels of Dorothy Richardson'. Towards the end of her life Richardson confirms Sinclair's characterization of the modernist novel, including *Pilgrimage*. Sinclair scholar Rebecca Bowler writes, 'But Richardson *did* agree with Sinclair's assessment of her novels as void of drama ("there is no drama, no situation, no set scene. Nothing happens"). She emphasises this herself, as late as 1952, in a letter to a critic, and extends it to include all the writers to whom the phrase "stream of consciousness" has been applied: "This, I feel, was a natural development from the move away from 'Romance' to 'Realism' (the latter being a critical reaction to the former). It dealt directly with reality. Hence the absence of either 'plot', 'climax' or 'conclusion'. All the writers concerned would agree with Goethe that drama is for the stage."' Rebecca Bowler 'Stream of Consciousness', 'Drama, and Reality' accessed 18 December 2019 https://maysinclairsociety.com/may-sinclair-and-stream-of-consciousness/.

20 Virginia Woolf, 'A Sketch of the Past' (1939), *Moments of Being*, edited by Jeanne Schulkind [1985], (London: Pimlico, 2002), p. 83.

21 Pier Paolo Pasolini, 'The Cinema of Poetry' [1965], in *Movies and Methods*, Vol. 1, edited by Bill Nichols (Berkeley: University of California Press, 1976), pp. 542–58. [Nichols's note: This text was read in Italian by Pier Paolo Pasolini in June 1965 at the first New Cinema Festival at Pesaro. The present version is from the French translation by Marianne de Vettimo and Jacques Bontemps which appeared in *Cahiers du Cinéma* No. 171, October 1965] Facsimile accessed 11 October 2018 at https://dilipshakya.files.wordpress.com/2013/04/pasolini1976-cinema-n-poetry.pdf, p. 10.

22 'The "cinema of poetry" becomes, therefore, an attempt to theorize a dual allegiance to formal experiment and to social referentiality, or realism. [. . .] the essay is characterized by one of the chief obsessions of Pasolini's entire corpus, from poetry to fiction to theatre and the cinema: the reconciliation of modernism and realism.' John David Rhodes, 'Pasolini's Exquisite Flowers: The "Cinema of Poetry"', in *Global Art Cinema: New Theories and Histories*, edited by Rosalind Galt and Karl Schoovoner (Oxford: Oxford University Press, 2010), p. 153.

23 Pasolini, 'The Cinema of Poetry' [1965], p. 10.

24 'What then does all this mean? It means that a common technico-stylistic tradition is in process of being formed: that is, a cinema language of poetry. [. . .] This emerging tradition is based on the collection of cinematic stylemes which have been constituted almost naturally in function of the irregular psychological characteristics of the characters chosen as pretexts, or, better: in function of a primarily formalist world-view of the author (informal in Antonioni, elegiac in Bertolucci, technical in Godard). Expressing such an inner vision necessarily requires a special language, with its technical and stylistic formulas simultaneously serving the inspiration, which, as it is precisely formalist, finds in them at once its instrument and its object. The "cinematic stylemes" which

have thus appeared and been classified in a tradition barely established and still without norms unless intuitive, pragmatic ones all coincide with typical procedures of cinematic expression. [. . .] Enumerating them amounts to outlining a possible "prosody," not yet codified, in gestation, but whose rules already exist in potential (from Paris to Rome and from Prague to Brasilia).' Pasolini, 'The Cinema of Poetry' [1965], p. 10.

25 Pasolini declares *Red Desert* a success in contrast to Antonioni's previous films since *L'avventura*, the earlier films imposing a formalist style not properly aligned with the perspectives of the characters: 'He [Antonioni] has finally succeeded in representing the world seen through his own eyes because he has substituted, wholly, the world-view of a sick woman for his own vision, which is delirious with aestheticism: a substitution justified by the possible analogy of the two visions.' Pasolini, 'Cinema of Poetry' [1965], p. 8. Pasolini wasn't always sympathetic to Antonioni, so declaring *Red Desert* a success because it expresses the bourgeois sickness of its auteur might be considered a back-handed compliment. The issues raised by the essay 'Cinema of Poetry' are, however, relevant to Pasolini's own later Marxist-modernist masterpiece *Theorem* (1968).

26 'The character-pretexts can only be chosen from the author's own cultural circle: therefore analogous to him by their culture, language and psychology: "exquisite flowers of the bourgeois class." If they happen to belong to another social world, they are always sweetened and assimilated via the categories of anomaly, neurosis or hypersensitivity. The bourgeois class itself, in sum, even in cinema, identifies itself, again, with all humanity, in an irrational interclassism. All this belongs to the general movement of recuperation, by bourgeois culture, of the territory it had lost in the battle with Marxism and its possible revolution. And this is a part of the somehow grandiose movement of the evolution – we shall call it anthropological of the bourgeoisie, along the lines of an "internal revolution" of capitalism, i.e. of a neo-capitalism, which questions and modifies its own structures and which, in the case which concerns us, re-attributes to the poets a pseudohumanistic function: myth and the technical awareness of form.' Pasolini, 'Cinema of Poetry' [1965], p. 11.

27 '*Style, in other words, comes to stand in for a class-consciousness that cannot otherwise appear in the cinema.*' (italics in original), Rhodes, 'Pasolini's Exquisite Flowers: The "Cinema of Poetry"', p. 149. Rhodes discusses the occasion of Pasolini giving the 'Cinema of Poetry' paper at the 1966 New York Film Festival on a panel alongside Andrew Sarris, Agnès Varda, Annette Michelson and Rene Allio (director of the Foucault collaboration *I, Pierre Rivière* a decade later). Pasolini was at the Festival to show *Uccellacci e uccellini / The Hawks and the Sparrows* (1966). When reading 'Cinema of Poetry' in terms of either Lukács or Adorno it should be remembered that at the end of *Hawks and Sparrows* Toto and Ninetto kill, cook and eat the Marxist crow.

Chapter 3

1 Mark Cousins, *The Story of Film* (London: Pavilion, 2004), p. 22.
2 Ibid., p. 37.
3 Ibid., p. 39.
4 Ibid.
5 Francois Truffaut, 'A Certain Tendency of the French Cinema', *Cahiers du Cinéma*, 31 January 1954.
6 Cousins, *The Story of Film*, p. 39.
7 Iris Barry, *D.W. Griffith: American Film Master* (New York: The Museum of Modern Art, 1940), p. 19 [facsimile at MOMA online: www.moma.org/calendar/exhibitions/2993].
8 Ibid., p. 37.
9 Ibid., p. 19.
10 Kracauer, *Theory of Film* I:4, p. 63. Kracauer cites Eisenstein, *Film Form: Essays in Film Theory*, edited and translated by Jay Leda (New York: Harcourt, 1949), p. 199.
11 *Modern Times* is of course a 'mute' rather than 'silent' film.
12 In France the avant-garde was associated with the French *cinéma pur* movement and the 'cineplastics' aesthetics endorsed by Éli Faure and which would come to represent a tradition to be opposed by Bazin and much postwar cinematic modernism.
13 Peter Wollen, 'The Two Avant-Gardes', *Studio International* 190, no. 978 (November/December 1975), pp. 171–5, accessed (no pagination) from Verso 23 February 2018 at https://www.versobooks.com/blogs/3634-the-two-avant-gardes. Also reprinted as 'The Two Avant-Gardes' (1968), in Peter Wollen, *Readings and Writings* (London: Verso, 1982).
14 Wollen, 'The Two Avant-Gardes' (1968).
15 Ibid.
16 Here Wollen is echoing the Godard-Gorin line that supported Vertov as 'revolutionary' against Eisenstein as 'revisionist'.
17 Wollen, 'The Two Avant-Gardes' (1968).
18 Wollen particularly favours Godard's *Le Gai Savoir* (1968) and sees *Tout Va Bien* (1972), with Yves Montand and Jane Fonda, as a retrograde step back to classical *modernist* film. Wollen's sympathies in 1975 clearly lay with the 'first avant-garde' and he is rather dismissive of the second: 'For most people, after all, cinema is unthinkable without words and stories. To recognize this fact is by no means to accept a conventional Hollywood-oriented (or Bergman / Antonioni / Bunuel-oriented) attitude to the cinema and the place of stories and words within it.' While Wollen's films with Laura Mulvey (*Riddle of the Sphinx* 1977) accord with these sympathies, Wollen was credited as co-writer of Antonioni's *The*

Passenger (1975), one of the greatest films of the 'second avant-garde', of cinematic modernism.

19 Murray Smith, 'Modernism and the Avant-Gardes', in *World Cinema: Critical Approaches*, edited by John Hill and Pamela Church Gibson (Oxford: Oxford University Press, 2000), p. 16.

20 Many of the great national cinemas of the silent era – Sweden, Japan – made films which shifted between and sometimes combined elements of expressionism, impressionism and naturalism, shifted between old-fashioned melodrama and a modern naturalism.

21 András Bálint Kovács, *Screening Modernism: European Art Cinema 1950–1980* (Chicago: University of Chicago Press, 2007), p. 17.

22 See David Bordwell and Kristin Thompson, *Film Art: An Introduction* (New York: McGraw-Hill, 1993), p. 462, presumably citing Georges Sadoul, *l'Histoire générale du cinema*.

23 Kovács, *Screening Modernism*, pp. 17–18.

24 Ibid., p. 18.

25 Bordwell and Thompson, *Film Art*, p. 463. The early modernist novel was sometimes called 'impressionist' – literary impressionism being an idea first popularized by Ford Madox Ford in 1914.

26 Jean Epstein, *Cœur fidèle / Faithful Heart* (1923), *La glace à trois faces / The Three-Sided Mirror* (1927), *La chute de la maison Usher / The Fall of the House of Usher* (1928), *Finis terræ* (1929). Epstein continued to make films into the sound era and his poetic realism sometimes prefigures neorealism in its themes and the use of Brittany locations and non-actors from the fishing communities. He also continued to write essays in film theory.

27 A similar 'impressionistic' development in poetic realism occurred in Japanese cinema in the silent era and then crossing over into the sound era in the films of Mizoguchi and Yamanaka from the 1930s.

28 David Bordwell, *On the History of Film Style* (Cambridge, MA: Harvard University Press, 1997), p. 13.

29 Ibid., p. 21. Paul Rotha, *The Film Till Now* (1930, revised edition, London: Spring Books, 1967).

30 Rudolf Arnheim, 'A New Laocoön: Artistic Composites and the Talking Film' (1938), in *Film as Art* (1933) (University of California 1957, fiftieth anniversary edition), pp. 199–230. One thing that connects early film theorists to theorists of modernism is their seemingly obligatory reference to Lessing's *Laocoön* (art vis-à-vis medium specificity).

31 André Bazin, 'The Stylistics of Robert Bresson' (*Cahiers du Cinéma* No.3, 1951), *What Is Cinema Vol.1*, translated by Hugh Grey (Berkeley: University of California Press, 1967/2005), p. 139.

Chapter 4

1 Cousins tracks the three phases of cinematic modernism across chapters 6, 7 and 8. Mark Cousins, *The Story of Film* (London: Pavilion, 2004).
2 Roger Leenhardt, 'Cinematic Rhythm', originally published in *Espirit* January 1936. Cited in Dudley Andrew, *What Cinema Is!* (Oxford: Wiley-Blackwell, 2010), p. 37.
3 Cousins, *The Story of Film*, p. 193.
4 Ibid., p. 191.
5 The American tradition of hard-boiled crime and detective novels, and also the gangster films of classical Hollywood going back to the 1930s and indeed going back to Griffith's The *Musketeers of Pig Alley* (1912) – written by Griffith and Anita Loos.
6 André Bazin, 'Un film libre et pur', *Le Parisien libéré*, 7 January 1956. Bazin had strongly supported Varda in the making of the film.
7 Given the centrality of quotation to Godard's films, it is difficult to know what is formalist self-reflexivity, what is homage and what is parody – the thirty-minute-sequence shot of Bardot and Piccoli quarrelling in their apartment in *Le Mépris Contempt* is probably all of these rather than a simple settling of accounts with Bazin.
8 The following is a (very) short *indicative* list of thirty films of the new wave era 1958–76 informed by *cinematic modernism* (this list is limited to one film per director):

- *The 400 Blows* (Truffaut 1958)
- *Pickpocket* (Bresson 1959)
- *Night and Fog in Japan* (Oshima 1959)
- *L'avventura* (Antonioni 1960)
- *Last Year at Marienbad* (Resnais 1961)
- *Cleo from 5 to 7* (Varda 1961)
- *Knife in the Water* (Polanski 1962)
- *8 ½* (Fellini 1963)
- *Le Mépris* (Godard 1963)
- *The Loves of a Blonde* (Forman 1965)
- *Persona* (Bergman 1966)
- *The Round-Up* (Jancsó 1966)
- *Closely Watched Trains* (Menzel 1966)
- *Accident* (Losey 1967)
- *Belle de Jour* (Bunuel 1967)
- *Theorem* (Pasolini 1968)
- *Faces* (Cassavetes 1968)

- *The Colour of Pomegranates* (Parajanov 1968)
- *My Night with Maud* (Rohmer 1969)
- *Love/Szerelem* (Makk 1971)
- *Walkabout* (Roeg 1971)
- *Out 1* (Rivette 1968–71)
- *The Bitter Tears of Petra von Kant* (Fassbinder 1972)
- *Aguirre, the Wrath of God* (Herzog 1972)
- *Last Tango in Paris* (Bertolucci 1972)
- *The Spirit of the Beehive* (Erice 1973)
- *Alice in the Cities* (Wenders 1973)
- *Mirror* (Tarkovsky 1974)
- *Jeanne Dielman* (Akerman 1975)
- *Taxi Driver* (Scorsese 1976)

9 Given that he saw montage as an integral part of Japanese culture, Eisenstein was perplexed that 'Japanese cinema is unaware of montage' – a mistaken view surely based on watching a limited range of films. Nevertheless, this misreading of Japanese cinema is interesting in light of the development of Mizoguchi, Ozu, Naruse, Yamanaka and others away from Soviet-style expressionist montage. Eisenstein, 'The Film Shot' (1929), in *The Eisenstein Reader*, edited by Richard Taylor (London: BFI, 1998), pp. 82–92.

10 Truffaut, *Foreword*, Bazin, *What Is Cinema* vol.2 1971, p. vii.

11 Although appreciated since the early 1960s by Tokyo-based critics like Donald Richie, Ozu did not become well-known internationally until the 1970s, his ascent to near universal critical acclaim coinciding with the emergence of minimalist cinematic modernism being a striking feature of film culture in the 1990s.

12 Siegried Kracauer, *Theory of Film: The Redemption of Physical Reality*, originally published 1960 by Oxford University Press (Princeton: Princeton University, 1997), pp. 187–8, see also Kracauer on Brakhage, p. 271, Deren, p. 190.

13 Spielberg's *Jaws* is a highly regarded film, however, it was the film that inaugurated the marketing strategies characteristic of the blockbuster and is seen as having put a stop to the 'New Hollywood'.

14 *Empire Magazine*, 'The Irishman Week: Empire's Martin Scorsese Interview' by Nick De Semlyen, *Empire Online*, 6 November 2019, at https://www.empireonline.com/movies/features/irishman-week-martin-scorsese-interview/ and 'Directors vs. Marvel: A Breakdown of the Criticism' by Jordan Moreau, at https://variety.com/2019/film/news/directors-vs-marvel-breakdown-everything-you-need-to-know-1203379604/.

15 Fernando E. Solanas and Octavio Getino, 'Towards a Third Cinema', *Movies and Methods: An Anthology*, edited by Bill Nichols (Berkeley: University of California Press, 1976), pp. 44–64.

16 A brief list of films associated with 'Third Cinema':

- Glauber Rocha, *Black God, White Devil* (Brazil 1964) *Entranced Earth* (Brazil 1967) *Antonio das Mortes* (Brazil 1969)
- Jorge Sanjines, *Blood of the Condor* (Bolivia 1969)
- Fernando Solanas and Octavio Getina, *Hour of the Furnaces/La Hora de Los Hornos* (Argentina 1968)
- Ousmane Sembene, *Black Girl/La Noire de . . .* (Senegal 1963) *The Money Order/Mandabi* (Senegal 1968) *Emitaï* (Senegal 1971) *Xala* (Senegal 1975)
- Djibril Diop Mambéty, *Badou Boy* (Senegal 1970) *The Journey of the Hyena/Touki Bouki* (Senegal 1973)
- Timité Bassori, *The Woman with the Knife/La Femme au couteau* (Ivory Coast 1969)
- Med Hondo, *Soleil Ô* (Mauritania 1970)
- Sarah Maldoror, *Sambizanga* (France/Congo/Angola 1972)
- Souleymane Cissé, *Five Days in a Life/Cinq jours d'une vie* (Mali 1972) *The Girl/Den muso* (Mali 1975)
- Youssef Chahine, *The Choice/Al Ikhtiyar* (Egypt 1970) *The Sparrow/Al Usfur* (Egypt 1972)
- Shadi Abdel Salam, *The Night of Counting the Years/Al Momia* (Egypt 1969)
- Heiny Srour, *The Hour of Liberation Has Arrived/Saat El Tahrir Dakkat* (Lebanon 1974)
- Mohammad Lakhdar-Hamina, *Chronicle of the Year of Embers/Waqai Sanawat Al-Djamr* (Algeria 1975)
- Mrinal Sen, *Interview* (Bengal 1971)
- Shyam Benegal, *Night's End/Nishant* (India 1975)

17 All of Godard's films made with Gorin as part of the Dziga Vertov Group deployed variations on these 'Brechtian' strategies.

18 D. N. Rodowick, *The Crisis of Political Modernism: Criticism and Ideology in Contemporary Film Theory* (Urbana: University of Illinois Press), 1994.

19 Political Modernism – selected key films:

- Jean-Luc Godard, *Weekend* (1967) *La Gai savoir* (1968) *Tout va bien* (1972) *Numéro deux* (1975)
- Chris Marker, *Far from Vietnam* [with Godard, Ivens, Klein, Lelouch, Resnais, Varda] (1967)
- Pier Paulo Pasolini, *Hawks and Sparrows* (1966) *Theorem* (1968) *Pigsty* (1969)
- Danièle Huillet and Jean-Marie Straub, *The Bridegroom, the Actress, and the Pimp* (1968) *Othon* (1969) *History Lessons* (1972) *Fortini/Cani* (1976)
- Alexander Kluge, *Artists Under the Big Top: Perplexed* (1968) *Part-Time Work of a Domestic Slave* (1973)

- Volker Schlöndorff and Margarethe von Trotta, *A Free Woman* (1972) *The Lost Honour of Katharina Blum* (1975)
- Rainer Werner Fassbinder, *Fear Eats the Soul* (1974) *Chinese Roulette* (1976) *In a Year of Thirteen Moons* (1978)
- *Germany in Autumn* (Fassbinder, Schlöndorff, Kluge et al 1977)
- Theo Angelopoulos, *Reconstruction* (1970) *Days of '36* (1972) *The Travelling Players* (1975)
- Miklós Jancsó, *The Confontation* (1968) *Red Psalm* (1972) *Electra, My Love* (1975)
- Dušan Makavejev, *W.R.: Mysteries of the Organism* (1971) *Sweet Movie* (1974)
- Barbet Schroeder, *La Vallée/Obscured by Clouds* (1972)
- René Allio, *I, Pierre Rivière, Having Slaughtered My Mother, Sister and Brother. . .* (1976)
- Chantal Akerman, *Saute ma Ville* (1968) *Je Tu Il Elle* (1974) *Jeanne Dielman* (1975) *The Meetings of Anna* (1978)
- Jacques Rivette, *Celine and Julie Go Boating* (1974)
- Marguerite Duras, *Natalie Granger* (1972) *India Song* (1974)
- Alain Tanner and John Berger, *La Salamandre* (1971) *Jonah, who will be 25 in the year 2000* (1975)
- Laura Mulvey and Peter Wollen, *Penthesilea: Queen of the Amazons* (1974) *Riddles of the Sphinx* (1976)
- Bill Douglas, *My Childhood* (1972), *My Ain Folk* (1973) *My Way Home* (1978)
- Jon Jost, *Speaking Directly* (1973)
- Yoshishige Yoshida, *Eros Plus Massacre* (1969) *Heroic Purgatory* (1970)
- Nagisa Oshima, *Death by Hanging* (1968) *Diary of a Shinjuku Thief* (1969) *The Ceremony* (1971)

20 Noël Herpe, 'Sadness Will Last Forever', *Positif* (March 2003), reprinted in 'Maurice Pialat (1925–2003) – A Tribute', *Senses of Cinema*, March 2003 Issue 25, retrieved 17 July 2020 at http://sensesofcinema.com/2003/feature-articles/pialat/.

21 András Bálint Kovács, *Screening Modernism: European Art Cinema 1950–1980* (Chicago: University of Chicago Press, 2007), pp. 203–9.

Chapter 5

1 D. N. Rodowick, *The Virtual Life of Film* (Cambridge, MA: Harvard University Press, 2007), p. 74.

2 Jacques Rivette, 'Letter on Rossellini', *Cahiers du Cinéma* 46, April 1955, *Cahiers du cinéma: Vol.1: The 1950s: Neo-Realism, Hollywood, New Wave*, edited by Jim Hillier (London: British Film Institute, 1985), pp. 192–204.

3 For a general statement of Bazin's view, see 'An Aesthetic of Reality: Cinematic Realism and the Italian School of the Liberation', in André Bazin, *What Is Cinema?* Volume 2 [1971], essays selected and translated by Hugh Gray (Berkeley: University of California Press, 2005), pp. 16–40. This essay also has a particular influence on Deleuze's theory, see 'Beyond the movement-image', Gilles Deleuze, *Cinema 2: The Time-Image* (London: Athlone Press, 1989), pp. 1–23.

4 'One began to realize that the success [of Italian neorealism] was inseparable from a special conjunction of historical circumstances that took its meaning from the Liberation, and that the technique of the films was in some way magnified by the revolutionary value of the subject.' Bazin, 'Bicycle Thief', *What Is Cinema Vol.2*, p. 47.

5 Roland Barthes, 'The Reality Effect' [1968], *The Rustle of Language*, translated by Richard Howard (Berkeley: University of California Press, 1989).

6 Deleuze's occasional discussions of experimental film are in terms of its relationship to abstract painting, for example, *Cinema 2*, pp. 214–15.

7 'Not only Eliot and Pound, Joyce and Bely, Stravinsky and Picasso, Klee and Henry Moore, but also Yeats and Saint-John Perse, Pasternak and Blok, Ungaretti and Montale, Guillen and Garcia Lorca, Despiau and Rouault, all these, both groups, prove that the modern genius is essentially avant-gardistic.' Renato Poggioli, *The Theory of the Avant-Garde*, translated from the Italian by Gerald Fitzgerald (Cambridge, MA: Harvard University Press, 1968), p. 224.

8 Peter Bürger, *Theory of the Avant-Garde* [1974] (Minneapolis: University of Minnesota Press, 1984).

9 After 1968 Cornelius Cardew, formerly Britain's most promising avant-garde composer and assistant to Stockhausen, denounced both the rival avant-gardes (both Stockhausen and Cage) as reactionary and formed the Scratch Orchestra, aiming to make 'accessible' revolutionary music which could played by non-musicians. Cornelius Cardew, *Stockhausen Serves Imperialism* (London: Latimer, 1974), includes an essay 'John Cage: Ghost or Monster?' By the 1980s minimalism had become a mainstream popular brand of music, polemically opposed to the preceding modernist avant-garde in both its post-serial (Stockhausen) and aleatory (Cage) modes.

10 Peter Wollen, 'The Two Avant-Gardes', *Studio International* 190, no. 978 (November/December 1975), pp. 171–5, accessed (no pagination) from Verso 23 February 2018 at https://www.versobooks.com/blogs/3634-the-two-avant-gardes.

11 'They [Picasso and Braque] were intuitively felt, I think, very early on, to represent a critical semiotic shift, a changed concept and practice of sign and signification, which we can now see to have been the opening-up of a space, a disjunction between signifier and signified and a change of emphasis from the problem of signified and reference, the classic problem of realism, to that of signifier and

signified within the sign itself.' Peter Wollen, 'The Two Avant-Gardes' (Verso online, no pagination).

12 Wollen, 'The Two Avant-Gardes' (Verso online, no pagination).

13 Wollen, 'The Two Avant-Gardes', quote on Vertov from Eisenstein, 'Beyond the Shot' (1929). For revised translation, see *The Eisenstein Reader*, edited by Richard Taylor (London: BFI, 1998), p. 92.

14 'Cinema, I have stressed earlier, is a multiple system – the search for the specifically cinematic can be deceptively purist and reductive. For most people, after all, cinema is unthinkable without words and stories. To recognize this fact is by no means to accept a conventional Hollywood-oriented (or Bergman / Antonioni / Bunuel-oriented) attitude to the cinema and the place of stories and words within it.' Peter Wollen, 'The Two Avant-Gardes'. There is an irony here in Wollen co-writing the script for Antonioni's modernist *The Passenger* (1975).

15 Frederic Jameson, 'The Existence of Italy', in *Signatures of the Visible* (London: Routledge, 1992), p. 213.

16 Ibid., p. 213.

17 Ibid., pp. 217–34.

18 Ibid., p. 214.

19 Ibid., p. 215.

20 Ibid., p. 216.

21 Ibid.

22 Ibid., pp. 273–5.

23 David Bordwell, 'The Art Cinema as a Mode of Film Practice' [1979], *Film Criticism* 4, no. 1 (Fall 1979), pp. 56–64. Reprinted without revisions but with Afterword as chapter 5 in David Bordwell, *Poetics of Cinema* (London: Routledge, 2008), pp. 151–69.

24 Bordwell, 'The Art Cinema as a Mode of Film Practice' [1979], *Poetics of Cinema*, p. 151.

25 'In short, a realist aesthetic and an expressionist aesthetic are hard to merge. The art cinema seeks to solve the problem in a sophisticated way: by the device of *ambiguity*.' Bordwell, 'The Art Cinema as a Mode of Film Practice' [1979], *Poetics of Cinema*, p. 156.

26 London Film Society: BFI online at https://www.bfi.org.uk/sites/bfi.org.uk/files/downloads/bfi-the-film-society-1925-1939-a-guide-to-collections.pdf.

27 Bordwell, 'The Art Cinema as a Mode of Film Practice' [1979], *Poetics of Cinema*, p. 157.

28 Ibid., p. 158.

29 David Bordwell, *Narration in the Fiction Film* (London: Routledge, 1986).

30 Ibid., chapter 10, p. 310.

31 Ibid., p. 310. Bordwell's problem here is that there are many exceptions; parametric narration may be used in some classical or mainstream films.

32 David Bordwell, 'Afterword [2008]', 'The Art Cinema as a Mode of Film Practice' [1979], *Poetics of Cinema*, pp. 161–2.

33 David Bordwell, *On the History of Film Style* (Cambridge, MA: Harvard University Press, 1997). Chapter 4 is entitled 'The Return of Modernism' and looks at modernism in silent film, postwar art film and post-1968 political modernism in the context of a transition in the critical discourse from Bazin to Burch marked by a revival of overtly modernist ideas and tropes.

34 In his critical reading of Bordwell and Kovács, Mark Betz argues that far from being superseded by postmodernism, cinematic modernism – displaying the features of Bordwell's art cinema international style, especially parametric narration – has dispersed from its 1960s European centre to all over the world since the 1990s. Betz concludes that 'In short, one cannot dismiss so easily the possibility that parametric narration has in fact settled in, and cinematic modernism extended over, the past two decades in such a way as to become widespread and perceivable, but also more recognisable, watchable, and marketable, than Bordwell in his formalism and Kovács his historicalism would allow.' Mark Betz, 'Beyond Europe: On Parametric Transcendence', in *Global Art Cinema: New Theories and Histories*, edited by Rosalind Galt and Karl Schoonover (Oxford: Oxford University Press, 2010), p. 39.

35 András Bálint Kovács, *Screening Modernism: European Art Cinema 1950–1980* (Chicago: University of Chicago Press, 2007), pp. 203–9.

36 Ibid., p. 203.

37 Ibid., pp. 217–37.

38 Ibid., p. 394 Given that *Stalker* belongs to the science fiction genre (like *Solaris* 1972) and to the allegorical, this argument seems problematic but usefully suggestive regarding *Mirror*.

39 Ibid., p. 395.

40 Ibid., p. 400.

41 Ibid., p. 400.

42 Jacques Rancière, *Film Fables* (2001), translated by Emiliano Battista (Berg: Oxford, 2006).

43 Chapter 7, 'From One Image to Another? Deleuze and the Ages of Cinema', Rancière, *Film Fables*, p. 107.

44 Rancière, *Film Fables*, p. 108.

45 Godard, *Histoire(s) du cinema*, 3A. In this episode Godard also talks about the relationship of cinema to French painting and Manet as the first cinematographer. Sally Shafto writes the following illuminating commentary:

> 'In episode 3A (*La Monnaie de l'absolu*), especially dense in painting, Godard narrates a history of art compatible with traditional histories of modern painting. He dates the origins of the *cinématographe* to Edouard Manet. Similarly, the American critic Clement Greenberg traced the origins of modern painting to Manet, when painting began to liberate itself from representation in order to

concentrate on form and colour (a title-card in 3A, appearing during a series of paintings by Manet specifies that that painter was creating silent films: "C'était du cinéma muet.") In the Greenberg version, based on an idea of progressive evolution, modern painting reached its acme with the heroic paintings of the American Abstract Expressionists. In *Le Musée imaginaire*, Malraux also reveals a predilection for history on the progressive model, and likewise dates the beginnings of modern painting to Manet, while remaining less teleological. Godard similarly relies upon a notion of progress, while substituting the cinema as its culmination. Just as Greenberg had done for abstract painting, Godard makes a case for the exceptional nature of the cinema, his *parti pris* indicated above all in the repetition of the title of episode 2A "Seul le cinéma". Godard seems to say that only the cinema is capable of showing certain things. In 3B (*Une Vague nouvelle*), a voiceover spoken by Anne-Marie Miéville, quoting André Bazin, continues in this vein: in saying that "perspective was the original sin of Western painting. Niepce and Lumière were its redeemers.'"

Sally Shafto, 'On Painting and History in Godard's *Histoire(s) du cinéma*', *Senses of Cinema* 40 (July 2006), accessed 21 July 2020 at http://sensesofcinema.com/2006/the-godard-museum/histoires-du-cinema/. This article first appeared in French in a special issue ('Où en est le God-Art') of *CinémAction*, edited by René Prédal, no. 109 (2003), pp. 226–35.

46 Rancière, *Film Fables*, p. 109.

47 Ibid., p. 111.

48 Ibid., p. 117. Rancière has outlined his own aesthetic theory at length elsewhere, see for example Jacques Rancière, *The Politics of Aesthetics* (2000), translated by Gabriel Rockhill with Afterword by Slavoj Žižek (Continuum: London, 2004).

49 Rancière, *Film Fables*, p. 108. Rancière's anxieties over the 'modern' fetishization of the 'break', 'rupture' or *coupure* might reflect his own 'break' with Althusser?

Chapter 6

1 András Bálint Kovács, *Screening Modernism: European Art Cinema 1950–1980* (Chicago: University of Chicago Press, 2007).

2 Francis Fukuyama, 'The End of History?', *The National Interest* 16 (Summer 1989), pp. 3–18.

3 Fredric Jameson, *Postmodernism, or the Cultural Logic of Late Capitalism* (London: Verso, 1991), the main thesis initially appeared in an article of the same title in *New Left Review* 1/146, July/August 1984.

4 From this perspective, socialism and communism can be seen as secondary temporary localized 'solutions' to contradictions *within* capitalism as the dominant global system.

5 'The Disappearance of Nothingness', András Bálint Kovács, *Screening Modernism: European Art Cinema 1950–1980* (Chicago: University of Chicago Press, 2007), pp. 394–400.

6 For discussion and examples of modernism as something continuing today in the twenty-first century, see the essay collection: *The Contemporaneity of Modernism: Literature, Media, Culture*, edited by Michael D'Arcy and Mathias Nilges (London: Routledge, 2015). As discussed in Chapter 1 of this book, 'vernacular modernism' is a now ubiquitous category of modernism across the arts but developed out of film theory and debates over cinematic modernism, initially in the following article: Miriam Hansen, 'The Mass Production of the Senses: Classical Cinema as Vernacular Modernism', *Modernism / Modernity* 6, no. 2 (April 1999), pp. 59–77. The 'inclusive' critical approach known as 'The New Modernism' was initiated by the following article: Douglas Mao and Rebecca L. Walkowitz, 'The New Modernist Studies', *PMLA* 123, no. 3 (May 2008), pp. 737–48.

7 A google search for *2001* today immediately brings up multiple links along the lines of 'Is *2001* boring?', 'Is *2001* too slow?'. Perhaps *2001* was not only modernist but the original example of 'slow cinema'?

8 *Nouveau roman* novels such as Alain Robbe-Grillet *Les Gommes* (1953), *Le Voyeur* (1955), *La Jalousie* (1957) or Marguerite Duras *Le Ravissement de Lol V. Stein* (1964).

9 Chapter 9 'Nostalgia for the Present', Jameson, *Postmodernism, or, The Cultural Logic of Late Capitalism*, pp. 279–96.

10 This is basically the Lacanian reading of Lynch as developed across numerous interventions from Žižek, such as the discussion of *Blue Velvet* in *The Pervert's Guide to Cinema* (DVD, Fiennes, 2006). See also: Slavoj Žižek, *The Art of the Ridiculous Sublime: On David Lynch's Lost Highway* (Seattle: University of Washington Press, 2000).

11 Kovács, *Screening Modernism*, pp. 394–400.

12 The positive critical reception of *Mulholland Drive* was often couched in terms of a 'rehabilitation' of long-standing modernist narrative tropes from the empty excesses of postmodernism. In his *Village Voice* review J. Hoberman wrote that *Mulholland Drive* 'is certainly Lynch's strongest movie since *Blue Velvet* and maybe *Eraserhead*. The very things that failed him in the bad-boy rockabilly debacle of *Lost Highway* – the atmosphere of free-floating menace, pointless transmigration of souls, provocatively dropped plot stitches, gimcrack alternate universes – are here brilliantly rehabilitated.' J. Hoberman, 'Points of No Return', *The Village Voice*, 1 October 2001.

13 Jarmusch's first significant work in film was his involvement in Wim Wenders's documentary portrait of the dying Nicholas Ray, *Lightning over Water* (1980). Jarmusch was Ray's assistant.

14 As a 2005 retrospective profile of Jarmusch put it, *Stranger Than Paradise* 'permanently upended the idea of independent film as an intrinsically inaccessible avant-garde form'. Lynn Hirschberg, 'The Last of the Indies', *New York Times*, 31 July 2005. In 1984 Jarmusch described his film as 'a neorealistic black comedy in the style of an imaginary East European director obsessed with Ozu and *The Honeymooners* [American television comedy series]', cited by J. Hoberman, 'Americana, Right and Wrong', *Village Voice*, 2 October 1984, reprinted in Criterion Collection as *Paradise Regained*, 3 September 2007 at https://www.criterion.com/current/posts/568-paradise-regained. Hoberman adds: 'Structurally, the movie is a tour de force – a succession of brief vignettes punctuated by opaque film stock. There are no reverse angles, no point-of-view shots; each scene is a single take. [. . .] With its dislocated travelogue, *Stranger Than Paradise* suggests Wenders's *Kings of the Road*; the transcendently shabby moonscapes evoke Chantal Akerman's *News from Home*, and the absence of reverse angles her *Jeanne Dielman*.'

15 Kent Jones: 'There's been an overemphasis on the hipness factor – and a lack of emphasis on his incredible attachment to the idea of celebrating poetry and culture. You can complain about the preciousness of a lot of his movies, [but] they are unapologetically standing up for poetry. [His attitude is] "if you want to call me an elitist, go ahead, I don't care"', quoted in Jonathan Romney, 'Jim Jarmusch: How the Film World's Maverick Stayed True to His Roots', *The Guardian*, 22 February 2014 https://www.theguardian.com/film/2014/feb/22/jim-jarmusch-only-lovers-left-alive.

16 Mark Cousins, *The Story of Film* (London: Pavilion, 2004), pp. 421–2.

17 Antonioni's camera has its static moments and there are many other directors from Max Ophüls to Jancsó who adhere more to tracking shots and sequence shots, but Antonioni is the most influential modernist director in terms of the centrality of fluid sequence shots to his aesthetic.

18 This argument resembles Burch's thesis about the radical aesthetic consequences of the isolation of Japanese cinema under nationalist militarism in the 1930s: Nöel Burch, *To the Distant Observer: Form and Meaning in the Japanese Cinema* (Berkeley: University of California, 1981). Of course, for many Iranian viewers the underlying aesthetic continuity of Iranian new wave cinema relates to long-standing Iranian cultural traditions across the arts, pictorial and literary, especially poetry.

Chapter 7

1 The 'death of cinephelia' debate was triggered by the main published version of the essay (misleadingly edited according to Sontag): Susan Sontag, 'The Decay of Cinema', *New York Times Magazine*, 25 February 1996.

2 'The only time his [Scorsese] ardour dims is when the subject of Marvel comes up. "I don't see them," he says of the MCU. "I tried, you know?" But that's not cinema. Honestly, the closest I can think of them, as well-made as they are, with actors doing the best they can under the circumstances, is theme parks. It isn't the cinema of human beings trying to convey emotional, psychological experiences to another human being.' *Empire Magazine*, 'The Irishman Week: Empire's Martin Scorsese Interview' by Nick De Semlyen, *Empire Online*, 6 November 2019, at https://www.empireonline.com/movies/features/irishman-week-martin-scorsese-interview/.

3 *Variety* reported: 'At the Lumiere Film Festival this week, the "Godfather" director doubled down on Scorsese's comments. "Martin was being kind when he said it wasn't cinema," Coppola said. "He didn't say it was 'despicable', which is what I say." [. . .] "They're made as commodities . . . like hamburgers," [Ken] Loach said in a Sky News interview. "It's about making a commodity which will make profit for a big corporation. They're a cynical exercise. They're a market exercise, and it has nothing to do with the art of cinema."' *Variety*, 22 October 2019, 'Directors vs. Marvel: A Breakdown of the Criticism' by Jordan Moreau, at https://variety.com/2019/film/news/directors-vs-marvel-breakdown-everything-you-need-to-know-1203379604/.

4 It was noticeable that the positive critical reception of Tarantino's *Once Upon a Time in Hollywood* (2019) was often pitched as Tarantino achieving artistic maturity, going beyond trash postmodernism and finally producing something in line with cinematic modernism, something in the lineage of early 1970s New Hollywood.

5 Ulrich Köhler, 'Why I Don't Make Political Films', cited by Marco Abel, *The Counter-Cinema of the Berlin School* (New York: Camden House, 2013), p. 1, see also pp. 8, 18, 24, 274, 278.

6 Harald Martenstein, Berlin *Tagesspiegel*, cited by Abel, *The Counter-Cinema of the Berlin School*, p. 13.

7 Abel, *The Counter-Cinema of the Berlin School*, p. 15.

8 *The Berlin School and Its Global Context*, edited by Marco Abel and Jaimey Fisher (Detroit: Wayne State University Press, 2018).

9 Listed by Obama on Twitter on 29 December 2019, his list also included Jia Zhangke, *Ash Is Purest White* and Joanna Hogg, *The Souvenir*. See https://www.indiewire.com/2019/12/barack-obama-favorite-movies-tv-2019-1202199555/.

10 '[E]xperimental silent film maker Max Fleischer [. . .] patented the Rotoscoping process in 1917. [For *Waking Life*] the animators used inexpensive "off-the-shelf" Apple Macintosh computers. The film was mostly produced using Rotoshop, a custom-made rotoscoping program that creates blends between key frame vector shapes, which also makes use of virtual "layers", and created specifically for the production by Bob Sabiston.' Wikipedia: https://en.wikipedia.org/wiki/Waking_Life.

11 Original Ebert review of *Man Push Cart* dated 19 October 2006, https://www.rogerebert.com/reviews/man-push-cart-2006.

12 https://www.rogerebert.com/rogers-journal/eberts-most-hated.

13 A. O. Scott, 'Neo-Neo Realism', *The New York Times,* Sunday Magazine, 17 March 2009, https://www.nytimes.com/2009/03/22/magazine/22neorealism-t.html.

14 Richard Brody, 'About "Neo-Neo Realism"', *The New Yorker*, https://www.newyorker.com/culture/richard-brody/about-neo-neo-realism.

15 J. Hoberman, 'Wendy and Lucy', *The Village Voice*, 10 December 2008, https://www.villagevoice.com/2008/12/10/wendy-and-lucy/.

16 Richard Brody, 'Against "Wendy and Lucy"', *The New Yorker*, 10 December 2008, https://www.newyorker.com/culture/goings-on/against-wendy-and-lucy.

17 Figgis refers to Godard frequently in his DVD commentary to the theatrically released version of *Timecode* (the fifteenth and final version). *Timecode* (Optimum DVD, 2000).

18 Digital filming facilitates these greatly extended lengths. For *Rope* (1948) Hitchcock had to film ten-minute takes (for shooting the then maximum length of a film camera magazine, while reels for projection lasted twenty minutes) and then assemble them to *appear* like a single real-time eighty-minute take. In fact Figgis had to do something similar when transferring the digital version of *Timecode* to celluloid for theatrical release.

19 Richard Williams, 'Once Upon a Timecode', *The Guardian*, 11 August 2000, https://www.theguardian.com/film/2000/aug/11/culture.features.

20 My transcription from UK DVD, *Timecode* (Optimum DVD, 2000).

21 '*Under the Skin*'s Jonathan Glazer on the Movies He Loves', by Jake Mulligan, *Esquire*, 14 April 2014, https://www.esquire.com/entertainment/movies/interviews/a28284/jonathan-glazer-interview/.

22 For a reading of *Under the Skin* in relation to race and gender, see Zara Dinnen and Sam McBean, 'The Face as Technology', *New Formations* 93 (July 2018), pp. 122–37.

23 '*Under the Skin*: why did this chilling masterpiece take a decade?' interview with Jonathan Glazer by Danny Leigh, *The Guardian*, 6 March 2014, https://www.theguardian.com/film/2014/mar/06/under-the-skin-director-jonathan-glazer-scarlett-johansson.

24 'Jonathan Glazer Talks about His New FIlm "Under the Skin"', by Hank Sartin, *Roger Ebert.com*, 10 April 2014, https://www.rogerebert.com/interviews/jonathan-glazer-talks-about-under-the-skin.

25 In *Sight and Sound*'s review of the first decade of the twenty-first century, Jonathan Romney gave an overview of 'slow cinema', describing it as 'a varied strain of austere minimalist cinema that has thrived internationally over the past ten years'. See 'In Search of Lost Time', *Sight and Sound* 20 (2 February 2010), pp. 43–4. A debate on 'slow cinema' was then instigated in a subsequent editorial, see Nick James, 'Passive Aggressive', *Sight and Sound* 20 (4 April 2010), p. 5. Apparently claiming victory, in a 2013 editorial Nick James reported from Cannes 'on the absence of any film I saw there that fits the "slow cinema" category' and he suggests that this 'might signal the

end of that post-Tarkovskian approach to cinema', *Sight and Sound* 23 (7 July 2013), p. 5.

26 In the United States the controversy over slow cinema (and art-house films more generally) centred on the so-called 'cultural vegetables' debate, for a summary, see A. O. Scott and Manohla Dargis in conversation with Dan Kois, 'Sometimes a Vegetable Is Just a Vegetable', *The New York Times*, 17 June 2011, p. 10, https://www.nytimes.com/2011/06/19/movies/critics-discuss-cinema-thats-good-for-you.html.

27 Matthew Flanagan, 'Towards an Aesthetic of Slow in Contemporary Cinema', *16:9 in English*, number 29, November 2008, http://www.16-9.dk/2008-11/side11_inenglish.htm. Major recent books on 'slow cinema' include Emre Çağlayan, *Poetics of Slow Cinema: Nostalgia, Absurdism, Boredom*, (London: Palgrave Macmillan, 2018); Tiago De Luca and Nuno Barradas Jorge, eds, *Slow Cinema* (Edinburgh: University Press, 2016); Ira Jaffe, *Slow Movies: Countering the Cinema of Action* (London: Wallflower Press, 2014).

28 Flanagan, 'Towards an Aesthetic of Slow in Contemporary Cinema'. Flanagan references the quotation as: David Bordwell, *The Way Hollywood Tells It: Story and Style in Modern Movies* (Berkeley, London: University of California Press, 2006), pp. 129–34. Regarding Bordwell's analysis of 'intensified continuity' as a new mainstream Hollywood style, Flanagan cites David Bordwell, 'Intensified Continuity: Visual Style in Contemporary American Film', *Film Quarterly* 55, no. 3 (2002), pp. 16–28; David Bordwell, *Figures Traced in Light: On Cinematic Staging* (Berkeley, London: University of California Press, 2005); David Bordwell, 'Unsteadicam Chronicles', *Observations on Film Art* (online blog), 17 August 2007, http://www.davidbordwell.net/blog/2007/08/17/unsteadicam-chronicles/.

29 Although the *Bourne* films are thought to have taken fast cutting/short ASLs to a new extreme, montage-based cinema has often experimented with fast cutting. Vertov's *Man with the Movie Camera* (1929) has an average shot length of less than 2½ seconds. Michael Glover Smith, 'Dziga Vertov: Wild Man of Soviet Montage', *White City Cinema* (online blog), 4 March 2011, https://whitecitycinema.com/2011/05/04/dziga-vertov-wild-man-of-soviet-montage/.

30 David Bordwell, 'insert-your-favorite-bourne-pun-here', *Observations on Film Art* (online blog), 30 August 2007, http://www.davidbordwell.net/blog/2007/08/30/insert-your-favorite-bourne-pun-here/.

31 Ibid.

32 András Bálint Kovács, *Screening Modernism: European Art Cinema 1950–1980* (Chicago: University of Chicago Press, 2007), pp. 203–9.

33 Paul Schrader, 'Rethinking Transcendental Style', p. 2, *Transcendental Style in Film* [1971], new edition (Berkeley: University of California, 2018), p. 5.

34 'I sensed a bridge between the spirituality I was raised with and the "profane" cinema I loved. And it was a bridge of *style* not content.' Paul Schrader, 'Rethinking Transcendental Style', *Transcendental Style in Film*, p. 2.

35 Schrader, 'Rethinking Transcendental Style', p. 2. Schrader cites Susan Sontag, 'Spiritual Style in the Films of Robert Bresson', in *Against Interpretation* (1966) and 'Aesthetics of Silence' in *Styles of Radical Will* (1967).
36 Schrader, 'Rethinking Transcendental Style', p. 1.
37 Ibid., pp. 3–4. Schrader cites Deleuze, *Cinema II*, p. 17.
38 Schrader, 'Rethinking Transcendental Style', pp. 4–5. Schrader cites Deleuze, *Cinema II*, p. 2 and Bazin, *What Is Cinema?* vol. 2, p. 81.
39 Schrader, 'Rethinking Transcendental Style', pp. 7–8. Schrader cites Bazin, *What Is Cinema?* vol. 2, 64; vol. 1, 14; vol. 1, 26.
40 Schrader, 'Rethinking Transcendental Style', pp. 22–3.
41 Ibid., pp. 17–21.
42 Ibid., p. 9.
43 Criticism of Serra's films centres on the accusation that Serra deploys a trash aesthetic which is not camp (i.e. is uptight heteronormative trash). For a sceptical critique of Serra, see 'Enlighten Me' by Nick Pinkerton in *Reverse Shot Online*, 20 November 2014, http://www.reverseshot.org/reviews/entry/1952/story_of_my_death.
44 *Juventude em Marcha* was a slogan associated with the 1974 revolution meaning 'Youth on the March' and is used ironically by Costa to refer to the failed hopes of the revolution but also the exclusion from the revolutionary events of Black migrant workers such as Ventura, migrants who came to Lisbon in the 1970s to work on prestigious building projects only to be left in old age to rot in the Lisbon slums with no real home of their own. The English title is also ironic, referring to the classical Greek 'Kouroi' marble statues of noble youths, Ventura possessing a statuesque physique now embodying broken old age and the lost dreams of youth. The English title may also reference British post-punk band Young Marble Giants and their album *Colossal Youth* (1981); as a post-punk himself Costa presumably sanctioned this title.
45 As with *Casa de Lava* vis-à-vis Tourneur's *I Walked with a Zombie*, Costa's *Colossal Youth* as a whole is filtered through a 'quotation' from classical Hollywood, from John Ford: '*Colossal Youth* (2006) can be seen as a remake of Ford's theatrically lit *Sergeant Rutledge* (1960), with the traumatized Cape Verdean patriarch Ventura standing in for Woody Strode', Jonathan Rosenbaum, 'Films of the Future', *Chicago Reader* 15 November 2007, https://www.jonathanrosenbaum.net/2007/11/cinema-of-the-future/.
46 'Pedro Costa's Politics' in Jacques Rancière, *The Intervals of Cinema*, translated by John Howe, (London: Verso, 2014), p. 142. Rancière sees Costa and Tarr as representing the aesthetic options left after the end of modern(ist) cinema and Marxism and both options might be described as utilizing non-ironic stylistic pastiche. See also Jacques Rancière, *Béla Tarr, The Time After*, translated by Erik Beranek (Minneapolis: Univocal, 2013).
47 Serra is an admirer and friend of Sokurov 'I like Sokurov, always, even if he makes bad films or failed films, because he takes risks. And you can't spot any influences

there – perhaps Tarkovsky, a very far-off echo. I like some Béla Tarr films, even if they are too emphatic for my tastes.' Interview with Kieron Corless, 'Albert Serra: "I am the best one"', *Sight and Sound*, 18 July 2015, https://www2.bfi.org.uk/news-opinion/sight-sound-magazine/interviews/lff-2011-albert-serra-i-am-best-one. Comparing Serra with Sokurov, Szaniawski writes: 'Serra posits himself clearly as a filmmaker of *presence*: he gives an immediacy to the bodies of characters and their surrounding which are far more important than the narrative. A late modernist no doubt, the Catalan delivers an updated version of Gilles Deleuze's time-image, wherein pure visual and sonic situations ("opsigns" and "sonsigns") disrupt a traditional causal, "sensori-motor" schema and sequence of the action-image. Becoming secondary, even as it remains linear on paper, the narrative becomes an epic of presence and *photogénie*.' Jeremi Szaniawski, '"Whose Death, Whose Power?": Crystal Images and the Political Unconscious in the Films of Albert Serra and Alexander Sokurov', *Senses of Cinema*, issue 82, March 2017, at https://www.sensesofcinema.com/2017/feature-articles/albert-serra-and-alexander-sokurov/.

Chapter 8

1 Frederic Jameson, *The Geopolitical Aesthetic: Cinema and Space in the World System* (London: BFI, 1992), which contains his extended reading of Sokurov's *Days of the Eclipse*, pp. 87–111. In the 1990s Jameson made a distinction between the understandable bewilderment of nations vulnerable to the emerging 'global system' (including the collapsed Soviet Union, see pp. 109–11) and 'first world' nations. In the twenty-first century this sense of an inexplicable external force has spread to the first world, with its attendant prejudice, paranoia and conspiracy theories.

2 In her *Artforum* list of the top ten films of the 1990s Susan Sontag put *The Second Circle* at number one. Susan Sontag, *Artforum*, December 1999, p. 116 at https://www.artforum.com/print/199910/susan-sontag-753.

3 Jameson, *Geopolitical Aesthetic*, p. 105 and note 13 pp. 112–13.

4 Ibid., pp. 88–9; p. 96.

5 Tarr 'In each of the films, you can see a combination of faiths, beliefs and interests. But each faith is revealed as an illusion. And then it spreads thin and disappears. [. . .] all messiahs are generally just ordinary spies.' *A Brief Interview with Bela Tarr*, Steve Erickson, Stevee, home.earthlink.net at http://home.earthlink.net/~steevee/bela.html.

6 All description in this commentary on *Taste of Cherry* is mine and all dialogue is my transcription derived from English subtitles on the English DVD: *Taste of Cherry* (UK: Artificial Eye, 2005).

7 Susan Sontag, 'Against Interpretation', in *Against Interpretation and Other Essays* [1961] (London: Penguin Classics, 2009).

8 The coda has been cut from some circulating versions of the film and Kiarostami was interested in different audience reactions to the film with and without the coda, see Jonathan Rosenbaum 'Philosophical Treatises of a Master Illusionist: A Conversation about Abbas Kiarostami', posted 8 July 2016 at https://www.jonathanrosenbaum.net/2016/07/49489/.

9 This passage is my description of the closing scene of *Taste of Cherry*, including dialogue derived from the subtitles of the English DVD.

10 Roger Ebert dismissed the film as 'excruciatingly boring' and then added it to a list of his 'most hated movies of all time'! https://www.rogerebert.com/rogers-journal/eberts-most-hated.

11 Laura Mulvey, *Death 24x a Second* (London: Reakton, 2005), p. 124.

12 Tony Rayns, 'Review: *Stray Dogs*', *Film Comment* 50, no. 3 (May-June 2014), https://www.filmcomment.com/article/review-stray-dogs-tsai-ming-liang/.

13 Tsai Ming-Liang, *Goodbye, Dragon Inn* (2003), all references to the English DVD edition (UK: Second Run, 2020).

14 Ibid.

15 Ibid.

16 According to Tsai, the Fu Ho cinema in Taipei was a cruising site in the 1980s. See interview with Tsai on DVD and see essay 'Haunted' by Tony Ryans in the DVD booklet, p. 9. *Goodbye, Dragon Inn* (UK: Second Run, 2020).

17 Inga Pollman, 'The Forces of Milieu: Angela Schanelec's *Marseille* and the Heritage of Michelangelo Antonioni', in *The Berlin School and its Global Contexts: A Transnational Art Cinema*, edited by Marco Abel and Jaimey Fisher (Detroit: Wayne State University Press, 2018), p. 155.

18 Dialogue taken from English subtitled DVD. Angela Schanelec, *Marseille* (2004) (Berlin: Filmgalerie, 2005).

19 Chris Berry, 'Still Life', *Still Life* DVD (London: BFI, 2008), DVD booklet, p. 4.

20 Jia Zhangke, 'Images that Cannot be Banned – New Cinema in China from 1995', *Still Life* DVD (London: BFI, 2008), DVD booklet, p. 19.

21 Ibid., p. 18 ('image deprivation' also p. 18).

22 Jia Zhangke, 'Director's Statement', *Still Life* DVD (London: BFI, 2008), DVD booklet, p. i.

23 All description in this passage of commentary on *Still Life* is mine and all dialogue is my transcription derived from English subtitles on the UK DVD: Zhangke, *Still Life* DVD.

24 Ibid.

25 As elsewhere, challenging dominant narratives of colonial history has become a huge issue in South America. Around the same time as Martel's *Zama* (2017) Lisandro Alonso also addressed Argentina's colonial history in *Jauja* (2014) and

used similar strategies to 'deconstruct' the conventions of the historical 'period film'.

26 *The Headless Woman* contains cultural references in its music and fashions to Argentina in the dictatorship period (1976–83).

27 *The Headless Woman* is not without comic touches – Juan thinks he is going to have to confess to his infidelity with Vero before realizing that 'the situation' husband Marcos is referring to is the car accident.

28 Deborah Martin, *The Cinema of Lucrecia Martel* (Manchester: Manchester University Press, 2016), p. 25, footnote 24 and p. 93.

29 Pier Paolo Pasolini 'The Cinema of Poetry' [p. 8], in *Movies and Methods*, Vol. 1, edited by Bill Nichols (Berkeley: University of California Press, 1976), pp. 542–58.

30 'LM: Really I don't like to see the shifting of focus between characters. I guess it's also connected to the structuring layers of my films. AT: *I would have to see the film again to make sure of this, but I don't think that there are any subjective shots.* LM: No, there aren't.', 'Interview: Lucrecia Martel: Shadow of a Doubt' by Amy Taubin, *Film Comment*, July/August 2009 issue online at https://www.filmcomment.com/article/shadow-of-a-doubt-lucrecia-martel-interviewed/.

31 Kovács discusses Antonioni and 'continuity' as a key stylistic characteristic of postwar cinematic modernism at length in *Screening Modernism* (while qualifying the prevalence of the long take in Antonioni's own films), András Bálint Kovács, *Screening Modernism: European Art Cinema 1950–1980* (Chicago: University of Chicago Press, 2007), pp. 153–61 and pp. 206–7.

32 François Truffaut, *The Films in My Life* (New York: Simon & Schuster, 1978.) pp. 327–8. Martel mentions her attachment to Kim Novak and *Vertigo* in a number of interviews, for example, referring to *The Headless Woman*: 'And there is a kind of play with Kim Novak. I love *Vertigo*.' In 'When Worlds Collide: An Interview with Lucrecia Martel' by Chris Wisniewski, 17 August 2009, *Reverse Shot Online* http://www.reverseshot.org/interviews/entry/938/interview_lucrecia_martel.

33 Ben Rivers has been one of the best-known exponents of this type of cinema, see, for example *Two Years at Sea* (2011).

34 Dialogue taken from English subtitles of UK DVD edition. Lisandro Alonso, *Liverpool* (2008), UK DVD edition (London: Second Run, 2012).

35 '*Poetry*: Interview with Lee Chang-dong' by Sarah Cronin, *Electric Sheep*, 27 July 2011, http://www.electricsheepmagazine.co.uk/2011/07/27/poetry-interview-with-lee-chang-dong/.

36 *Burning* is loosely adapted from a short story 'Barn Burning' by Haruki Murakami (the barns become greenhouses in Lee's film). Faulkner wrote a short story 'Barn Burning' in 1939.

37 With regard to fragmented narrative structure and multiple unreliable narrators, the four most relevant Faulkner novels would be *The Sound and the Fury* (1929), *As I Lay Dying* (1930), *Light in August* (1932) and *Absalom, Absalom!* (1936).

38 Dialogue transcribed from English subtitles of UK DVD edition. Lee Chang-Dong, *Burning* (2018), UK DVD edition (London: Thunderbird, 2019).

39 Roland Barthes, 'Dear Antonioni' ['Cher Antonioni', *Cahiers du Cinéma* 311, May 1980] translated by and in G. Nowell-Smith, *L'avventura* (London: BFI, 1997), pp. 63–9.

40 *Burning* is full of little homages to Antonioni. Near the beginning of the film Hae-mi performs a mime for Jong-su, initially juggling a ball and then peeling and eating a tangerine, and explaining that the important thing in mime is to forget that what is being imagined is not actually there – evoking the famous scene of the mime tennis match at the end of *Blow Up*. Hae-mi's apartment is overlooked by the Seoul Tower, evoking the EUR water tower overlooking the flat where Vittoria and Riccardo argue and break up at the beginning of *L'Eclisse*. And of course the sudden mysterious disappearance of Hae-mi from the narrative and Jong-su's investigation into her disappearance recalls *L'avventura*.

41 Barthes, 'Dear Antonioni', *L'avventura* (London: BFI, 1997), p. 63.

42 *An Elephant Sitting Still* was written as a novella before being adapted into a film.

Appendix

1 This selective list (unfortunately limited to films actually seen by the author) relates to the films discussed in this book and is mostly limited to films which adhere to the aesthetic of cinematic modernism as outlined in this book. Late films by veteran directors from the postwar era of cinematic modernism such as Godard, Rivette and Varda have not been included. Overtly satirical films and 'new extreme' films from the recent 'cinema of cruelty' have also not been included, regardless of any modernist formalist trappings they may display.

Selected Filmography

1 This selected filmography lists 150 of the films discussed in the book, along with relevant films discussed by Bazin, Kracauer and the other major theorists in the book. The commonly known English title is given first, if the non-English title is generally used it is given first.

Bibliography

Abel, Marco. *The Counter-Cinema of the Berlin School*. Rochester, New York: Camden House, 2015.

Abel, Marco, and Jaimey Fisher (eds). *The Berlin School and its Global Context*. Detroit: Wayne State University Press, 2018.

Adorno, Theodor. 'Transparencies on Film' (1966), translated by Thomas Y. Levin. *New German Critique* 24–25 (Fall-Winter 1981–1982): 199–205.

Adorno, Theodor, Walter Benjamin, Ernst Bloch, Bertolt Brecht, and Georg Lukács. *Aesthetics and Politics*. London: Verso, 1992.

Andrew, Dudley. *What Cinema Is! Bazin's Quest and its Charge*. Oxford: Wiley-Blackwell, 2010.

Andrew, Dudley, and Hervé Joubert-Laurencin (eds). *Opening Bazin: Postwar Film Theory and its Afterlife*. Oxford: Oxford University Press, 2011.

Arnheim, Rudolf. *Film as Art* [1938]. Berkeley: University of California, 1957.

Arnheim, Rudolf. 'Melancholy Unshaped'. *The Journal of Aesthetics and Art Criticism* 21, no. 3 (Spring 1963): 291–7.

Badiou, Alain. *Cinema*. Cambridge: Polity Press, 2013.

Barry, Iris. *D.W. Griffith: American Film Master*. New York: The Museum of Modern Art, 1940.

Barthes, Roland. 'The Rhetoric of the Image'. In *Image Music Text*, edited by Stephen Heath, 32–51. London: Fontana, 1977.

Barthes, Roland. 'The Reality Effect' [1968]. In *The Rustle of Language*, edited and translated by Richard Howard, 141–8. Berkeley: University of California Press, 1989.

Baudelaire, Charles. 'The Painter of Modern Life' [1863]. In *Modern Art and Modernism: A Critical Anthology*, edited by Francis Frascina and Charles Harrison, 23–8. London: The Open University, 1982.

Bazin, André. *The Cinema of Cruelty*. 1975. Edited by Francois Truffaut, translated by Sabine d'Estrée. New York: Arcade, 1982.

Bazin, André. *What is Cinema?* Volume 1. 1967. Essays selected and translated by Hugh Gray. Berkeley: University of California Press, 2004.

Bazin, André. *What is Cinema?* Volume 2. 1971. Essays selected and translated by Hugh Gray. Berkeley: University of California Press, 2005.

Beckman, Karen, and Jean Ma (eds). *Still Moving: Between Cinema and Photography*. Durham: Duke University Press, 2008.

Bell, Clive. 'The Aesthetic Hypothesis' [1914]. In *Modern Art and Modernism: A Critical Anthology*, edited by Francis Frascina and Charles Harrison, 67–74. London: The Open University, 1982.

Bell, Clive. 'The Debt to Cezanne' [1914]. In *Modern Art and Modernism: A Critical Anthology*, edited by Francis Frascina and Charles Harrison, 75–8, London: The Open University, 1982.

Benjamin, Walter. 'The Work of Art in the Age of Mechanical Reproduction'. In *Illuminations*, translated by Harry Zohn, edited by Hannah Arendt. London: Fontana, 1992.

Berman, Marshall. *All That Is Solid Melts Into Air: The Experience of Modernity*. London: Verso, 1983.

Betz, Mark. 'Beyond Europe: On Parametric Transcendence'. In *Global Art Cinema: New Theories and Histories*, edited by Rosalind Galt and Karl Schoonover, 31–47. Oxford: Oxford University Press, 2010.

Bickerton, Emilie. *A Short History of Cahiers du Cinéma*. London: Verso, 2009.

Bordwell, David. 'The Art Cinema as a Mode of Film Practice'. *Film Criticism* 4 (Fall 1979): 716–24.

Bordwell, David. *Narration in the Fiction Film*. London: Routledge, 1986.

Bordwell, David. *On the History of Film Style*. Cambridge, MA: Harvard University Press, 1997.

Bordwell, David. *Poetics of Cinema*. London: Routledge, 2008.

Bordwell, David, Janet Staiger, and Kristin Thompson. *The Classical Hollywood Cinema: Film Style and Mode of Production to 1960*. London: Routledge, 1988.

Bordwell, David, and Kristin Thompson. *Film Art: An Introduction*. New York: McGraw-Hill, 1993.

Bray, Patrick M. (ed.). *Understanding Rancière, Understanding Modernism*. London: Bloomsbury Academic, 2017.

Bresson, Robert. *Notes on the Cinematograph* [1975]. New York: New York Review of Books, 1986.

Burch, Noël. *Theory of Film Practice*. Princeton: Princeton University Press, 1981.

Burch, Noël. *To the Distant Observer: Form and Meaning in the Japanese Cinema*. Berkeley: University of California, 1981.

Burch, Noël. *Life to Those Shadows*. Berkeley: University of California Press, 1990.

Bürger, Peter. *Theory of the Avant-Garde* [1974]. Minneapolis: University of Minnesota Press, 1984.

Çağlayan, Emre. *Poetics of Slow Cinema: Nostalgia, Absurdism, Boredom*. London: Palgrave Macmillan, 2018.

Cardew, Cornelius. *Stockhausen Serves Imperialism*. London: Latimer, 1974.

Cavell, Stanley. *The World Viewed: Reflections on the Ontology of Film* [1971]. Enlarged edition. Cambridge, MA: Harvard University Press, 1979.

Chaudhuri, Shohini. *Contemporary World Cinema*. Edinburgh: Edinburgh University Press, 2005.

Ciment, Michel, and Laurence Kardish (eds). *Positif: 50 Years – Selections from the French Film Journal*. New York: Museum of Modern Art, 2003.

Clark, T.J. *Farewell to an Idea: Episodes from a History of Modernism*. New Haven: Yale University Press, 2001.

Codell, Julie F. (ed.). *Genre, Gender, Race, and World Cinema: An Anthology*. Oxford: Blackwell, 2007.

Corbett, David Peters. *The Modernity of English Art 1914–1930*. Manchester: Manchester University Press, 1997.

Cousins, Mark. *The Story of Film*. London: Pavilion, 2004.

Daney, Serge. *Postcards from the Cinema*. Oxford: Berg Press, 2007.

D'Arcy, Michael, and Mathias Nilges (eds). *The Contemporaneity of Modernism: Literature, Media, Culture*. London: Routledge, 2015.

De Luca, Tiago, and Nuno Barradas Jorge (eds). *Slow Cinema*. Edinburgh: Edinburgh University Press, 2016.

Deleuze, Gilles. *Cinema 1: The Movement-Image*. Translated by Hugh Tomlinson and Barbara Habberjam. London: Athlone Press, 1986.

Deleuze, Gilles. *Cinema 2: The Time-Image*. Translated by Hugh Tomlinson and Robert Galeta. London: Athlone Press, 1989.

Dinnen, Zara, and Sam McBean. 'The Face as Technology'. *New Formations* 93 (July 2018): 122–37.

Doan, Mary Ann. *The Emergence of Cinematic Time: Modernity, Contingency, The Archive*. Cambridge, MA: Harvard University Press, 2002.

Donald, James, Anne Friedberg, and Laura Marcus (eds). *Close Up 1927–1933: Cinema and Modernism*. London: Cassell, 1998.

Fainaru, Dan (ed.). *Theo Angelopoulos: Interviews*. Jackson: University Press of Mississippi, 2001.

Flanagan, Matthew. 'Towards an Aesthetic of Slow in Contemporary Cinema', *16:9 in English* 29 (November 2008), online at http://www.16-9.dk/2008-11/side11_inenglish.htm.

Ford, Hamish. *Postwar Modernist Cinema and Philosophy: Confronting Negativity and Time*. New York: Palgrave Macmillan, 2012.

Forgacs, David, Sarah Lutton, and Geoffrey Nowell-Smith (eds). *Roberto Rossellini: Magician of the Real*. London: British Film Institute, 2000.

Frascina, Francis, and Charles Harrison (eds). *Modern Art and Modernism: A Critical Anthology*. London: Harper and Row, The Open University, 1982.

Fry, Roger. 'An Essay in Aesthetics' [1909]. In *Modern Art and Modernism: A Critical Anthology*, edited by Francis Frascina and Charles Harrison, 79–88. London: The Open University, 1982.

Fusco, Katherine, and Nicole Seymour. *Kelly Reichardt*. Urbana: University of Illinois Press, 2017.

Galt, Rosalind, and Karl Schoonover (eds). *Global Art Cinema: New Theories and Histories*. Oxford: Oxford University Press, 2010.

Grant, Catherine, and Annette Kuhn (eds). *Screening World Cinema*. London: Routledge, 2006.

Greenberg, Clement. 'Modernist Painting' (1965). In *Modern Art and Modernism: A Critical Anthology*, edited by Francis Frascina and Charles Harrison, 5–10. London: The Open University, 1982.

Gunning, Tom. 'The Cinema of Attraction: Early Film, Its Spectator and the Avant-Garde', *Wide Angle* 8, no. 3–4 (1986): 63–70.

Gunning, Tom. 'Modernity and Cinema: A Culture of Shocks and Flows'. In *Cinema and Modernity*, edited by Murray Pomerance, 297–315. New Brunswick: Rutgers University Press, 2006.

Hames, Peter (ed.). *The Cinema of Central Europe*. London: Wallflower Press, 2004.

Hames, Peter. *The Czechoslovak New Wave*. London: Wallflower Press, 2005.

Hansen, Miriam Bratu, 'Introduction to Adorno, "Transparencies on Film" (1966)'. *New German Critique* 24–25 (Fall-Winter 1981–1982): 186–98.

Hansen, Miriam Bratu. *Cinema and Experience*. London: University of California Press, 2012.

Hansen, Miriam Bratu. 'The Mass Production of the Senses: Classical Cinema as Vernacular Modernism'. *Modernism / Modernity* 6, no. 2 (April 1999): 59–77.

Harrison, Charles. *English Art and Modernism 1900–1939*. New Haven: Yale University Press, 1994.

Hill, John, and Pamela Church Gibson (eds). *World Cinema: Critical Approaches*. Oxford: Oxford University Press, 2000.

Hillier, Jim (ed.). *Cahiers du Cinéma: Vol.1: The 1950s: Neo-Realism, Hollywood, New Wave*. London: British Film Institute, 1985.

Horton, Andrew. *The Films of Theo Angelopoulos : A Cinema of Contemplation*. Princeton: Princeton University Press, 1997.

Horton, Andrew. *The Last Modernist: The Films of Theo Angelopoulos*. Westport: Praeger, 1997.

Huyssen, Andreas. *After the Great Divide: Modernism, Mass Culture, Postmodernism*. Bloomington: Indiana University Press, 1986.

Issa, Rose, and Sheila Whitaker. *Life and Art: The New Iranian Cinema*. London: British Film Institute, 1999.

Jaffe, Ira. *Slow Movies: Countering the Cinema of Action*. London: Wallflower Press, 2014.

Jameson, Frederic. *Postmodernism, Or, The Cultural Logic of Late Capitalism*. London: Verso, 1991.

Jameson, Frederic. *Signatures of the Visible*. London: Routledge, 1992.

Jameson, Frederic. *The Geopolitical Aesthetic: Cinema and Space in the World System*. London: British Film Institute, 1995.

Jameson, Frederic. *A Singular Modernity: Essay on the Ontology of the Present*. London: Verso, 2002.

Jameson, Frederic. *The Modernist Papers*. London: Verso, 2007.

Jameson, Frederic. *The Ancients and the Postmoderns: On the Historicity of Forms*. London: Verso, 2015.

Jones, Peter (ed.). *Imagist Poetry*. London: Penguin, 1972.

Kermode, Frank. *Continuities*. London: Routledge, 1968.

Kermode, Frank. *The Romantic Image* [1957]. London: Routledge, 2001.

Kolocotroni, Vassiliki, Jane Goldman, and Olga Taxidou (eds). *Modernism: An Anthology of Sources and Documents*. Edinburgh: Edinburgh University Press, 1998.

Kovács, András Bálint. *Screening Modernism: European Art Cinema 1950–1980*. Chicago: University of Chicago Press, 2007.

Kovács, András Bálint. *The Cinema of Béla Tarr: The Circle Closes*. London: Wallflower Press, 2013.

Kracauer, Siegfried. *Theory of Film: The Redemption of Physical Reality* [1960]. Princeton: Princeton University Press, 1997.

Levenson, Michael. *A Genealogy of Modernism* [1984]. Cambridge: Cambridge University Press, 1995.

Levenson, Michael (ed.). *The Cambridge Companion to Modernism*. Cambridge: Cambridge University Press, 2011.

Lindsay, Vachel. *The Art Of The Moving Picture* [1915]. Denver: Denver Art Association reprint, 1922.

Lukács, Georg. *The Meaning of Contemporary Realism*. London: Merlin Press, 1979.

Ma, Jean. 'Tsai-Ming-Liang's Haunted Movie Theater'. In *Global Art Cinema: New Theories and Histories*, edited by Rosalind Galt and Karl Schoonover, 334–50. Oxford: Oxford University Press, 2010.

MacCabe, Colin. 'Bazin as Modernist'. In *Opening Bazin: Postwar Film Theory and its Afterlife*, edited by Dudley Andrew and Hervé Joubert-Laurencin, 66–76. Oxford: Oxford University Press, 2011.

Mao, Douglas, and Rebecca Walkowitz. 'The New Modernist Studies'. *PMLA* 123 (2008): 737–48.

Marcus, Laura. *The Tenth Muse: Writing about Cinema in the Modernist Period*. Oxford: Oxford University Press, 2007.

Marcus, Laura. *Dreams of Modernity: Psychoanalysis, Literature, Cinema*. Cambridge: Cambridge University Press, 2014.

Marcus, Laura. 'Modernist Literature and Film'. In *The Bloomsbury Companion to Modernist Literature*, edited by Ulrika Maude and Mark Nixon, 153–70. London: Bloomsbury, 2018.

Margulies, Ivone. *Nothing Happens: Chantal Akerman's Hyperrealist Everyday*. Durham: Duke University Press, 1996.

Martin, Deborah. *The Cinema of Lucrecia Martel*. Manchester: Manchester University Press, 2016.

Maude, Ulrika, and Mark Nixon (eds). *The Bloomsbury Companion to Modernist Literature*. London: Bloomsbury, 2018.

Morgan, Daniel. 'Bazin's Modernism'. *Paragraph* 36, no. 1 (2013): 10–30.

Mulvey, Laura. *Death 24x a Second*. London: Reakton, 2005.

Nagib, Lúcia, Chris Perriam, and Rajinder Dudrah (eds). *Theorizing World Cinema*. London: I.B. Tauris, 2012.

Nichols, Bill (ed.). *Movies and Methods*, Vol. 1. Berkeley: University of California Press, 1976.

Nowell-Smith, Geoffrey. *L'avventura*. London: British Film Institute, 1997.

Orr, John. *Cinema and Modernity*. Oxford: Blackwell / Polity Press, 1993.

Orr, John. *Romantics and Modernists in British Cinema*. Edinburgh: Edinburgh University Press, 2012.

Pasolini, Pier Paolo. 'The Cinema of Poetry' [1965]. In *Movies and Methods*, Vol. 1, edited by Bill Nichols, 542–58. Berkeley: University of California Press, 1976.

Perry, Ted (ed.). *Masterpieces of Modernist Cinema*. Bloomington: Indiana University Press, 2006.

Phillips, James. *Cinematic Thinking: Philosophical Approaches to the New Cinema*. Stanford: Stanford University Press, 2008.

Poggioli, Renato. *The Theory of the Avant-Garde*. Cambridge, MA: Harvard University Press, 1968.

Pollman, Inga. 'The Forces of Milieu: Angela Schanelec's *Marseille* and the Heritage of Michelangelo Antonioni'. In *The Berlin School and its Global Contexts: A Transnational Art Cinema*, edited by Marco Abel and Jaimey Fisher, 154–73. Detroit: Wayne State University Press, 2018.

Pomerance, Murray (ed.). *Cinema and Modernity*. New Brunswick: Rutgers University Press, 2006.

Rancière, Jacques. *The Politics of Aesthetics*. Edited and translated by Gabriel Rockhill. London: Continuum, 2004.

Rancière, Jacques. *Film Fables*. Translated by Emiliano Battista. Oxford: Berg, 2006.

Rancière, Jacques. *The Future of the Image*. Translated by Gregory Elliot. London: Verso, 2009.

Rancière, Jacques. *The Emancipated Spectator*. Translated by Gregory Elliot. London: Verso, 2011.

Rancière, Jacques. *Béla Tarr, The Time After*. Translated by Erik Beranek. Minneapolis: Univocal, 2013.

Rancière, Jacques. *The Intervals of Cinema*. Translated by John Howe. London: Verso, 2014.

Rascaroli, Laura, and John David Rhodes (eds). *Antonioni: Centenary Essays*. London: Palgrave Macmillan, 2011.

Rhodes, John David. 'Pasolini's Exquisite Flowers: The "Cinema of Poetry"'. In *Global Art Cinema: New Theories and Histories*, edited by Rosalind Galt and Karl Schoonover, 142–62. Oxford: Oxford University Press, 2010.

Rivette, Jacques. 'Letter on Rossellini' [1955]. In *Cahiers du Cinéma: Vol.1: The 1950s: Neo-realism, Hollywood, New Wave*, edited by Jim Hillier, 192–204. London: British Film Institute, 1985.

Rodowick, D.N. *The Crisis of Political Modernism: Criticism and Ideology in Contemporary Film Theory*. Urbana: University of Illinois Press, 1994.

Rodowick, D.N. *Gilles Deleuze's Time Machine*. Durham: Duke University Press, 1997.

Rodowick, D.N. *The Virtual Life of Film*. Cambridge, MA: Harvard University Press, 2007.

Rodowick, D.N. (ed.). *Afterimages of Gilles Deleuze's Film Philosophy*. Minneapolis: University of Minnesota Press, 2010.

Rodowick, D.N. *Elegy for Theory*. Cambridge, MA: Harvard University Press, 2014.

Rohdie, Sam. *Montage*. Manchester: Manchester University Press, 2006.

Rohdie, Sam. *Film Modernism*. Manchester: Manchester University Press, 2015.

Rosenbaum, Jonathan. *Essential Cinema: On the Necessity of Film Canons*. Baltimore: John Hopkins University Press, 2004.

Rosenbaum, Jonathan, and Adrian Martin. *Movie Mutations: The Changing Face of World Cinephelia*. London: British Film Institute, 2003.

Roy, Rajendra, and Anke Leweke. *The Berlin School: Films from the Berliner Schule*. New York: The Museum of Modern Art, 2013.

Saeed-Vafa, Mehrnaz, and Jonathan Rosenbaum. *Abbas Kiarostami*. Urbana: University of Illinois Press, 2018.

Schickel, Richard. *D.W. Griffith: An American Life*. New York: Simon & Schuster, 1984.

Schrader, Paul. *Transcendental Style in Film* [1971]. New enlarged edition. Berkeley: University of California, 2018.

Shail, Andrew. *The Cinema and the Origins of Literary Modernism*. London: Routledge 2012.

Silverman, Kaja, and Harun Farocki. *Speaking about Godard*. New York: New York University Press, 1998.

Sinclair, May. 'The Novels of Dorothy Richardson', *The Egoist* 5, no.4 (April 1918): 58.

Solanas, Fernando E., and Octavio Getino, 'Towards a Third Cinema'. In *Movies and Methods: An Anthology*, edited by Bill Nichols, 44–64. Berkeley: University of California Press, 1976.

Sontag, Susan. *Against Interpretation and Other Essays* [1966]. London: Penguin Classics, 2009.

Suchenski, Richard (ed.). *Hou Hsiao-Hsien*. Vienna: Austrian Film Museum Books, 2014.

Suchenski, Richard. *Projections of Memory: Romanticism, Modernism, and the Aesthetics of Film*. Oxford: Oxford University Press, 2016.

Tapper, Richard (ed.). *The New Iranian Cinema: Politics, Representation and Identity*. London: I.B. Tauris, 2002.

Taylor, Richard, and William Powell (eds). *The Eisenstein Reader*. London: British Film Institute, 1998.

Temple, Michael, and James S. Williams (eds). *The Cinema Alone: Essays on the Work of Jean-Luc-Godard 1985–2000*. Amsterdam: Amsterdam University Press, 2000.

Trotter, David. *Cinema and Modernism*. London: Blackwell, 2007.

Verstraten, Peter. *Film Narratology*. Toronto: University of Toronto Press, 2009.
Watts, Philip. *Roland Barthes' Cinema*. Oxford: Oxford University Press, 2016.
Westfall, Joseph (ed.). *The Continental Philosophy of Film Reader*. London: Bloomsbury, 2018.
Williams, Christopher. *Realism and the Cinema*. London: Routledge / British Film Institute, 1980.
Williams, Raymond. *The Politics of Modernism*. London: Verso, 1989.
Witt, Michael. *Jean-Luc Godard, Cinema Historian*. Bloomington: Indiana University Press, 2014.
Wollen, Peter. *Readings and Writings*. London: Verso, 1982.
Wollen, Peter. 'The Two Avant-Gardes' [1968]. In *Readings and Writings*, edited by Peter Wollen, 92–104. London: Verso, 1982.
Wollen, Peter. *Raiding the Icebox: Reflections on Twentieth-Century Culture*. London: Verso, 1993.
Wollen, Peter. *Signs and Meaning in the Cinema* [1969]. London: British Film Institute, 1998.
Wood, Michael. 'Modernism and Film'. In *The Cambridge Companion to Modernism*, edited by Michael Levenson, 217–32. Cambridge: Cambridge University Press, 2011.
Woolf, Virginia. *Selected Essays*. Oxford: Oxford University Press, 2008.
Zhangke, Jia. 'Images That Cannot be Banned – New Cinema in China from 1995', *Still Life*, DVD booklet, 18–26. London: British Film Institute, 2008.
Žižek, Slavoj. *The Art of the Ridiculous Sublime: On David Lynch's Lost Highway*. Seattle: University of Washington Press, 2000.
Žižek, Slavoj. *The Fright of Real Tears: Krzysztof Kieślowski Between Theory and Post-Theory*. London: British Film Institute, 2001.

Index

Ackerman, Chantal 62, 95, 116, 118, 150–2, 155–7
Jean Dielman 175–7
Adorno, Theodor 20–1, 33–41, 67, 115, 171
Alonso, Lisandro 114, 255–9
Liverpool 256–9
American Indie Film 106, 152–7, 174–81
Antonioni, Michelangelo 4, 31–2, 98, 117–18, 127, 137–9, 164–5, 231, 240–2, 244, 263–4
La Notte 38
L'avventura 62, 64, 101, 252
Red Desert 64–7, 243, 253
Arnheim, Rudolf 18, 20, 88, 114
avant-garde 8, 14, 16–17, 20, 24, 37, 46–7, 101, 106, 112, 120, 144–5, 174
silent film era avant-garde 76–82, 84, 85
theories of the avant-garde 123–7, 131–2, 135

Barry, Iris 72–4, 131
Barthes, Roland 15, 42, 122–3, 263
Bazin, André 4, 5, 14, 18–23, 88–9, 93, 102, 116–17, 164–7, 169, 196–8, 242
Bazin and Kracauer 23–7, 39, 100, 104, 143, 145, 176
Bazin and modernism 28–9, 56–7, 73, 106, 119–20, 138–40, 144–5
Bazin and neorealism 95–9, 141–2
Bell, Clive 10–12
Benjamin, Walter 21, 23, 34–44
Bergman, Ingmar 6, 7, 14, 127, 148, 210, 241
Bergman, Ingrid 3, 27–8, 97–9, 120
Berlin School 170–4, 237, 240, 241
Bordwell, David 85–6, 130–6, 193–5, 261
Brakhage, Stan 26, 82, 106, 126, 128, 154–5, 174
Bresson, Robert 4, 19, 25, 100, 106, 117–18, 120, 134, 137, 163–4, 169, 195–200
Bürger, Peter
Theory of the Avant-Garde 124–5

Cahiers du cinema 7, 18–19, 26, 48, 71, 92–3, 97, 101–6, 114, 116, 120, 123, 129, 131, 144, 169
Cavell, Stanley
The World Viewed 8, 29–33
Chaplin, Charlie 8, 24, 36–7, 43, 70–1, 85, 131
Modern Times 43, 75
Shoulder Pads 75
Close Up [film journal] 7, 51, 57
Coppola, Francis Ford 44, 106–7, 148, 168–9
Costa, Pedro 118, 201–7
Cousins, Mark
The Story of Film 6–7, 68–72, 90–4, 100, 162

Daney, Serge 18
Deleuze, Gilles 4, 30, 95, 99, 121–3, 140–2, 197–9
Deren, Maya 26, 106, 128, 154
De Sica, Vittorio
Umberto D 18, 23, 25, 29, 89, 94–7, 122, 180, 197, 267
Duras, Marguerite
Nathalie Granger 95, 152

Eisenstein, Sergei 7, 40, 52–7, 59, 74, 77, 83, 126, 131–2, 144, 193, 197
experimental film 13–14, 24, 26, 29, 65, 80, 106, 116, 123–8, 130, 150–2, 154, 174, 177, 183, 190, 198, 200

Fassbinder, Rainer Werner 4, 7, 112–13, 170, 175, 185, 201, 207, 210–11, 231, 243
fast cinema
  Bourne series 182, 193–5
Fellini, Federico 6, 61, 66, 90, 95, 101–2, 117, 190, 195, 207
Figgis, Mike 182–4
Flaherty, Robert 25, 27, 32, 87, 144, 198, 204
Flanagan, Matthew 191–4
Fry, Roger 8–12

German Expressionist Film 22, 24, 49, 77, 82–5, 92, 131
Glazer, Jonathan 184–5
  Under the Skin 185–8
Godard, Jean-Luc 6, 7, 14, 42–3, 80, 90, 116–17, 125–7, 133, 171, 181–3, 194–5, 240–1, 243
  Histoire(s) du cinema 142, 181
  Le Gai savoir 109
  Weekend 110–11, 241
Greenberg, Clement 8, 11–15, 31, 67, 124–5, 144, 149, 153
Griffith, D.W. 1, 42, 52, 54, 58, 70, 72–4, 85–6, 144

Hansen, Miriam Bratu 33
  Cinema and Experience 34–40
  Theory of Film (Kracauer) 21–2
  Vernacular Modernism 41–4
Herzog, Werner 37, 111, 113–14
Hitchcock, Alfred 7, 24, 83, 89, 92–3, 97, 99, 105, 120, 123, 131, 163, 215, 230
  Vertigo 254
Hogg, Joanna 188–90
Hou, Hsiao-hsien 118, 157, 160–1, 169
  City of Sadness 161–4
Hu, Bo 264
  An Elephant Sitting Still 195, 265–8

Italian neorealism 3, 18, 23, 25, 27, 29, 38, 66, 90–100, 107–8, 117, 120–1, 129, 136–7, 142, 169, 178–80, 196–8, 242

Jameson, Fredric 127–36, 146–7, 153, 213–14, 216
Japanese Cinema 26, 42, 102–4, 163
Jarmusch, Jim 148, 154–7
  Stranger than Paradise 156
Jia, Zhangke 157, 164, 242–4
  Still Life 245–9
Joyce, James 6, 9, 15, 29, 57, 59–60, 73, 98, 124, 135

Keaton, Buster 8, 36, 48, 70, 75, 85
Kermode, Frank
  'Modernisms' 16, 17
Kiarostami, Abbas 61, 157, 166, 222
  Taste of Cherry 67, 179, 223–30
Kohler, Ulrich 171
  Bungalow 172–3
Kovács, András Bálint
  Screening Modernism 7, 82–4, 104, 117, 137–9, 146, 147, 153, 195, 253
Kracauer, Siegfried 14, 18, 20–1, 23–7, 34–5, 44, 65, 104, 106, 120, 176
  Theory of Film 1–5, 22–3, 38–41, 74, 100

Lee, Chang-dong 259–60
  Burning 260–4
Leenhardt, Roger 91–2
Lindsay, Vachel 51–2
Linklater, Richard 177
  Waking Life 175–6
Lumière Brothers 2, 11, 23, 59, 68, 70, 85
Lynch, David 84, 148, 152, 154
  Blue Velvet 148, 153

Malraux, André 19, 91–2, 110
Marcus, Laura
  The Tenth Muse 8, 51–2, 59
Martel, Lucrecia 249
  The Headless Woman 250–4
Méliès, Georges 23, 69, 85
Mizoguchi, Kenji 93, 100, 102–4, 123, 162, 164
modernism
  drama 9, 47–50, 57, 71, 88, 109–14, 133, 135, 192–3, 205
  music 7, 12, 38, 46, 109–10, 112, 125, 134
  novel 2, 6–10, 15, 17, 29, 40, 42, 57–67, 84, 88–9, 92–3, 111, 121–2, 126–7, 192–3, 262

painting 7, 9–14, 31, 36, 39, 45–6, 51, 71, 73, 76–7, 82–3, 125–6, 141, 144
poetry 9, 33, 50–7, 65–7, 135, 242
mumblecore 152, 157, 174–8

neo-neo realism 174, 178–9
New Iranian Cinema 157, 165–7

Ozu, Yasuhiro 102–4, 117, 132, 134–5, 162–4, 169, 196–8, 200

Pasolini, Pier Paolo 7, 14, 64, 207, 210, 231, 253
Cinema of Poetry 65–7, 112
Petzhold, Christian 171, 173
Pialat, Maurice 116–17, 172, 189, 190
Poggioli, Renato 123
Theory of the Avant-Garde 124
Political Modernism 7, 42, 80, 90, 103, 109–16, 132–4, 138
Positif 92, 101, 117, 191
postmodernism 15, 16, 41, 45, 125, 127–30, 134–9, 146–50, 152–6, 167, 173, 175–7, 180, 182, 188, 214
Pound, Ezra 50–6
imagism 51, 53
Proust, Marcel 6, 40, 57, 59, 130, 135, 176, 193

Rancière, Jacques 23, 139–45, 207
Reichardt, Kelly
Wendy and Lucy 179–81
Renoir, Jean 9, 29, 32, 85, 92, 100, 132
Richardson, Dorothy 61–3
Rivette, Jacques 19, 111–13, 117, 120, 144, 154, 198
Rodowick, D.N. 7, 42, 114, 119, 133
Roeg, Nic 105, 122, 184–6
Rohdie, Sam
Film Modernism 7
Rossellini, Roberto 3, 7, 25, 48, 57, 61, 66, 73, 82, 89–91, 94–7, 100, 116–18, 120, 133, 137, 139–40, 145, 164–6, 180, 195, 212
Journey to Italy 98–9, 101, 138, 179, 192, 197, 222
Stromboli 27–9
Rotha, Paul 86

Schanelec, Angela 170, 173–4, 182, 237–8
Marseille 238–42
Schrader, Paul
Transcendental Style in Film 196–200
Scorsese, Martin 29, 44, 106, 148, 168–9
Serra, Albert 192, 201–2, 207–12
Birdsong 209–10
Honor of the Knights 207–8
Story of My Death 211
significant form 10–12, 20, 46, 53, 145
silent film 7–8, 42, 61, 68–88, 128–9, 142
slow cinema 3, 62, 152, 179, 181, 190–6, 198–200, 256
Smith, Murray
[on silent avant-garde film] 80–1
Sokurov, Alexander 129, 157, 170, 184, 192, 214–16
Days of the Eclipse 215–16
Sontag, Susan 39, 168, 196, 226
Straub, Jean-Marie and Danièle Huillet 7, 42, 126–7, 133, 204

Taiwan New Cinema 136, 146, 157–65, 169
Tarantino, Quentin 149, 156, 169, 175
Tarkovsky, Andrei 4, 44, 82, 117–18, 123, 169, 197–8, 200, 213–14, 216
Mirror 7, 137–8, 243
Tarr, Béla 61, 114, 129, 157, 216, 264
Sátántangó 164, 192, 194, 196, 217–21
Third Cinema 107–9, 115, 133
Trotter, David
Cinema and Modernism 8
Tsai Ming-liang 118, 165, 231–2, 241
Goodbye, Dragon Inn 232–7

Varda, Agnes 116
La Pointe Courte 100–1, 192
Vertov, Dziga 7, 40, 42, 57, 80, 84, 90, 111, 126–7, 143, 184
Man with a Movie Camera 21, 77–9, 87, 132–3
Vigo, Jean 29, 32, 82, 85, 92, 100

Welles, Orson 43, 73, 82, 84, 90–3, 99, 105, 123, 140, 143–5, 197
Citizen Kane 42, 89, 91, 93, 97, 100, 196, 262
Williams, Raymond 8
Politics of Modernism 47–8
Wollen, Peter 42, 115
'*The Two Avant-Gardes*' 76–80, 123–7, 132, 152
Woolf, Virginia 6, 9, 10, 12, 50, 59, 176, 193
To the Lighthouse 60–1

Yamanaka, Sadao 102
Yang, Edward 158, 160
Terrorizers 164–5

Zavattini, Cesare 18, 94

Printed in Great Britain
by Amazon

55682007R00187